The Art of Efficient Reading

THE ART OF EFFICIENT READING

second edition

George D. Spache
Head, Reading Laboratory and Clinic
University of Florida

Paul C. Berg
Director, Reading Clinic
University of South Carolina

THE MACMILLAN COMPANY, NEW YORK
COLLIER-MACMILLAN LIMITED, LONDON

© COPYRIGHT, THE MACMILLAN COMPANY, 1966

All rights reserved. No part of this book
may be reproduced or utilized in any form
or by any means, electronic or mechanical,
including photocopying, recording or by
any information storage and retrieval
system, without permission in writing from
the Publisher.

First Printing

Earlier edition © copyright 1955
by The Macmillan Company.

LIBRARY OF CONGRESS CATALOG CARD NUMBER: 66-19579

THE MACMILLAN COMPANY, NEW YORK
COLLIER-MACMILLAN CANADA, LTD., TORONTO, ONTARIO

Printed in the United States of America

PREFACE

Like the students who have used the first edition during the past nine years, we have modified our concepts of the reading process. As a result, this second edition is completely rewritten with the intention of improving its effectiveness for its users. Our basic concepts of the purposes of this book, however, remain unchanged. It is our purpose to help students understand more clearly various ways of approaching their reading tasks, and to provide sufficient practice in these techniques to enable them to achieve flexibility. We continue to believe that success in the reading-studying aspects of college life is to be found only by fitting the approach to the nature and purpose of the work at hand.

The sequence of chapters in the first section is planned to lead the student through a series of reading approaches that later may be selectively integrated in the acts of studying and critical reading. Although these techniques will result in greater speed and effectiveness, an increased rate of reading and simple practice in answering questions of comprehension are not panaceas for college reading problems. Sheer increase in speed of reading will make only a very small contribution to improvement. In fact, if applied indiscriminately, increased speed in reading college-level materials results in marked loss in effectiveness and comprehension. Repeated practice in reading without changes in techniques and approaches offers no permanent gain for the intelligent student.

The second section offers detailed suggestions for handling the problem of vocabulary in college reading. A system for analyzing difficult words is proposed, and attention is given to the meaningful elements of word structure and to that universal vocabulary tool, the dictionary. These chapters will aid students in handling the difficulties inherent in the breadth, variety, and depth of the vocabularies of college courses.

The final section presents an opportunity for the student to apply his newly acquired reading and vocabulary skills in a variety of passages from college reading sources. Each selection is presented as it might be by an instructor who has more or less definite purposes in mind. After trying the selection, the student is aided in evaluating his choice of approaches and his success in mastering the material in the expected ways.

Our indebtedness to our colleagues in college and adult reading-improvement work is obvious. We have drawn from their ideas and experiences, combined these with our own daily clinical observations, and prepared a program of training that will enable college or college-bound students to achieve their academic purposes more effectively.

G. D. S.
P. C. B.

CONTENTS

Contents   ix

PART I

Flexibility in Reading

CHAPTER 1

PREVIEWING: THINKING
BEFORE READING

Reading well is no small task. Not many people ever become highly skilled at it except in relatively few areas of knowledge. The reason is that each area requires not only highly developed general reading ability but also special skills for special reading tasks. For example, a broad general vocabulary is needed for accurate, fluent reading in any area; but a vocabulary of special meanings is also needed to read in each particular area of knowledge. Also necessary are particular ways of thinking for understanding best what each writer has to say. Reading newspapers requires the skill of being able to "read between the lines" or to read critically in order to detect bias or insufficient proof of statements. Reading literature also requires critical analysis, but not so much for judging truth or bias as for discovering the writer's tone and mood, as well as his point of view. Reading in mathematics and science requires specific steps of reasoning and special attention to detail. Reading in social studies calls for skill in organizing facts if the reader is to understand time-space sequences or to follow cause-effect relationships dealing with human behavior. These examples indicate only a few of the many kinds of skills required for good reading.

The efficient reader must also know how to select the right combination of skills for a particular purpose, taking into account the depth of comprehension he needs. Assignments, directions, formulas, or statements of scientific principles must, of course, be read carefully and, as a rule, slowly. But one need not have a high level of comprehension for everything he reads: in some instances, a quick and superficial reading will suffice. Yet some persons—especially those who have narrow reading interests—regard everything as important and prod and pull out every small detail. Although such persons may have satisfactory comprehension, they may read very little, probably only in their areas of major interest, never finding time to read for pure enjoyment or entertainment. Some things are not worth careful reading or remembering, and others, though important, can be scanned quickly for all the necessary information.

As you can see, a mark of efficient reading is being able to select quickly the skills you need to read a particular selection in keeping with the purpose you have for reading it. To select the proper skills, you must spend some time thinking about a selection or book before reading it completely. This thinking process preceding a reading, based on certain questions that you may raise about the selection, is called *previewing*. Previewing should help you to form several opinions about the material to be read, including an estimate of your interest and background for it, the level of comprehension needed to satisfy your purpose for reading, the kinds of skills that will help to accomplish your purpose, and the rate at which you can read the material effectively. You may in fact find that a preview will give all the information you need from a particular article, or it may show just what part of an article will contain the ideas you are looking for.

How to Preview

Previewing starts with questions about the topic or title and then goes on to other items that can quickly tell you what to expect. You might begin by asking, "What do I know about this title? What experiences have I had or what reading have I done that gives me information about this material?" Then you should look at the author's name and see whether it or the author's affiliation will give you any leads about the probable content of the writing. If you are about to study an unfamiliar book, its copyright date will help to judge how up-to-date it is, and a reading of the preface may tell something of the purpose the author had for writing it. A careful study of the table of contents is particularly important in previewing. This table provides a description of the book in a compact form and shows the relationship of ideas and the way they will be presented throughout.

If you wish to know whether the author defines his terms, look for a *glossary* in the back. If you want to see whether he lists any of the background data from which he wrote his book, look for and study the *appendix*. Check the *index* to find the pages bearing on a particular phase of the author's presentation. This simple skimming technique not only will help you to preview a book you are about to study, but it will save time and effort when you need to choose a book on a particular subject from the library.

Before reading a chapter from a book, or a magazine or journal selection, these further steps for previewing will help you organize the material for better understanding during reading and for greater retention of the ideas and details: Read the chapter or article title and any headlines that may appear. Read any typographical aids, such as subtitles, marginal summaries, and italicized words, and briefly examine charts, graphs, and any other aids that may quickly give you some idea of the content and purpose of the writing. If no such aids are present, read the first paragraph and the first sentence of each of the other paragraphs. If a summary paragraph is given, read it carefully.

Remember, you are really asking questions about the purpose of the writing, the kind of information it will contain, and the apparent difficulty of the material, based on your own background for it. This will help you to decide what reading techniques you need—whether you need to note carefully each detail, whether you need to read critically or analytically, or whether a summary is all that is needed. You can also decide whether you need to read slowly and carefully or whether you may read rapidly and less carefully. Practicing this type of previewing will soon teach you what, and how much, previewing you probably will need to do in most instances.

A logical way to begin using the previewing technique is to preview the book you are now holding: *The Art of Efficient Reading*. Here are some questions to help you.[1]

1. What are some of the ways of reading that will be discussed in this book? _____
   _____
   _____
   _____
   _____
   _____
   _____

2. Who are the authors? _____
   _____

3. What are the authors' qualifications for writing this book? _____
   _____
   _____
   _____
   _____

4. What is the copyright date? _____

5. Looking at the titles in the Table of Contents, what can I infer about the practice articles used in this text? Are they strictly reading exercises, or do they cover topics of varied interest? _____
   _____

6. In previewing quickly through the book, does it appear to be written in a fairly easy style, or will it require careful concentration to follow its meaning? _____

7. Does the vocabulary appear to be fairly simple, or quite technical?
   _____

You may compare your answers on the last two questions with those of a classmate or consider them thoughtfully by yourself. These answers are

[1] NOTE: Don't expect to keep all seven questions in mind while previewing. Preview to answer one or two, then try the others in turn.

subjective and will vary from person to person. For example, the style of writing is meant to be fairly easy, as is the vocabulary. If you have a particularly weak vocabulary, however, or if your comprehension tends to be poor, you may need to concentrate more carefully than will another reader. Thus, you must be the judge.

Previewing Exercises

In the following selections, use these questions to help you with your thinking *while* you are previewing:

1. Am I familiar with the topic of the selection?
2. Does the selection appear to be written in a fairly easy style, or will it require careful concentration to follow its meaning?
3. Does the vocabulary appear to be simple, or technical?
4. Is the selection literary in style, or factual and/or scientific?
5. For high comprehension, would I need to read material of this type slowly and carefully, or could I read at an average or comparatively rapid rate?
6. What seems to be the writer's purpose?
7. What is his main idea?
8. What significant questions can be answered from the selection? (Be prepared to write at least four or five.)

►   *PREVIEWING EXERCISE I*

The first selection is quite short and can be previewed very quickly. After the title, read the italicized "lead-in" and then read the subheadings and an occasional first sentence after the subheadings if you need more information. This should not take you more than thirty seconds. As you preview the selection, write down five questions that you believe the selection can answer for you. You can frame these questions by turning the subheadings or certain key phrases and sentences into questions. After you have written your own questions, answer the five questions at the end of the selection.

Remember these steps:

1. Read the lead-in.
2. Read the subheadings.
3. Occasionally read the first sentence after a subheading.
4. Write down questions that you expect to be answered by complete reading. (Space is provided at the end of the selection.)
5. Then answer the questions printed at the end of the selection, using the information gained during your preview.
6. Time yourself in minutes and seconds, beginning with the moment you start to read the title.

TIME: 30 SECONDS

After the Honeymoon, What?*

Over 200,000 June brides will walk down the aisle this month—one-eighth the year's total. They will be young (two out of three under 21) and brimming with bright expectations of married life ahead. As a group their destinies are predictable, within limits. Based in part on trends reported by the Population Reference Bureau, here are the June bride's prospects.

THE MARRYING KIND

Girls marry earlier than they used to. They are more matrimony-minded than the generation before them. About 12% (or over 170,000) of girls now in college are married. About 73,000 newlywed girls are still in high school.

PARENTHOOD COMES EARLY

The average young mother has her first child at 20 or 21, her last child by the time she is 28. She can expect to see the last one leave the nest— either career-bound or college-bound—while she and her husband are still in robust middle age. Then no longer will their lives be child-centered.

HOW MANY CHILDREN?

Three or more for most wives. (The population remains static when the figure is at 2.27—a "physically preposterous but statistically quite acceptable feat.") Few families stop with one child any more. Childless couples are becoming rarer, and adoption by such couples is increasingly common.

FAMILY LIFE

The young marrieds are quick to acquire things. They may start out in an apartment, but home ownership is the goal for most. They go into debt readily (after all, the future will take care of *that*). They expect good living, good incomes, bright prospects. Since they are embarking on the matrimonial seas at a time when the sailing is smooth, they are perhaps justified in their optimism.

THE WIVES WHO WORK

For thousands of new brides, the end of the honeymoon signals a return to work as well as assumption of wifely chores. When babies arrive, domesticity becomes a full-time job for most. But in the growing-up years —when children are between 6 and 18—over 40% of mothers go back to work. The reasons are primarily economic: to help pay for everything from music lessons to orthodontic braces. College expenses put another

* Reprinted by permission from *Changing Times*, the Kiplinger Magazine (June 1964). Copyright 1964 by The Kiplinger Washington Editors, Inc. 1729 H Street, N.W., Washington, D.C. 20006.

severe strain on family budgets, and the extra pay check earned by mother often becomes indispensable. At the present rate, between a third and a half of the new brides can expect to take on outside jobs during their married life.

THE SPECTER OF DIVORCE

Most young brides (and grooms) say that they worry, deep down, about the durability of their bond. One out of four of the newly married couples will wind up in the divorce courts. When they do, the odds are that at least one child will have to be raised without benefit of one natural parent. On the bright side, though, the divorce rate has receded from the record peaks it reached in the years immediately following World War II.

HEAD OF THE HOUSEHOLD

Almost one out of ten of the new brides will at some time in her married life find she is the main breadwinner—either because of separation or divorce, or because of death or disability of her spouse. About three out of 100 of the new grooms will one day have to take on the job of running the house and raising the kids by themselves.

MOST WILL OUTLIVE THEIR HUSBANDS

The sober truth is that by the time they reach their early seventies, at least half of today's brides will be widows. These may be lonely years or they may be rich with activity and interests, depending on how well they have been planned for. Be that as it may, as the years wear on for both husband and wife, there will accumulate the memories and reflections of a lifetime together that now, in June, is just beginning.

STOP TIMING HERE

Write the questions you gained by previewing here. _____

_____

_____

_____

_____

_____

_____

_____

_____

_____

_____

_____

_____

Without referring to the selection, answer the following questions:

1. Does this article appear to be based on research or opinion?
   a. Research.   b. Opinion.
2. Who compiled the information included in this article?
   a. Population Reference Bureau.   b. U.S. Department of Health, Education, and Welfare.
3. What type of information is given in this article?
   a. Advice to young married couples.   b. Statistics on marriage.
4. This article indicates that—
   a. most wives will outlive their husbands.   b. most husbands will outlive their wives.
5. What might also be an acceptable title for this article?
   a. Predictions for Young Marrieds.   b. How to Have a Happy Marriage.

For comparison, here are some questions you might have written while previewing:

1. What problems are involved in the trend toward earlier marriages?
2. What problems arise because young married people are quick to acquire a family and possessions?
3. What happens to young marriages when wives work?
4. How frequent is divorce among young married couples?
5. Do many young women become heads of the households?
6. What happens to the children in young marriages that end in divorce?

If your questions differ greatly from these, read the selection to determine whether your questions are answered.

► **PREVIEWING EXERCISE II**

In the second selection, "Thunderbolts in Harness," a brief review of scientific experiments with lightning is offered. As you will see, the selection is divided into a number of parts. The sentence immediately after each heading, or the last sentence just before each new heading in many instances summarizes the idea the author wishes to present about the subtopic.

Before you begin your preview, check again the questions listed at the beginning of this section. Because this is one of your earliest attempts, the following additional steps are outlined for you:

1. Read the title of the selection. (What questions can you ask about the title?)
2. Check to see where the selection originally appeared.
3. Read the "lead-in."

4. Read the headings and the first sentence following each.

5. If you need more information for preview purposes, read the last sentence in the last paragraph of each subtopic.

6. Time yourself accurately (in minutes and seconds), beginning the moment you begin to read the title. You should be able to preview this article (writing your own questions as you go) in two minutes.

TIME: 2 MINUTES

Thunderbolts in Harness:
A Story of Man's Conquest of Lightning*

Man's attempts to control, understand and create lightning have had marked success in the last twenty-five years. This article briefly reviews some of the ways in which this scientific effort has developed.

For century upon century men watched in awe and fear as stormy skies cast jagged streaks of lightning earthward with ominous crashing. Surely, it was the ire of the gods, they said. And they made sacrifices to appease these angry deities. The bold Teutons of northwestern Europe believed it was the god of war, who amused himself by hurling bolts of lightning into their forests.

The first faint inkling of the truth about lightning is recorded in American history books. It is the story of one of the founders of the United States, the statesman-philosopher-inventor Benjamin Franklin and his experiment with kite and key. Franklin discovered that lightning is electricity. He then invented the lightning rod to protect buildings from it.

A BOLT WRITES IN FIRE

We may say that Benjamin Franklin was the author of the prologue to *Thunderbolts in Harness*. The first chapter wasn't written until nearly two centuries later, when engineers began experiments to reproduce lightning in the laboratory.

It was a hot afternoon in August, 1920. The story told by the brief flash of electricity might have gone unnoticed if the bolt hadn't struck the summer camp of one of the few men who could and would read it—in the broken pieces of a mirror.

The man was a short, bearded, German-born genius, with a twisted, dwarfed body—Charles Proteus Steinmetz.

A STORY IN A MIRROR

The lightning struck Steinmetz' small cottage, perched on a bank close to the Mohawk River, a few miles from his General Electric labora-

* Adapted from *Thunderbolts in Harness,* published by the General Electric Company. Reprinted by permission of the General Electric Company.

tory in Schenectady, New York. No one could tamper with the trail it left. Steinmetz went over the place like a detective hunting clues to a murder. He pieced the damaged mirror together, and thus began the first scientific study of lightning.

The day of electricity to do man's work had arrived, and power stations and power lines were fanning out in all directions in ever-increasing numbers. Lightning, the unconquered "weapon of the gods," was a very real menace. When it struck it wrought havoc to man's spiderweb of electric lines. Interrupted electrical service was a commonplace occurrence. The more man depended on electricity, the more serious became its interruption.

Steinmetz puffed a cigar and reasoned that the best solution to the problems created by lightning was to study lightning itself. Easily said, but not so easily done, since no one knew where or when lightning would strike.

But why not make lightning?

1922 Is Historic Date

There were scoffers, naturally, when the wizened little wizard began building his first artificial-lightning generator in 1921. It was a queer contraption, with stacks of large glass plates, coated with metal foil, and connected here and there with wires. But it worked, and in 1922, the first sizeable man-made bolt of lightning using power equipment flashed across a gap, accompanied by a loud clap of artificial thunder. With a potential of 120,000 volts and 1,000,000 horsepower, it was only about one five-hundredth as powerful as natural lightning. But scientists and engineers could control it; they could study it. They knew when, where, and what it would strike.

The next year a larger and more powerful lightning generator was built; but Steinmetz never got the chance to use it. He died before it was completed.

In Pittsfield, Massachusetts, another General Electric scientist, Frank W. Peek, Jr., who had come from Schenectady in 1913, was testing high-voltage electric power equipment. The following year the first high-voltage laboratory was built under his direction, and soon after that time work began with high-voltage impulses, in connection with the design of lightning arresters.

Peek Takes Up Study

It is not surprising that in his quest for better and better power transformers and distribution equipment Peek took up the study of lightning where Steinmetz had left off. In 1928 he built a 3,600,000-volt lightning machine—a "big gun."

But lightning research was progressing rapidly, and before many years the "big gun" was superseded. Peek went on to develop a 5,000,000-volt, and then a 10,000,000-volt lightning generator. The 10,000,000-volter's bolt jumped 30 feet.

A Bout with Lightning

Dr. Karl B. McEachron was at that time engaged in high-voltage research on lightning arresters. He became the director of the high voltage laboratory after Peek was killed in an automobile accident in 1933. Dr. McEachron has the dubious distinction of having once come in contact with 33,000 volts of electricity and living to tell about it. (It sent him to the hospital for nine weeks.)

The knowledge which scientists had gained from studying artificial lightning in the laboratory led them back to the source of their work—natural lightning. The twentieth-century lightning-hunters had tools which Benjamin Franklin never dreamed of—high-speed cameras whose film traveled past the lens at a mile a minute, oscillographs for recording the waves of electricity in a lightning stroke, and other sensitive electrical instruments. But like Franklin, they needed lightning.

A Vigil in the Clouds

Each summer, in the "thunderstorm season," a man, who has to be part electrical engineer, part photographer, and part night watchman, takes up his vigil watching for lightning bolts to strike the mooring mast atop New York's loftiest skyscraper. Most of his work consists of sitting around waiting for thunderstorms, but when one comes he has to go into action fast.

Special high-speed rotating cameras focused on the top of the Empire State building are located in another skyscraper eight blocks away. Oscillographs and recorders are atop the Empire State building. When a storm is building up sufficient intensity to produce a stroke, these devices are automatically turned on by an electrical corona device. When the building is struck, the oscillographs automatically measure the stroke's characteristics.

A phone call warns the lightning watcher that a storm is approaching. No matter what time of night, he grabs a cab and rushes to the camera location and waits. Many times nothing happens except at distances too far to obtain good records. Frequently, however, the watch is rewarded by obtaining good lightning photographs.

A Youngster's Theory

When a bolt does strike, though, the lightning watcher is busy taking pictures and speaking into a voice recorder, describing what he sees as it happens.

Similar photographic research is carried on during the summer months in Pittsfield, from an observatory located on the roof of one of the city's tallest factory buildings. There, too, lightning watchers make the mad dash to the camera when a thunderstorm approaches.

One scientist's five-year-old daughter was slightly confused by the procedure. Many times at night, when the best lightning pictures are taken, she would hear father get up to answer the telephone, then dress quickly and hurry out. Soon it would rain and there would be thunder and lightning. Convinced that her father had something to do with the storm, the little girl begged her mother to "tell daddy to turn it off."

THE HIGH-VOLTAGE LABORATORY

Twenty-five years had passed since a bolt of lightning shattered a mirror in the Mohawk River camp of the late Charles Proteus Steinmetz and aroused his curiosity. Research on natural lightning had grown like a snowball rolling downhill. As Julius Hagenguth assumed directorship of the high-voltage laboratory at General Electric's Pittsfield plant, he had knowledge and equipment which had been gained and built up by a quarter century of hard work. Steinmetz had built a 120,000-volt lightning generator; Peek also was doing research, followed by McEachron. They contributed a 3,600,000-volt generator, a 5,000,000-volt generator, increasing better defense for power equipment, observations atop the Empire State building, and then a 10,000,000-volt lightning bolt that was in the limelight at the [1939] New York World's Fair, also much that was new concerning lightning as a phenomenon, providing data which hitherto had been lacking.

In June 1949 press, radio, and newsreel representatives sat in the gallery as "the world's largest man-made lightning center" opened with the flash and crash of a 15,000,000-volt bolt of lightning—a bolt which jumped a gap of 50 feet.

This bolt jumped at the *premiere* of General Electric's new High-Voltage Engineering Laboratory at Pittsfield, which was constructed under Hagenguth's direction.

A $2,000,000 CENTER

There are three other sections to this $2,000,000 lightning laboratory. In an adjoining building are seven high-voltage test areas. In one, experiments with powerful currents are conducted. In others, other electrical phenomena are studied. Less space is required for this equipment than is needed in High-Voltage Hall. Also in the same building is a controlled-temperature room, where tests are made under varied temperature and humidity conditions. Then there is an area of offices, a lecture room, five photographic darkrooms, chemical and physical laboratories, mechanical and electrical workshops, and other special test rooms.

Though the lightning "shows" are probably most impressive to the visitor, the primary purpose of the High-Voltage Engineering Laboratory is not entertainment. Far from it. All the expensive equipment and highly trained personnel are there for one basic reason: to develop better and lower-cost high-voltage electric power equipment. Though lightning is the most colorful, it's only a part of the research in high-voltage electricity.

STOP TIMING HERE

What significant questions could be answered by reading this selection? _____

_____

_____

_____

_____

_____
_____
_____
_____
_____
_____
_____
_____
_____
_____

Now answer the following questions without referring to the selection:

1. Is this selection technical or nontechnical?
   a. Technical.   b. Nontechnical.

2. What is the purpose of the selection?
   a. To help the reader better understand lightning.   b. To inform the general public about General Electric's experiments with lightning.

3. Is the selection literary in style, or factual and/or scientific?
   a. Literary.   b. Factual.

4. Should this probably be read quite slowly for best comprehension, or may it be read rapidly?
   a. Slowly.   b. Rapidly.

5. Does the article seem to be based on opinion, or research?
   a. Research.   b. Opinion.

6. To what area of learning is this selection most nearly related?
   a. Social sciences.   b. Science.   c. Literature.   d. Mathematics.

Some of the preview questions you might have written are the following:

1. How has man gradually learned to control lightning?
2. Who began the scientific study of lightning?
3. What were some of the first steps in the study of lightning?
4. What was the high-voltage laboratory?
5. Of what use is the study of lightning?
6. Who were some of the men active in the early study of lightning?
7. When were the first experiments in lightning attempted?

If your preview questions differ greatly from these, read the selection to determine whether your questions are answered.

► **PREVIEWING EXERCISE III**

Although the following selection is longer than the previous one, its careful organization and clearly defined subheadings and italicized key sentences make it easy to preview. Read the headings and the topic and summary sentences, and note the key sentences that are set off by special typographic treatment. Allow yourself one minute for preview. While previewing the selection, write down five questions that you would like to have answered and that you believe can be answered from the selection.

Preview by—
1. Reading the title.
2. Reading the headings.
3. Reading the topic and summary sentences under each subheading.
4. Noting key phrases and sentences.
5. Writing down questions to be answered by complete reading.

Then answer the questions printed at the end of the selection.

TIME: 1 MINUTE

What Makes a Floor Plan Good?*

How convenient, efficient and livable a house proves to be depends on how well it is laid out. If there are defects in the floor plan, you'll know it soon enough—after you move in. But how do you spot those defects before you buy?

If you go house shopping often enough and do it thoughtfully enough eventually you acquire a knack for sizing up floor plans at a glance. The flaws reveal themselves immediately. Most people, though, hunt houses only three or four times in a lifetime. They never have a chance to develop this valuable skill.

So unless you are an expert in this line, your only hope of figuring out the faults or merits of a floor plan is to take time to study it and see how it works.

GET IT ON PAPER

Make a point of getting a floor plan of every house you seriously consider buying, a plan you can take home to analyze and ponder. If none is available, make your own. Carry pencil, paper and tape measure with you. Take the dimensions of each room on the spot and sketch out the floor plan roughly, including the location of doors, windows and closets.

When you get home, transfer these rough notes and sketches to a simple scale drawing of the plan. You can do this easily by using quadrille-ruled paper divided into $\frac{1}{5}$-inch or $\frac{1}{4}$-inch squares. If you let

* Reprinted by permission from *Changing Times,* the Kiplinger Magazine (December 1963). Copyright 1963 by the Kiplinger Washington Editors, Inc., 1729 H. Street, N.W., Washington, D.C. 20006.

each square equal 2 feet, you can reproduce the floor plan in a small space in a matter of minutes. A larger scale, of course, would be even better.

Study and discuss the plan. You will be astonished at how much it reveals that never entered your mind when you were in the house.

If you have several houses under consideration, do this for each one. Then you will be able to compare at leisure and avoid getting one house confused with another, easy enough to do when you trust to memory without notes.

THE TESTS THAT TELL THE TALE

Now suppose you have a floor plan spread out before you. You want to decide whether it is a good plan or poor. How can you judge? What should you look for?

We've distilled the problem to its essence for you by devising six tests that you can apply to any floor plan, right in your favorite chair. They call for no expert knowledge, no equipment but your homemade scale drawing of the layout, a pencil and an hour.

A floor plan that passes all six tests is an excellent plan. Most floor plans will show some shortcomings. Whether they are serious enough to warrant crossing the house off your list will be for you to determine.

Putting any floor plan through the six tests, incidentally, will do a lot to teach you the elements of good planning. The experience will make you a better shopper next time you go house hunting.

To begin with, remember that a house has to accommodate three different types of activity:

There must be space for certain kinds of *work,* including food preparation, laundering, sewing, perhaps workship chores related to repair and maintenance of household equipment.

There must be space for *group activities,* including dining together, entertaining, children's play, shared leisure and recreation.

There must be space for *private activities,* including sleeping, dressing, individual study, individual recreation, or just getting away from everybody.

The space required to meet these needs varies from family to family. A family with two children of the same sex, for example, may not need as many bedrooms as a family with two children of opposite sexes. A family that entertains often will need a separate dining room. One that lives more informally and entertains less may not need a dining room nearly as much as room to eat in the kitchen. A family with teen-age children may need a place for parents to hide out more than it needs a recreation room.

You are the world's best expert on your family's requirements. No one can appraise a plan from this point of view better than you. So make this kind of critical examination the first phase of your evaluation. Hence . . .

Test 1. Does the plan provide all the different kinds of living space you require?

Now look at the plan in another light. To be a good plan, it must not only permit your family to carry on the normal activities of its daily life, but it ought to provide separate places for different kinds of activity.

This is important because many things you do are incompatible. Your children can't do good homework, for instance, if they have to study in the kitchen at the same time that dinner dishes are being washed. Similarly, it is impossible to sleep, rest or be quietly sick in peace if your bedroom is separated by only a thin wall from the room where the hi-fi or TV is in use. And it hardly contributes to gracious living if the noise of the shower or a flushing toilet is plainly audible in the living room where you are entertaining guests.

Such considerations lead to the concept of *zoning*, the principle that there is a right place and a separate place for all activities incompatible with other expectable activities.

You should be able to identify three general zones on the floor plan— a zone for living, a zone for working, a zone for sleeping. Furthermore, these zones should be separated by something more than an ordinary partition. Otherwise their separation will be theoretical rather than real. So look for barriers between the zones, buffers such as closets back to back or seldom-used spaces between frequently used spaces.

You'll find it easier to visualize the zoning of the plan—or lack of it— if you take a pencil and lightly circle the areas that belong in each of the three zones. If the circles are distinctly separate, the floor plan passes the zoning test. If they overlap, or impinge on each other, be careful. This may be the tip-off to a poorly zoned plan.

Test 2. Is the plan distinctly zoned, with buffers between the zones?

Now take up the problem of how you move around inside the house, the traffic pattern. Here the expressway idea should govern. That is, you should be able to get from here to there—wherever you are and wherever you are bound—without taking devious routes or traversing congested areas.

This aspect of the planning is called *circulation*. To analyze it, draw these paths on your study plan:

From the service entrance (maybe you call it the back door or kitchen door) to each of the other rooms of the house, including bedrooms and bathrooms.

From the main entrance (front door) to each of the other rooms, including kitchen, bedrooms and baths.

From each bedroom to the nearest bath.

From the kitchen to living room, dining room, bedrooms and bathrooms.

It is very unlikely that all these pathways will be separate. Many of them probably will overlap. Indeed they should.

When you have all the journeys penciled in, take a look at what they do to the plan. Was it possible to make each trip from one room to another without passing through a third room? In a good plan, it will be possible.

Pay particular attention to traffic in the living room. This room should be a dead end, a destination and not a crossroad. If you find the living room slashed with traffic lanes, it will not be a calm, relaxed room. Furthermore, it won't even be a good traffic route. Either it will be an obstacle course impeded by tables and chairs or you will not be able to furnish it properly because you have to keep space open for circulation. And either way makes for an unsatisfactory living room and indicates a poor plan.

Test 3. Is the circulation pattern direct, efficient and uncluttered?

Next, consider the provisions for storage, of which you will need plenty. And you will need it everywhere, near the main entrance for coats and hats, in the kitchen for foods and utensils, in utility areas for ironing boards and cleaning equipment, in bedrooms for clothing, in bathrooms for linens and medicines, in laundry areas for soap powders and soiled and clean washables, in the living room for records, books and games— plus general storage areas for seldom-used bulky articles, sports and hobby gear, seasonal equipment and outdoor equipment.

How much storage should you have? That's hard to say because families have possessions in different quantities. It is helpful, though, to compare the storage space shown on the plan with what you have now. In all likelihood you will want more in your new home. The rule is to look for lots of storage. Hardly anyone ever has too much.

To get a good idea of how much of the interior of the house is given over to storage, crosshatch the closets and storage rooms on the floor plan so that they stand out clearly.

Test 4. Is there adequate—or abundant—storage space in every room of the house?

Floor plans can be deceptive if you look on all the space shown as usable space. In reality, a good deal of the floor area is not usable, at least as living space.

In carefully-thought-out plans, a high proportion of the available space is usable. In poor plans, much of the area is wasted by being taken up for nonliving uses.

To see how the plan you are studying functions in this respect, take up your pencil again. You already have crosshatched the storage areas, which are one kind of nonliving space. And you have drawn in the traffic lanes. Now shade in those pathways to make them as wide as they have to be for unrestricted movement. Those paths, too, are nonliving space.

Do the same thing for all hallways, shading in their entire width because they usually have no other use than carrying traffic. Finally, shade in the floor areas that must be kept free to allow doors to swing.

Then you can see at a glance whether a lot or a little of the total floor area is lost to these nonliving uses.

Test 5. Does the plan efficiently preserve a high proportion of the available space for living use?

The last test concerns dimensional adequacy. Are the rooms big enough?

One of the best ways to judge this factor is, again, to compare with the rooms you now occupy. No doubt you have firm ideas on whether they are big enough or too small. Be sure to make your judgment on the basis of actual measurements, though. Your eye can easily mislead you about the size of empty rooms or rooms furnished with furniture that may differ in quantity or scale from yours.

Another useful device is to make paper cutouts of your furniture to the same scale you used in drawing your study plan. Then you can put the pieces on the plan, move them around, and see just how they would fit into the room. When you do this, though, remember to take window sill levels and door swing space into account.

Test 6. Will the rooms accommodate the furniture you intend to put into them—and still leave enough space to move about?

If there are major flaws in the floor plan you are studying, these six tests will expose them. As you can see, though, the tests aim at general principles, the fundamentals of good planning. Let them be suggestive, stimulating you to check the plan for the specifics that matter most to you.

STOP TIMING HERE

Write your preview questions here. _____

_____

_____

_____

_____

_____

_____

_____

_____

_____

_____

_____

_____

After you have written your own questions, answer the following without referring to the selection:

1. From what source was this selection taken?
   a. *Today's Health.*   b. *Changing Times.*

2. Before buying or renting a home, your first step should be—
   a. to study a floor plan.   b. to investigate the neighborhood.
3. In judging the layout of a house, you should give particular attention to—
   a. the space your family might need for work, group, and private activities.   b. the amount of play and living areas.
4. Other significant factors in house selection are—
   a. the age and roominess of the house.   b. the circulation pattern and storage space.
5. Does the author suggest any minimum amount of space for each member of the family?
   a. No.   b. Yes.

Check your answers to these questions by referring to the Answer Key. Then look back to the selection and check your own questions against its content. Were your questions answered in the article? Were your questions too general? Were they too specific? Write in a sentence or two what you believe your problem was, if you could not find the answers to more than two of your questions. _____

_____

_____

_____

_____

_____

_____

If you have followed the reasoning of previewing up to this point, you should already have learned ways of thinking about reading that will help you with your daily assignments. Let us review the ideas behind previewing again. Keep clearly in mind *why* you preview. Previewing is a way of setting the mind in order for a maximum of comprehension. You are looking for the general topic of the selection, the writer's purpose, the level of difficulty of the material, whether it is literary or a presentation of factual data, and clues that indicate the writer's biases, opinion, and so on. You should also be able to grasp some of the major details that support the main ideas. This preparation for reading is accomplished by asking questions as you preview—by turning headings and other key phrases or sentences into questions. *Why, who, when,* and *how* should be included in some of your questions as you jump rapidly from one subheading to the next.

►   ***PREVIEWING EXERCISE IV***

The following selection is somewhat more difficult to preview than the earlier articles. It does not have subheadings, and its style is less compact and precise. Yet the major ideas the author wishes to present are nearly all contained in the first sentences of its paragraphs. Thus, even in materials that are less formally written, previewing is a practical method of gaining ideas about a writing before reading it completely.

Select your own points for preview-reading, but gain as much information as you can that will help you later to read completely for maximum comprehension. Allow yourself three minutes for preview. While previewing, write down five questions that you would like to have answered and that you believe can be answered from the selection.

Preview by—

1. Reading the title.
2. Reading the headings.
3. Reading the topic and summary sentences.
4. Noting key phrases and sentences.
5. Writing down questions to be answered by complete reading.

Then answer the questions at the end of the selection.

TIME: 3 MINUTES

How Your Right to Vote Was Won*

Our struggle through history to guarantee voting rights to all is told in this second in a series of election articles. —ALFRED BALK

One of the most frequently cited reasons for Americans' unenviable poor voting record is a lack of appreciation of the precious privilege that voting represents. Yet the privilege to step up to a ballot box, or voting machine, and freely select the leaders who will make the laws under which one will live is one of the most valued and hard-won opportunities yet gained by man—one which even today fewer than half the world's population can claim. Consider its history and some of the marvelous machinery which implements and protects this right.

For centuries there was no such thing as voting. Leaders gained and held power by spear, club, and sword. Men could be made serfs or slaves, denied education and property rights, be allowed to move about purely at the whim of the wealthy and strong. Anyone born outside favored cliques had no real voice in community affairs.

Then the ancient Greeks, seeking to lift man from this backward and uncertain status, instituted the idea of selecting leaders and deciding public questions by common consent. For minor issues an open-air assembly and voting by a show of hands sufficed. To elect leaders or vote on banishment of citizens into exile, however, balloting was done by dropping pebbles into a warrior's helmet or a Grecian urn, the first demo-

* Adapted from Alfred Balk, "How Your Right to Vote Was Won," *Today's Health,* **42** (February 1964), pp. 52–54. Reprinted by permission of *Today's Health,* published by the American Medical Association.

cratic balloting as we know it. Light-colored stones signified "yea," or acquittal; dark ones, "nay," or exile.

In the 10th century A.D., the idea of voting was revived in Italy long enough to give birth to the words "ballot" and "balloting." A "ballota," or small ball, was used for voting in Italian city-states. So widespread was the discontent with despotic kings that in 1215 British noblemen won basic rights from the King in the famed Magna Charta (Great Charter). By the 16th century, noblemen and property owners of several states obtained the right to elect local officials.

But it was not until the American Revolution that the real breakthrough came. Britain's king forced American colonists to pay heavy taxes, restrict their trade, and quarter British soldiers in homes, all without consent of the colonists. The king appointed and removed colonial officials on impulse, punished members of any publicly elected body which complained, and refused accused persons a trial by jury.

Finally the colonists revolted. They issued the Declaration of Independence, insisting that "all men are created equal" and "governments [derive] their just powers from the consent of the governed." They fought six years against overwhelming odds for their independence, and won— establishing for the first time a government under which men were guaranteed the right to determine their own laws and leaders.

Even then all Americans could not vote. So the problem today of who should be allowed to vote need not be looked upon as something new.

The framers of the Constitution gave much thought to the voting question. They considered an outright rigid decision on who could vote and how to vote so touchy that these subjects were left completely out of the document.

In fact, at the time of our nation's birth, our leaders did not believe in giving every man the right to vote. Our Constitutional fathers were definite on one other subject related to voting, too. They opposed direct elections, and the Constitution itself is singularly silent as to how the American voting process will take place.

In 1787, when the Constitution was framed, less than one-quarter of adult Americans were permitted to vote. Laws in 11 of the 13 original colonies restricted all voting rights to property owners and taxpayers.

In 1868, the 14th Amendment was proclaimed. It provided that all persons born or naturalized in the United States and subject to its jurisdiction are citizens, and that no state shall make or enforce any law which shall abridge their privileges or immunities, including the right of adult males to vote. Excluded from these rights, however, were Indians, who were not taxed. This amendment was slow in ratification, taking a good number of years. In fact, the last state to ratify it was Maryland in 1959, 91 years from the time of the amendment's proclamation.

It required a Civil War and ratification of the 15th Amendment, in 1870, to establish that "the right of citizens of the United States to vote shall not be denied or abridged by the United States, or any State, on account of race, color, or previous condition of servitude."

And it was a half-century later before women could vote. Then, in

1920, culminating a 70-year campaign during which 10,000 women once had marched in Washington, the 19th Amendment guaranteed them that right.

Few persons realize it, but for more than a century voters also were denied the right to elect U.S. senators. State legislatures retained this power until ratification of the 17th Amendment in 1913.

(Technically, Americans also are prohibited from voting directly for president and vice president. The Constitution reserves this right for an Electoral College whose members are elected in November. The electors then meet the following January to select a president. In practice, of course, with few exceptions, electors traditionally award their state's entire electoral vote to the candidate receiving the largest popular vote in the state.)

The mechanics of voting also have evolved slowly over the years. When Americans first voted, most merely walked into a polling place, signed a voting register, or asked an election official to sign it, wrote the names of the candidates they favored on a blank piece of paper, and dropped the ballot into a hat.

Abraham Lincoln, for one, apparently voted in this manner during his early years in New Salem, Illinois. An election-day register of voters, in which his name is inscribed, still is on file in the Illinois State Historical Library.

For a time, political parties themselves were allowed to print ballots of different colors and hand them to voters at polling places. Unethical party workers even handed out tissue paper ballots which could be stuffed surreptitiously into the ballot box in quantity—the genesis of the term "stuffing the ballot box." Only in the 1870's did the states begin printing official ballots, and only in 1888 was a secret, uniform, non-partisan ballot adapted from a type that originated in Australia—assuring all Americans, for the first time, complete independence and freedom from embarrassment as they voted.

The advent of voting machines has refined election procedures even more, decreasing both the time required for voting and the chances of error or fraud in vote-counting. The first practical machine, invented by a safe-maker named Jacob H. Myers, was used in a municipal election in Lockport, New York, in 1892. Today, at least half of all Americans' votes reportedly are cast on voting machines.

Carrying out these carefully prescribed procedures for voting and vote-counting is expensive. The City of New York alone, for instance, budgets some $4 million for expenses in each national election. Citizens of smaller cities pay proportionately.

"But most Americans," according to Brendan Byrne, executive director of the American Heritage Foundation, "realize that this is one of the finest investments that any citizenry can make. Thousands of Americans have paid with their lives for this privilege."

The official balloting apparatus is only one, component of the marvelous machinery of free elections, however. Many others are required to make elections work. Candidates must be screened and nominated, for example, campaign funds raised, campaign organizations staffed, issues clarified and dramatized, and balloting and vote-counting policed. In this country, for the most part, these things are accomplished through local and national political parties.

Efforts of the two major parties may go unappreciated by many, but a visit to the offices of the Republican and Democratic National Committees in Washington, D.C., readily reveals their indispensability. Republican headquarters occupies most of the second floor of the modern Cafritz Building, and Democratic offices are virtually around the corner in a large seventh-floor section of the equally modern Riddell Building.

There, walking past busy staff members and their secretaries, who work in rooms and cubicles jammed with printed materials and files, one sees researchers at work culling dozens of newspapers for material for their voluminous files. Activities of candidates and office holders of the opposing party, and the most pressing issues in various areas—all are noted. National chairmen are rarely seen in the offices. Both maintain speaking and travel schedules which keep them away half the time.

Both offices publish newsletters and fact books for local and state party officials, answer barrages of questions from party members, mail thousands of fund-raising letters, oversee preparation of campaign materials, coordinate registration drives, channel requests for speakers, and supervise arrangements for the vast presidential nominating conventions. Both, like other branches of the party at various levels, depend heavily on housewives, college students, and other volunteer staff members.

"But this," says the Democratic chairman, "is only the visible part of the iceberg. Actually, the major work and strength in both parties is at the grass roots in county and state party organizations."

It is noteworthy, too, that both parties, like American government itself, are built upon free voting and a pyramid of representation of members. Ward or township committeemen, or precinct captains who are elected in party primaries govern the party's county organization, and choose its chairman. The county chairmen, in turn, constitute a state central committee, and each state organization, by various means, selects two national committeemen as well as delegates to the quadrennial national nominating conventions which select the party's presidential and vice presidential nominees.

Both parties also recruit and assign election judges and poll-watchers to polling places, and both recruit volunteers who, by phoning, preparing, and distributing literature, and performing other services, such as chauffeuring voters to the polls, help contribute to the success of elections by getting out the vote.

"No matter how routine these things seem," says the Republican chairman, "they're important. It is only through a representative turnout that an election means anything, and it is in the precincts that elections are won or lost."

Running for office nowadays is expensive. In 1960, the national elections cost the two political parties, their candidates, and their supporters, an estimated $20 million. Of this, $14 million went for radio-TV time, and members of each party spent at least $1 million on campaign buttons, lapel tabs, bumper stickers, window stickers, cards, and similar materials.

The 1962 congressional campaigns cost more than $18 million, and the 1962 total for all offices, estimates the authoritative *Congressional Quarterly*, was $100 million. Almost every presidential campaign ends with huge deficits which both parties must work for months, even years, to erase. In 1960, these amounted to $700,000 for the Republicans and $3.8 million for the Democrats.

One authority estimates that it costs at least a quarter-million dollars to run for the U.S. Senate, and a half-million dollars or more to run for governor. Even mayoral candidates, or contestants for the state legislature, may be required to raise $5000 to $10,000 or more in campaign funds. "In a modern democracy," comedian Will Rogers once said, "it takes a lot of money even to get beat with."

But candidates and their supporters willingly assume this burden. They sacrifice leisure time, ring doorbells, and shake hands to the point of exhaustion, and outline their views in speeches until even the hardiest become hoarse—all to fulfill their part in the only practical method yet devised for making freedom and self-government work. All they ask in return is some degree of help from those who believe as they do, and the willingness of every citizen to use the miraculous machinery of elections to make his interests and preferences known. For they know that the immortal observation by the great statesman Edmund Burke is an implacable truth:

"All that is necessary for the forces of evil to win the world is that enough good men do nothing."

STOP TIMING HERE

Write your preview questions here. _____

_____

_____

_____

_____

_____

_____

_____

_____

_____

_____

_____

_____

_____

_____

After you have written your own questions, answer the following without referring to the selection.

1. Who were the first people to grant voting privileges?
   a. The Romans.   b. The Greeks.
2. From what language does "ballot" originate?
   a. Latin.   b. Italian.
3. Did the framers of our Constitution believe in giving every man the right to vote?
   a. Yes.   b. No.
4. What is the purpose of this selection?
   a. To give a short history of the evolution of voting.   b. To show that the strength of our country is based on the right to vote.
5. Besides voting, what other topic is discussed in this selection?
   a. The expense of running for office.   b. The philosophies of the two major parties.
6. In what field of study would this article most likely appear?
   a. Science.   b. History.

Check your answers to these questions, using the Answer Key. Then *read* the selection and check your own questions against its content. Were your questions answered in the article? Were you unable to find the answers to three or more of your questions? If so, why? In a sentence or two, explain any miscalculations you may have made concerning the kind of information the writer would give you. _____

_____

_____

_____

_____

_____

_____

_____

_____

_____

►   *PREVIEWING EXERCISE V*

A final selection for previewing is excerpted from a college text on the psychology of personal and social adjustment. Choose your own points for previewing, but allow yourself *one and one half minutes* only. As you preview, write down five questions that you would like to have answered and that you believe can be answered from the selection.

TIME: 1½ MINUTES

Understanding Our Behavior:
The Psychology of Personal and Social Adjustment*

AREAS OF ADJUSTMENT

Life consists of many experiences that need to be interwoven or integrated from day to day. A normal adult probably is, or at some time in his life has been, motivated by the desire to marry, rear children, experience a happy home life, and earn success in a chosen vocation. In addition, he desires to enjoy the companionship of friends and associates of his choice, and to spend his leisure time in interesting and relaxing activities. He also strives to achieve a position of respect among his associates, to enjoy democratic rights, and to establish the foundation of an economically and socially secure old age.

Children, adolescents, and adults are faced with the problem of so ordering their attitudes and behavior that they achieve maximum success and satisfaction in their home, school, work, and social activities, without interfering with or limiting the interests, ambitions, and activities of other members of the group. Adjustment to environmental conditions and human interrelationships is a gradually developing process that begins early in childhood and continues throughout life. Moreover, an understanding of what constitutes good adjustment and a willingness to become a well-adjusted person probably can be achieved best through the study and application of the psychological principles that are basic to the development of healthful living and wholesome behavior.

Family adjustment. The family is the basic unit of society. It is generally agreed that as the home is so will be the larger social group. The intimate relations that are inherent in home and family life may build up either closely knit loyalties or disrupting discords.

Bickering, faultfinding, resentments, display of extreme individualism, disregard for the rights of others, and shirking of responsibility in the home are more than likely to be carried over into other group relationships. Through the centuries the home has changed gradually from an independent autocracy dominated by the "head" of the family into a more or less loosely organized social unit. Former rigid parental control of child behavior and more recent child self-assertion can find a meeting ground through a conscious effort to build the home upon a foundation of cooperative family interrelations that are aimed at the healthful development of every member of the family group.

Educational adjustment. A young person's degree of successful adjustment in his learning experiences is affected by many factors: the learner's degree of mental ability; learning readiness; interests and ambitions; appropriateness of curricular offerings; teacher attitudes; and teaching techniques. Problems of adjustment arise in the school life of a young person when or if any one of these factors is inadequate to help him select and engage in the kind of educational experiences that will prepare him for successful participation in his present and future life activities.

To provide proper financial support for education is the responsibility of the nation, state, and local community. The value of education as a means of improved educational adjustment is receiving increased recognition. Better educational facilities are made available for children and adolescents; educational opportunities are being extended to meet adult needs for continued schooling. Adequate financial aid is needed to provide extensive and intensive education. Yet money alone cannot solve all the educational problems of the school community. Educational leaders are faced with the problem of supplying the kind of education that will help young and older learners achieve success in their marital, family, occupational, and social adjustments.

A well-balanced, forward-looking educational program is essential to the development of individual and group adjustment to personal and social demands. The task of organizing and administering such a program is tremendous. Will individual communities be able to meet this responsibility? How much state aid will be needed? Should the federal government give financial assistance when or if a community cannot meet its educational obligations? Are taxpayers willing to support nursery schools and kindergartens? To what extent is the public responsible for maintaining junior colleges, colleges, universities, and special schools? What is to be the content of study? How extensive can be the equipment? What is to be the maximum of educational preparation and of remuneration for teachers? How can community facilities and resources be utilized as learning aids? These are some of the educational problems that are closely related to educational adjustment.

Occupational adjustment. Job adjustment is dependent upon job conditions, worker attitudes, and degree of efficiency. A worker's chances to perform adequately on the job and to experience personal satisfaction in the work are conditioned by: vocational selection based upon personal interest in the work and ability to meet its demands; appropriate and adequate preparation; available job opportunities; healthful working conditions; intelligent and understanding supervision; pleasant co-worker relationships, and adequate financial remuneration. Poor worker adjustment in any one of these areas may give rise to worker inefficiency, discontent, resentment, feelings of frustration, or seriously maladjusted behavior.

This is a critical period of occupational and economic adjustment. High cost of living has brought about disagreement concerning adequacy of remuneration. Technological changes are opening new occupation fields and closing others. Fear concerning economic security interferes with the occupational adjustment of the worker; uncertainty as to the most effective ways in which human resources and occupational opportunities can be integrated constitutes a serious problem of management adjustment.

Social and community adjustment. Participation in organized or informal group activity is a test of an individual's power to adjust his own attitudes and interests to the interests, needs, or rights of other people.

His interest in community welfare and his cooperative attitude toward community projects are as important as is the exercise of similar interest and attitudes in home and work relationships. In all these associations a person experiences many problems of adjustment that become increasingly serious as group needs and interests change with changing conditions.

Community problems that demand intelligent leadership and citizen cooperation include safety regulations, recreational facilities, health protection, adequate housing, and efficient transportation. Community well-being is dependent not only upon the provision of these environmental conditions, but also upon the displayed attitude and the behavior of community members. Good individual or group adjustment can be hindered by frequent occurrences of asocial acts committed by some of the group members. Accounts of burglaries, muggings, assaults, reckless driving, heavy drinking, fights, and illicit sex relations are featured in the daily newspapers. Apprehension of offenders and prevention of antisocial behavior constitute important areas of community concern.

STOP TIMING HERE

Write your preview questions here. _____

_____

_____

_____

_____

_____

_____

_____

_____

_____

_____

_____

_____

_____

After you have written your own questions, answer the following without referring to the selection.

1. What is the probable purpose of *Understanding Our Behavior?*
   a. It is a practical attempt to assist adults in gaining greater understanding of human behavior.   b. It is a theoretical discussion of medical and psychiatric research.

2. The terminology used in this selection is—
   a. nontechnical.   b. technical.

3. Which of these types of adjustment is not mentioned in the selection?
   a. Family adjustment.   b. Educational adjustment.   c. Marital adjustment.   d. Occupational adjustment.
4. What do the authors say is a criterion of one's ability to adjust to the interests, needs, and rights of other people?
   a. The number of organizations in which he holds membership.
   b. His ability to participate in group activity.
5. Which area of adjustment am I most interested in? In which area do I find my greatest difficulties? (These answers, of course, are your own.)

After you have checked your answers to these questions, *read* the selection and check your own questions against its content. Were your questions answered? If not, what error are you making in anticipating the authors' thoughts? Perhaps you did not carefully define the basic purpose of the writing, or perhaps you thought it was more detailed with specific information than it was. If you found difficulty in anticipating the writers' ideas, explain in a sentence or two why you apparently miscalculated. _____

_____

_____

_____

_____

_____

_____

Summary

Continued practice in previewing is necessary if you expect to add this technique to your study methods. Use previewing each time you pick up a book, magazine, or newspaper. At first, previewing followed by reading will probably take you longer than the methods of study you presently use. When you have become skilled in the previewing reading method, however, you will find that it is both fast and effective.

Here are some suggestions that may help you with your practice:

1. First of all, be willing to give the technique an honest trial. You may at first find it difficult to accept the fact that "skimming off" the surface of a chapter or article will make a significant difference in your comprehension of the material when you later read it completely.

2. Overcome the need to read every word or sentence in a paragraph by reading the first sentence, then looking aside and trying to guess what the rest of the paragraph will say. What does the writer imply in these first few words that reveals the idea he will develop in the rest of the paragraph? Now read the second sentence, again look away, and attempt to further develop your first idea about the meaning within the paragraph. Go through the entire paragraph, anticipating after each sentence what the rest will be

about. As you practice, you will learn to infer more and more meaning from smaller and smaller units of a given selection.

3. Practice in perceptual alertness will also help in previewing. Cover the first line of a paragraph with a small card. Fix your attention toward the beginning of the covered line, quickly pull the card down and push it back again. How many words did you see? Were you able to infer the meaning of the sentence? Try again, this time looking at the second line. How did you do this time? Can you infer the meaning of the first and second lines and from it guess at the main idea of the paragraph?

4. In each of your own textbooks study the table of contents. Skim half way down the first page of each and then see how well you can guess at the titles of the next consecutive chapters. This practice will help you to think in terms of the writer's purpose and the fact that textbooks are developed logically toward some goal.

HELP YOURSELF

The following books offer further suggestions and practice material in previewing; use them if you need more work in this area.

Brown, James I. *Efficient Reading.* Revised edition. Boston: Heath, 1962.

Leedy, Paul D. *Read with Speed and Precision.* New York: McGraw-Hill, 1963. See Chapter 2.

McDonald, Arthur S., and George H. Zimmy. *The Art of Good Reading.* Indianapolis: Bobbs-Merrill, 1963. See Chapter 2 and exercises 20–23.

CHAPTER 2

SKIMMING: A WAY OF
RAPID READING

In the preceding chapter you were introduced to previewing. The skill that is used for previewing is *skimming*—the technique of allowing your eyes to travel over a page very quickly, stopping only here and there to gain an idea. You learned that the purpose of previewing-skimming is to help you get ideas about a selection before actually reading it. You learned that you can make reading more vivid by looking for the answers to questions you have raised during previewing, and that you can mentally outline or organize the author's main points to ensure better comprehension when you later read the selection completely.

In this chapter skimming is presented as a systematic, rapid-reading skill, more thorough than previewing, and useful when you do not intend to read the selection completely at a later time. This skill has many uses—skimming the newspaper, keeping up with news magazines and other periodicals, and gaining a broad background of general information from many sources about a particular topic. Often in this type of skimming, a particular paragraph that you wish to read completely may attract your attention. After you have read such a paragraph thoroughly, however, don't forget to continue the skimming activity.

How to Skim

Skimming as a rapid-reading technique makes use of the previously learned skills of previewing, but it requires more careful attention to the structure and content of the individual paragraphs than you would ordinarily use during preview-skimming. Read a few words in each paragraph: read the first sentence; scan the paragraph for clue words that may tell you *who, what, when, where, how many,* or *how much;* and then, perhaps, read the last sentence. Let your eyes "float" down over the content of each page, looking for other clues, such as names, places, unusual words, numbered sequences, and so on. Look also for the writer's direction words. Such words as *more, furthermore,* and *also* suggest that the preceding thought is still being discussed. Words such as *however, yet,* and *on the contrary* suggest that the thought is apt to reverse itself or take another direction.

What do you think is the author's purpose in the way he writes a particular paragraph? Does the paragraph offer an opinion or make a statement and then offer proof or support? Perhaps its purpose is to describe a process, behavior, or appearance, or to offer chronological steps in a sequence of events. The purpose may be to present a free flow or association of ideas, as is often found in fiction. Sometimes a paragraph simply repeats or summarizes ideas that have been presented earlier.

The skill of sensing, during high-speed skimming, the purpose for which a writer selects his words in constructing a paragraph takes much practice. As you begin skimming, try at once to "connect" with the author's general purpose; then try to sense the way he develops each paragraph. Note how he uses a series of sentences to develop an idea and then how he develops a transition to another thought.

Some paragraphs are built like an equilateral triangle. They start at the top with a small point, and then broaden out by adding more details until they reach a firm base, the main idea. Other paragraphs resemble an inverted triangle. They begin with a broad statement, the main idea, and then add a series of details that support that idea. Some paragraphs can be compared to a structure of two triangles balanced point to point. Such a paragraph begins with a strong statement (the topic sentence) then offers a series of details to support the main idea. These details then build up again into a strong idea, the summary sentence, or the conclusions.

Sometimes this arrangement of details and main ideas implies a cause-and-effect relationship—a series of causes add up to a certain effect or result. In some paragraphs, the presentation is simply chronological: this happens first, then this, then this, and so on. In other paragraphs, the details are gradually built up into a conclusion or judgment or inference. In some there may be only details, and no main idea.

These are only a few of the ways in which a writer develops his ideas in one or a series of paragraphs. As you skim these and other types of paragraphs, your understanding will be improved if you try to recognize the author's plan—in other words, to sense his purpose and organization. Obviously, the more quickly you recognize how a paragraph is built, the more quickly you will know what portion to read and what to skip.

Skimming Exercises

You will practice skimming as a rapid-reading technique in the selections that follow. Remember that your purpose is somewhat different from what it is when previewing. You will be trying to learn more of the content, and you will not need to give attention to organizing an over-all method of attack for more careful reading later on. Questions at the end of each selection will help you determine whether you have gathered some of the more important facts from skimming, and whether you have noted main ideas, purposes, and so on.

These steps for skimming are suggested to help you get started:

1. Read the title.
2. Note the author's name and source of selection.
3. Read the first paragraph completely.
4. Read subheadings and first sentences of remaining paragraphs.
5. Alternately read and "float" over the body of the material, looking for the following:

   a. Main ideas of paragraphs, with some of the more important supporting details.

   b. Clue words, such as names, dates, and qualifying adjectives.

   c. Direction words, indicating the writer's agreement or disagreement with the idea under discussion.

   d. Numbered sequences and ideas set off by attention-getting markings, such as italic or boldface type, arrows, asterisks, and so on.

6. If the final paragraph appears to be a summary, read it completely.
7. You should be able to skim-read most of the selections at 1,000 words per minute. The suggested time for skimming each selection is based on this rate.

► *SKIMMING EXERCISE I*

TIME: 1½ MINUTES

Our Rarest Mammal? *

The Auther—Lt. Charles L. Homolka, USAF, is a jet pilot instructor at Connally Air Force Base near Waco, Texas. He is a 1960 graduate of the University of Nebraska with a Bachelor of Science degree in conservation. Nature writing, birdwatching and fossil collecting occupy his spare time.

The black-footed ferret is so scarce that even the National Park Service can't find one to study. A decade ago, a seven-year survey found only 70. —CHARLES L. HOMOLKA

* Charles L. Homolka, "Our Rarest Mammal?" *Audubon Magazine*, **66** (July–August 1964), pp. 244–246. Published by permission from *Audubon Magazine*.

Another species of wildlife may soon vanish from the American scene. The object of concern is the black-footed ferret (*Mustela nigripes*), a mysterious, seldom seen and little understood species.

Its life history is not thoroughly understood, its range is not certain and the number of individuals which survive is still less certain. Even the National Park Service has little information on the black-footed ferret.

Walter H. Kittams, regional biologist in the Midwest, says "the Park Service has participated in a survey to locate specimens of this rare species. We are hopeful that animals can be located in a favorable habitat where they can be studied . . . [but] we have yet to locate animals which will be attractive for study by a university."

Wildlife conservationists agree that the black-footed ferret is near extinction. It may be the rarest mammal in the United States today.

A member of the weasel family, the black-footed ferret looks like a yellow-tinted mink. It is buffy-yellow with lighter underparts but is easily distinguishable by the tip of its tail, its black feet, and the black mask across the face.

Its range apparently has coincided with that of the prairie dog on which it preys. Its closest relative, the South Siberian ferret (*Mustela eversmanni*), also known as the masked polecat, occurs in Eastern Asia. The black-footed ferret may have crossed from Siberia when a strip of land joined America and Asia across the Bering Sea.

John J. Audubon and John Bachman were the first naturalists to describe this mammal. Their description was based on an imperfect skin sent to them from the lower waters of the Platte River of Nebraska by naturalist Alexander Culbertson in 1851. Nearly 25 years passed before the animal was reported again. During this time other naturalists began to doubt whether it even existed.

In 1877 Elliott Coues wrote that he was able to obtain only five or six fragmentary skins. When Clinton Hart Merriam wrote his *Synopsis of the Weasels of North America* in 1896, he reported having less than half a dozen specimens with which to work. This shows that the black-footed ferret has always been quite rare, even when the West was first being explored and settled. The Wildlife Management Institute calls it "one of the very rare species . . . on the danger list for many years."

Several years ago Walt Disney and his staff were able to trap three black-footed ferrets in the central part of South Dakota for the motion picture, *Vanishing Prairie*. The ferrets were later released in Wind Cave National Park in South Dakota. As to their whereabouts, Jess H. Lombard, park superintendent, reports: "Insofar as we know, they are still here, although they are rarely observed and are of unknown sex. The nocturnal habits of the ferret make it difficult to determine their presence. Efforts have been made to secure additional black-footed ferrets to supplement this nucleus of three."

In 1961 American Museum of Natural History scientists visited Wind Cave National Park to make a study of this natural history rarity, but could find no specimens for study. . . .

Specialists in Indian culture have long known that it is a part of the

tradition of the Blackfoot tribe to use the tawny hides of the black-footed
ferret as part of a chief's headdress. There is no evidence, however, that
the Indians have been able to find black-footed ferrets for many years.

Little is known about the habits of this ferret. It is believed to be
almost entirely dependent upon the prairie dog for its existence. Seldom
is it found in an environment other than that of a prairie dog town. That
the ferret breeds in prairie dog burrows is largely conjecture based on
the fact that its prey is principally the prairie dog.

Other victims may include rodents, birds and reptiles but there are
few reports to substantiate this theory. In Custer County, Nebraska, a
ferret was seen carrying a thirteen-lined ground squirrel. Years ago a
ferret reportedly lived under a wooden sidewalk in Hays, Kansas, where
it killed rats.

Since the prairie dog still is being wiped out in many areas, the black-
footed ferret also is vanishing. Originally, with the advance of civilization, the prairie dog population increased. Many of its predators such as
wolves, coyotes, hawks and eagles were killed or driven from the prairie.
The removal of the buffalo and other large game eliminated an important
competitor for forage, and the introduction of crops increased the food
supply.

About the turn of the century full-scale war was declared on prairie
dogs. They competed with domestic livestock for grass. It was estimated
that 32 prairie dogs consumed as much as one sheep and 256 as much as
a cow. The validity of these figures is questionable, but the fact remains
that the prairie dog was an important competitor with livestock for food.

At first, large scale destruction was accomplished by poisoning with
cyanide of potassium or strychnine or by fumigation with bisulphide of
carbon. About 1928 thallium sulfate was introduced; this was more effective and poisoning was intensified. After World War II poisoning resumed
its original pace with the introduction of a still more effective chemical,
sodium fluoroacetate—called 1080.

The prairie dog's original range extended from the Missouri River in
Montana and the Dakotas southward through Texas. Its western limit was
the Rocky Mountains except in the South where it extended into Arizona.
The eastern limit was roughly the 97th meridian. The black-footed ferret
was once found in this same general area.

In 1952 the plight of the black-footed ferret was discussed by the
executive committee of the American Committee for International Wild-
life Protection. This group then conducted a survey, led by Victor H.
Cahalane, to determine the number and the distribution of this species.
It canvassed field employees of the U.S. Fish and Wildlife Service, Soil
Conservation Service, and the National Park Service for information.

The survey yielded 42 acceptable reports involving 90 ferrets. Most of
the ferrets reported were sighted between 1948 and 1952. In some cases
duplication of reports was suspected and the actual number of animals
seen may have ranged as low as 50 or as high as 60 or 70. Nearly one
third of the reports involved dead ferrets, most of which had been shot,
trapped, run over on roads, or had died in captivity.

Of the ferrets observed alive, most were reported in prairie dog towns then being eradicated. Although it is not known if they eat poisoned prairie dogs, the ferrets still may be killed by fumigation. Also, whenever a town is eliminated, the ferrets, if they have been lucky enough to survive, must move to more favorable habitat—if they can find it.

South Dakota reported the most ferrets—followed by Montana, Nebraska, Colorado, North Dakota, Wyoming, Texas, New Mexico, and Utah. They appear to be most numerous in the area from Central and Western Nebraska to the southwest corner of North Dakota.

Texas, Kansas and Oklahoma have generally been excluded from the range of this animal. The only ferret reported from Texas was observed near Dalhart in the extreme northern portion of the Panhandle.

Two recommendations have been made to aid the perpetuation of this species. One would establish populations of ferrets in sanctuaries where prairie dog colonies can survive. This was attempted in Wind Cave National Park when steps were taken with the three ferrets used in the Walt Disney picture. Live-trapping and relocation in suitable habitat was favored as the best approach.

However, ferrets are so rare and little understood that other biologists recommend a life history study in order to determine the ferret's basic needs for survival.

In a recent prairie dog report of the Conservation Foundation and the New York Zoological Society, biologist Carl B. Koford observed that a study of the life history of the black-footed ferret "is a project that will require patience, skill, resourcefulness, and luck."

There may not be much time for such a project. The National Wildlife Federation says "this ferret may be near extinction." The Colorado Cooperative Wildlife Research Unit, combining efforts of Colorado State University, the State of Colorado, the Wildlife Management Institute, and the U.S. Fish and Wildlife Service, says it has "no information on the black-footed ferret other than that it is nearly extinct."

STOP TIMING HERE

Answer the following questions without referring to the selection:
1. What do you think is the main idea of this selection?
   a. The black-footed ferret is both rare and almost unknown.
   b. The black-footed ferret is likely to become extinct.   c. Each of us should make a real effort to do something about the black-footed ferret.   d. Conservation policies in the United States are, on the whole, very ineffectual.

2. How many ferret sightings were reported in the Survey of 1952?
   a. 25.   b. 70.   c. 90.   d. 130.

3. What is the major food source of the black-footed ferret?
   a. Plant life.   b. Fish.   c. The prairie dog.   d. Rodents.

4. In what area of our country is the black-footed ferret found?
   a. Northeastern states.   b. Central plains states.   c. Southeastern states.   d. Western states.

5. What is assumed to be the reason that the black-footed ferret is nearly extinct?
   a. His food supplies have been destroyed.   b. The Blackfoot Indians killed most of them for headdresses.   c. They have more than their share of natural predatory enemies.   d. This ferret is unusually susceptible to disease.

6. Why was a full scale war waged against the prairie dog at the turn of the century?
   a. The prairie dog was found to be a prime carrier of rabies.
   b. The prairie dog killed too much small game.   c. The prairie dog's ground holes became the refuge for reptiles and rodents.
   d. The prairie dog competed with domestic livestock for grass.

7. How long has it appeared that the extinction of the ferret was imminent?
   a. Since the turn of the century.   b. During the last decade.
   c. Since the intrusion of domesticated animals to their natural feeding grounds.   d. The ferret has always been quite rare.

8. What group was mentioned as having trapped three black-footed ferrets some years ago?
   a. Walt Disney and his staff.   b. National Park Service.   c. Audubon Society.   d. Wildlife Management Institute.

9. Why should we be concerned about the possibility of the black-footed ferret becoming extinct?
   a. It is an important fur-bearing animal.   b. The author does not offer any reasons for our concern.   c. Without ferrets to control them, prairie dogs become an increasing nuisance.   d. This member of the weasel family is an important mammal.

10. Which of these methods was mentioned as a way to perpetuate the species?
    a. Live-trapping and relocation.   b. Artificial breeding.
    c. Placing the animals in the artificial protection of large zoos.
    d. Introduce more stringent legislation regarding their protection.

Were you able to secure a fair degree of comprehension of the selection? If you answered seven or eight of the questions correctly your comprehension was adequate.

Had you previously realized how much time skimming can save you in reading material in which complete, detailed comprehension is not necessary? Compare the time required to skim the next selection and the time you would have spent if you had read in your usual fashion.

► **SKIMMING EXERCISE II**

TIME: 1½ MINUTES

**Psychology for Today's Living
Part II:
Love, Romance, and Marriage***

*Northeast High School, Philadelphia,
Pennsylvania* —HYMAN M. BOODISH

In our Western culture, the ideal way of choosing a husband is through the process of falling in love. Fortunate is the woman who, through this process, obtains the kind of husband she really wants, not only at the time of marriage but for all the remaining years of married life. Is it a great deal to ask of love?

One wonders how some of the great love stories of fiction might have ended if the two lovers had been permitted to marry. On the basis of the knowledge we have today of personality and human behavior, it would probably have been an extremely unfortunate marriage if, for example, Romeo and Juliet had been united in wedlock, for they were both highly immature youngsters. Had they been married their intense love might even have turned into bitterness and resentment. And what of their children! If Hamlet and Ophelia had married each other, theirs would have made an even worse match, for both were not only immature but highly unbalanced mentally. Cyrano de Bergerac and Roxanne might perhaps have made a good marriage, but Roxanne was in such a fog that when she finally became aware of her love for Cyrano, she was an old woman and he a very old man breathing his last breath.

Of the real-life romances there are few authentic case histories from which we could obtain scientific conclusions regarding the effectiveness of romantic love as a sound basis for choosing a husband. Certainly the large number of divorces and separations of couples who apparently had at one time "been in love" is evidence that love cannot in all cases be relied upon as a *sure way* of getting the right husband or the right wife. The great wonder among many sociologists is that a large number of marriages are relatively successful in spite of the fact that they commenced as love marriages.

Falling in love, in the sense with which we are all familiar, is basically a characteristic of emotional immaturity. With most people it is a necessary step in growing up, although some of us seem to grow up without ever falling in love. In our culture, people begin to fall in love during their teens or early twenties. As in the case of the measles, mumps, or chicken pox, some individuals are stricken by the "love bug" at a later age or are never bothered by it at all. A fairly large number of persons never become immune to it even after they have had it once.

* Hyman M. Boodish, "Psychology for Today's Living, Part II: Love, Romance, and Marriage," *The Social Studies,* LV (April 1964), pp. 143–145.

They fall in love, or at least manifest the symptoms characteristic of being in love, several times during their lifetime. The majority of people find that falling in love once is enough.

Persons who have been in love report it as being a thrilling experience. An amazing fact about love is that people who have never actually experienced being in love can write such beautiful things about it. Another amazing fact about love is that a great deal of the creative powers of men are devoted to it. Composers create endless numbers of musical scores and songs about love. Poets, novelists, dramatists, scenario writers, painters and sculptors make love the central theme of their creations. Even our comic books have of late been devoting their pages to "true love romances." All in all, therefore, the average person, by the time he is able to go to school, is made to feel that falling in love is the grandest of all human experiences.

For two young people, falling in love may or may not be the beginning of a good marriage. If they have potentially mature personalities and necessary qualities which are important to successful marriage, then romantic love for them can serve as an additional binding or cementing force to the marriage relationship. However, for most young people falling in love is inevitable, and marriage is a natural consequence. Furthermore, it is not the falling in love that makes a good marriage. Success in marriage depends much more on the maturity of the two people—how well they can solve or resolve the many problems they will ultimately face as man and wife.

All marriages, whether they commence because the two persons are "deeply in love" or result from a mature understanding, entail a most intimate living-together relationship. For each partner it involves "getting used to" all the idiosyncrasies, some lovable and many distasteful, of the other partner. It necessitates coming to workable agreements on a host of matters ranging all the way from such simple things as personal habits in the bathroom or taste for clothes to such complex matters as choice of friends, relationship toward each other's family, spending money, rearing children, and sex compatibility. Two people are fortunate indeed if their marriage, based originally on the strength of their love feelings, fulfills their basic expectations. Even in such relationships, the "love" after marriage is not of the same variety as that which the two people had for each other during the period of courtship. Love is a dynamic force. It is constantly undergoing change, imperceptible though this may be. The kind of love that exists between two persons must change because the needs of people change as they grow older.

All love springs, basically, from selfish motives. Our first love, as an infant, is self-centered. Later, as we mature, we come to love our mother, father and friends because they somehow fulfill needs that we have— needs for food, for support, for warmth, for guidance, and for love itself. During adolescence, our various needs, such as the needs for security, recognition, status, and companionship, become blended with the need for sex gratification and romantic love. Depending upon the strength of each need, the individual tends to fall in love with the person who seems best able to fulfill one or more of these needs. Thus a young woman who has been denied and therefore desires warmth and affection from her parents may fall in love with a man who makes her his idol and showers her with affection. A youth seeking recognition and admiration may feel a strong love for a girl who worships his musical talents. So it goes.

Unfortunately, the intensity of a person's needs at nineteen or twenty and the resulting love feelings evoked by a person of the opposite sex, who somehow fulfills those needs, may blind the two individuals to their other basic needs, particularly as they will be manifested five, ten, fifteen years later. To a girl of eighteen or nineteen, a young man's ability to dance, to say pretty things, and to be generally romantic and affectionate may fulfill a very dominant need at the time. But, at thirty or forty years of age, and as a married woman, this same woman's love will center more on the kind of home her husband can provide, the kind of father he is to their children, and how he treats her family and friends.

For a marriage to be successful, therefore, it is much more important that the two people possess the basic qualities which will enable each to fulfill the other's basic needs, than for them to fall romantically in love. For men and women over thirty this is especially true since, as we pointed out, their chances for falling in love are considerably reduced. Instead of looking for romantic love, a woman over thirty will do better if she will look for *mature love*—the kind of love that exists between two grown-up people who are able to fulfill one another's basic needs. Mature love can come after marriage as well as before marriage. Indeed, for two people who intelligently consider and weigh each other's qualities with reference to marriage, mature love may result more readily than for two people who marry for romantic love reasons but who are otherwise ill-suited to each other. The biggest obstacle a woman over thirty has to overcome in her quest for mature love in marriage is her desire to fall in love with her husband before she marries him. If that feeling is very strong, she may profitably consult a marriage counselor. But, if she is able to accept the fact that falling in love is primarily for adolescents, her battle is half won.

STOP TIMING HERE

Now answer the following questions without referring to the selection.

1. What is the main idea of this selection?

   a. A successful marriage depends more on the ability to meet each other's basic needs than for the partners to "fall in love."   b. A marriage cannot hope to be successful unless it is consummated by two persons who are truly "deeply in love."   c. Falling in love is basically a characteristic of emotional immaturity.   d. True love is ageless: behavior and ideals springing from true love will continue to satisfy at all ages for the couple involved.

2. What does the author state is the basis of love?

   a. True love is made in heaven.   b. A mature personality.
   c. Selfish motives.   d. Physical chemistry.

3. What does the writer believe would have been the outcome had the two lovers of some of the great love stories of fiction finally married? a. He believes that it would have been unfortunate.   b. He believes that they would have made ideal unions.   c. He believes that one cannot foresee the fate of love.   d. He believes that not enough is stated in most instances to make any prediction.

4. With whom are we most likely to fall in love?
   a. That person who can satisfy our most pressing needs.   b. That person who is most completely our opposite in personality.
   c. That person for whom we hold the greatest respect.   d. That person for whom we hold the greatest sympathy.

5. At what age is a person most likely to fall in love?
   a. During his teens.   b. During his late twenties.   c. During his early forties.   d. Falling in love is no respecter of age.

6. According to the author, what is one of the biggest obstacles a woman over thirty has to overcome in her quest for mature love in marriage?
   a. She feels that she should fall in love before getting married.
   b. She believes that there are no eligible men her age.   c. She falls in love so easily she does not dare trust her feelings.   d. She has to face her own inferiority feelings for not having married earlier.

7. According to the author, who are the first persons we love?
   a. Our parents.   b. Our brothers and sisters.   c. Ourselves.
   d. Our friends.

8. How plentiful are authentic case histories that attest to romantic love as a sound basis for choosing a mate?
   a. Very plentiful.   b. Very scarce.   c. Plentiful enough to prove the point.   d. Nonexistent.

9. This selection was originally given as a talk to a chapter of one of the national associations listed below. To which one of these do you believe the remarks would be most appropriate?
   a. American Psychological Association.   b. American Personnel and Guidance Association.   c. National Secretaries Association.
   d. American Bar Association.

10. What is the final criterion of a successful marriage?
    a. Ability to maintain a high level of romantic attachment.
    b. Ability to get used to all of the idiosyncrasies of the marriage partner.   c. Ability to always be thoughtful and kind.   d. Ability to like the same things as the marriage partner.

Check your answers against those in the Answer Key. If you answered seven or more questions correctly, your comprehension was adequate.

► **SKIMMING EXERCISE III**

All of us occasionally write business letters, but how successful are we in our attempt? Skim the following selection and learn how much you know about new approaches to business correspondence.

TIME: 1½ MINUTES

Letters That Get Results*

A well-known training team which has gained national recognition for their use of role-playing in communication training, lets you in on some fresh approaches to the problems of business correspondence and to the task of training people to write better letters in less time.

—JOSEPH R. HAYES and DUGAN LAIRD
Education and Training Center United Air Lines, Chicago, Illinois

Few American businessmen are happy about the flood of paper flowing across their desks and crowding their file cabinets. According to the New York Times this flood reaches the frightening total of 345 billion sheets of paper each year.† One way to stem the flood is to get the results you want with the first letter.

Stop to think about it. Isn't action the ultimate goal of all communication? Understanding is usually an intermediate step: people must respond to one another as people before they can take common steps toward common goals. We really write in order to take these steps—to take action! Our letters, then, need to build action-oriented understanding. We hope that the writing will cause people to agree with us, to send us some facts or some opinions, to send a payment, to say "yes." How can you get them to say "yes" to your first letter?

Four simple, common-sense methods can help your letters hit their target. First of all, *come to the point at once.* Don't keep your reader guessing. You're not writing a murder-mystery, so let him know in the very first paragraph why you are writing. Frequently you are simply providing information which he can use; he may even have requested it in a letter to you. Tell him so: "Here is the information you requested," or "We thought you would like to know that . . ."

Very often you are writing to get information. If so, admit your interrogative purpose. Use it as your beginning. Questions like "Can you help us . . . ?" or "Would you give us some information?" or "What do you think about . . . ?" are considerate and direct. Contrast them with the

---

* Joseph R. Hayes and Dugan Laird, "Letters That Get Results," *Personnel Journal,* **43,** Number 7 (July–August 1964), pp. 380–381, 388. Reprinted by permission.
† T. Irwin, "Six Copies Please," *The New York Times Magazine,* November 17, 1963.

roundabout (and too-typical) "We require the following information relevant to . . ." or "Information is requested on the subject . . ."

Even if the mission of your letter is persuasive, this law of primacy helps get results. When you are seeking acceptance of your position, you obviously will explain the reasons for your beliefs. How can your reader follow your logic if you wait until the end (or leave unstated) such "big picture" statements as "Do you agree with us that . . ." or "We are seeking your concurrence on . . ."

In giving your purpose at the start of your letters, take a moment to express the desired response from your reader's viewpoint. Notice the implied flattery of "Can you help us?" opposed to the dogmatic "We require your advice." The newsboy doesn't sell his last papers by telling passerbys how cold he is. As a letter writer you won't easily get results by opening with "We cannot complete our manpower budget until we hear from you." In just a moment you can figure out what your reader will gain by supplying the data which help you complete that budget. He will respond more readily if you start with something like "To secure your 1964 manpower approvals, would you . . . ?"

Secondly, if you *maintain the integrity of the paragraph*, you will speed results. Readers of the English language are accustomed to the "signal of the white space." The break between paragraphs tells the reader that you're going on to a different aspect of the purpose which unifies the entire letter. The particular sub-topic of each paragraph should be put into print just as near the start of the paragraph as possible. Don't make your reader plod through three or four lines before learning that you have left clerical manpower and are now discussing personnel for the warehouse. Once you've named the sub-topic, exclude from this paragraph anything about any other sub-point. A reader doesn't expect salary expense data in a paragraph about sales quotas any more than he would expect to pick apples from a pear tree. Remember that fussy English Composition teacher and her passion for "topic sentences"? Well, this is one point at which she had something worthwhile to say to the letter-writing businessman.

Next, *indenting and listing* helps guarantee responses from readers because the device itself (like paragraphing) shows the logical structure of your message. Indentations tell the reader that the indented material is a sub-point of the preceding statement. The numbers beside the items in the list (of statements, requests or questions) remind him to respond to all your message rather than just a part.

Finally, *be as conversational as possible.* This doesn't mean (repeat: *doesn't*) that you should write the way you talk. Far from it. The long sentences, the vocal and facial inflections, the feedback—none of these operates from the printed page. But to the degree that you can sound like a human being, a reader visualizes you. And to the degree that you do sound human, he is inclined to make the response you desire.

How can your writing be conversational? There are many ways, so let's look at a few of them right now. For one thing, keep your sentences short. This may sound strange, since conversation uses long sentences.

But remember, the reader is not here with you; he cannot hear the vocal inflections which clarify and add meaning as you speak. He has to find the subject-verb-object pattern to make sense of your writing. Help him find them quickly and easily by keeping your sentences short. Do so, and you will read like a considerate conversationalist.

Then too, you can vary the length of your sentences to add personality. Do you agree? A "quickie" like that last sentence does much to relieve the monotony of long expository statements. You'll notice also that it was a question. You can give the variety of real talk to your letters by mixing the declarative (statement of fact) with the imperative (requests or commands) and the interrogative (question). What about commands? They can seem terribly dictatorial on the printed page. One antidote is to convert them to questions: "Could you reply by the 15th?" seems less autocratic than "Please reply by the 15th."

Finally, vary your punctuation marks. Why? A long series of declarative sentences, stuffed with commas and spiced with only a rare semicolon in the longer, more complex sentences is hard to follow and deadly dull. (If you're skeptical, re-read the sentence you just finished!) Furthermore, a parade of declarations indicates that you want to get ideas off your chest—but that you aren't thinking of the reader or his responses while unburdening yourself. Why not let readers of your business letters enjoy the enriched meanings which come from the varied punctuation of personal letters? We use them in conversation. We drop our voice to imply that an idea is parenthetical: why not put closely related background (such as definitions of technical jargon) in parentheses on the printed page? In speech, we emphasize key words and ideas by speaking louder. On the printed page we can use a dash just before the important idea—and the dash gives emphasis to the idea. It's just possible that you'll want to use some contractions!

The use of questions is worth repeating here. We've discovered several good reasons for using them liberally in business correspondence:

1. Frequently the real purpose of our letter is to ask a question. If so, why not state that purpose in an interrogative format?

2. The question is a healthy antidote for the monotony of declarative sentence after declarative sentence after yet one more statement of fact.

3. The question is an effective way of taking the curse off requests and commands.

4. Here's still another advantage to questions: they give your reader a sense of involvement. Instead of just passively reading your statements, he is encouraged to make a direct response. He feels as if the two of you were closer together—and perhaps you are!

Now when you use oral communication, you need to summarize. The minister and the teacher agree that they must tell people what they're going to tell them, then tell them, and conclude by telling them what they've told them. This is not true of the business letter. The summary and conclusion may easily insult the intelligence of your reader. If you've done a good job of stating your purpose first, isolating subpoints—but no! In this article we'll practice what we preach: no summary!

STOP TIMING HERE

Answer the following questions without referring to the selection.

1. What do the authors say is the ultimate goal of all communication?
   a. Understanding.   b. Getting the recipient to agree with us.
   c. Action.   d. Economic gain.

2. Which one of the following is a good beginning to a business letter?
   a. "We require the following information about . . ."   b. "Information is requested on . . ."   c. "Can you help us . . . ?"   d. "We require your advice . . ."

3. Which one of the following sentences is most likely to get the desired response?
   a. "We cannot complete our records until we hear from you."
   b. "So that you may secure your bonus payment, please help us to complete your records."   c. "Please fill out the following forms and return immediately."   d. "Your previous refusals to complete and return the enclosed forms have caused this firm much embarrassment."

4. What do the authors mean by suggesting that business letters be as conversational as possible?
   a. One should write the way he talks.   b. Be chatty—interject humor and "catch phrases."   c. Keep your punctuation fairly consistent, with little variation.   d. Write so the reader can visualize you as a human being.

5. What do the authors feel about summarizing a business letter?
   a. There should be no summary at all.   b. The summary should be complete and detail all that has preceded it.   c. The summary should be short and include only the more important items.   d. It is better to summarize after each main idea than to wait until the end of the letter.

6. According to the authors, how can we help to stem the flood of business mail that crosses our desks each year?
   a. Include more in each of our own letters, thus cutting down the number of separate communications needed in response.   b. Write our first letter in such a way that it gets the results we want.
   c. Return all but first-class mail to the senders.   d. Refuse to answer any mail that is not of direct importance to us.

7. How should a business letter be introduced?
   a. The first paragraph should include some friendly or personal remarks.   b. Come to the point of your letter at once.   c. Do not state the purpose of your letter in the introduction—arouse your

reader's curiosity first.   d. A business letter should always begin with a question.

8. How does a writer "maintain the integrity of the paragraph"?
   a. By writing clearly and honestly.   b. By summarizing each paragraph in a concluding statement.   c. By placing the topic sentence in the concluding sentence.   d. By including only one subtopic and its details in a given paragraph.

9. Through what method of training have the authors gained national recognition?
   a. Lecture method.   b. Small-group discussion.   c. Role playing.   d. Individual counseling.

10. In which of these journals did the article first appear?
    a. *The Journal of Developmental Reading.*   b. *Personnel Journal.*
    c. *American Psychologist.*   d. *Journal of Educational Research.*

If you compared your skimming with your usual reading rate, you probably discovered that skimming permits you to cover material much more quickly. It is true that the skimming rate is not an actual measure of the words per minute you read. In skimming you do not read all the words. But it is valid to compare the time required for skimming with that required for more complete methods of reading. You can easily cut your reading time by half if you will skim where it is appropriate.

► **SKIMMING EXERCISE IV**

The following selection, "Our Restless Earth," is typical of a parallel reading for a course in geology. See whether you can skim it in the time suggested and then answer most of the questions correctly.

TIME: 1 MINUTE

Our Restless Earth*

—MAYNARD M. MILLER, PH.D.

The Author: Maynard M. Miller, Professor of Geology at Michigan State University, has twice made glaciological studies under grants from the National Geographic Society's Committee for Research and Exploration—in Alaska in 1961, and with the 1963 Mount Everest Expedition. In Alaska he studied earthquake effects on glaciers, following up the classic Society-sponsored research of Ralph S. Tarr and Lawrence Martin in 1909–11.

* Maynard M. Miller, Ph.D., "Our Restless Earth," *National Geographic Magazine,* **126**, Number 1 (July 1964), pp. 140–141. Reprinted by permission of the National Geographic Society.

When the earth shook, the Algonquian Indians used to say, the Great Tortoise who supported the world was shifting his weight. Aristotle had an equally mistaken notion: He thought earthquakes were caused by powerful subterranean winds.

What really does happen when the ground trembles violently, causing destruction and suffering as it did in Alaska on last Good Friday? Scientists still do not know for sure. But we have theories.

A simplified cross section of the earth shows four regions: inner and outer cores totaling about 4,300 miles in diameter, believed to be largely iron and nickel; then a mantle of rock, about 1,800 miles thick, that is neither liquid nor solid, but plastic, so that it yields or flows with infinite slowness under pressure; and, finally, a solid, generally brittle, outer crust, like the shell of an egg, only 3 to 30 miles in thickness.

Today's most widely accepted theory holds that many quakes are caused by titanic shifts in the crust along cracks or fracture lines called faults. Portions of the crust are under constant tension, like a bent bow. At frequent intervals, when the strain becomes intolerable, the rock gives way at some weak point, often far beneath the surface.

As the crust makes this sudden shift, it releases pent-up energy in enormously powerful waves that make the whole earth vibrate like a giant bell. Some of the waves circle the globe; others may pass completely through the earth at speeds of more than eight miles a second. All record their passing in the jiggling of pens on sensitive measuring instruments called seismographs.

But what creates these enormous stresses in the earth's crust? Years ago it was thought that the earth was cooling; as it shrank, the crust presumably buckled and cracked. Today most geologists believe exactly the reverse: The earth's interior is a mighty furnace, producing prodigious heat through the breakdown of radioactive elements such as uranium and thorium. I have felt that heat two miles deep in a mine in the Kolar gold fields of Mysore, India. There the rock walls registered 156° F.

Tests indicate that heat increases steadily with depth; at the base of the crust it may reach 1,300° F, the temperature of molten aluminum. Only enormous pressure keeps the mantle from becoming totally liquid.

Possibly, as some geologists believe, this heat causes expansion of the earth, stretching the crust like a balloon. Or it may be, as others suggest, that temperatures and pressures cause abrupt molecular changes in the rock, just as these forces can change graphite into diamond in the laboratory. Accompanying changes in volume could cause uplift or subsidence and a shifting of the crust.

Still another theory—most attractive to me—pictures the plastic material of the upper mantle seething in slow convection currents, somewhat like jam boiling on a stove. These currents, though infinitesimally slow, drag against the solid crustal rocks, in places pulling and torturing them until they rupture, with shocking release of power.

Whatever the actual mechanisms that trigger earthquakes and their aftershocks, they seem to be associated with the same forces that build mountains. Preliminary reports indicate that some of Alaska's coastal land mass has been thrust upward six feet or more by the 1964 Good Friday quake.

Earthquakes also are intimately related to volcanoes. Four out of five of the world's shocks are recorded on the Pacific rim, called the "rim of fire" because of its many volcanic peaks. Alaska suffers because it lies within this earthquake belt, one of earth's most unstable areas.

Many active fault lines constantly threaten Alaska with tremors. Four of these lines—the Lake Clark, Cook Inlet, Seldovia, and Fairweather Faults—are bent and compressed in the recent quake region. Three converge near Anchorage. This ominous pattern may well be the key to the Alaska shock.

However, it was not the rock slippage itself, but rather the vibration, sliding, and settling of loose glacial-alluvial deposits, that caused the heavy damage. These deposits respond to shocks much as grains of sand dance on a board when it is struck.

EARTH TREMBLES MANY TIMES A DAY

During the course of a year there may be a thousand shocks that do some damage, and another 100,000 that could be felt by human beings. But the 1,200 seismograph stations around the globe may detect half a million tremors in 12 months' time.

This constant quivering of our restless planet, strange as it seems, has beneficial as well as destructive results. Seismic waves provide almost our sole means of studying the earth's deep interior.

But, more important, repeated uplifting of earth's crust, with its attendant quakes, is essential to life as we know it. Mountains are constantly eroding; if they were not raised again, the world would become an awful place of stagnant seas and swamps.

Thus these seismic tremors that sometimes alarm and hurt us are the inexorable ticks of our planetary clock, the pulse beats of earth. Were they to stop, ours would indeed become a dead world.

STOP TIMING HERE

Now answer the following questions without referring to the selection.
1. What did Aristotle believe to be the cause of earthquakes?
    a. Shifts in the earth's crust.   b. Powerful subterranean winds.
    c. Shrinking of the earth's crust.   d. Molecular changes in the earth's crust due to heat and pressure.
2. What is the most widely held theory today concerning the cause of quakes? They are caused by—
    a. shifts in the earth's crust along fractures or faults.   b. expansion of the earth's crust due to intense internal heat.   c. chain reaction from volcano eruptions.   d. convection currents within the plastic material of the upper mantle.

3. How many quakes are detected by seismograph stations in a year's time?
   a. 100,000.   b. 1,200.   c. 1,000.   d. Half a million.
4. What is a beneficial result of earthquakes?
   a. They create an uplifting of the earth's crust, protecting the earth's surface from stagnation and swamps.   b. They are related to stabilization of the earth's weather.   c. They move alluvial deposits from one place to another, thus enriching the soil.   d. They have no beneficial results.
5. What is the earth's most unstable area?
   a. The "rim of fire," lying within the Pacific.   b. A spot in Outer Mongolia.   c. Northern Japan.   d. California.
6. What is the author's profession?
   a. He is director of an Alaskan seismograph station.   b. He is a geologist for the U.S. Department of the Interior.   c. He is a physicist with the U.S. Department of Mines.   d. He is Professor of Geology at Michigan State University.
7. What Alaskan city is near the point of convergence of three active fault lines?
   a. Fairbanks.   b. Juneau.   c. Anchorage.   d. Seward.
8. What was the actual cause of the great damage to Alaska in the 1964 earthquake?
   a. Rock slippage.   b. Vibration, sliding, and settling of loose earth deposits.   c. Repeated uplifting of the earth's crust.   d. The bending and compression of the rock faults.
9. What does the author call earthquakes?
   a. The pulse beats of earth.   b. Rims of fire.   c. The primal causes of dead worlds.   d. The progenitors of stagnant seas and swamps.
10. What is almost the sole way of studying the earth's deep interior?
    a. With instruments like radar and sonar.   b. Observing earthquake shock waves.   c. By observations made in deep mines.
    d. By measuring the effects of man-made explosions.

Summary

We have outlined here a method of skimming based upon your ability to preview. In other words, if you have learned how to preview, you can simply expand this approach into the rapid-reading skill of skimming. There are, of course, other ways of skimming, some of which you may have already discovered or attempted. If you haven't learned to skim in one way or another, it may help you to think about the following patterns.

1. One method of skimming is to read the first few words and the last words of each sentence. In this fashion, the reader skips what he considers

to be the less important parts of the sentence. This method may or may not result in comprehension of the sentence, depending upon its complexity and structure.

2. A second method of skimming follows a preview of the material. Having read the opening and closing sentences of each paragraph, the reader returns to pick up quickly the facts and ideas offered elsewhere in each portion. He then skims rapidly through the body of each portion to identify the significant phrases or key words.

3. A third method of skimming is to read rapidly the first part of each line. The reader hugs the left-hand margin (or sometimes the right-hand one) and reads about a third of each line throughout the page.

4. A fourth method of skimming is quite similar to margin-hugging. In this method, however, the reader reads only the central third of each line. Thus he reads only in the middle of the page, but reads some on almost every line.

5. A fifth method is to look only for key words or phrases set off by numbering, italics, quotation marks, capital letters, underlining, or some other typographical sign. This method may result in fragmentary comprehension, and that mainly of details rather than main ideas.

6. A sixth method of skimming is to move down the page in a more or less diagonal pattern. The reader may jump from the beginning of the line to the middle or end of the next line, back to the left or the middle, and so on down the page. Occasionally he may read a complete sentence, if it seems significant.

The method we have suggested resembles the second method described above. It has the advantages of more adequate coverage of material than some of the other methods. However, you may find by observing yourself in the act of skimming that you find it more natural and equally effective to use one of the other methods described.

The next step in mastering the art of skimming is one only you can take. Keep using this technique as frequently as you can. Use previewing to help sort your reading materials according to their difficulty and your purpose. Then skim those requiring more attention to details. Your skill in comprehension will also grow as you use this technique. As you continue to overcome habits of slow, cautious reading, you will continue to improve in skimming.

Continue to practice skimming—

1. When reading newspapers and magazines.
2. When you need only the "gist" of an article.
3. When you wish to sample a book in the library before deciding to take it out.
4. When you wish to sample a number of opinions and ideas on a particular subject.
5. When you need to gather material for a talk or paper.

HELP YOURSELF

If you need materials in which to practice skimming, in addition to practicing in your study assignments, your instructor may help you to select one of the following.

Berg, Paul C., Stanford E. Taylor, and Helen Frackenpohl. *Skimming and Scanning.* Huntington, N.Y.: Educational Developmental Laboratories, 1962. *Offers both a textbook and a workbook for practice in these skills in a variety of materials.*

Brown, James I. *Efficient Reading.* Revised edition. Boston: Heath, 1962. $3.00.

McDonald, Arthur S., and George H. Zimny. *The Art of Good Reading.* Indianapolis: Bobbs-Merrill, 1963. See chapter 6 and exercises 15–19.

Shaw, Phillip B. *Effective Reading and Learning.* New York: Thomas Y. Crowell, 1955. See Chapter 2.

Spache, George D., and Paul C. Berg. *Faster Reading for Business.* New York: Thomas Y. Crowell, 1958. See Chapters 4 and 10.

CHAPTER 3

SCANNING: FINDING
FACTS QUICKLY

This chapter will introduce scanning, another skill of efficient reading. Scanning means looking very quickly over a piece of reading matter to find the answer to a specific question. You already use this skill when looking for a name in a telephone directory, but it can be useful to you in many other situations as well. For example, from a particular selection you may wish to find a name, date, statistic, or other fact. Or you may wish to find a phrase or general idea that will support a theory or clarify a thought. Scanning is invaluable when you are reviewing, doing research, writing a paper, or seeking specific information for other purposes. It is the usual way you work with directories, dictionaries, tables, indexes, and maps.

How to Scan

Scanning is not reading in the ordinary sense. Instead, you let your eyes run rapidly over several lines of print at a time, looking for a specific fact or idea. Above all, you must keep in mind exactly what it is you are searching for. If you hold the image of the word or idea clearly in mind, the item you are looking for will appear to show itself more clearly than the surrounding words as you approach it.

If the material is familiar or relatively brief, you may be able to scan the entire body of the selection in a single search. If the material is lengthy or difficult, a preliminary skimming to find the part of the selection in which to scan for particular information will be more profitable.

If you learn to scan effectively, there is hardly a limit to the amount of print you can cover in a minute. You will not understand all the words, nor will you even fully perceive them. Your purpose does not require that all the words be understood. But what you want—namely, to find a word, a number, or an idea on a page—will be accomplished. You may find, after you have practiced scanning for a while, that you can locate a fact or figure from fifteen or twenty thousand words in a minute or two.

Scanning Exercises

In order to give you exercises for practice, we have selected several short articles, each preceded by questions that you are to answer as quickly as possible.

Follow these steps:

1. Note the time when you start the exercise.
2. Read the first question at the beginning of the first selection.
3. Scan, but do not read in the usual way, the paragraphs that follow to find the answer to this question. Let your eyes move very rapidly over the sentences until you come to the sentence that gives you the answer. Read this sentence. Check no further in the selection.
4. Mark your answer to the question by circling the letter preceding the correct response.
5. Repeat this process for each question. When you have answered the questions for one selection, go on immediately to the next; complete all questions to all selections.
6. Make a note of your finishing time.

►   *SCANNING EXERCISE I*

STARTED   ———————————   FINISHED   ———————————
TOTAL TIME   ———————————

Discoverer of the Stethoscope*

Question 1. In what year was the first essay published describing cardiac and pulmonary sounds heard through a stethoscope?
a. 1812.   b. 1816.   c. 1819.   d. 1825.

Question 2. What is medical diagnosis called that has as its basis the listening for sounds produced by the body?
a. Auscultation.   b. Audiology.   c. Stethoscopy.   d. Encephalography.

Question 3. Who was the inventor of the stethoscope?
a. Dr. Laennec.   b. Dr. Corvisart.   c. Dr. Pasteur.   d. Dr. Curie.

One spring day in 1816, a young French physician—Rene Theophile Laennec—was relaxing in a Paris park. His duties as chief surgeon in a major Parisian hospital were heavy and he welcomed these periods of relaxation.

He watched strolling couples and youngsters at play, and then a new sound caught his ear. The more he listened, the more significant became

* "Discoverer of the Stethoscope," *Today's Health,* **42,** Number 3 (March 1964), p. 68. Reprinted by permission of *Today's Health,* published by the American Medical Association.

the sound. Two children were tapping messages to each other from the opposite ends of a discarded hollow log.

The longer Doctor Laennec listened, the more his mind recalled a similar sound—one from his childhood—when he used to watch the thumping on large barrels by men who employed the method to determine how full the barrels were. But now the sounds were magnified as he listened to them through that hollow log upon which the children were thumping. He also vividly recalled a technique of his former teacher, Dr. Jean Corvisart, who thumped a patient's chest and listened intently for the resulting sounds.

Doctor Laennec remembered the hollow log incident the next time a heart patient visited his office. He made a make-shift tube from a piece of paper and listened. To his medically trained ears came the beating of a heart more clearly and distinctly than he had ever heard one beat before. That little paper tube, and beating heart gave the ingenious doctor a new idea.

He constructed a wooden stethoscope, and in 1819 he published an essay detailing the information on all the cardiac and pulmonary sounds he had heard through the wooden stethoscope. And so it was that Doctor Laennec ushered in an era of medical diagnosis in the field of "auscultation." Auscultation is the art of listening for sounds produced in the chest, abdomen, and other parts of the body to determine abnormal conditions.

But for Doctor Laennec's ingenuity, physicians of today still might be thumping the chest and other parts of the anatomy and listening for any unusual sounds which might indicate an abnormal condition. However, without the stethoscope as we know it, the extensive examinations of today would be impossible.

GO ON TO THE NEXT SELECTION

The Telephone†

Question 1. The frequency of a vibration is described by—
a. its pitch.   b. its loudness.   c. the number of vibrations per second.   d. its speed.

Question 2. Sound waves travel—
a. 900,000 feet per minute.   b. One thousandth of an inch per second.
c. 186,000 miles per second.   d. 1,075 feet per second.

Question 3. The early telephone employed—
a. amplification of the voice.   b. steel organ reeds over electromagnets.
c. the principles of harmony.   d. a very short circuit.

Question 4. Alexander Graham Bell was helped in his telephone experiments by—
a. his knowledge of vocal-cord vibrations.   b. a great many assistants.
c. his great manual dexterity.   d. his broad knowledge of science.

† From *The Magic of Your Telephone,* published by the American Telephone and Telegraph Company. Reprinted by permission.

MECHANICAL VIBRATIONS

Your telephone *rings*. You answer it and the person calling *speaks* to you. As you converse you are faintly aware of the wind *howling* around the corner of your house and a street car *rumbling* past. Somewhere in the distance a train *whistles* and in another part of the house a door *slams*.

Those sounds are *vibrations*—mechanical vibrations—that set air waves to vibrating against your eardrum, which causes a message to be transmitted to your mind. Each of them has its own number of vibrations per second—that is called *frequency*.

The motion which you give to the molecules of air when you speak is not like that of the wind where a multitude of air molecules sweeps along. In a spoken word, or in any musical sound, the molecules dance back and forth. First they advance, pushing against the eardrum, and then they retire and the membrane of the ear springs back. Over and over again this happens, hundreds and even thousands of times every second. The higher pitched the voice of the speaker, the higher the frequency and the more rapid is the dance. And yet it is a dainty dance, for the weight of a snip of human hair only about one thousandth of an inch in length would press as heavily upon the sensitive eardrum.

Sound waves do not travel very far or very fast. Actually they poke along at only 1,075 feet per second and the farther they travel the more faint they become. But when their electrical counterparts travel, as in a telephone circuit, their speed may be increased as much as 900,000 times. Though they, too, weaken as they travel along, they may be amplified at intervals and repeated with practically the same clarity and tone as when they were spoken, no matter how far they have traveled.

Alexander Graham Bell was able to invent the telephone because, as an expert in instructing the deaf, he had extensive knowledge both of vocal-cord vibrations and of the operation of the human ear. His interest in the electrical transmission of speech grew naturally out of his broad knowledge of acoustics and his experiments with an invention intended to send several telegraph messages at one time over a single wire. This "harmonic telegraph," as he called it, utilized strips of steel organ reeds mounted so that they would vibrate over electromagnets.

GO ON TO THE NEXT SELECTION

1, 10, 100, 1,000, . . .‡

Question 1. When did the United States adopt the base-ten system for its currency?
a. At the close of the Civil War.   b. During the Colonial Period.
c. At the close of the War of 1812.   d. At the close of the American Revolution.

Question 2. What two countries of Europe and the Americas have failed to adopt the gram-centimeter-second system?

‡ Theodor Benfey, "1, 10, 100, 1,000, . . . ," *Chemistry*, **37**, Number 5 (May 1964), p. 3. Copyright © American Chemical Society, 1964. Reprinted by permission of the copyright owner.

a. Great Britain and the United States.   b. France and Canada.
c. Germany and Mexico.   d. Italy and Paraguay.

Question 3. How long is it expected to be before all countries of Europe and the Americas participate fully in the metric system?
a. Fifty years.   b. Thirty years.   c. A decade or two.   d. Five years.

About 3,000 years ago the Babylonians used a decimal system for numbers, as well as a system based on the number 60. Since then we have adopted the Arabic "base ten" numerals, whose beauty was the ease of multiplying and dividing by powers of ten. For the Romans $L \times X = D$. How much simpler to write $50 \times 10 = 500$. What is $D \times X$? Soon you run out of letters. You never run out of Arabic numbers. But though we use the base-ten notation, we persist in behaving as if it had not been discovered—$1'2'' \times 10 = 11'8''$; 1 lb 3 oz $\times$ 10 = 11 lb 14 oz. This computation might be useful for arithmetic exercises but it does not foster speed and efficiency in science, industry, or trade.

Immediately after the French revolution the French appointed a commission to do something about the discrepancy between number systems and measuring systems. The commission, of which Lavoisier for a while was secretary-general, developed the metric system, which in addition to being based on the base-ten number system, tied the mass standard directly to the length standard. One gram is the mass of one centimeter cube of water at its temperature of maximum density.

After the United States had its revolution, it adopted the base-ten system for its currency but not for its weights and measures. By 1925 every country in Europe and the Americas except Great Britain and the United States had adopted the gram-centimeter-second system. Now, in both these countries moves are afoot that will almost certainly lead to transition to the metric system within one or two decades. By the time most children now in our schools leave college, the metric system may be the official system of units in this country. Will they have some feel for the units they must then employ? Will they know that a speed of 90 kilometers an hour is not excessive on most open highways, that a meter is about a yard, and a kilogram approximately 2.2 lbs.? Students should demand that they be properly prepared for the world in which they will have to find their way. And the best way to get used to the metric system is not to convert inches to centimeters and vice versa, but to use the metric system in as many situations as possible.

Following the example set by several other magazines, *Chemistry* plans to use the metric system exclusively (with maybe occasional lapses) as well as the Centigrade temperature scale.

We need to familiarize ourselves with the metric system not only because we will soon be using it in daily life. We are also an integral part of the world community and the most advanced country scientifically and technically. If we go overseas—teaching chemistry in the Peace Corps or working in an overseas division of a U.S. industry—we will find ourselves at a great disadvantage if we are not thoroughly familiar with the metric system. Our effectiveness in sharing scientific knowledge will be greatly hampered.

Standard weights and measures were developed to ease communication and trade. When most of the world has accepted a scientific and simple set of standards, the most scientifically and industrially developed country should accept any temporary inconvenience and join the metric fold.

GO ON TO THE NEXT SELECTION

Focus on Norway*

Question 1. How many islands are included in the geography of Norway?
a. 150.   b. 1,500.   c. 15,000.   d. 150,000.
Question 2. What is the population of Norway?
a. 4 million.   b. 8 million.   c. 12 million.   d. 16 million.
Question 3. What portion of the natural resources for hydroelectric power are utilized in Norway?
a. One twentieth.   b. One tenth.   c. One fifth.   d. One half.

Since the fierce Vikings sailed the North Atlantic, more than 1,000 years ago, the men of the land that is today Norway have won fame as some of the world's most skillful seamen. Wed to the sea along 12,500 miles of cliffbound, fjord-riven coast, Norway is essentially a maritime nation, operating the world's third-largest merchant fleet. Although fishing remains a major industry in Norway, with a recent year's catch of nearly one million tons, its share in the national product has decreased in recent years owing to growing industries ashore. These have risen along with the development of the land's great hydroelectric-power resources, now about one-fifth utilized. Agriculture and forestry also figure prominently in the nation's economy.

The land, described by the Norwegian Poet Björnson as rising "furrowed and weatherbeaten above the sea," is the most mountainous in Europe and includes about 150,000 islands. The Western part of the country is warmed by the Gulf Stream and enjoys warm summers and mild winters. The Northern reaches lie well above the Arctic Circle where the sun does not set from the middle of May to the end of July and does not rise from late November to late January. Here the nomadic Lapp tribes tend great herds of reindeer. Norway's people, nearly 4 million in number, enjoy a high standard of living and a comprehensive system of social welfare. Their government is a hereditary monarchy under a constitution, which was 150 years old in May of this year.

STOP TIMING HERE

How well were you able to scan for the preceding questions? Even with time out for recording your answers, the first exercise should not have taken you more than four minutes. What happened when you searched for a fact

* "Focus on Norway," *The Rotarian*, **105**, Number 1 (July 1964), p. 64. Reprinted by permission.

or single idea? Did it appear clearer to you than the other words on the page?

Did you have to read more of the text to find some answers to questions than you did others? The time you need for scanning and the actual amount you read tend to vary with the form in which the answer is found. When the answer is a single word or statistic, little actual reading need take place. The word seems to pop out of the context because the word or number you have in mind is in the same form as the wording in the text. When the answer involves paraphrasing or interpretation of words in the text, more reading is naturally demanded.

The speed of your scanning is the critical element in evaluating your success. With enough time, of course, you would have been able to give correctly the answers to all the questions. The amount of time needed will vary, depending upon the length of the material to be scanned, where the answer occurs in the text, and how much difference in wording there is between the question and the way the answer appears in the text.

Now try the second scanning exercise. The content is relatively difficult in vocabulary and concept, and is based on statistical reasoning with which you may not be familiar. You will find, however, that you can understand most of the writer's ideas by using the headings as questions as in previewing, or by asking a question and searching for its answer within the text as in scanning. You may not understand all the statistical proof the writer uses, but that does not mean that you cannot understand most of his findings.

In this exercise, the questions you are to answer are placed within the selection. First, read the "lead-in" and the introductory paragraph. Then read the first question and its answer choices carefully. Third, scan each paragraph following the question, looking only for the answer; as before, mark only the answer you choose. Keep going until you have answered all questions. You should be able to complete the exercise in 1½ to 2 minutes.

► *SCANNING EXERCISE II*

STARTED ——————————   FINISHED ——————————

TOTAL TIME ——————————

A Comparative Study of Problems of Married and Single Students†

Single and married students differ in some respects but not in others in their adjustments to and satisfaction with their roles as students. The differences found by this study relate to living conditions, economic concerns, and

† Laurence L. Falk, "A Comparative Study of Problems of Married and Single Students," *Journal of Marriage and the Family*, **26**, Number 2 (May 1964), pp. 207–208. Reprinted by permission.

*study quarters; similarities relate to time spent
studying and academic achievement. Within
the married group, no clear relationship appears between marital adjustment and academic achievement.*   —LAURENCE L. FALK
                                  Concordia College

The married college student undoubtedly has problems which are
unique to his particular combination of roles as parent, spouse, employee,
and student. Consequently, it is important to consider whether married
students experience more difficulty than single students in living adjustments, in finding time, in worrying about finances, etc. Furthermore, if
these differences exist, do they influence academic achievement? Earlier
studies indicated that married students were academically superior to
single students. However, more recent studies indicate that no significant
difference exists between the two groups.

This study compared single and married students in order to determine
if married students experience greater difficulties in following their
academic pursuits than do single students. Seven null hypotheses which
pertain to this problem were tested.

PROCEDURES

Question 1. How many matched pairs of students were used in this
study?   a. 10.   b. 20.   c. 30.   d. 40.

The subjects for this study consisted of 40 single and 40 married
students attending Concordia College (Minnesota) during the academic
year 1962–63. Each married student was individually matched with a
single student according to age, college year, sex, and academic potential.
Academic potential was estimated by the composite score of the Psychological Examination of the American Council on Education where this
score was available. Where this score was not available, students were
matched on the basis of their rank in their high school graduation class,
taking into account size of school. To equate somewhat the course load,
students were selected who were carrying a minimum of 12 course hours
at the time of the completion of the questionnaires. The completed sample
consisted of 40 single students matched with 40 married students.

FINDINGS

Question 2. Do married or single students find their living conditions
more satisfactory?
a. Married students.   b. Single students.   c. No significant difference.

1. *Married students were more satisfied with their living conditions
than were single students.* The questionnaire consisted of statements indicating satisfaction with living conditions. Statements were so worded as
to be suitable for either married or single students. Subjects responded to
each statement by circling a value from 1 to 7, indicating the degree to
which they felt each statement applied to their situation.

The sum of the values from these statements become a "satisfaction" score suitable for statistical analysis. The mean score for married students was 34.6 and for single students, 31.1. The *"t"* value for this hypothesis is 5.843, $p < .001$. On this basis, the null hypothesis was rejected, leading to the conclusion that the married students were more satisfied with their living conditions than were the single students.

Question 3. Were economic concerns for married students greater, less, or about the same as for single students?
a. Greater.   b. Less.   c. About the same.

2. *Economic concerns for the married students were less than those for single students.* This finding is based on a similarly constructed questionnaire. The higher the score, the greater is the concern with finances. The mean score was 20.3 for married students and 23.0 for single students ($t = 2.914$, $p < .01$). Though one might reasonably assume that the opposite would be true, in this sample no more married than single students found it necessary to subsidize their finances through employment. It is possible that favorable financial circumstances contributed to the decision to marry before completing college.

Question 4. Did married or single students more easily find a suitable place to study?
a. Married students.   b. Single students.   c. No significant difference.

3. *Finding a suitable place to study was less difficult for married students than for single students.* The mean score for married students was 19.2 and for single students was 21.5 ($t = 3.165$, $p < .01$), indicating that single students had more difficulty in finding a suitable place to study. Disturbances in dormitory living or at other study locations seemed to be greater than those associated with the domestic living situation.

Question 5. Which group indicated the greatest amount of time spent in study?
a. Married students.   b. Single students.   c. No significant difference.

4. *Married students spent about the same amount of time studying as did single students.* The subjects were requested to state the average number of hours a week that they spent in studying. On the basis of this figure, the correlated *"t"* test shows no significant difference. The mean number of hours that married students spent in studying was 19.9, and the mean for single students was 20.5 ($t = 0.550$, $p < .60$).

5. *No significant difference existed between the grade averages of married and unmarried students.* The grade average was obtained for each single and married student for the academic year (first and second semesters) of 1962–63. The mean grade average for single students was 1.993 and for married students, 2.019 ($t = 0.351$, $p < .80$).

6. *The grade averages of students who married in college either did not change or rose from their grade averages before marriage.* Married students responded to the question, "If you are married, and if you

married while in college, after marriage did your grade average go up, go down, or remain about the same?" Of the 38 students responding to this question, 18 indicated that their grade average went up, one that his grade average went down, and 19 that their averages remained about the same. Assuming the accuracy of this reporting, grades either remained about the same or rose after marriage. However, as Cohen *et al.* found in their study, both single and married students' grade averages tend to rise as students become more mature.

Question 6. Is marital happiness positively related to grade averages? a. There is a high positive relationship.   b. No clear relationship was found between marital adjustment and grade average.

7. *Marital happiness was not related to grade average.* A simple scale for measuring marital adjustment was developed on the basis of a preliminary study by Videbeck. The questionnaire consisted of 14 items, each of which was responded to by circling a value from 1 to 6. The sum of these responses becomes the marital adjustment score. Both these scores and the grade averages were divided into those falling above and below their median. The "median test" was used to estimate the relationship between marital adjustment and grade average. The Chi-square value for this relationship is 3.600 ($p < .10$). Since this does not attain the .05 level acceptable for this study, the null hypothesis is not rejected, and no clear relationship is found between marital adjustment and grade average.

Conclusions

This study examined seven hypotheses related to the life of the married student to determine if problems faced by married students are any more intense than those faced by single students and if any difference exists in academic achievement. It was found that single students are more concerned with their finances, find it more difficult to find adequate study surroundings, and are generally less satisfied with their present living conditions than are married students. However, these factors affect neither academic achievement nor the amount of time spent in studying. Considering the married students alone, no clear relationship appears between marital adjustment and academic achievement.

STOP TIMING HERE

Are you conscientiously scanning to find the answers to the questions? Be sure that you read the question *first,* then scan for the answer.

In the first two exercises on scanning, multiple-choice answers were given to guide your search. In the third exercise, the questions preceding the paragraphs cannot be answered by a word or short phrase, and multiple-choice answers are not given. You will be looking for an idea in which the exact wording is unknown to you. The directions for answering are changed also. Instead of checking a multiple-choice answer, you need only place the *line number* in which the answer is found in the space after the question.

Review the directions again:

1. Record the time when you begin to scan.
2. Read the first question before the selection or paragraph.
3. Scan the material for the answer.
4. Write the line number in which the answer is found in the space after each question.
5. Scan for the answer to each question and record the line number.
6. Stop timing and figure your total time.

▶   **SCANNING EXERCISE III**

STARTED ——————————   FINISHED ——————————
TOTAL TIME ——————————

Stalagmites and Stalactites*

Question 1. What agent acts as a catalyst to cause limestone to become soluble in water? ————
Question 2. Where do stalactites form? ————
Question 3. Where do stalagmites form? ————
Question 4. What happens if limestone is placed in distilled water?
————

1 Stalactites are icicle-like structures most commonly found hanging
2 from the ceilings of caves in limestone-rich areas, and stalagmites are
3 complementary masses that develop on cave floors. Both result from
4 slow precipitation of material from ground water. Most stalactites and
5 stalagmites are made up of two forms of calcium carbonate—calcite
6 and aragonite—although some small stalactites are composed of
7 gypsum, gibbsite, opal, and chalcedony.
8 Limestone is the most soluble of the common rocks, and nearly all
9 great caves are in limestone areas. Pure limestone is composed of
10 calcium carbonate derived mainly from shells of marine organisms.
11 In an alkaline environment, limestones are chemically stable, but
12 they are subject to slow leaching when exposed to rain water and
13 subsurface ground water, which are acidic.
14 If several small pieces of limestone are placed in distilled water
15 they will show no noticeable changes, even during a period of several
16 years. Should the water be charged with carbon dioxide, however,
17 carbonic acid is formed and the limestone will show a measurable
18 weight loss in only a few days because some of the calcium carbonate
19 of the limestone is converted to calcium bicarbonate which is soluble
20 in water. If this solution is allowed to evaporate, it will become super-
21 saturated with calcium carbonate, which, in turn, will be precipitated
22 as calcite or aragonite.
23 In nature, rain water falling to the earth becomes charged with
24 carbon dioxide from the atmosphere. After it hits the earth it comes
25 in contact with organic acids in the soil. The water percolates through

* Edward O'Donnell, "Stalagmites and Stalactites," *Natural History*, LXXIII (May, 1964), 23–25. Reprinted by permission.

26 the soil until it reaches bedrock, where it follows fractures and bed-
27 ding planes. If the rock is a limestone, solution occurs, and after
28 a long period of time, perhaps several thousand years, passages are
29 formed that range in size from small channels to great caverns. Size
30 depends on how long the process has worked, the volume of water in-
31 volved, and its acidity.
32   Stalactites form when carbonate-enriched ground water reaches a
33 cavern. The water drips slowly from the ceiling, but before each drop
34 falls, a small amount of evaporation takes place. The drop becomes
35 saturated with calcium carbonate and an infinitesimal amount is
36 precipitated. When the drop falls to the cave floor, the same thing
37 happens again, and a stalagmite begins to develop.
38   The rate at which stalactites grow is not definitely known. Certainly
39 the speed of formation will depend on the amount of water that is
40 available and how much calcium carbonate is in solution. Sir Archi-
41 bald Geikie, the great Scottish geologist of the late nineteenth cen-
42 tury, recorded stalactites one and a half inches in diameter beneath
43 a one-hundred-year-old bridge in Edinburgh. They had grown from
44 lime leached out of the cement in the bridge. All evidence points to a
45 slow rate of formation, and it is estimated that stalactites grow ap-
46 proximately one cubic inch in every century.

GO ON TO THE NEXT SELECTION

Improving Cotton Fabrics*

Question 1. How do the growth rings of cotton differ from those of a
tree? ————

Question 2. Is it possible to produce cotton without growth rings?

————

Question 3. What type of cotton has the greatest elastic properties?

————

Question 4. What chemical is used in mercerizing cotton? ————

1   Cotton fibers are complex structures. Their internal structure is
2 a tube with growth rings much like those in a tree, except that in
3 cotton, the rings grow from the outside in. One ring is produced for
4 each day of growth. This complex structure makes the job of under-
5 standing cotton fibers a slow process, according to scientists who are
6 working on them at Stanford Research Institute (SRI) Southern
7 California Laboratories. But as their research progresses, they expect
8 its results will be useful in improving cotton fabrics.
9   Growth rings in cotton are made up of tiny fibers called "fibrils"
10 that run spirally along the axis of the fiber. Unaccountably, these
11 may reverse in direction many times along the length of the fiber, the
12 SRI scientists point out. What causes these separate construction fea-
13 tures, what functions they serve, and what effect each has on the
14 characteristics of the final fabric all need to be studied.

* Research Reporter, "Improving Cotton Fabrics," *Chemistry*, **37**, Number 3 (March
1964), pp. 23–24. Copyright © American Chemical Society, 1964. Reprinted by permission
of the copyright owner.

15 As part of SRI's cotton fiber research, plant physiologist Harris
16 Benedict has produced cotton without growth rings. He grows the
17 ringless cotton in chambers maintained at constant temperature and
18 humidity and with continuous light, varied from 5000 foot-candles for
19 12 hours to 10 foot-candles for 12 hours. His is not the first ringless
20 cotton grown in a laboratory, Mr. Benedict explains. U.S. Department
21 of Agriculture scientists conducted this experiment some 25 years ago,
22 but it was never repeated until SRI started its current research pro-
23 gram. Mr. Benedict also has grown three-ring cotton and one-ring
24 cotton by moving plants out of the controlled environment chamber
25 into a normal night-and-day environment for three days and for one
26 day, respectively, and then returning them to the controlled en-
27 vironment.
28 L. P. Berriman and Vincent Monteleone of SRI have subjected the
29 ringless cotton fibers to numerous tests of physical and chemical prop-
30 erties. For example, their work shows that ringless cotton is more
31 elastic than field-grown cotton. Its ability to return to normal length
32 after being severely stretched is greater, and it can be stretched far-
33 ther before breaking. Further, mercerizing (treating cotton with
34 sodium hydroxide to increase fiber strength) is more effective when
35 applied to the ring-free cotton.

GO ON TO THE NEXT SELECTION

A New Concept for a Navigation Satellite System†

Question 1. What is a fundamental deficiency of the ground-based radio
navigation system? ———
Question 2. Do international regulations require that ships at sea notify
their traffic-control agency of their positions at special intervals? ———
Question 3. How effective are ground-based navigational systems for
ships far from shore? ———
Question 4. When are the present navigational systems most likely to
prove their lack of effectiveness? ———

*A new navigational system that uses comput-
erized control stations and satellite relays is
proposed for world-wide navigation and
traffic control for ocean-crossing ships and
aircraft.*

1 Today's advances in space and electronics technology have made
2 possible a new kind of world-wide navigation and traffic-control sys-
3 tem. Satellites orbiting the earth are the key to a navigation system that
4 could direct traffic, locate distressed craft, and direct rescue vessels.
5 Such a system would be invulnerable to weather and would enable
6 ships and aircraft to cross oceans more safely, efficiently, and eco-
7 nomically. This satellite navigation concept has resulted in a feasi-

† E. S. Keats, "A New Concept for a Navigation Satellite System," *Westinghouse Engineer*, **24**, Number 4 (July 1964), p. 105. Reprinted by permission of the Westinghouse Electric Corporation.

8 bility study by Westinghouse under contract to the National Aero-
9 nautics and Space Administration.

NEED FOR A NEW NAVIGATION SYSTEM

10   During the past twenty years, more than two dozen ground-based
11 radio navigation systems have been put into service in various loca-
12 tions around the world. A fundamental deficiency in all of these
13 navigation systems is that they are inherently incapable of providing
14 position information to anyone other than the ship or aircraft using the
15 system. Air traffic-control agencies, air-sea rescue services, and operat-
16 ing companies are thus isolated from the craft after departure until
17 and unless the navigator radios his calculated position. Despite many
18 advances in communications equipment, timely position reports from
19 ships or aircraft in mid-ocean are often difficult to receive. Ground-
20 based radio navigational aids are ineffective far from shore; in bad
21 weather, navigators are unable to use the stars to locate position;
22 and reported position is always vulnerable to human errors in calcula-
23 tion and transmission.

24   International air regulations require that aircraft inform the air
25 traffic-control agency of their positions at specific intervals when
26 communications can be established. Ships, however, are not required
27 to radio position information to shore, and, because it is often difficult,
28 do so less frequently.

29   The inadequacies of our present navigational systems are high-
30 lighted during emergencies or disasters, when ships and aircraft are in
31 trouble or lost. Too much time is spent in just discovering that an
32 emergency situation exists, finding the vessel or its survivors is dif-
33 ficult, and the problem of determining which rescue craft is near a
34 disabled craft is frustrating.

35   Improved communications between ships and aircraft at sea and
36 control centers ashore is a partial solution. This solution, however,
37 would still require personnel on the ship or aircraft to take the
38 initiative in calculating the craft's position. Position calculation can
39 be a time-consuming task even for the most rapid system; failure
40 to perform it regularly, and perhaps not at all, during an emergency
41 situation would disable the system at times when it is needed most.

42   A far better and safer way to provide accurate navigation in-
43 formation is to remove the work of position calculation from the craft
44 and perform these computations at established land bases. Accurate
45 position information could then be transmitted automatically, quickly,
46 and reliably to ships, to aircraft, and to traffic routing and safety
47 agencies at periodic intervals. Such a system could also provide ships
48 and aircraft with weather reports and forecasts, notices of unusual
49 dangers, warnings to avoid collisions, and other information useful
50 to insuring a safe passage. A system using satellites can provide these
51 and many additional benefits that cannot be provided with present
52 land-based navigational methods.

GO ON TO THE NEXT SELECTION

Cooperation and the Growth of Knowledge*

Question 1. Why must there be cooperation between men of knowledge? _____

Question 2. Is the contribution of the single individual less today than in earlier centuries? _____

Question 3. Why cannot any scientific organization impose detailed standards upon its members? _____

Question 4. Is the human character becoming more cooperative by nature? _____

1 Leonardo da Vinci has often been cited as one of the last men
2 capable of knowing all that was known in his time. Usually (though
3 not in *Chemistry*, January 1964, p. 18) such statements are coupled
4 with words expressing nostalgia. Why? Many of us, it seems, would
5 like to be masters of all knowledge either because of insatiable
6 curiosity or because we don't want to be dependent on anyone.

7 Was Leonardo more brilliant than Einstein or Picasso? Probably
8 not. If Einstein or Picasso had lived 400 years ago, they too would
9 almost certainly have mastered all knowledge. Minds have not
10 shrunk, the amount of information has grown. Leonardo was ignorant;
11 as far as knowledge was concerned he should be pitied, not remem-
12 bered with longing.

13 How then do we handle this increased knowledge, assuming we
14 would need some from many fields, both for our scientific work and
15 for the problems of our daily life? The answer is pretty obvious. Since
16 we cannot know all that we need to know, we must rely on others to
17 become experts in areas outside our own competence. And they in turn
18 become dependent on us for information in our area of specialization.
19 We find ourselves forced to cooperate and trust each other, not be-
20 cause the human character is becoming markedly more cooperative by
21 nature, but because of the conditions of daily life and scientific work.

22 The team approach in much scientific work is likely to stay. The
23 discovery of xenon tetrafluoride was reported in *Science* 138, 136
24 (1962) over the names of 17 research scientists. The synthesis of the
25 tranquilizer reserpine (*J. Amer. Chem. Soc.* 78, 2023 [1956]) was
26 reported by a group of five chemists.

27 This trend in no sense demonstrates that the contribution of a
28 single individual is less important now than in earlier centuries. The
29 exact opposite is the case. A community of experts depends on the
30 quality of the contribution of each member. Any failure to maintain
31 high standards in his own work endangers the work of all others.

32 One other consequence: The community, the "organization," can-
33 not impose detailed standards on an expert because he is usually the
34 only one in the group who knows the problems of his particular field.
35 Being a member of a properly operating team of scientists is there-
36 fore a very different matter from being a member in most other

* Theodor Benfey, "Cooperation and the Growth of Knowledge," *Chemistry*, **37**, Number 3 (March 1964), p. 3. Copyright © American Chemical Society, 1964. Reprinted by permission of the copyright owner.

37 teams. It can only mean willingly sharing expert information and
38 judgment in order to increase knowledge.

STOP TIMING HERE

Graphs, Tables, and Charts. Graphs, tables, and charts are, by the nature
of their content, most often read by scanning. There are several times during
the study act when they are used. During the preview, the reader rapidly
examines charts and graphs to establish their general nature and discover
what they can quickly tell him about the text. During the complete reading
of the text he may study these visual aids again more carefully, checking
from the text to the graph or chart by scanning. Some of these graphic aids
may of course be skipped during the reading act, if, during the preview,
they were understood by a first glance or found to be insignificant.

Perhaps the most important act in reading these visual aids is first to
find out what the graph or chart is intended to indicate and exactly what
each column or line shows. Time is wasted and confusion multiplied when
you attempt to get meaning from a figure, bar, or line graph without first
carefully checking the headings that explain the itemized data. Once the
organization of the particular visual aid is understood, there is no difficulty
in finding and understanding the data it offers.

In the materials for the following scanning exercise, graphs, tables, and
charts are used. Find the answers to the questions preceding each visual
aid, and check the correct answer response.

Remember to follow these steps:

1. Read the title.
2. Read the column headings or the scale.
3. Then scan for the answer to each question.

►   *SCANNING EXERCISE IV*

STARTED   ————————————   FINISHED   ————————————
TOTAL TIME   ————————————

Reasons Given for Dropping out of College*

Question 1. What was the reason given most often by women students
for dropping out of college?
a. Unsure about what to study.   b. Couldn't afford the cost.

Question 2. What was the reason given only 1 per cent of the time by
both men and women for leaving college?
a. Faculty discouraged me.   b. Few of my friends were in college.

Question 3. What was the reason given most often by men students for
dropping out of college?
a. Unsure about what to study.   b. College not relevant to my goals.

* Alexander W. Astin, "Personal and Environmental Factors Associated with College
Dropouts Among High Aptitude Students," *Journal of Educational Psychology,* **55,** Number
4 (August 1964), Table 1, p. 222, "structured items" only. Reprinted by permission of the
American Psychological Association and the author.

Reasons Given for Dropping Out of College

Reason	Male Dropouts[a]		Female Dropouts[b]	
	% giving reason	Rank	% giving reason	Rank
Structured items:				
Unsure about what to study	62	1	32	4
My grades were unsatisfactory	55	2	14	7
I was tired of being a student	51	3	33	3
Couldn't afford the cost	49	4	60	1
I wanted to go to work	31	5	26	6
Not sure I had the ability	21	6	11	8
My scholarship was terminated	20	7	8	9
College not relevant to my goals	16	8	31	5
Wanted to devote more time to family	11	9	56	2
Faculty discouraged me	8	10	3	10
Pressure from draft board	4	11	1	12
Few of my friends were in college	1	12	1	11

GO ON TO THE NEXT SELECTION

Attrition Among First-Semester Engineering Freshmen And Father's Occupation†

Question 1. Which occupational group seems to have the greatest percentage of college dropouts from all causes?
a. Service and semi-skilled.   b. Skilled.

Question 2. Which of these groups had the greatest college dropout by withdrawal?
a. Service and semi-skilled.   b. Unknown.

Question 3. Which of these groups had the least attrition from all causes?
a. Professional.   b. Mother guardian.

Father's Occupation

Father's Occupation Classified as	Per Cent of Students Classified According to Father's Occupation			
	Total Group	Dropped after 1 Semester	Trans. after 1 Semester	Withdrew
Professional	16.1	12.9	15.6	10.0
Managerial and official	16.3	9.7	18.7	14.0
Clerical and sales	13.9	9.7	9.4	5.0
Service and semi-skilled	16.6	22.6	9.4	18.0
Skilled	12.7	22.6	9.4	14.0
Agricultural	9.4	12.9	12.5	10.0
Unknown	4.8	3.2	15.6	24.0
Retired	2.6	. . .	9.4	5.0
Mother guardian	7.5	6.4	. . .	. . .

GO ON TO THE NEXT SELECTION

† Lois B. Greenfield, "Attrition Among First Semester Engineering Freshman," *The Personnel and Guidance Journal*, XLII (June 1964), Table 7, p. 1008. Reprinted by permission.

Statistic of the Month‡

Question 1. What was the approximate number of high school graduates for each 100 persons 17 years of age for the year 1920?
a. 25.   b. 17–18.

Question 2. Of the 1963 high school graduates, what occupation did the most women choose?
a. Clerical and kindred work.   b. Sales.

Question 3. What occupation did the least number of men enter of the 1963 high school graduates?
a. Managers, officials, proprietors, except farm.   b. Private household workers.

GO ON TO THE NEXT SELECTION

Statistic of the Month

High school graduates: 1963 and 1964

Approximately 2.3 million young people—the largest number in our history—were graduated from high school in 1964 (most of them in June, but about 3 percent in January). This is an increase of more than 300,000 over the class of 1963.

The size of the 1964 graduating class reflects the high birth rate that followed World War II and the increasing tendency of young people to remain in school at least until high school graduation. During the past century, as the accompanying chart shows, the proportion of high school graduates has steadily increased, decade by decade. Between 1870 and 1963 the number of high school graduates for each 100 persons in the population 17 years old rose from 2.0 to 70.7.

About half of the 1964 graduates, or some 1.15 million, will enter colleges and universities in September. The Office of Education estimates that there will be 1.25 million first-time college students this fall, including some graduates of earlier classes. For hundreds of thousands of 1964 graduates, high school graduation marked the end of formal education. A sample survey of the graduating class of 1963, conducted by the Bureau of Labor Statistics, U.S. Department of Labor, in October 1963, provides some indication of what we may expect for the 1964 graduates who do not enter college. In the fall of 1963, 90 percent of the boys and 72 percent of the girls who had not entered college were in the labor force—either employed or seeking employment. Many of the boys were employed as semiskilled operatives and laborers; a majority of the girls held clerical jobs. About 18 percent of the graduates in the labor force were unemployed. The table shows the percentage distribution of the types of positions held by the 1963

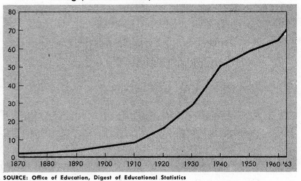

Number of high school graduates for each 100 persons 17 years of age, United States, 1869–70 to 1962–63

SOURCE: Office of Education, *Digest of Educational Statistics*

Percentage distribution of 1963 high school graduates [1] employed in October 1963, by sex and by occupation group

Occupation group	Total	Male	Female
All occupation groups................	100.0	100.0	100.0
Professional, technical, and kindred workers.....	2.6	2.6	2.6
Managers, officials, and proprietors, except farm.	1.5	2.6	.6
Clerical and kindred workers..................	37.1	10.9	57.8
Sales workers..............................	6.1	4.0	7.8
Craftsmen, foremen, and kindred workers........	4.4	8.4	1.2
Operatives and kindred workers...............	19.8	35.4	7.5
Private household workers....................	4.5	.7	7.5
Service workers, except private household.......	10.2	8.4	11.6
Farm laborers and foremen...................	4.0	5.5	2.9
Laborers, except farm and mine...............	9.8	21.5	.6

[1] Includes persons 16 to 24 years of age in the civilian noninstitutional population.

NOTE.—Because of rounding, detail may not add to totals.

SOURCE: U.S. Department of Labor, Bureau of Labor Statistics, *Monthly Labor Review*, May 1964.

high school graduates in October 1963.

For additional information on young persons in the labor market, see "Employment of High School Graduates and Dropouts in 1963," an article in the May 1964 issue of *Monthly Labor Review* (vol. 87, No. 5). This issue may be purchased from the Superintendent of Documents, U.S. Government Printing Office, Washington, D.C., 20402, for 75 cents a copy.—*W. Vance Grant, educational statistician, Office of Education.*

‡ *School Life,* **46,** Number 9 (August 1964), p. 7.

Needs Selections by Occupations*

Question 1. Which occupational group finds job security its most important need?
a. Clerical.   b. Trades.

Question 2. Which group has the least need for leadership qualities among its members?
a. Trades.   b. Service.

Question 3. Which occupational group has the greatest need for "interesting duties"?
a. Professional.   b. Clerical.

Needs Selections (%) by Occupations

		A	B	C	D	E
	Job security	71	70	53	27	11
Most	Money security	24	20	22	19	8
prepotent	Congeniality	34	30	33	21	16
needs	Respect	36	24	14	7	13
Average	Independence	25	41	14	19	26
	Leadership	5	6	8	19	13
Less	Interesting duties	33	34	60	54	70
prepotent	Advancement	19	13	24	33	39
needs	Self-actualization	19	18	36	58	70

A=Trades   D=Managerial-Official
B=Service   E=Professional
C=Clerical

GO ON TO THE NEXT SELECTION

Daily Requirements Covered by the Basic Foods†

Question 1. How many calories are contained in a pint of milk?
a. 250.   b. 340.

Question 2. Which has more calcium: four ounces of round steak or one orange?
a. Four ounces of round steak.   b. One orange.

Question 3. Who should have the greater daily intake of calories: a grown man or a growing male teen-ager?
a. A grown man.   b. A teen-ager.

Question 4. Which has the greater amount of iron: one egg or one-half cup of green leafy vegetable?
a. One egg.   b. One-half cup of green leafy vegetable.

* Boris Blai, Jr., "An Occupational Study of Job Satisfaction and Need Satisfaction," *The Journal of Experimental Education*, **XXXII** (Summer 1964), Table I, p. 386. Reprinted by permission.
† "What to Eat and Why," The John Hancock Mutual Life Insurance Company, 1961, chart, p. 24. Reprinted by permission.

Daily Requirements Covered by the Basic Foods

Food	Amount	Calories	Protein (Gm.)	Calcium (Gm.)	Iron (Mg.)	Vitamin A (I.U.)	Thiamine (Mg.)	Riboflavin (Mg.)	Niacin (Mg.)	Ascorbic acid (Mg.)
Milk	1 pint	340	17.0	0.58	0.4	780	0.19	0.83	0.5	5
Citrus fruit	1 orange (sm'l)	50	0.9	0.03	0.4	190	0.08	0.03	0.2	50
Other fruit	5 prunes	125	0.6	0.01	1.0	470	0.02	0.04	0.4	....
Green leafy vegetable	½ cup	50	3.9	0.23	2.2	6540	0.12	0.35	0.8	25
Potato	1 small	85	2.0	0.01	0.7	20	0.11	0.04	1.2	17
Another vegetable	½ cup	70	3.4	0.03	1.8	540	0.11	0.06	0.9	8
Egg	1	75	6.4	0.03	1.4	570	0.06	0.17	0.1	....
Round steak	4 oz.	250	28.0	0.02	4.4	....	0.21	0.18	6.4	....
Ceral	1 cup	100	3.1	....	1.1	....	0.06	0.04	1.3	....
Bread—white enriched	4 slices (thin)	260	8.4	0.06	2.0	....	0.24	0.15	2.2	....
Margarine or butter	1 tbsp.	100	....	....	....	430	....	....	....	....
Total		1505	73.7	1.00	15.4	9540	1.20	1.89	14.0	105

Recommended Daily Dietary Allowances

	Calories	Protein (Gm.)	Calcium (Gm.)	Iron (Mg.)	Vitamin A (I.U.)	Thiamine (Mg.)	Riboflavin (Mg.)	Niacin (Mg.)	Ascorbic acid (Mg.)
Man (physically active)	3200	65	0.8	12	5000	1.6	1.6	16	75
Woman (moderately active)	2300	55	0.8	12	5000	1.2	1.4	12	70
Girl (13–15 yrs. old)	2500	80	1.3	15	5000	1.2	2.0	13	80
Boy (16–20 yrs. old) Athletic	3800	100	1.4	15	5000	1.9	2.5	19	100

STOP TIMING HERE

Summary

Continued practice in the use of scanning will improve your reading and help you to save many hours when scanning, rather than a complete reading, will suffice. You will find many opportunities for application of scanning to your daily work. Finding facts and figures; using directories; reading maps, graphs, and charts; collating information; and even locating main ideas may be best accomplished by a scanning technique. Let the facts come to you rather than reading for them laboriously line by line. Use scanning when you are not trying to secure a continuous flow of ideas but rather are looking to find specific facts or ideas that are in the printed material.

HELP YOURSELF

If you want additional practice materials to try this type of reading, try one of the following:

Berg, Paul C., Stanford E. Taylor, and Helen Frackenpohl. *Skimming and Scanning.* Huntington, N.Y.: Educational Developmental Laboratories, 1962. *The textbook and parallel workbook provide a wide variety of practice materials.*

Leedy, Paul D. *Read with Speed and Precision.* New York: McGraw-Hill, 1963. See Chapter 6.

CHAPTER 4

THE ART OF READING RAPIDLY

In earlier chapters we have pointed out that the first consideration for reading is to outline in your own mind just what your purpose is. Once you have thoughtfully detailed for yourself what you need to find out and have noted the difficulty of the material and considered your familiarity with it, you are then ready to select the particular skills you need to read the material most efficiently. Sometimes your purpose for a reading is to learn only the general trend of ideas in the selection, or to quickly brush-up or review. In such instances skimming is useful. At other times a particular fact is all you need to obtain from a selection. Scanning is recommended for this purpose.

How to Read Rapidly

Frequently your purpose is simply to read for entertainment. Novels, newspapers, magazines, or any reading that is easy for you may come under this heading. Often, you may read such materials by skipping the less important words; you will still not miss the meaning of the material. Depending again on your purpose, there are times when the same approach is suitable for reading in literature, the social sciences, parallel selections for courses, and familiar selections.

Instead of reading for words, you may read "idea groups," which give the meaning not only more rapidly but also in a form that is more in keeping with the rapid pace at which the plot or sequence of details may move. Several of the selections of this chapter help to illustrate and give practice in reading for ideas rather than words. Only the more important words are printed; blank spaces appear where the less important words have been deleted. Because the word-by-word flow of the material is broken up, leaving only "idea words" and "idea groups," you must gain the author's train of thought through these word groupings, rather than by trying to follow the writer's ideas simply by adding all the writer's words together into the usual sentence or paragraph structure. With practice, you can soon learn to grasp such "idea groups" by wholes, eliminating words unnecessary for meaning, significantly speeding up your reading. This process leads not only to more rapid reading but also to better comprehension.

Just what words you will leave out as a rapid reader the writers of this book cannot say. However, we can say that if you become a rapid reader you will learn to look for idea groupings, skipping various words that to you are not necessary to convey the full meaning of the writer. In this kind of reading you do not intentionally select certain words to "skip." Obviously such performance would take you much longer than reading the entire text word for word. On the contrary, *you do not see certain words* because you do not need them to complete the writer's thought. Thus you read along from idea group to idea group, really not conscious of the words you literally are not seeing.

In these practice exercises, words that in our opinion seem less important have been left out; a blank space remains in their places. Attempt to read through these selections, grasping the thoughts presented by the words remaining and weaving all together into meaningful information. Do not try to guess what words are missing; try to gain meaning from the words and word groups that are present. Don't puzzle over a sentence that seems to mean nothing to you. Keep moving forward, constantly putting together the information you have gathered into a pattern of meaning.

The very short selection "What is Petroleum?" is presented as an example. In the left-hand column it appears as printed in its original text. In the right-hand column it is printed with over 40 per cent of its words deleted. Compare the two printings carefully. Do you think any words have been deleted that are really necessary for meaning? What words would you probably have read had you been selecting words for meaning?

What Is Petroleum?*

Petroleum is a mineral found underground in "fields" scattered over the earth. Its name is derived from two Latin words: *petra*, rock and *oleum*, oil.

Petroleum is also called "crude oil." It exists as a liquid, in solid form, and as natural gas. Crude oil and natural gas are usually, but not always, found together.

Ordinarily, crude oil is a dark, greasy fluid, but there are endless varieties. They range from nearly colorless, through amber, light green, and dark green to dark brown, and black. They also vary greatly in fluidity. Crude oil may flow like water or like syrup. Or it may be of such tarlike thickness that it will scarcely flow at all unless it is heated.

For thousands of years, men have known about petroleum because it seeped from the earth in small quantities in many different locations. But, as history reveals, it was only recently that science made possible the vast benefits of petroleum.

The first well ever drilled to find oil—and which did find it—was drilled in 1859—less than one hundred years ago. Since then thousands of ways have been devised to make petroleum serve man's needs.

A century ago, nearly all the power used to farm the land, to make things, and to move material and people from place to place was supplied by the muscles of men and animals. Machines did only six per cent of the work. Today, in the United States, nearly all of our heavy work, 94 per cent of it, is done by machines.

Petroleum (including natural gas) provides more than three-quarters of the energy we use today. From it comes power to propel our transportation system, and power to drive our farm machinery. It drives the vast machines in our mines and factories. It provides the light and heat we use in our homes and buildings.

Moreover, without lubricants from petroleum, all our modern machinery would soon cease to run. There is no other adequate source of the oils and greases machines require for lubrication.

Petroleum also serves many other purposes. Truly, it is one of man's most useful servants.

---

* "What is Petroleum?" from *Petroleum in Our Age of Science,* booklet published by the American Petroleum Institute, New York, p. 3. Reprinted by permission.

Petroleum   mineral   underground   "fields" scattered over
        earth. Its name   derived   Latin words: *petra*, rock
oleum, oil.
        Petroleum   "crude oil."   liquid, in solid form,
and   natural gas. Crude oil and natural gas   usually,   ,
found together.
        Ordinarily, crude oil   dark, greasy fluid, but   endless
varieties.   range   nearly colorless, through amber, light green,
        dark green   dark brown,   black. They   vary
fluidity. Crude oil   like water or   syrup. Or   tarlike
thickness   scarcely flow   unless   heated.
        thousands   years, men   known about petroleum
seeped from   earth   small quantities   different locations.
        ,   ,   only recently   science made possible
        vast benefits   petroleum.
        first well   drilled   find oil—   —   1859—
        . Since   thousands   ways   devised   make
petroleum serve man's needs.
        century ago, nearly all   power   farm   land,
make things,   move material   people   place to place
supplied by   muscles   men   animals. Machines   six
per cent of   work. Today,   United States,   heavy work,
94 per cent   ,   done by machines.
        Petroleum (including natural gas) provides more than three-quarters
        energy   use today.   power   propel   transporta-
tion system,   power   drive   farm machinery.   drives
        vast machines   mines   factories.   provides   light
        heat   homes and buildings.
        , without lubricants   ,   modern machinery   cease to
run.   no other   source   oils   greases   for lubrication.
        Petroleum   serves   other purposes.   ,   one of man's
most useful servants.

Rapid-Reading Exercises

In these practice exercises, words that in our opinion seem less important have been left out; a blank space remains wherever one or more
words are missing. Attempt to read through the selections, grasping the
thoughts presented by the words that remain and weaving all together into
meaningful information. Do not try to guess what words are missing; try to
gain meaning from the words and word groups that are present. Don't
puzzle over a sentence that seems to mean nothing to you. Keep moving
forward, constantly putting together the information you have gathered into
a pattern of meaning.

Follow these steps in reading the selections:

1. Begin each exercise by previewing the title and some of the first
sentences of paragraphs. Organize in your mind what you believe the article
is about.

2. Read the selection. See how quickly you can grasp the meaning from the "idea groups" and remaining single words; then weave them into a pattern of main ideas. Start timing as you begin to read.

3. Answer the questions at the end of the selection.

4. Use the Chart at the end of the book to find your rate in words per minute. Because the word count for each selection given is the original number of words before any were deleted, you should be able to read at half again your average rate.

▶   *RAPID-READING EXERCISE 1—700 WORDS*

STARTED ——————————   FINISHED ——————————
TOTAL TIME ——————————   WORDS PER MINUTE ——————

Sound*

Before you read   far   , close   eyes   listen
sounds around   . What   you hear?   hear   clock,
car horn, people talking,   dog barking,   wind or rain,   leaves
rustling? If   winter, can   hear   snow falling?
Some sounds   readily heard, even through   closed window.
Others   cannot hear,   though   ear   close to them.
Sounds differ   , both   kind   loudness.   many sounds
some animals   hear,   we cannot.   machines   make
some sounds   too high   human to hear, but   see them on
special instruments   analyze sounds   project them as wavy lines
on   screen similar   television screen. Sounds   locate objects,
communicate   other people,   produce music,   interpret
mechanical operations (squeaks   mean   machine needs grease).
doctor determines   condition   your heart   interpreting
sound   thumps   stethoscope.   other uses   sound
you know   ?

Sound Is Vibration

Whenever   object vibrates,   produces   sound. Sometimes   vibration   too fast   too slow   our ears   hear,
but often   do hear   vibration. To see   things   do
vibrate   produce sounds, turn on   radio   place   fingers
on it. If   man   talking, or music   played do you get   buzzy
sensation   your fingers? Do you feel more   buzz   low sounds
high sounds?
Go to   piano,   one hand on   top   and strike   low
note. Can   feel   vibration   through   wood? Now strike
higher note. Does   feeling   vibration change? Try   very
high note and see if you   feel   vibration. Some things   as

* Verne N. Rockcastle, *Sound*. Cornell Science Leaflet, **54**, Number 1 (October 1960), pp. 3–5.

high notes   piano vibrate so fast   your fingers cannot feel
very well.
     Place   ruler on   table, with most   projecting beyond
edge   table. Hold   other part firmly against   table   one
hand. Press down slightly   free end,   let   snap up.   see
     vibrate?   looks blurred when   moves up   down.
hear   musical sound as it moves? Move   ruler back on   table with
less   projecting,   try again. Does   sound of   note change?
Can   still see   ruler   blurred as   vibrates?
     tuning fork   made   vibrate   constant rate.   rate
     vibration   determined when   instrument   made   .
If   strike   tuning fork against   rubber heel, then hold
near   ear,   hear   tone.   tuning forks vibrate   fast,
     ,   cannot see   move. Touch   prongs   one to   glass
     water after   struck and   see how   prongs of   tun-
ing fork spatter   water.   would not spatter water if   not
moving.
     Hang   ping-pong ball by   thread   foot long.   , glue
one end   thread to   ball, or fasten   adhesive tape. When
     ball hangs motionless, strike   tuning fork and   touch
side   one prong to   ping-pong ball. What happens to   ball?
This   evidence   prongs really vibrate.
     Examine   vibrations   various objects   materials around
you. Watch   strings   piano or   violin as   instrument
     played.   see them move? Feel   throat of   person speak-
ing.   feel   vibration from   vocal cords? Put   hand on
     radiator grille   car while someone toots   horn. What
feel? Remember   every sound   made   something vibrating.

STOP TIMING HERE

Questions—Sound

Indicate whether the following statements are true or false in the selection that you have just read by putting T or F in the space provided.

——— 1. Sounds can be viewed on special instruments although we may
          not be able to hear them with our ears.
——— 2. Sound is produced by vibration.
——— 3. Sound cannot be felt through any sensory organ except the ear.
——— 4. High-pitched sounds can be felt through touching the object
          producing the sounds while low-pitched sounds cannot.
——— 5. The vibration of tuning forks can be observed by sight.

At this point you may say, "I would have been able to answer those
questions without reading the selection." That is probably true. The facts
presented in the selection were relatively simple and direct and were also
undoubtedly familiar to you. As was mentioned in the introduction to this

material, rapid reading techniques are used when the ideas presented are not complex and when you are already familiar with the material to be read. As you can now see, reading this material slowly and carefully is not necessary; rapid reading meets your needs as well as a slower rate would have. If you think a moment, you will realize that much of your recreational daily reading from newspapers or magazines is of this type—a noting of simply-presented ideas, many of them already familiar.

Here is another selection from which the less important words have been deleted. As in the preceding article, read the words or groups of words that are present; don't try to fill in all the missing words. Although occasionally you may fail to understand a sentence completely, don't go back and reread it unless you think it absolutely necessary. Keep moving forward from one group of words to the next and you will see, when you are finished, that you have understood the ideas presented in the selection.

►   *RAPID-READING EXERCISE II—1,700 WORDS*

STARTED   ——————————   TOTAL TIME ——————————

FINISHED   ——————————   WORDS PER MINUTE ————————

Your Job*

Assuming   we average eight hours sleep   night, those   us must work   a living spend   third   waking hours at jobs—   total   hundred thousand hours. A   large chunk your life,   ?   when   think of   terms   day-to-day living,   tremendous factor   sum total   emotional experience, determines   mental health.

best insurance   wholesome satisfaction   your daily work careful choice   vocation   suits your   peculiar needs. Young men   women entering   business world   are fortunate   vocational guidance is   universally available. High schools   colleges provide   personnel   specific purpose. Employment agencies   equipped   determine   lines of work for applicants,   industry   adopted efficient systems   testing aptitudes   fitting   individual to   job.

ARE YOU USING YOUR TALENTS?

are   things   a job   do for you if   get anything besides   weekly pay check. First   the work   must challenge   abilities. If   whiz at arithmetic,   not much   strain mathematical skill   punch 65 cents   cash register give out   change.   striking   monthly balance   double entry bookkeeping-   is   chore   requires a little know-how

* "Your Job," New York State Department of Mental Hygiene, *Guideposts to Mental Health,* No. 4, 1949.

figures. In   same way   pumping gas   make much use
all   motor magic   learned   Tank Corps,   if
get   chance   get under   hood   tinker   , you feel
you're doing something.

Sometimes   challenge is   less tangible   —salesmanship,
instance.   girl   can fit   size 42 customer   size 14
ideas   send   away happy   making   use   style sense,
knowledge   practieal psychology (even if   doesn't realize
as such) and   persuasive charm.

These   satisfactions   don't measure in dollars.   triumph
achievement   not lie   size   significance   accomplishment,   in   knowledge   you gave   all   you had.
job   demands this from day to day is   one   makes   feel
meeting life   and giving   good account of yourself.

You Want Creative Satisfaction

important   your feeling   accomplishment   work
accompanied by   conviction   is worth while.   must
know   your daily stint helps   create something   could not
exist if   particular job   not performed.   idea
creative work   many people identified   the arts—   writing,
painting, sculpture, music. But   automobile   creative product   every   member of   production line—   drafting
board   salesroom—   had a share.   man   sole contribution
tighten bolt A   part B   played   essential part   making   sleek,   machine.   without   man who drives
tractor-trailer transporting   factory   market,   well as
innumerable clerks,   , bookkeepers   salesmen involved in   ,
fine product   industrial genius   never serve   purpose
hands   the customer.

Jobs   provide services   community—policemen, firemen,
doctors, teachers,   , barbers,   —have   obvious   public
value.   many jobs seem   remote   society   ultimately
benefit.   must learn   see   particular job   relation
whole productive process   is a part.

You Need to Belong

Just as   need   feel   we belong   our family,
cannot   be happy   work unless   we feel   we belong.
First   identify   with   working unit,   whether   construction crew,   department   sales force   office staff.
must have   feeling   working together   common goals, taking
pride   achievements   group and sharing   dismay   failure.

Beyond   feeling   belonging   working group,   is
important   to know   are part   larger organization.
people   proud   say   work for   G.E.,   New
York Central,   Metropolitan Life.   develop   loyalty
more personal basis   in a small business,   if   firm   highly

regarded   community. All   contributes   to another factor
    carries   weight   our   emotional adjustment   daily
work,   significant feeling   importance.

We All Want to Be Big Shots

While   chief concern   emotional satisfactions derived   the
course   our work,   must recognize   fact   our job
part   our lives not   in between 9 a.m.   5 p.m.,   reaching over   leisure-time conversation,   social contacts,   our
standing   community.   is   ·   natural   should all want
      kind of job   gives us prestige—   sets us apart   com-
mands the respect   fellow workers   our neighbors.   is well
      remember   standards   values vary   one group   to
another.   job   surrounded   glamour   one town   just
routine   another.   one   circle   important thing   be
      salary   pays;   another   will be   education
training   involves; and   another   may be   special talents
      abilities   requires.
            can't all hold glamour jobs. Someone   take   responsi-
bility   doing   routine   that are necessary   progress
      public welfare.   own attitude toward   job   go
long way   shaping   attitude   your associates   . If
regard it   essential part   important public service   will give
it   dignity   its own, no matter   unimportant   may appear.
      significance   such jobs   our social scheme   definitely
recognized   recent years   various   ways.

Security Is a Basic Need

          with   recent benefits   come   general provision,
      in ·industry   ,   job security.   security   we
need   two areas—first, economic   ,   right to work,   as-
surance   retaining   job   provision for income   illness
      old age.   basic requirement   peace of mind   bread-
winner   obtainable   union contracts, seniority,   tenure, sickness   accident insurance,   pension systems.   second type
      relation   job   .   know what   expected   what
      expect from   job.
          supervisor   foreman   do much   establish
security.   employee   learn   whys   wherefores   work
      receive   instruction   satisfactory performance. He
know   will receive fair treatment   not   subject   prejudices   favoritism. He   entitled   recognition   good work
      constructive criticism   poor work.
      Your   working conditions may fall short   one   more
      important respects.   needn't worry   ,   , unless
definitely making   unhappy.   situation   involves various personalities,   sometimes   no amount   effort   your part
      remedy   unwholesome relationship   may become necessary
      seek   change.   large   organization   request

transfer   another department. If   not feasible   conditions   serious,   look   employment elsewhere.

Before   drastic action,   ,   good idea   have
heart-to-heart talk   supervisor   if   fails,   personnel manager.   may discover   alteration   own attitudes   work
habits   bring   pleasanter relationship with   supervisor   fellow
workers.   ,   take stock   yourself   beginning,   evaluating   own actions   their effect   others, you   able
improve things than   imagined.   helps   you try   understand   people act   way   they do.   boss   irritable
unreasonable   worrying about   sick child.

Work No Fun? There's Always Play

must realize   no such thing   perfect job. Every job
advantages and   drawbacks.   weigh one against   other.
If   not getting   satisfactions   daily work   ,   something   do about it besides gripe. (griping   all right   ,
up to   point.   healthy sign   aware something   wrong.
healthy, however,   when   leads   constructive action.)

When   find   vocation   failing   meet   emotional
needs,   feel tied down   dull routine   yearn   opportunity
exercise   real talents,   time   look   for   avocation,   leisure-time activity   affords   fun   doing what we
think   meant to do.   man   knows   executive ability
have no chance   apply   daily work,   he can organize
neighborhood campaigns   turn   ability   fine purpose.
woman   sits at   machine   dress factory   find   outlet
creative ideas   designing clothes   family   friends.
Often   avocation leads   real business; successful custom dress-
maker started   this way.

Sometimes   ,   stuck with   jobs.   remember   —
, we can choose   hobbies.   fascinating things   leisure
hours   more than   emotional gratification   derive   day
to day. They provide   lasting interest   will stay   through
years, giving   constructive,   satisfying activity   fill
lives when   no longer necessary or   possible   have
full-time daily job.

STOP TIMING HERE

Questions—Your Job

Decide whether the following statements are true or false as they relate
to the selection that you have just read.

_____ 1. The large portion of time in our lives spent at work makes job
satisfaction an important part of our mental health.

_____ 2. Choice of vocation should be made in terms of our own particular needs.

——— 3. It is not very easy to get good advice on choosing a vocation.

——— 4. There are other values on a job more important than the weekly pay check.

——— 5. A job must challenge our abilities if we are to be happy in it.

——— 6. A job must make us feel we are doing something worthwhile or even creative.

——— 7. Even complex industrial products are dependent upon the contribution of every worker.

——— 8. To be happy in his job, each worker must be conscious of its social value.

——— 9. Our enjoyment of a job is independent of our feeling of belonging to the working group.

——— 10. Job satisfaction seriously influences our lives when away from work.

——— 11. An adequate economic return is often more important than the prestige value of a job.

——— 12. It is possible to feel the social values and contributions of any honest job.

——— 13. The aspects making for security may be summed up in the meeting of economic needs, such as union contracts, seniority, tenure, and various insurances.

——— 14. If your present working conditions do not suit you it is best to start looking at once for other work.

——— 15. Whatever your job, you should expect it to satisfy all your emotional and social needs.

Although the following selection is quite short, you may find it somewhat more difficult to read for high comprehension. It covers a subject with which you are probably unfamiliar, and the questions asked at the end deal with details presented in the article.

►   *RAPID-READING EXERCISE III—650 WORDS*

STARTED   —————————   TOTAL TIME —————————

FINISHED   —————————   WORDS PER MINUTE ————

The Magic Box That Tests Your Driving Skills*

Someday,   not too distant future,   driving skills   tested by   electro-mechanical device when   apply   driver's license. Or if   a student attending   driver training class,   abilities at   wheel   measured   same remarkable gadget.   device Drivometer.   small, rectangular "magic" box   fits   glove compartment   automobile and   linked   car's basic con-

* Hal Butler, "The Magic Box That Tests Your Driving Skills," *Ford Times,* 57, No. 8 (August 1964), pp. 36–37. Used by permission of *Ford Times.*

trols—steering wheel, brakes   accelerator.   ticks off   continuous record   performance   driver, measuring   over-all
driving ability and building   efficiency score   indicates where
rank   fine art   operating   motor vehicle.

   Drivometer   developed   University of Michigan's Transportation Institute,   research grant   Ford Motor Company Fund.
   principals behind   development   Dr. Bruce Greenshields,
assistant director   U of M's Transportation Institute,   Fletcher
N. Platt, manager   Ford's Traffic Safety and Highway Improvement
Department.

   Through   measurements,   reveals driver reaction   sensitive situations—traffic jams, passing   truck, normal   abnormal
flows of traffic.   evaluates   driver's behavior behind   wheel,
including emotional reactions   traffic patterns.   judgment
levied   ten counters on   face   magic box.   record steering wheel reversals (movements   right or left), accelerator reversals,
brake applications   speed changes—   gauges   determining
   driver's skill.

   One   most important checks   steering wheel reversal rate.
   number   times   driver must move   steering wheel
   track accurately provides   measure   ability   concentrate
   task   driving. If   ability   stay within   lanes
good,   reversal rate per minute   low.   also indicates
looking well ahead as   drives   anticipating situations   ,
making lane changes   erratic movements less necessary.   movement   ⅜   inch   chalk up   point   Drivometer,
total count per minute   between 20   25   considered good.
Beyond 25, questions   driving ability   raised.

   However, too low   score   also   suspect. If   normally
average between 20   25, and, after several hours   driving,
steering reversals slip to 15—you're tired. Fatigue will result   notice-
ably lower score because   not controlling   car as   should
but are "drifting." Someday,   ,   buzzer   added   car
   sound off   time   warn   insidious danger.

   Accelerator motions   indication   whether   driver
impulsive   erratic   control   car.   better drivers post
   lower rate   speed changes, showing   have good coordination
   control   automobile.   driver   keeps within   traffic
flow   anticipates situations developing ahead   will post
good score   2½-mile-per-hour change   speed registers   count.
   Good drivers use   brakes less.

   number   times   apply   brakes   factor
prime importance.   pre-set route,   better drivers   post
lower score   this area.

   300 drivers have been tested   Drivometer to date, so
definite good-driver scoring pattern   established under most traffic
conditions.

   Fletcher Platt says   "four areas   Drivometer shows potential."

determine individual driving ability, improve driver-training procedures, evaluate   safety characteristics   vehicles,   test drivers   licensing purposes."

         don't be surprised if, when   drop in for   driver's license
someday,   find   these automatic backseat drivers ticking off
talents—and faults!

                                                          STOP TIMING HERE

Questions—The Magic Box That Tests Your Driving Skills

Indicate whether the following statements are true or false in the selection you have just read by putting T or F in the spaces provided.

—— 1. Driving skills may be tested by an electro-mechanical device.
—— 2. The Drivometer was developed by Ford Motor Company.
—— 3. The Drivometer is capable of measuring twenty different
       driver responses at a time.
—— 4. In straight driving, a 2½ mile-per-hour change in speed is reg-
       istered on the Drivometer as a count against the driver.
—— 5. Fletcher Platt, co-developer of the Drivometer, says that the
       instrument has potential for use in eight different areas of
       driver training and evaluation.
—— 6. Twenty or twenty-five steering movements of three eighths of
       an inch or more are expected in normal driving each minute.
—— 7. More than six hundred drivers have been tested already by the
       Drivometer.
—— 8. The Drivometer's mechanism fits into the glove compartment
       of the automobile.
—— 9. Good drivers use their brakes less.
—— 10. Ability to stay within lanes is in inverse proportion to the
       driver's steering wheel reversal rate per minute.

The last article selected for this chapter is 1,900 words in length and is
presented without any word deletions. Read the selection, using the following steps:

1. Preview-skim the selection, reading the title and subheadings and
an occasional first sentence in selected paragraphs. Do not take more than
one minute for skimming.

2. Begin timing.

3. Read the selection, looking for the writer's idea for each sentence.
Read only as many words as you need to grasp the idea, and as soon as you
understand it, move on to the next sentence.

4. Complete the reading and note the time elapsed.

5. Answer the questions.

6. Find your rate in words per minute, using the table at the end of the
book.

▶　　　　　　*RAPID-READING EXERCISE IV—1,900 WORDS*

STARTED ─────────────　　　TOTAL TIME ─────────

FINISHED ─────────────　　　WORDS PER MINUTE ─────────

Don't Let Stereotypes Warp Your Judgment*

*Stereotyped ideas can rob you of true under-
standing, can sour your human relations and
impair your general effectiveness. Here is the
way to recognize and eradicate stereotypes.*
　　　　　　　　　　—ROBERT L. HEILBRONER

Is a girl called Gloria apt to be better-looking than one called Bertha?
Are criminals more likely to be dark than blond? Can you tell a good
deal about someone's personality from hearing his voice briefly over the
phone? Can a person's nationality be pretty accurately guessed from his
photograph? Does the fact that someone wears glasses imply that he is
intelligent?

The answer to all these questions is obviously, "No."

Yet, from all the evidence at hand, most of us believe these things.
Ask any college boy if he'd rather take his chances with a Gloria or a
Bertha, or ask a college girl if she'd rather blind-date a Richard or a
Cuthbert. In fact, you don't have to ask: college students in questionnaires
have revealed that names conjure up the same images in their minds as
they do in yours—and for as little reason.

Look into the favorite suspects of persons who report "suspicious
characters" and you will find a large percentage of them to be "swarthy"
or "dark and foreign-looking"—despite the testimony of criminologists
that criminals do *not* tend to be dark, foreign or "wild-eyed." Delve into
the main asset of a telephone stock swindler and you will find it to be a
marvelously confidence-inspiring telephone "personality." And whereas
we all think we know what an Italian or a Swede looks like, it is the sad
fact that when a group of Nebraska students sought to match faces and
nationalities of 15 European countries, they were scored wrong in 93
percent of their identifications. Finally, for all the fact that horn-rimmed
glasses have now become the standard television sign of an "intellectual,"
optometrists know that the main thing that distinguishes people with
glasses is just bad eyes.

How is it, then, that we continue to entertain such cockeyed notions
about the world?

TYPES FROM A GRADE B MOVIE

The answer seems to be an inveterate trait in all of us to type-cast
people—to imagine them, even to *see* them, not as they really are, but
as if they stepped out of a Grade B movie. Introduce someone to a poet
or a politician, a Texan or a teacher, and before he even shakes hands, he

* Robert L. Heilbroner, "Don't Let Stereotypes Warp Your Judgment," *THINK,* 27, (June,
1961), pp. 7–8. Reprinted by permission of the author.

"knows" what the other person will be like: the poet, of course, will be a dreamer; the politician a glad-hander who's probably never read a book or been inside a museum in his life; the Texan an oil man or a cattle rancher; and the teacher mousy and pedantic. Of course, the poet *might* be like Wallace Stevens, who was an insurance executive, or the politician *might* be like Nelson Rockefeller, who is an art connoisseur, or the Texan *might* be a pianist, like Van Cliburn, or the teacher *might* be a comedian like Sam Levenson. But we wouldn't expect them to be.

What we *would* expect are the stereotypes by which we commonly picture professions, nationalities, races, religions. Just name an occupation, and its stereotype image lights up: tough truck driver, stuffy banker, dumb cop. Mention a nationality and its ready-made portrait jumps up from the page: excitable Latins, stolid Swedes, hot-tempered Irish. Think about any group of people—mothers-in-law, teen-agers, women drivers, young marrieds, cannibals—and what Walter Lippmann once called a "standardized picture" forms in our heads.

The Dark World of Prejudice

Stereotypes, in other words, are a kind of gossip about the world, a gossip that makes us prejudge people before we ever lay eyes on them. Hence it is not surprising that stereotypes have something to do with the dark world of prejudice. Explore most prejudices (note that the word means prejudgment) and you will find a cruel stereotype at its core.

For it is the extraordinary fact that once we have type-cast the world, we tend to see people in terms of our standardized pictures. In another demonstration of the power of stereotypes to affect our vision, a number of Columbia and Barnard students were shown 30 photographs of pretty but unidentified girls, and asked to rate each in terms of "general liking," "intelligence," "beauty" and so on. Two months later, the same group were shown the same photographs, this time with fictitious Irish, Italian, Jewish and "American" names attached to the pictures. Right away the ratings changed. Faces which were now seen as representing a national group went down in looks and still farther down in likability, while the "American" girls suddenly looked decidedly prettier and nicer.

Why is it that we stereotype the world in such irrational and harmful fashion? In part, we begin to type-cast people in our childhood years. Early in life, as every parent whose child has watched a TV Western knows, we learn to spot the Good Guys from the Bad Guys. Some years ago, a social psychologist showed very clearly how powerful these stereotypes of childhood vision are. He secretly asked the most popular youngsters in an elementary school to make errors in their morning gym exercises. Afterwards, he asked the class if anyone had noticed any mistakes during gym period. Oh, yes, said the children. But it was the *unpopular* members of the class—the "bad guys"—they remembered as being out of step.

The Stereotype Joke

We not only grow up with standardized pictures forming inside of us, but as grown-ups we are constantly having them thrust upon us. Some of them, like the half-joking, half-serious stereotypes of mothers-in-law, or country yokels, or psychiatrists, are dinned into us by the stock jokes we hear and repeat. In fact, without such stereotypes, there would be a lot fewer jokes. Still other stereotypes are perpetuated by the advertisements we read, the movies we see, the books we read. For instance, a Columbia University group has pointed out that whereas 40 percent of our national population is a member of some minority racial, national or religious group, less than 10 percent of our magazine fiction heroes belongs to such a group.

And finally, we tend to stereotype because it helps us make sense out of a highly confusing world, a world which William James once described as "one great, blooming, buzzing confusion." It is a curious fact that if we don't *know* what we're looking at, we are often quite literally unable to *see* what we're looking at. People who recover their sight after a lifetime of blindness actually cannot at first tell a triangle from a square. A visitor to a factory sees only noisy chaos where the superintendent sees a perfectly synchronized flow of work. As Walter Lippmann wrote in his book, *Public Opinion,* nearly 40 years ago, "For the most part we do not first see, and then define; we define first, and then we see."

Stereotypes are one way in which we "define" the world in order to see it. They classify the infinite variety of human beings into a convenient handful of "types" towards whom we learn to act in stereotyped fashion. Life would be a wearing process if we had to start from scratch with each and every human contact. Stereotypes economize on our mental effort by covering up the blooming, buzzing confusion with big recognizable cut-outs. They save us the "trouble" of finding out what the world is like —they give it its accustomed look.

They Make Us Lazy

Thus the trouble is that stereotypes make us mentally lazy. As S. I. Hayakawa, the authority on semantics, has written: "The danger of stereotypes lies not in their existence, but in the fact that they become for all people some of the time, and for some people all the time, *substitutes for observation.*" Worse yet, stereotypes get in the way of our judgment, even when we do observe the world. Someone who has formed rigid preconceptions of all Latins as "excitable," or all teen-agers as "wild," doesn't alter his point of view when he meets a calm and deliberate Genoese, or a serious-minded high school student. He brushes them aside as "exceptions that prove the rule." And, of course, if he meets someone true to type, he stands triumphantly vindicated. "They're all like that," he proclaims, having encountered an excited Latin, an ill-behaved adolescent.

Hence, quite aside from the injustice which stereotypes do to others, they impoverish ourselves. A person who lumps the world into simple categories, who type-casts all labor leaders as "racketeers," all businessmen as "reactionaries," all Harvard men as "snobs," and all Frenchmen as "sexy," is in danger of becoming a stereotype himself. He loses his capacity to be himself—which is to say, to see the world in his own absolutely unique, inimitable and independent fashion.

Instead, he votes for the man who fits his standardized picture of what a candidate "should" look like or sound like, buys the goods that someone in his "situation" in life "should" own, lives the life that others define for him. The mark of the stereotype person is that he never surprises us, that we do indeed have him "typed." And no one fits this strait-jacket so perfectly as someone whose opinions about *other people* are fixed and inflexible.

Impoverishing as they are, stereotypes are not easy to get rid of. The world we type-cast may be no better than a Grade B movie, but at least we know what to expect of our stock characters. When we let them act for themselves in the strangely unpredictable way that people do act, who knows but that many of our fondest convictions will be proved wrong?

How to Avoid a Stereotype Lapse

Nor do we suddenly drop our standardized pictures for a blinding vision of the Truth. Sharp swings of ideas about people often just substitute one stereotype for another. The true process of change is a slow one that adds bits and pieces of reality to the pictures in our heads, until gradually they take on some of the blurriness of life itself. Little by little, we learn not that Jews and Negroes and Catholics and Puerto Ricans are "just like everybody else"—for that, too, is a stereotype—but that each and every one of them is unique, special, different and individual. Often we do not even know that we have let a stereotype lapse until we hear someone saying, "all so-and-so's are like such-and-such," and we hear ourselves saying, "Well—maybe."

Can we speed the process along? Of course we can.

First, we can become *aware* of the standardized pictures in our heads, in other peoples' heads, in the world around us.

Second, we can become suspicious of all judgments that we allow exceptions to "prove." There is no more chastening thought than that in the vast intellectual adventure of science, it takes but one tiny exception to topple a whole edifice of ideas.

Third, we can learn to be chary of generalizations about people. As F. Scott Fitzgerald once wrote: "Begin with an individual, and before you know it you have created a type; begin with a type, and you find you have created—nothing."

Most of the time, when we type-cast the world, we are not in fact generalizing about people at all. We are only revealing the embarrassing facts about the pictures that hang in the gallery of stereotypes in our own heads.

STOP TIMING HERE

Questions—Don't Let Stereotypes Warp Your Judgment

Indicate whether the following statements are true or false in the selection you have just read by putting T or F in the spaces provided.

—— 1. Matching faces to their national origin can be done with a fairly high degree of accuracy.

—— 2. Stereotypes are the basis of most prejudices.

—— 3. Stereotypes only help to add confusion to an already highly confused world.

—— 4. Walter Lippmann once wrote, "For the most part we do not first define and then see; we see first, and then we define."

—— 5. Stereotypes tend to give the world an "accustomed" look.

—— 6. Stereotypes are substitutes for observation.

—— 7. The person who views a stereotyped world is very likely stereotyped himself.

—— 8. We should be suspicious of judgments that we allow exceptions to prove.

—— 9. When we form a stereotype, we are really generalizing about people.

—— 10. The habit of stereotyped thinking should be suddenly and completely stopped by the right-thinking person.

Summary

Improvement in rate of comprehension, once the idea of reading by thought units is understood, is probably best practiced by reading light, easy material, such as a short popular novel, within a time limit. For example, if such a novel of a hundred pages, with 350 to 400 words to a page, would ordinarily take you three or four hours to read, set a two-hour limit and attempt to read it in this shorter time. Check yourself every twenty-five pages or so, and if you are lagging behind, try to catch up to your schedule in the next twenty-five pages. Such timing by fairly large units allows for individual differences among specific pages and parts of the story. You may wish to read one part slowly, another part much more rapidly. By practicing this way you are applying flexibility in rate, which is very important to good reading.

The next time you pick up a magazine or newspaper, try reading more rapidly than normally. As you do so, you will be forced to avoid certain words and select others that are more important.

There are differences between the longer book and the shorter article that make the reading of them somewhat different. Their purposes and the way in which they are organized are different, and therefore practice in reading just one will not train you thoroughly for the other. Continued practice both in book-length material and in short stories, articles, and other forms will make rapid comprehension more and more a part of your reading skills.

CHAPTER 5

READING FOR STUDY PURPOSES

In the preceding chapters we have discussed ways of selecting reading skills for a variety of reading tasks. In this chapter we shall examine how the skills you have learned, with the addition of some new ones, can be organized into what is called studying.

As you know, the proper selection of reading skills depends on many things—the nature of the material, your familiarity with it, your interest in it, your background, and your purpose for reading. We shall assume for each of the exercises in this chapter that your purpose is careful study. The nature of the material is different for each selection; one selection is on the skill of listening, the others represent the areas of history, science, and sociology. Of course, your approach will differ in certain details for each. However, each exercise will be developed around a study plan commonly called the *PQRST* method.

Before describing this *PQRST* study plan, which is really a collection of all the reading techniques you have practiced thus far in this book, let us consider ways in which you approach various kinds of study materials. As a student, most often your purpose is the careful study of facts and ideas in order to retain them. You will be trying to learn both main ideas and some details when you study. In some materials, you will also be trying to make judgments, react emotionally or analytically, or even memorize certain small portions. Occasionally, your study materials require you to make an over-all evaluation or reaction, or recognize the author's hidden purpose or prejudice, or even make comments on his style, diction, ideas, and so on.

When your purposes for reading vary in these ways, the manner in which you study must also vary—in degree of concentration, in speed, in attention to details, in the type and amount of note-taking, and in other ways. We shall outline for you here a basic method of studying, the *PQRST* method. We do not claim that it is a perfect system, nor do we expect you to use it every time you study. But we do hope you will learn it by practicing it in the selections of this chapter. When you have given it a fair trial in this chapter, you may then begin to modify it in terms of your purposes in each study situation. You will gradually learn to stress certain steps more—for example, the *Read-Summarize* step when your purpose for study demands more detailed comprehension, or the *Preview* step when your purpose is more analytic or interpretive. Let us begin by describing the complete study plan.

The PQRST Study Plan

The steps of the *PQRST* study plan are as follows:

P—Preview the selection by reading the title, headings, first and last sentences of paragraphs, and introductory or summary paragraphs.

Q—During the preview, raise as many *questions* as you can about the content. Turn the headings into questions and try to anticipate the possible answers the writer may offer. Steps *P* and *Q* work together; keep an active, questioning attitude, posing questions and jotting them down for reference during the *R* and *S* steps.

R—Read, trying to answer the questions written down during the *P* and *Q* steps.

S—Summarize during your reading by making brief notes based on the answers to your questions. Most of your questions (unless you have asked some very detailed ones) should be answered by recognizing the central idea of each paragraph, if there is one. Therefore, in addition to reading to answer your questions, read to determine the writer's main idea for each paragraph and state it in your own words in a brief sentence. When you have finished, you not only will have answered your questions but you will have outlined the selection as well.

Now look at your point-by-point outline. You will see that several paragraphs can be brought together to form a more inclusive idea. These clusters in turn can be grouped to pull all the points together into one over-all main idea. Accurate and more rapid comprehension is built up as you learn to grasp quickly units of ideas, summarizing them, if possible, into a final, general, main idea for the selection. (In practical daily application, you probably will not make a paragraph-by-paragraph *written* summary each time. However, the mental process will be much the same.)

T—Test your understanding of the selection by attempting to answer your preview questions without referring to the material or your notes. Make up some true-false questions based on your comprehension that you believe might resemble questions an instructor might give as a quiz.

▶   *STUDY EXERCISE I*

Before you study the first selection, review the steps again:

1. *P—Preview* the material.
2. *Q*—Jot down *questions* from your preview. (Write these in space provided at the end of the selection.)
3. *R—Read* to answer your questions.
4. *S—Summarize* by (a) making brief notes based on the answers found to your preview questions; (b) noting the main idea of each paragraph; (c) stating a final main idea for the selection. (Write your notes for *b* and *c* at the end of the selection. The paragraphs have been numbered to assist you in *b*.)
5. *T—Test* your comprehension by referring to your preview questions.

Listening with the Inner Ear*

The experts say that most of us retain only half of what we hear—an expensive handicap in business, education, practically every kind of work. Here is what we can do to develop good listening habits.   —RALPH G. NICHOLS
                                     with LEONARD A. STEVENS

1. Are we a nation of "half-listeners"? For several years at the University of Minnesota we have tested the listening ability of college students and business people who attend adult education courses. The results show that the average person remembers only about 50 per cent of what he has heard immediately after he has listened to someone talk—no matter how carefully he thought he listened. A couple of months later he is doing well to remember 25 per cent of what was said. These figures have been substantiated at a number of other universities.
2. Bad listening is a handicap to businessmen because their affairs are largely conducted by the spoken word, and its effectiveness is directly related to how people listen. When their listening is poor, it causes trouble at all levels of a business.
3. Not long ago, for example, a group of employees in a Long Island factory were given oral instructions concerning the operation of a new forge. The men all seemed to listen carefully, but in a short time, one of them hung a hot grappling iron on a wall where, according to instructions, only cool irons were to be placed. Another employee grabbed the hot iron which burned and stuck to his hand. The burns permanently impaired his ability to work.
4. The art of listening, as we shall consider it here, is defined as the ability to understand and recall the spoken word. This process is a

---

*Ralph G. Nichols with Leonard A. Stevens, "Listening with the Inner Ear," *Think*, XXIV, (June 1958), pp. 11–13. Reprinted by permission from THINK magazine, Copyright 1958 by International Business Machines Corporation.

skill—the same as reading is a skill—and when treated as such, we find that listening can be improved through training. It is already being taught at the University of Minnesota and other schools and colleges around the country.

5. In the past, however, listening has been the neglected stepchild of education, while reading has been the favored son. In our opinion, this imbalance was produced by several false assumptions held by educators.

6. Teachers assumed, for example, that reading instructions would automatically improve listening. But actually the two skills are different from one another. The reader, for instance, has a body of words before him, and he can ordinarily read and reread them for understanding and retention. The listener, however, must receive words that come and go, one at a time, at a pace determined by the speaker. Effective listening, therefore, requires skills not developed by reading instruction.

7. In the schools that were attended by today's adults, reading received about six years' formal attention, but listening ability was neglected. The typical student was graduated, as a fairly good reader and a poor listener, into a world of telephones, radios, critical conferences and trials by jury—all depending upon an understanding of the spoken word.

8. Most people do not realize how much time they spend just using their ears. A survey made by Paul T. Rankin as supervising director of research and adjustment for the Detroit Public Schools, showed that the average adult spends 45 per cent of his communicating time listening. The remainder is divided up among reading, writing and speaking.

9. Other surveys substantiate Rankin's findings. Some of them have been made by businessmen who have found that white-collar workers sometimes receive from 40 to 80 per cent of their salaries for using their ears. When they don't know how to listen well, these employees are unduly expensive. The effects of their bad listening—in addition to causing costly errors—are reflected in a number of ways throughout a business.

10. Bad experiences with listening compel many businessmen to avoid oral communication if messages have the slightest importance. This tendency whips up a snowstorm of memos.

11. Two businessmen at the Madison, Wisconsin, airport were overheard discussing a purchase order that was urgently needed from their home office in Chicago.

"Did you let John know how to prepare the order and exactly where to send it?" asked one man.

"Yes, this morning," said the other.

"How? Did you wire him?"

"No, by telephone."

"Good Lord, no! Don't ever depend upon John getting anything straight verbally. You've got to get it into writing for him, so that it'll stare him in the face."

12. Because of the rule to "Put it into writing!" industry's filing cabinets are overstuffed with written messages that should have been spoken. Poor listening is thereby forcing people away from the spoken word, which can be a faster, more economical means of communication than the written word.

"UPWARD COMMUNICATION"

13. The need for improved listening shows up more and more as a business firm grows. For example, it acquires importance in "upward communication." The top man of a large business has many channels for communicating downward through an organization, but he has few channels for the upward flow of information from all those who work under him. For the top man, it's like speaking to a person who doesn't answer. The more he talks, the more uncertain he becomes of the reaction he produces below. Many methods are tried to induce upward communication (the suggestion box, for one) but few work well.

14. There's one obvious upward channel in operation every day. The foreman listens to the man at the bench, the superintendent listens to the foreman, and so on up the line. All would be fine except for the bad listeners along the way. They either stop or twist the upward-bound information, making it useless. Here is a place where improved listening could serve industrialists well.

15. The smooth horizontal flow of information also becomes increasingly important in growing industries. Without it one department soon loses track of another. Salesmen, for instance, get into trouble because they don't know what production people are up to. When this occurs, departments need to get together, and the best way is through conferences which, of course, depend upon talking and listening. The talking at a conference usually takes care of itself, but it only burns up oxygen if it isn't heard and absorbed. Indeed, an efficient conference, if you think about it, requires far more listening than talking. This, coupled with the fact that businessmen conduct their most important affairs at meetings, really calls for listening improvement among executives.

16. The skill of listening has a crucial role in the human relations area of business. For instance, it's important for most people to talk and be heard, to voice their problems, to get things off their minds. Executives are frequently called upon as listeners for this purpose, because subordinates are likely to turn to superiors for a sympathetic ear. When it isn't there, strange things have been known to happen.

17. At a large plant near Chicago a few years ago, a promising young superintendent slowly became sullen and uncommunicative to the point of being useless. He was to be fired or demoted. The parent company, an electrical equipment manufacturer, sent a trained counselor to see the man. By listening sympathetically, the counselor eventually encouraged the superintendent to talk freely about his problems. Here, very briefly, is the tale told by the superintendent:

18. At one time he was away from work because of family trouble. He

tried expressing his problems to the plai t manager who refused to listen. "Don't bring family troubles here," said the manager. "They're no excuse for being absent." With no other outlet, the superintendent's problems grew in his mind.' They slowly reduced his effectiveness on the job. By the time the counselor arrived, the problems had turned into mental monsters.

19. With the opportunity to talk out his problems, he saw them more realistically. Slowly, he found the flaws in his own thinking, and was soon on the way to being useful again.

20. Too many businessmen feel that they can only listen to the most pertinent of their subordinates' statements. This is a mistake. At times an executive can be of service to those who work for him, and to his organization, simply by acting as a sounding board, by being a sympathetic listener.

The Value of Aural Skills

21. Once people become aware of the importance of good listening, they are likely to show some improvement almost automatically. Telephone operators, for instance, are usually good listeners, not necessarily as a result of special training in the aural skills, but because they know the importance of good listening. At times, their abilities to retain what they hear has been valuable far beyond the line of duty.

22. A Streetman, Texas, operator plugged into her switchboard one day to hear an excited farmer calling her. He said that a car driven by two men had just run off the road near his home. While he went for help, the men disappeared. As he returned to the empty car, he found a Missouri license plate and two guns hidden nearby.

23. "What'll I do?" he asked the telephone operator.

"Tell me what the men looked like," she said. The farmer described the men, and the operator quickly rang the sheriff's office. Before going on duty, she told the sheriff, she had heard a news broadcast saying that six Springfield, Missouri, police officers had been shot to death. The broadcast had described the killers, and the description, said the operator, fitted the two men who had ditched the car. Following her tip, the police caught up with the two outlaws in Houston, Texas.

24. The development of such acute listening habits within most people also requires an understanding of what produces effective aural skills. For this reason, let's consider some of the more technical aspects of listening.

25. What do you listen for when someone is talking, and you really want to understand him? A common answer to this question is: "I listen for the facts." The intentions are good, but we've found that "I-get-the-facts" listening doesn't work well. Here's what happens:

26. Let's say your boss is giving you instructions made up of facts that we will label A to Z. The boss begins to talk. You hear Fact A and think: "I've got to remember it." So you begin a memory exercise of repeating, "Fact A, Fact A, Fact A, ..." Meanwhile, the boss is re-

lating Fact B. Now you have two facts to remember, and you're so busy doing it that you miss Fact C completely. And so it goes up to Fact Z. You catch a few, garble others and completely miss the rest.

27. When a person talks to you, he usually wants to put across an idea or two. He uses facts to support the ideas, like building blocks. A good listener naturally hears the facts, but he concentrates on finding what they all add up to. He weighs one against the other, trying to recognize their relationships. In so doing, he looks for the main idea the speaker wishes to impart. When this happens, the listener is likely to get the most meaning from what he hears.

28. Regardless of what you listen for, aural concentration is a problem—and for a special reason. It's made difficult by the way people talk. The average person speaks at a speed of about 125 words per minute. Most of us think at about four times that rate (if we measure thought in words), and it's impossible to slow down. Therefore, we have about 400 words of thinking time to spare every minute that we listen to someone talk. What the listener does with this spare time determines how well he concentrates aurally.

29. The bad listener uses the excess time to make mental excursions away from the spoken line of thought entering his ears. He starts following the speaker, but then, knowing that he has time to spare, he thinks his own thoughts for moments here and there. These brief side excursions continue until his mind tarries too long upon some enticing but irrelevant subject. Then when his mind returns to the speaker, the would-be listener finds he's losing track of what is being said. Now it's harder to follow the speaker and easier to take more side excursions. Finally, the listener gives up, allowing his mind to remain in a world far off from the speaker.

WHAT TO LISTEN FOR

30. In listening improvement courses, we try to help students with this problem of aural concentration. It's done by suggesting ways that the listener may apply all of his thinking time to the spoken words. To do this, he should:

31. Try to anticipate what a person is going to talk about. On the basis of what the speaker has already said, the listener should ask himself: "What's he trying to get at? What point is he going to make?"

32. Mentally summarize what has been said. What point has the speaker made already, if any?

33. Weigh the speaker's evidence by mentally questioning it. If he gives facts, illustrative stories and statistics, the listener should ask himself: "Are they accurate? Do they come from an unprejudiced source? Am I getting the full picture or is he telling me only what will prove his point?"

34. Listen "between the lines." A person doesn't always put everything that's important into words. The changing tones and volume of his voice may have meaning. So may his facial expressions, the gestures he makes with his hands.

35. With these principles in mind, a person is on the way to improved listening—but he won't arrive unless he works hard aurally. This means doing some listening that requires mental effort. Too many of us turn a deaf ear to words more difficult than those of a TV comedian. If an oral explanation is hard to understand, we say: "Make it easier or I won't listen." If a talk seems uninteresting, we quit listening, saying: "That fellow is a bore, therefore he can't have much to say." Such habits form a downward spiral leading to the lowest common denominator of listening ability.

36. One who wishes to improve his aural abilities must sometimes listen to talk that requires a degree of mental strain for understanding. The right kind of practice can be found, for example, in certain radio and TV discussions or speeches, in educational lectures, in a number of spoken-word recordings now on sale and in the ever-present possibility of reading aloud to one another at home.

37. In the past, there has been confusion about communication responsibility between speakers and listeners. Almost all of the responsibility has been placed upon the speaker. The listener has said, "If you can't catch my attention and make me understand, it's your fault." But this is absurd if you remember that the listener is on the receiving end. At least half—perhaps more—of the communication responsibility should fall to him. When this concept is more widely realized, we will find better listeners everywhere.

Questions—Listening with the Inner Ear

Write your preview questions for "Listening with the Inner Ear" here. Then compare them with those offered in the Answer Key.

61984

Write the main idea of each paragraph here (if there is one).

1. _____
_____

2. _____
_____

3. _____
_____

4. _____
_____

5. _____
_____

6. _____
_____

7. _____
_____

8. _____
_____

9. _____
_____

10. _____
_____

11. _____
_____

12. _____
_____

13. _____
_____

14. _____
_____

15. _____

16. _____

17. and 18. _____

19. _____

20. _____

21. _____

22. _____

23. _____

24. _____

25. and 26. _____

27. _____

28. _____

29. _____

30. _____

31. _____
_____
_____

32. _____
_____
_____

33. _____
_____
_____

34. _____
_____
_____

35. _____
_____
_____

36. _____
_____
_____

37. _____
_____
_____

Were many of your preview questions answered in the main ideas of each paragraph? They should have been, if your previewing was successful in anticipating the content of the article.

Compare your main ideas for each paragraph and those found in the Answer Key. You will see that in some instances several paragraphs fit together, one paragraph explaining, illustrating, or supporting another. These could readily be pulled together to form one basic idea. For example, paragraph three supports or illustrates the idea of paragraph two. The statement "bad listening is a handicap to businessmen" can summarize both paragraphs.

Paragraphs five, six, and seven also stand together. These could be summarized to read: "Because educators have falsely assumed that instruction in reading skills automatically transfers to better listening skills, schools have not taught listening, and the present generation of adults has never been trained in this skill."

Paragraph nine of course elaborates more fully on paragraph eight, and paragraphs ten, eleven, and twelve as obviously form a single idea, which can be worded as the summary for paragraph ten: "Poor listening skills force many businessmen to rely on written directives only."

Continue through the selection, pulling together each group of closely related paragraphs into a more inclusive statement. Your organization may be somewhat different from what ours would be. Compare your ideas with those of a classmate.

Put your restated, regrouped main ideas here. _____

_____

_____

_____

_____

_____

_____

_____

_____

_____

_____

_____

_____

_____

_____

_____

What would you give as the writer's main idea for the complete selection? Put your statement here. _____

_____

_____

_____

_____

_____

_____

(Check the Answer Key for our suggestions.)

Now test your comprehension by answering your own preview questions without referring to the selection.

►   *STUDY EXERCISE II*

The second selection is taken from a history textbook. Study it, using the following steps:

1. *Preview.*

2. Write down *questions* that come to you as you preview. (Use the space at the end of the selection.)

3. *Read.*

4. Look for the answers to your preview questions as you read.

5. Write the answer after each question. Be brief in your statements.

6. *Summarize* by pausing at the end of each paragraph or cluster of paragraphs to phrase mentally a main idea line.

7. Reread *only* those paragraphs that are not clear to you.

8. *Test* your comprehension by answering your own preview questions.

Roman Culture in the Republican Age*

INFLUENCE OF GREEK CULTURE

Of the early literature, art, and philosophy of Rome almost nothing remains, and historians entertain a probably well-founded suspicion that very little existed. The interests of the sturdy farmers, soldiers, and statesmen of the early republic did not run naturally in those directions, while their remarkable lack of commercial contact with the outside world kept them for a long time free from the influence of more advanced civilizations. The conquest of the Greek cities of southern Italy and Sicily brought the Romans into direct contact with Greek culture, but it was not until toward the end of the third century B.C. that they seem to have become fully aware of its charm. Having become aware of it, however, the educated class in Rome set about absorbing Greek literature and thought with all the enthusiasm of the recent convert. During the second century, as the eastward trend of foreign policy brought the republic into ever closer relations with the Greek world, a knowledge of Greek became a necessary part of a Roman gentleman's education and, by the following century, it had become a second mother tongue to the Roman literati. Greek slaves and freedmen swarmed into Rome, bringing the artistic techniques of the Hellenistic East and, in many instances, serving as tutors to the sons of wealthy families. The beginnings of Roman literature and philosophy date from the beginning of the Greek influence and, throughout, they retained the character imprinted upon them by Greek forms and Greek thought. But, as they developed, they became adaptations rather than imitations of the Greek models. Roman culture was built upon a Greek foundation, but the structure was Roman, and it had the lasting quality peculiar to Roman buildings. It still stands today as one of the great monuments of human civilization, preserving for us not only much Greek thought that would otherwise have been lost, but also much that was the original expression of Roman genius.

LATIN DRAMA

The drama dominated the early period of Latin literature. Plays adapted from the Hellenistic New Comedy or the older Greek tragedies brought entertainment and intellectual stimulus to a public not yet fully accustomed to reading in any extensive fashion. The first dramatist of whose quality we can judge from plays that have survived intact was

* Wallace K. Ferguson and Geoffrey Brunn, "Roman Culture In The Republican Age," *A Survey of European Civilization* (Boston: Houghton Mifflin Company, 1958), pp. 59–62. Reprinted by permission of the Houghton Mifflin Company.

Plautus (c. 254–184 B.C.), who wrote boisterous, rollicking comedies based on Greek plots. These seem intended for popular consumption and must have received a hearty response from the groundlings. In the next generation, the more subtle shadings of Greek comedy were presented in an infinitely more refined, literary Latin by Terence (c. 195–159 B.C.), a member of the aristocratic circle of the younger Scipio, though born a slave in Africa. At the same time Ennius (239–169 B.C.) reproduced in Latin the best tragedies of Sophocles and Euripides, with variations that brought them into harmony with the characteristic Roman conceptions of morality. Drama continued to be the most prolific form of Latin literature through most of the second century. As the educated Romans developed more consistent reading habits, however, it declined, its place being taken by other types of poetry and prose.

POETRY

The early imitations of Greek poetry were rendered somewhat awkward by the intractability of the Latin tongue. Long practice under Greek guidance was needed before it acquired the flexibility that would enable the Roman poets to rival their Greek models. By the middle of the first century it had reached that stage, and the Roman writers had by then so thoroughly absorbed the spirit and forms of Greek literature that they were able to work freely, without the cramping effect of too close imitation. The lyric poetry of Catullus (c. 84–54 B.C.) has all the spontaneity and ease of a native literature despite his use of Greek forms. The charming lyrics addressed to Lesbia, in particular, have a youthful freshness that makes them more appealing than any of the Hellenistic poetry that has survived. The men of this generation perfected the poetic vocabulary, the meters and rhythms of Latin poetry and prepared the way for the great poets of the Augustan Age.

PROSE

While the Golden Age of Latin poetry was yet to come, the prose writers of the late republican era created a Latin style that has never since been surpassed. Latin oratory flourished in these years under conditions similar to those which had developed the rhetorical style of republican Athens, and partly under the influence of Greek models. The hectic political life of the dying republic placed a premium on oratory, and every young Roman aristocrat devoted himself to the study of rhetoric as the essential training for a career in public office, in the Senate, or in the law courts. Cicero (106–43 B.C.), the unrivaled master of Latin prose, had a long and distinguished career in public office and was one of the most intransigent leaders of the conservative senatorial party in opposition to the dictatorial senatorial party and in opposition to the dictatorial ambitions of Caesar and the triumvirate. His rhetorical style was developed in the heat of political controversy. His orations against Catiline, whom he prosecuted for conspiracy against the state, are models of their kind, as are also the bitter attacks on Mark Antony after the murder of Caesar, which Cicero, incidentally, approved. The orations against Antony were in fact all too effective. They were the last acts of a courageous and cantankerous career, for they led to Cicero's being proscribed and killed by the victorious triumvirate. Cicero's fame as a prose writer, however, does not rest solely upon his orations. His familiar letters to his friends are also models of their kind. They show a more amiable side of the great controversialist's character and are filled with priceless reflections of the social life of republican Rome. Finally, in the philosophical treatises *On Friendship, On Duty, On Old Age,* etc., he demonstrated the capacity of the Latin language to express the finest shades of meaning, while at the same time transmitting to the Latin world the best moral teaching of the Greek philosophers. Julius Caesar, too, was a master of prose style, although of a more simple and direct sort. His *Commentaries on the Gallic Wars,* a report to the Roman people on his conquest of Gaul, have served as an introduction to Latin prose for countless schoolboys. They constitute also a masterpiece of historical literature. This same generation of politically active writers produced one other popular historian, Sallust (86–34 B.C.), whose accounts of the Catiline conspiracy, from a point of view very different from that of Cicero, and of the war against the Numidian king Jugurtha, have been greatly admired for their vigorous style, if not always for their reliability.

RELIGION

The religion of Rome was native to the country, but like other aspects of Roman culture it was transformed by Greek influence, while Roman philosophy was in origin an importation from Greece. The early Roman religion consisted of a formalized worship of *numina* or spirits who pervaded the household, the fields, and the woods. Later, as the state developed, the conception of household gods was adapted to the needs of the state and a ritualistic state religion evolved as a significant factor in practical politics. It was only after the Greek cultural invasion, however, that the impersonal *numina* or gods acquired an anthropomorphic character and a mythology. By the simple expedient of identifying the native gods with their Olympian prototypes, the Romans took over the literary heritage of Greek mythology. As a result of this process, Latin literature was greatly enriched, but the Roman religion lost its indigenous character and much of its hold on the faith of the educated classes. By the Age of Augustus it had degenerated into a literary convention, a "poets' religion," while the religious emotions of the mass of the people were being fed by Hellenistic cults that were beginning to be imported from the East.

PHILOSOPHY

The most cultured of the Roman aristocrats were turning meanwhile from religion to philosophy for comfort and guidance. As a rule they lacked the interest in metaphysical speculation about the nature of the universe which was characteristic of the Greeks of the classical age, but like the later Hellenistic philosophers they were greatly concerned with practical morality. They asked of philosophy how a man should live so as to achieve peace and the good life; and many of them found satisfactory answers according to their temperament in either Epicureanism or Stoicism, both of which had originated in Greece in the third century B.C. . . . Epicureanism gained many adherents among the wealthy Romans who were disillusioned and repelled by the violence of republican politics. Stoicism, on the other hand, made its strongest appeal to the conscientious statesmen, public officials, and judges who were the mainstay of the Roman state. It was a stern and somewhat arid philosophy, but for centuries it inspired men like Cicero and the Emperor Marcus Aurelius.

Questions—Roman Culture in the Republican Age

Write your preview questions here. _____

_____
_____
_____
_____
_____
_____
_____
_____
_____
_____
_____
_____
_____
_____
_____
_____

Answer your preview questions here. Then compare your questions and answers with those in the Answer Key. _____

_____
_____
_____
_____
_____
_____
_____
_____
_____

_____

_____

_____

_____

_____

_____

_____

_____

►   *STUDY EXERCISE III*

The third selection for your study is taken from science. In general format this particular material is not unlike the previous excerpt from history. This selection does contain a greater concentration of "facts" such as stellar distances, temperature comparison, and chemical and other environmental characteristics that are necessary to support life as we know it. The kind of methodical thinking that will best help you achieve adequate comprehension is, however, probably much like the kind of thinking you did for the history selection.

One difference may be in the way you find answers to your preview questions. If your questions are particularly detailed or specific, scanning to find the answers may be the best technique.

Use the following steps in a study of the material:

1. *Preview.*
2. Write down *questions* that come to you as you preview.
3. *Read.*
4. Look for the answers to your preview questions as you read.
5. Write the answer after each question. Scan for the answers to questions that require the use of figures you may not remember accurately.
6. *Summarize* by pausing at the end of each paragraph or cluster of paragraphs to phrase mentally a main idea line.
7. Reread *only* those paragraphs that are not clear to you.
8. *Test* your comprehension by writing some true-false questions on the selection. Try to frame questions like those your instructors might use.
9. *Test* yourself by answering the questions at the end of the selection.

Life's Home[*]

THE VAST UNIVERSE

We live in an incredibly vast universe. Traveling at about 186,000 miles per second, light takes over 4 years to reach us from the nearest star. That works out at roughly 23,500,000,000,000 miles to the *nearest*

[*] From *Life: An Introduction to Biology* by George G. Simpson, Colin S. Pittendrigh, and Lewis H. Tiffany, © 1957, by Harcourt, Brace & World, Inc., pp. 13–16. Reprinted with permission of Harcourt, Brace & World, Inc., and Routledge & Kegan Paul Ltd.

star. It takes light about 200,000 years to travel across our particular cluster of stars. That is, our home galaxy is some 200,000 light-years in diameter. Out beyond this galaxy are innumerable other galaxies, millions of light-years distant and more. The most distant object visible with the naked eye—the spiral nebula in Andromeda—is about 900,000 light-years away, but modern telescopes reach far beyond that. As larger telescopes are built, the astronomers see (or, in practice, photograph) farther and farther, revealing more of the same and no signs of a limit. There are ingenious and interesting theories about limits to our universe, but the fact is that no one knows how large it is.

THE SOLAR SYSTEM

Until someone actually produces the "time drive," so common in science fiction and so entirely unknown to science, only one cozy little part of this awesomely immense universe has any direct interest to the biologist. Our solar system consists of nine planets and a variety of other objects (satellites of the planets, asteroids, comets, meteors) revolving around the sun. The sun is a rather commonplace or second-rate star, as stars go, about 860,000 miles in diameter and with a surface temperature of about 11,000°F. With exceptions of no real importance, all the energy used by living things comes as radiation from the sun. This is true even of the energy used by human industry. For instance, the energy in your automobile is solar energy. It was radiated by the sun long ago, fixed in chemical form by living organisms, turned into petroleum by a series of other transformations, and finally made into gasoline at a refinery. . . . Atomic or, more strictly, nuclear energy, does not come from solar radiation, but its extensive industrial use is not yet at hand.

THE PLANET EARTH: FITNESS FOR LIFE

Our earth is an intermediate planet in position and size. It is the third from the sun, at an average distance of some 93,000,000 miles, and is about 8,000 miles in diameter. It is the densest planet, 5½ times as dense as water. Its temperature at the surface varies greatly but generally averages between 50° and 60°F throughout the year over the whole surface and only rarely and locally falls much below 30°F or rises far above 100°F. It has a deep atmosphere, about ⅕ oxygen and ⅘ nitrogen, with considerable water vapor and carbon dioxide. It has a great deal of liquid water on and near the surface. It also has quantities of other chemical substances in various forms at and near the surface, where they are available for the use of living things.

Such facts about the nature of the earth, its climatic conditions, chemical composition, and so on could be greatly expanded. The reason for listing a few of them here is to point out that the earth is well fitted to the life that inhabits it. All the chemical elements necessary for all known expressions of life are here in available form and adequate amounts. And the physical characteristics of the earth are right: it has a suitable atmosphere; it is neither too close to the sun nor too far away.

Take the matter of temperature. In the universe, temperatures range from 524° below zero (Fahrenheit) to at least 35,000,000° above; 524°F below is absolute zero—no heat at all—and 35,000,000°F is approximately the temperature at the center of the sun. Higher temperatures doubtless exist. In all this tremendous scale, there is only a tiny range of 100°F or so in which life normally operates. Living things become quiescent and eventually die with long-sustained temperatures much below the freezing point of water. Few of them can long survive above 100° or 150°F; none can live near or above the boiling point of water. Just this insignificant part of the temperature scale of the universe includes the usual temperatures on earth.

Earth has other qualifications fitting it for life. For instance, water as a liquid is an absolutely indispensable part of all living matter. Water happens to be abundant on the earth. It also happens to be liquid from 32° to 212°F (or a little below and a little above, depending on pressure and dissolved substances)—again neatly within usual earth temperatures. With a little study of chemistry, too, you will find that certain elements common on earth have special properties without which life as we know it would be quite impossible. This is particularly true for hydrogen, oxygen, and carbon, the three elements most abundant in all living things. It is true to a lesser degree of nitrogen, the next most abundant element in living matter.

All this shows that adaptation is a two-way proposition. It is not something that living things have or acquire. Adaptation is a relationship between living things and their environment. The environment has to fit them just as much as they fit the environment; otherwise—no life!

Why is the earth so well fitted to life? It seems peculiar, even downright providential, as our ancestors thought it literally was. As with so many knotty scientific problems, the answer is really simple if a little common sense is applied. Life, this particular state known to us as "life," is on earth precisely because it arose here and under these conditions. If the earth were not fit for living things, they would not be here but, if anywhere, on some other planet in some other solar system. If the earth had quite different conditions and something like life had nevertheless arisen, then that "life" would not be life as we know it but something quite different, perhaps not even recognized by us as truly alive.

Life on Other Worlds?

You would doubtless be a Venutian right now if Venus had, throughout its history, had the conditions that in fact have prevailed on earth, and earth had had Venus's history. Are there real Venutians waiting for us to land a spaceship? Trying to answer that question may not be very serious science, but it is certainly interesting. If we try to answer it scientifically, that is, by applying common sense and logic to what facts we actually know, the answer is disappointing for the fans of science fiction. From what was said above about the earth as a home for living things, it is evident that two different questions are really involved. First, are there other places where life as we know it could exist? Second, are there other possible sorts of living that could exist under quite different conditions from those on earth?

Let us briefly consider the first question first. Life as we know it could exist only on a planet. The only planets we really know anything about are the nine of our own solar system. Of these, seven (including Venus) have conditions so different from those on earth that it is as certain as can be that life like that of earth does not exist on them. It is just conceivable that some particularly tough—and to us rudimentary and nonhuman— earthlike living things could exist on Mars. It is a far cry from saying that such a thing perhaps *could* live on Mars to saying that it *does*.

It is sometimes said that there are probably millions of planets much like earth elsewhere in the universe, even though there are no others in our own solar system. Among these millions, the argument runs, some must have developed living things like those on earth, and even what the science fiction writers call "humanoids." No planets at all like the earth are *known* to exist outside our solar system. The *chances* that earthlike planets exist elsewhere depend on theories as to how our own solar system originated. Was it a rare accident? In that case the chances are slim for other, similar systems. Or was it a fairly usual incident of stellar evolution? In that case chances would be relatively good.

There are still current half a dozen different theories about how our solar system originated. There are objections to all of them, and there is at present, anyway, no really decisive way to establish any one of them as correct. That life like ours *may* exist somewhere else, perhaps a million light-years distant, is an interesting speculation. That is all. It rests on no direct evidence, either one way or the other.

Then what about the second possibility, that life of a sort might exist under conditions quite different from those of earth? It is chemically possible, or perhaps we should say "conceivable," that ammonia, for instance, could play the role that water does here. Since pure ammonia boils at more than 90° below zero, other conditions of temperature, pressure, and so on would have to be very different from those of earth. This entails all sorts of other differences, such as those of energy exchange and other reactions at very low temperatures, high pressures, or both. In short, "organisms" on these planets would be so very different from ours that we would hardly recognize them as living in our usual sense of the word. That they could be recognizably "humanoid" is incredible. Beyond that, all is baseless speculation.

Questions—Life's Home

Write your preview questions here. _____

_____

_____

_____

_____

_____

_____

_____

_____

_____

_____

_____

_____

_____

_____

_____

_____

_____

Write your true-false questions here. _____

_____

_____

_____

_____

_____

_____

_____

_____

_____

_____

_____

_____

_____

_____

_____

Answer the following questions, writing your answers immediately after each question. Compare answers with the Answer Key.

1. How long does it take for light from the nearest star to reach the earth? _____

2. What is known about the limits to our universe? _____

_____

3. Although almost all energy on earth is produced by solar radiation, what is a notable exception? _____

4. What is the density of the earth in comparison to water? _____

5. In the tremendous range in temperature throughout the universe, how large is the range in which life normally operates? _____

6. What relationship must be established if adaptation is to take place?

7. Of the nine planets in our solar system which one conceivably could support a rudimentary form of life?_____

8. What evidence do we have that life may exist on other planets? _____

Summary

We could go on offering selections from various fields for your practicing the *PQRST* method. But you have many more realistic samples to study right at hand in your college assignments. If not, there are a number of selections from typical college-level materials in Chapter 11. You may turn to these now, if you want further practice in the *PQRST* method at this time.

Your biggest problem will be that of transferring the ideas you have learned here into your usual study assignments. Out of our experience in teaching the *PQRST* method to many college students, let us point out some of their mistakes and their failures to transfer efficiently. Some students react negatively to the idea of changing their study habits. They believe, with some degree of justification, that their present system must be fairly adequate or they wouldn't have progressed as far as they have in their schooling. Other students are willing to change only slightly by adding one or two of the *PQRST* steps to their own method. Unfortunately, both of these attitudes may be based on false premises.

The habits of study adopted by most students have evolved by trial and error, by fumbling to find ways of studying successfully. Sometimes they are really efficient; more often they are not, for very few college students have ever been trained in improving their study habits. Ineffective methods of study, such as repeated rereading, excessive underlining, and over-memorizing can result in good grades for some students. But this does not prove the efficiency of these study habits. It simply shows that if a student works hard enough and long enough, even with poor learning methods, he may learn enough to make good marks. Even though your grades in the past may have been reasonable, you may be achieving these by means that are wasteful of time and effort.

There is nothing sacred about the sequence of the *PQRST* steps. A few students of superior intelligence and strong academic background may not need to follow the system precisely. But before you decide to modify the system on your own, you should realize that each step has been carefully evaluated in many learning experiments and has demonstrated its superiority in comparison with other student habits. Each step in *PQRST* has been shown to aid retention and comprehension to a significant degree. Before you decide whether to adopt the *PQRST* in whole or in part, read the introduction to Chapter 11 and all of Chapter 12. Then begin to modify your study habits, retaining those of your present methods that parallel our suggestions, and adding any of the recommended steps that you do not now use.

Give each new step a fair trial for a month or two before you decide whether to retain it. Evaluate each new habit in terms of its effect upon study time, ease of learning, and your understanding and retention of material. Don't be disturbed by the fact that you may feel uncomfortable or even disorganized during the first week or two of trial with a new habit. This is a normal experience in changing or discarding an old habit, as you may know from having observed someone who was trying to stop smoking or break some other habit. Wait until this period of change has passed before trying to weigh the values of each new procedure. Then make your decisions regarding the best study steps for you. You are certain to improve your effectiveness by evaluating your present methods and combining the best of them with new steps that prove to be useful.

Problem Solving in Mathematics

If you have difficulty in reading mathematical materials, or in solving problems, this section is addressed to you. Many otherwise good readers experience special difficulties in reading problems and in dealing with mathematical concepts. The skills that seem to work so well in literature, the fine arts, and social sciences just don't seem to help in this area of reading. Good readers in science, on the other hand, often have similar success in mathematics because of the common elements of logic, reasoning, and problem solving. Perhaps this is an indication that there are certain skills and ways of thinking that are of particular importance in various types of problem solving. Research on reading has not answered all the questions on how to read in mathematics. But we shall attempt to point out such facts as are known, and some of the difficulties readers have in this area. If you can recognize some of the mistakes or omissions you may make in reading problems, you may be able to take corrective steps.

Reading Too Rapidly.   Some individuals read problems too quickly and superficially for real understanding. They seem to expect the solutions to be obvious or the relationships to be quite apparent, without careful reading. Now it is true that a first, quick reading of a problem is recommended by many reading authorities, for the purpose of previewing or to gain a general concept. But this first reading must be followed by a second, careful reading, even by scientists or mathematicians. A rapid, first reading may not reveal all the relationships or steps that may be present. Nor does this reading result in a complete memorization of the exact figures or numbers involved. The detailed nature of many mathematical materials does not lend itself to rapid reading, for most of us, if we really intend to follow through with an attempt at solution.

For example, use the title of the following paragraph as a clue to its content. Then read it carefully.

Ways of Using Equations*

All of the equations, so far, have been of a simple type and easily solved. Thus, in studying perimeters, we found equations of the form $120 = 6s$. In studying triangles we used equations like $4x + 2x + 5x = 180$ to express the sum of angles. The equation $x + 3x = 90$ may mean that two angles are complementary, and $m + 4m = 180$ may mean that two angles are supplementary. The acute angles of a right triangle satisfy relations like $a + 6a = 90$. The circumference of a circle is found by means of the formula $c = nd$. Similar triangles lead to equations like $x/5 = 8/15$.

All these illustrations show that one cannot go very far in the study of mathematics without a knowledge of algebra (in which letters are often used for numbers), in particular of equations.

How many uses of the equation are mentioned? If you can recall fewer than five, you have read too rapidly.

Visualizing or Restating the Problem. Problems involving measurement or geometric relationships often should be visualized or even drawn on paper before a solution is attempted. In this manner, the reader clarifies for himself the conditions with which he is about to deal. Also, by the visualization or drawing, he provides another way of thinking (or looking at) the problem and thus promotes clearer understanding. Problems that do not lend themselves to visualization or to diagramming are best approached by an attempt to translate or restate the facts in the reader's own words. Having read once quickly, the reader may try to rephrase his comprehension of the basic idea of the problem. Some individuals benefit from expressing this restatement aloud, thus reinforcing their comprehension by hearing themselves.

Can you visualize while following these directions for mounting a photograph? As you read, put a check in the margin for each distinct step.

Mounting a Print†

To determine the size and proportions of the card on which the print should be mounted, place the print on the card and with a pair of L-shaped pieces of card alter the space and proportions of the area surrounding the print and study the effect. In general, the margins at the

* Ernst R. Breslich, *Junior Mathematics* (New York, The Macmillan Company, 1924).
† C. B. Neblette, F. W. Brehm, and E. L. Priest, *Elementary Photography* (New York: The Macmillan Company, 1936). Reprinted by permission of the Eastman Kodak Company.

sides and at the top should be the same width and the bottom slightly greater. The exact width of the margins depends upon the print and upon personal taste and judgment. For the print about 3 × 4 inches, a margin of 2 inches at the sides and top and 2¾ inches at the bottom is sufficient. Cut from the sheet of cardboard a piece a little larger than the finished mount is to be in order to allow for trimming afterwards.

The next step is to lay out and draw the lines which are to outline the print. The size of the outlined space should be from ¼ to ⅜ of an inch larger on all sides than the print. Thus, if the print is 3 × 4 inches, the outlined space should be at least 3½ × 4½ inches. This leaves a margin of ¼ inch between the edge of the print and the line on each side.

Cut a piece of cardboard (any kind will do as it is not a part of the mount) the exact size the outlined space is to be. Locate this on the mount so that there is an equal space at the top and on both sides. Hold the card firmly in place with one hand and with the other draw a line around its edges with a sharp pencil.

Place the print on the mount within this outlined area so that the space between the two is equal on all four sides. Hold the print in place with one hand and outline the two upper corners of the print with a sharp lead pencil. These marks are used to place the print accurately within the outlined area and should not be too heavy as they will be erased after the print has been mounted.

Remove the print and apply a thin line of glue or mucilage to the back about ⅛ of an inch from the top of the print. Do not put the glue or mucilage too close to the edge or it will come out along the edges of the print when it is put under pressure to dry. Only a small amount should be applied; too much will leave raised places on the print.

Lay the print down carefully on the mount so that the upper corners will be just within the location lines previously made for this purpose.

Place the mounted print under pressure for 15 to 20 minutes. A heavy book or convenient weight will do nicely.

How many steps do the directions indicate? Could you visualize each of the approximately ten steps?

Recognizing the Essentials. Many problems are stated in roundabout ways and may even contain material which is not essential to the solution. For example, "Find the circumference of a circle whose radius is 4 feet and whose diameter is 8 feet." Because the length of the radius is given, the length of the diameter is irrelevant to the solution if we use the formula $C = 2\pi r$. This fact is included only to catch the unwary, or perhaps to trap the too-rapid reader who may use this figure in this formula for circumference.

Can you recognize the essential facts in this problem?

A boy 12 years of age weighing 79 pounds can run from the courthouse to High Street in 8 minutes. He can walk this distance in 15 minutes. If the courthouse is 8 blocks from High Street, how long will it take him to run a block?

The only essential facts in this problem are (1) the distance from the courthouse to High Street and (2) the time to run this distance. The other facts and figures given are irrelevant to the solution. When do you sort out the essential facts from those not needed—in your first reading of a problem, or your second?

Another group of essential facts to be found in each problem are the steps needed for solution. These steps are not necessarily presented in the wording of the problem in the order in which they will be employed. In many instances, the second, careful reading of the problem may require some change in the normal progression from the top line to the bottom. It may be better for understanding to retrace through the problem beginning with the last or some other sentence, rather than the first, in order to identify the steps to solution, and to secure the figures needed for computation. As in so many other reading tasks, the best results are obtained by a flexible approach, rather than a stereotyped manner of reading.

The following example may serve to illustrate the point in reading flexibly and carefully to identify the proper sequence of steps in solution.

> How much reduction in taxes will Mr. Smith achieve if he computes his medical deduction? His gross income is $10,000, his net income after all deductions, $8,000. His income will be taxed at the rate of 22%. During the year, he and his family have incurred medical expenses of $800. He is permitted to deduct any amount in excess of 5% of his gross income.

There are at least two ways of expressing the possible steps in solution. Which did you think of?

Solution A

a. Subtract 5% of gross income from total medical expenses.
b. Find 5% of gross income.
c. Find 22% of the deductible medical expenses.
d. Find 5% of net income.

Solution B

a. Subtract 5% of $10,000 from $800.
b. Find 5% of $10,000.
c. Find 22% of the answer to *a*.
d. Find 5% of $8,000.

Solution *A* represents a rephrasing of the steps of the problem, an approach we have recommended to aid in visualizing the problem. Solution *B* represents the actual computations needed, which should not be attempted until the translation or rephrasing has been done. We recognize, of course, that to some readers this problem is so obvious that they seem to skip over the rephrasing of Solution *A*, yet such thinking actually does occur. Some readers do this translation while reading the problem, a few during the first rapid reading, others during the second reading. For successful solution, the problem must be translated or rephrased in terms the reader can understand, whether this is done as a separate step or occurs during the actual reading.

In any event, the proper sequence of steps in Solution *A* or *B* is *b, a, c*. But this is not the order in which the facts are presented. The essential facts for step *b* are contained in the last sentence and the second sentence. The facts for step *a* are suggested in the answer to step *b* and the fourth sentence of the problem. Step *c* depends upon the answer to step *a* and the third sentence. To establish mentally the proper order of steps, you have to skip around in this problem, either during the second reading, or during a mental rephrasing.

In this problem, as in many others, some irrelevant facts not needed for the solution were introduced—for example, Mr. Smith's net income after all deductions is $8,000. Did you ignore this extraneous matter, or were you trapped into using step *d*?

Recognizing Relationships.   Some one has estimated that there are more than 20,000 ways of presenting problems that require only elementary school arithmetic knowledge. Yet some students have a habit of trying to force a series of problems into the same type, or into the same steps and relationships. They expect each problem to be similar to that used for demonstration in the text or classroom. Even when they sense that there are some differences present in the series, they look through for a magic word or an obvious clue that will tell them exactly what to do. Other readers who have been using a certain formula struggle to force the facts of each successive problem into this pattern regardless of its true nature. You may remember using such words as *of* as a clue to multiplication, as in "½ of . . .", "20% of . . ."; or using *less than* as a cue to subtract. Are you still looking for such magic words rather than reading the problem carefully? When you are assigned a group of problems, do you tend to expect them to fall into the same pattern of solution? Each problem must be attacked in terms of its own peculiar conditions. A preconceived notion that it must fall into a certain category is self-defeating for the reader.

Summary of Problem Solving.   We have pointed out and illustrated four sources of difficulty in problem solving: reading too rapidly; failing to visualize or restate; failing to identify carefully the essential facts and steps; and missing the nature of the problem because of a prereading set or attitude. Most of these and other problem solving troubles may be controlled by such approaches as these:

1. Previewing the problem to understand its general nature or type.

2. Carefully rereading the problem, in a sequence that follows the steps as presented, rather than the printed order; identifying the essential facts and relationships; and eliminating the nonessential.

3. Trying to visualize or restate the problem during or after the second reading.

4. Beginning the computations, being certain to recheck the figures as given, in order to be certain of accuracy in copying them.

Some authors recommend a more formal series of steps in problem solving, such as "What is given?" "What is to be found?" "What steps should be taken?" "What is an approximate answer?" And so on. The research on this point by one of the authors and others in the field indicates that this type of approach cannot be successfully superimposed on the thinking of many individuals. Even when trained in these steps, most students do not adopt and use them. If you have found this sort of approach helpful, by all means continue with it. But if you have not adopted it or are still having troubles with problem solving, we strongly recommend that you consider the corrective steps we have outlined here.

CHAPTER 6
CRITICAL READING

All the training in reading that schools and colleges offer and all the practice in various reading skills have one basic purpose. That purpose is to prepare the reader for critical reading—the ability to read with analysis and judgment. Or as Dr. Frances Triggs, a noted reading specialist, says: "Critical reading requires a contribution by both the author and the reader and an interplay which usually results in a new understanding."

Critical reading requires a wide variety of reactions on the part of the reader. Foremost, of course, is the ability to comprehend precisely what is being said. Before he can evaluate such aspects as the author's purpose, accuracy, or implications, the reader must be able to identify the facts. Only then is the reader ready to begin to apply his tools of critical evaluation. These tools include first, examining the source—the reliability, recency, accuracy, and competence of the writer. In addition, the reader will try to identify the author's obvious and hidden purposes or viewpoints and assumptions. He will try to distinguish between material representing an opinion and that founded on facts.

Second, the reader will examine the implications present in the material. What are the author's implications? What inferences does he intend the reader to make? What inference is suggested by his tone, choice of words or style? Finally, the reader will react to the author's use of devices to influence his thinking. He will note the attempt to appeal to some of his common personal or social needs for security, status, approval, acceptance, and so on. He will examine the logic of the author's viewpoint, the soundness of his premises, and the accuracy of his conclusions.

Together these judgments and reactions by the reader produce the skill we call critical reading. Together they spell the difference between the reader who is being controlled by the author and the reader who adapts what he reads to his own intelligent purposes.

We cannot provide enough planned practice in critical reading to prepare the reader for all reading situations. At best, we can simply provide a wide variety of examples in which critical reading should be applied. The task for the reader is not to learn exactly what questions should be asked of each author or when to ask certain probing questions. Rather, the intelligent, critical reader asks questions of every bit of material that attempts to induce him to accept a fact or a viewpoint.

The Non-Sequitur

The following is an excerpt from a speech by Alfred M. Landon, one-time Republican candidate for the Presidency, as reprinted in the *Congressional Record* for May 2, 1963.

> Let me point out that this 88th Congress is simply being criticized for refusing to pass legislation recommended by the President that the preceding 87th Congress refused to pass. And there has been an election in between. Therefore, it must be evident that this Congress is representing the thinking and the philosophy and the convictions of the people in their districts and their States.

What is he saying? Do you agree with him?

1. Mr. Landon suggests that we should not criticize the 88th Congress—
   a. because they have just been elected.   b. because they don't represent the views of the people who elected them.   c. for failing to pass legislation that the 87th Congress also refused to pass.
   d. for ignoring the President's recommendations regarding legislation

What does he imply?

2. He believes the 88th Congress is justified in its actions because—
   a. since they were just elected, they must represent the people's views.   b. they agree with the preceding Congress.   c. they refused to pass certain legislation.   d. they alone know what the public wants.

What is he assuming?

3. How many of these assumptions is Mr. Landon making?
   a. Members of the 88th Congress were elected because the people approved of the actions of the 87th Congress.   b. Voters knew the voting records of their congressmen and showed their approval by their ballots.   c. The 88th Congress is justified in defying the President's legislative recommendations because the 87th Congress did.   d. Congress should not be guided by the President's legislative suggestions.

Like many office-seekers, Landon assumes that being elected is tantamount to receiving the voters' approval of all a candidate's actions—both personal and political. Unfortunately, this is only theoretically true, for many factors influence the outcome of an election. Among these are demagogic appeal, political labels, the size of the campaign fund, personal characteristics of the candidate, the effectiveness of the political organization, and the like. Not many local elections are decided solely by the candidate's expression of opinions on specific issues clearly understood by the electorate.

A teacher of logic might point out the implicit syllogism present in Mr. Landon's reasoning in this fashion.

Major Premise: An election is an implicit approval of the legislative acts of congressmen. (In this case, rejecting the President's recommendations.)

Minor Premise: The 88th Congress was elected (or in some cases reelected.)

Conclusion: Therefore, the 88th Congress should follow the example of the 87th in rejecting the President's legislative program.

Mr. Landon makes at least two unwarranted assumptions, as phrased in answers *a* and *b* in question 3. This type of reasoning may be called an example of *non-sequitur* logic, in which two unrelated incidents are interpreted as proof of each other. Even if the entire 87th Congress was reelected, this does not prove that the general public approved of their actions in frustrating the President's legislative program. Voters seldom know what their Congressmen vote for or against in their legislative sessions. Do you disagree? Then recall, if you can, how your two senators voted this year on any issues you think were significant.

False Statements

At the request of Senator Kuchel of California the following text was inserted in the Congressional Record of May 2, 1963, page 7637. Numerous copies of this leaflet were received by the Senator from his constituents. The text reads, in part, as follows. What does it mean to you?

The United States Has No Army, No Navy, No Air Force*

For doubting Thomases who think this statement in not true, Senate Bill No. 2180 entitled "The Arms Control and Disarmament Act" was approved by the House of Representatives as House Bill 9118 and was signed into effect as Public Law 87-297 on September 26, 1961, by John F. Kennedy, President of the United States. This bill was prepared to expedite a plan already proposed at Geneva by our administration and State Department . . . to affect the "legal" connotation to disarmament.

The only thing that keeps our Army, Navy and Air Force from being

---

* Prepared by United Societies of Methodist Laymen, Inc., Austin, Texas.

wiped out of existence is public opinion. At any time he chooses the
President of the United States can now transfer our Army, Navy and
Air Force (your husband, father, son or brother) to the command of
Eugene D. Kiselev (Russian) who is Secretary of the United Nations
Security Council (World Police Force).

Actually this bill established the Arms Control Agency (a frightening
title?) under the direction of the Secretary of State for the acquisition of
practical knowledge about disarmament, to conduct research in that field,
and to coordinate work now being conducted in that field by other government agencies. The interpretation given the bill by the distributors of the
leaflet quoted above is completely false. As Senator Kuchel aptly terms it,
this leaflet is "fright mail" calculated to scare the average American out of
his wits. *Who would publish such material?* This piece was distributed
widely by the "American Opinion Speakers Bureau" operated by the John
Birch Society. *Who would believe it?* Copies of the leaflet were enclosed in
hundreds of letters received by the Senator, written by individuals who
demanded that he do something about this terrible situation.

Here is a second but milder example of this use of the bald statement
of a highly questionable fact used to shock or frighten the reader into following the speaker's suggestions.

In the preface to *Why Johnny Can't Read and What You Can Do About
It,*° by Rudolf Flesch, you will find this statement:

> What I found is absolutely fantastic. The teaching of reading—all
> over the United States, in all the schools, in all the textbooks—is totally
> wrong and flies in the face of all logic and common sense. Johnny
> couldn't read until half a year ago for the simple reason that nobody ever
> showed him how. Johnny's only problem was that he was unfortunately
> exposed to an ordinary American school.
>
> You know that I was born and raised in Austria. Do you know that
> there are no remedial reading cases in Austrian schools? Do you know
> that there are no remedial reading cases in Germany, in France, in Italy,
> in Norway, in Spain—practically anywhere in the world except in the
> United States? Do you know that there was no such thing as remedial
> reading in this country either until about thirty years ago? Do you know
> that the teaching of reading never was a problem anywhere in the world
> until the United States switched to the present method around about
> 1925?

What is Dr. Flesch saying? Do you agree with him?

4. Dr. Flesch is telling us that—
   a. reading instruction in America needs some improvement.
   b. reading instruction in America is poorer than that in many European countries.   c. American reading instruction is completely

° Rudolph Flesch, *Why Johnny Can't Read and What You Can Do About It* (New York:
Harper & Row, 1955), p. ix.

wrong and bad.   d. remedial reading instruction is a recent development in American and European schools.

What is he implying?

5. He wants us to believe that—
    a. American reading instruction is so bad it produces retarded readers.   b. America should imitate the instructional methods of Europe.   c. If America used the methods current in Europe, it too would have no retarded readers.   d. No country in the world had any retarded readers until the last thirty years.

Actually, Flesch is offering all these implications, without a shred of proof. It is his purpose to prepare us to believe these implications by first destroying any faith we may have in the American system. Then he will have an easier time of convincing us of the infallibility of European (his) reading instruction. The administrators of European schools would profoundly wish that Dr. Flesch was correct. But, unfortunately, he is not. In several of these countries there are, as in America, organized societies of professional teachers who devote a good deal of their time to the study of the cure or prevention of current failures in reading. Several of these associations publish journals regularly describing the extent of the reading problem in their respective countries and the research being conducted in this field. Failures in reading are neither peculiar to America nor to the last thirty years.

Why would a skilled, professional writer make a statement such as this? Simply because he knows that the average reader is unable to confirm or refute his facts and will be shocked into attending carefully to the author's program for curing this imaginary problem. *Who would believe this?* Dr. Flesch's book was on the best-seller lists for an unfortunately long period of several months after its publication.

Irony and Satire

Sometimes the clever writer makes his point by deliberately saying the opposite of what he means. If his audience realizes his true meaning, and is amused by the play on words, it tends to accept his viewpoint without critical evaluation. For example, in his description of the ideal college he would create, Stephen Leacock makes these remarks.*

> What I mean is that our studies have drifted away, away from the single-minded absorption of learning. Our students of today live in a whirl and clatter of "student activities." They have, in any large college, at least a hundred organizations and societies. They are "all up!" for this today and "all out!" for that tomorrow. Life is a continuous rally! a rah,

---

* From "On the Need for a Quiet College." Reprinted by permission of Dodd, Mead & Company from *Model Memoirs* by Stephen Leacock. Copyright, 1938, by Dodd, Mead & Company, Inc.

rah! a parade! They play no games: they use teams for that. But exercise, and air, is their life. They *root,* in an organized hysteria, a code of signals telling them what to feel. They *root,* they rush, they organize, they play politics, run newspapers—and when they step from college into life, they fit it absolutely, having lived already.

No one is denying here what fine men and women college makes, physically fine and mentally alert. Any one of them could run an elevator the day he steps out of college. But there's something wanting: do they *think?* Or is there anything after all to think about? And yet, surely, in the long run the world has lived on its speculative minds. Or hasn't it?

What is he really saying? Do you agree with him?

6. Leacock believes that—

a. student activities really prepare students for life.   b. college life produces young men and women eminently prepared for life.
c. student activities help a student have a well-rounded experience in college.   d. student activities are simply a mad whirl, signifying nothing.

7. Leacock's concept of the true purpose of college is—

a. to prepare students to run an elevator.   b. to provide an exciting round of activities.   c. to produce fine young men and women.   d. to teach students how to think.

How does he produce the feeling of excitement in describing student life? How do such words as *whirl, clatter, rally, rah-rah,* and *parade* impart the author's feelings about student activities? Does Leacock make his point stronger by building the reader up to a climax and then startling him with an unexpected conclusion?

Here is a letter written to the editors of a national magazine.†

Business Week
330 West 42nd Street
New York 36, New York

Dear Sirs:

May I draw your attention to the steadily growing plight of a significant portion of our population—the Davy Crockett hat-makers?

As *Business Week,* with its extensive and up-to-date market coverage is well aware, prices on Davy Crockett hats have been plummetting, and an industry and way of life heretofore exuberantly expanding is now faced with the prospect of mass unemployment. Raccoons that have been encouraged to produce now find that there is no market.

It is not necessary that this happen because several remedies are at hand that have had long and successful histories in other segments of our economy. Specifically, these remedies are:

1. That the Tariff Commission take off its rose-colored glasses and

† From a letter in "Readers Report," *Business Week,* November 26, 1955. Used by permission.

face up to the fact that the peril point has been reached in the Davy Crockett hat industry, that prohibitive duties be levied, that a quota be imposed to reassure the foreigners that we are still interested in some trade, and that all imported Davy Crockett hats be so identified, such as by being dyed bile green, so that American purchasers will know they are not purchasing skins from healthy well-fed American raccoons processed by healthy well-paid American workers. In addition, to prevent evasion of the intent of this regulation, its provisions should be extended to all hats made from raccoons that are not born in the U.S. or territories thereof.

2. That a price support program be inaugurated perhaps under the jurisdiction of the Bureau of Wildlife and Fisheries but preferably under a brand new agency that will draw upon the staff of the aforementioned Bureau, of the Dept. of Agriculture, and of the Historical Division of the Smithsonian Institution. This agency should engage in a two-pronged attack on the problem.

It should support Davy Crockett hats at a full 100% of parity, the parity base period to be a time when the industry was in healthy condition, e.g., the first half of 1955. It is possible that surpluses may pile up, but this is a calculated risk. This program is essential if we are to maintain Davy Crockett hatmaking as a way of life in our society, a way of life that springs from the most deeply loved traditions and most inspiring history of our heritage. Where would our country be today if it weren't for Davy Crockett and men like him!

The other task of the agency should be to actively increase effective demand. Such means can be used as giving Davy Crockett hats to schools with underprivileged children, perhaps tying them in with the Free Lunch program. It should also arrange that a specified portion of our foreign aid or loans be spent to purchase hats; such a gift from us would indeed be twice blessed because it would not only be aid but would introduce foreigners to basic elements in the American spirit and to the foundations of the American standard of living.

We do not believe in paternal government, and therefore in addition to our legislative program we have a vast, industry-wide program under consideration. On our designing boards are thrilling plans that will, we feel sure, make every household a two—and maybe three—Davy Crockett hat household. In addition, we are in the process of preparing a communication to all magazines and newspapers that have carried pictures of people wearing live raccoons, pointing out the disadvantages of a live raccoon as compared to a bona fide Davy Crockett hat. . . .

Sincerely,
ELEANOR SHLIFER

How many of the well-worn clichés did you recognize—rose-colored, American . . . , way of life, and so on? Is the inconsistency in the last paragraph, in claiming not to believe in a "paternal government," deliberate? Which political philosophy is the author satirizing—Republican, Democratic, or Socialist?

Emotionally Toned Language

Although words have obvious meanings, they also carry connotations or values that often are not quite so obvious. Words appeal to our senses, to our feelings, to our convictions and prejudices and to our needs. Some words call up visual images—*Uncle Sam, beatnik, Lincoln Memorial, John F. Kennedy*. Others appeal to other senses—*putrid, spicy, squeak, garbage*. Another group arouses more complex connotations, as in *radical, security, Communism, inflation* and *anti-American*.

Because of these connotations, writers and speakers pay very close attention to their choice of words. Almost every word may be weighed and considered in terms of the reactions it may evoke and its fitness for achieving the purpose of the writer. A motion picture is not just "great"; it is "stupendous" or "magnificent." A political opponent is not simply "mistaken" in his views; he is "ignorant," or "deceitful." A toothpaste is not "pleasant-tasting"; it is a "bacteria-fighter" or a "decay-preventative."

Here are examples of the use of emotionally-toned language in advertising. What sort of common need or feeling is each intended to appeal to?

> Automated Speed-Reading Course—The New Teaching Machine Course that is Guaranteed to Double Your Reading Speed in Just 30 Days.

8. This ad appeals to your need for—
   a. security.   b. social status.   c. patriotism.

> Protect youngsters, invalids and elderly folks from dangerous falls and slips. Sturdy Tub-Seat offers safe, secure, sit-down comfort.

9. This ad appeals to your need for—
   a. security.   b. social approval.   c. patriotism.

> An Income She's Sure of as Long as She Lives?—There's one way that guarantees it! How can you best protect your wife and family against the unforeseen? By assuring her a lump sum of money? Or by guaranteeing her a steady income? The answer depends on your individual circumstances. Fortunately, your life insurance offers both choices.

10. This ad appeals to your need for—
    a. social approval.   b. security.   c. social status.
11. Among the terms it employs to achieve its effect upon the reader are: guarantees, protect, unforeseen, assuring, ———— and ————.

Just to see how an appealing advertisement is written, make the choices of the emotionally-toned words you think the copy writer inserted in the blanks.

> As though you were born with it, your hair can be ———— (pretty, attractive, radiant) with ———— (nice, many, beautiful) curls and waves. In the ———— (trial, use, miracle) of one simple application and

set even difficult to curl hair develops ———— (pretty, attractive, fascinating) waves as natural-looking as naturally wavy hair. . . . Just
comb and back into place fall those ———— (homemade, natural,
lovely) curls and waves. And, equally important, your hair gleams
———— (nicely, brightly, radiantly), is so soft, so ———— (natural,
well-groomed, glamorous).

Apparently most of those who write this sort of material believe strongly
in the effectiveness of exaggeration. In each case, the writer used the superlative, the strongest term, as given in the third alternative for each blank.
You might have hesitated to use such exaggerated words as *radiant, miracle,
fascinating,* but the advertiser does not. He has learned that even the most
extravagant claims produce sales, provided that the descriptive terms carry
the appropriate connotations for the reader.

Playing upon the connotations of words and their effects upon the reader
is certainly not confined to the ad-writer. Almost every type of reading you
will encounter, with the possible exception of strictly factual matter, has
been written in a manner that is intended to influence your thinking or your
behavior. Compare, if you will, these two brief reviews of the same Canadian history textbook, *Ordeal by Fire; Canada, 1910–1945,* by Ralph Allen
(Doubleday, 1961). This book is the fifth volume of the Canadian History
series; it is presumably a factual account of the development of Canada
during the first third of this century.

Ordeal by Fire—First Review

—EUGENE GRIFFIN

in the *Chicago Sunday Tribune**

For the colorful story of Canada's growth as a nation there is no more
lively reading than the Canadian History series edited by Thomas B.
Costain, and this fifth volume is another rich slice of anecdotes, vivid
characterizations of public figures, and fascinating insights into the life
of America's northern neighbor. . . . It is enlightening to see history
from the Canadian perspective.

How does the reviewer create the favorable tone he desires to set? What
six words with pleasing connotations does he select for this purpose? In
fact, does he employ a single neutral or derogatory adjective? Yet, has he
told you anything objective about the book or its author—its accuracy and
completeness, the viewpoint and competence of the author, or his use of
documentary or research sources?

If you were seeking a good Canadian history book, would the review
just quoted influence you to make *Ordeal by Fire* your selection? Before
you make a final decision, read the second review of the same book, which
follows. As you read, decide whether the second reviewer favors the book.

* October 29, 1961, p. 12; reprinted by permission of the *Chicago Tribune.*

Ordeal by Fire—Second Review

—Canadian Forum†

The *Ordeal* is excellent journalism (even assuming that accuracy is still an aim of the journalist) and bad history. Indeed, it is not really a history at all, but a collection of tales told by a man of considerable ability but signifying very little. Quite clearly readability and drama were the author's paramount aims; significance, balance, and accuracy were well down the list. . . . Even accepting Mr. Allen's apparent aims and assumptions he can be faulted for inadequate knowledge and poor historical judgment. . . . Nonetheless, Allen achieved his major object. He has written a colorful and dramatic book. His generalizations are fascinating: sometimes brilliant in insight and imagery, sometimes daring, sometimes absurd. If he cares little for issues, his treatment of people is often superb. *Ordeal by Fire* will not last long, but it is good fare.

Here again the reviewer has used descriptive terms with definite connotations, but in a different fashion. Note how he contrasts *excellent* with *bad* in the first sentence, and *considerable ability* with *signifying very little* in the second. Almost every sentence presents this parallelism comparing what the author offered with what he should have done. The reviewer could have simply listed his adverse criticisms one after the other. But by opposing every positive comment with a negative one, the reviewer makes his effect cumulative and more devastating. He destroys the author not by direct attack but by undercutting every possible positive value of the book.

Now, would you use this book as a source of historical information? If not, for what purpose might you read it?

Repetition

Do these slogans sound familiar?

Us ———— smokers would rather fight than switch. (Tareyton)

————. They satisfy. (Chesterfield)

Strongest in the pain reliever that doctors recommend most. (Anacin)

Get ———— for fast, fast, fast relief. (Bufferin)

You can be sure, if it's ————. (Westinghouse)

Don't be half-safe, use ———— to be sure. (Arrid)

Not too strong, not too light, ————'s got the taste that right. (Viceroy)

Use ———— with your detergent every time you wash. (Clorox)

Nothing else does as much to relieve the congestion of head colds as ————. (Contac)

It's what's up front that counts. (Winston)

Advertising slogans are the commonest use of the technique of constant repetition intended to fix an idea in the minds of readers or listeners. But this same device has been used in many other fields with equal effectiveness.

† June, 1962, p. 66; reprinted by permission of the *Canadian Forum*.

Some of the following have started wars, created or destroyed nations, inspired elections—and have been just about as meaningful as the advertising slogans.

No Taxation Without Representation. (American Revolution)
Uncle Sam Needs You. (World War I)
54–40 or Fight! (James K. Polk, 1884)
Keep America Safe for Democracy. (World War I)
Go West, Young Man, Go West. (Horace Greeley, 1851)
The Aryan Race Will Live for a Thousand Years. (Hitler)
Vote Yourself a Farm. (Abraham Lincoln, 1860)
You Shall Not Crucify Mankind upon a Cross of Gold. (William Jennings Bryan, 1896)
A New Deal for the Forgotten Man. (Franklin Delano Roosevelt, 1932)
Drang Nach Osten [Push Toward the East]. (Austria-Hungary, 1914)

Looking back at these trite phrases, we wonder at their appeal. How could these have inspired people to vote, to go to war, or to practice mass murder? Certainly not because of their literal meanings, but because of the emotions they aroused and the fact that they were dinned into the ears and minds of gullible listeners. Repeated often enough, loud enough, and with strong emotion, these sayings produced the desired effects. And such phrases continue to produce every day in the fields of advertising, politics, and nationalism.

Summary

In this first chapter on critical reading we have attempted to introduce you to a few of the types of reading matter that demand careful judgments and reactions. You have seen how a writer may influence his audience by careful choice of emotional language, by faulty logic, or even by bold untruths. These are only a few of the pitfalls for the uncritical reader. Many others will be illustrated in the next chapter.

Before you go on to further practice, you should be aware of several facts about critical reading. To read critically, it is essential that you first clearly understand what the author is saying. You must get the facts before you evaluate or judge them, or your interpretation will be faulty. To see the facts clearly, any emotional reaction or prejudice regarding the author or the material must be controlled. You may dislike the author or his style, or be angry with his viewpoint—*after* you are certain you understand what he is saying.

Many adults never learn to read analytically and hence never learn to deal successfully with materials with which they disagree. They allow their negative reactions to the author—his nationality, race, religion, or viewpoint—to distort their comprehension of his meaning. Other readers are impressed by the writer's reputation or name and thus are led to accept his implications without first examining the facts. In the rest of your efforts at critical reading, try to follow this two-step approach: first, be sure you understand the facts; then evaluate critically.

How does one read critically and intelligently? There are no set answers to this question, because each kind of situation may demand a different type of thinking or reaction by the reader. To avoid being convinced by false statements or non-sequiturs, you may need to question the facts offered. Is this statement true? What proof is being offered? Does the result the writer predicts always follow these facts?

To recognize that the speaker is ironically saying the opposite of what he really means, or that he is ridiculing the follies of his opponents in satire, may require other questions in your reactions. Does he really mean this? Are his taunts and criticisms accurate and fair? To keep from being swept along in the stream of emotionally toned words the speaker uses, you may require another kind of reaction. Of what is he trying to convince me? Why is he trying so hard? What will he gain if I agree? If his facts are accurate, why does he have to stress them so emotionally, to try to appeal to my feelings instead of my intelligence?

To deal with meaningless slogans, commercials, and catchwords, you may need to do more than turn off the TV or try to ignore the repetition. What does this phrase really say, if anything? What actions are implied? Do I want to take these actions? Could I justify these actions? To sum up this point, the critical reader responds by questioning the facts offered, the implications between the lines, and the author's hidden purposes before making his final judgments.

CHAPTER 7

MORE ABOUT CRITICAL READING

One of the constant tasks facing the intelligent reader is to discriminate between opinion and fact. Even in what appears to be strictly factual material, these decisions must continually be faced. Truth must be sorted out from half-truths; feelings or beliefs, separated from things as they are. The reader must constantly submit what he reads to the test of credibility, using his reasoning, his own knowledge or experience, or other sources as guides.

Opinion Versus Fact

Can you discriminate opinion from fact? Here are quotations from respected sources such as textbooks, editorials, speeches, and book reviews. Which are opinion; which are factual?

1. From the *Library Journal:**

> The Venetian Affair is a sorrily inflated claptrap job in conception and the heavier for Miss MacInnes's Scottish insistence upon a moral lesson. The tale is contemptuously clever, and the undisguised intention (an editorial on East/West relations) is not really novel enough for all of this worldly disguise.

2. From the *Congressional Record:*

> It is tragic that in a society grown great through freedom we now endeavor to stay great by enforced taxation, Federal programs and the substitution of Federal Government schemes for private initiative.

---

* From a review of *The Venetian Affair* by James Sandoe in *Library Journal,* September 1, 1963, p. 3105. Reprinted by permission.

3. From a leading newspaper:

> The steel industry will continue to increase production, but the chances are excellent that fewer workers will be needed in 1970 than today because of automation.

4. From a prominent speaker:

> When a union has a closed-shop contract, a refusal of membership in the union means that the worker is deprived of his livelihood.

5. From a management advisor:

> Until management realizes that employees are even more complex than the machines they operate, cooperation and working efficiency will seldom be achieved.

6. From a leading medical researcher:

> Medical science will win important new victories in its fight against illness and death, in the next five to ten years. As a result, Americans now alive can look forward to lengthening life expectancies.

7. From an editorial:

> The chief issue in the developing presidential campaign, so far at least, is foreign policy. Unfortunately, the debate is generating more heat than light.

Taken at face value, every one of these statements reflects the opinion of the speaker. From this viewpoint, none is truly fact. Some, such as the third and the next-to-last, may prove to be true. But, however sound they may seem, we would have to wait five or ten years for them to be proven to be correct forecasts. For the moment, then, they continue to be opinion, not fact.

The False Dilemma

In political as well as private arguments, a favorite trick is to present your opponent with two possible solutions to a problem—yours and one he can't possibly accept. The logician calls this device a false dilemma—a dilemma because there is no real choice offered, and false because there really are other possible solutions to the situation. Another version of the false dilemma is to propose only one direct solution for a problem that is very real to your listener.

An example may be taken from the *Congressional Record* of February 1963 in which Senator J. Lausche of Ohio is speaking against the adoption of the College Academic Facilities and Scholarship Act. He is opposed to the intention of the Act to grant individual scholarships of up to $1,000 per academic year to college students.

One phase of the arguments made on the floor of the House was as follows: a student who refuses to attend an institution of higher learning unless he is given an outright grant, instead of a loan, in all probability does not possess the moral fabric to justify making the grant to him.

I repeat that if our youth have reached a stage where we cannot get them to go to college unless we fully or substantially pay their tuition, we ought to begin to wonder what is wrong with what we in Congress have been doing and what has broken down the moral fabric of our youth, when a young fellow says: I will not go to college and I will not study, even though I have an alert mind, unless you give me the money I need to have in order to go to college.

Which of these is the Senator implying?

    a. Students who would accept these grants don't deserve to go to college.
    b. Students should be willing to go to college without any grants.
    c. Only morally weak students would ask for a grant before attempting to go to college.   d. The moral fabric of our younger generation is deteriorating.

In a sense, he is implying all these, but emphasizing *c* most of all.

Why does the choice between morally sound students who wouldn't want a grant and morally unsound students who would want grants constitute a false dilemma? What false assumption is he making regarding the financial resources of many students who want to go to college? Are we supposed to believe that every ambitious and energetic student who wants to go to college can either work his way through or receive ready aid from existing scholarships and loans? Does the average cost of a college year ($1,400 to $1,800 in public institutions and $2,500 in private) have any relationship to the average income ($6,140) of families in which the parents are in the 35-to-54 years of age group?

Does the Senator even believe his own arguments? Reread carefully the last few lines of his remarks, in which he quotes the imaginary thoughts of one of the "weak" students. Does the Senator unwittingly admit that some students might *need* money to go to college?

False dilemmas are readily offered for the solution of difficult political, national, or personal problems, such as the current cold war with Russia, the effects of smoking upon cancer, the danger of inflation, and many others. Here are some you may have overheard lately. As you read them, decide whether you can accept the speaker's conclusions.

"You know as well as I do we are in a war with the Russians. They've told us they intend to bury us. I say we should hit them hard first, and get this thing settled." (Are the only alternatives frustration in dealing with the Russians or all-out nuclear war?)

"You have no choice—either you give up smoking or you get lung cancer." (Do all smokers die of lung cancer?)

"The trouble with this country is we have too many _____. We ought to send them all back where they came from." (You fill in the blank, according to your own prejudices. Then point out how this solution would solve any of America's problems—if you can.)

"What we ought to do to stop crime is stop coddling prisoners. We should go back to the whipping post." (Or thumbscrews or the rack? What evidence is there that harsher punishments reduce crime? Is there no other possible solution?)

Fallacious Reasoning

Almost all the illustrations we have used thus far demand critical reading because of the fallacious reasoning present. Whether we call them false dilemmas, appeals to emotion, errors in logic, or something else, the crux of each is faulty thinking. The writer or the speaker has consciously or unconsciously attempted to convince the reader by clouded reasoning. Only skill in thinking critically will enable the reader or listener to deal with these situations. Being able to label the falsity properly is not important: being able to recognize and refute it is.

Here is a final group of examples of faulty reasoning. How would you attempt to answer each? Compare your criticisms with those offered in the Answer Key.

1. I succeeded in business, and what was good enough to educate me is good enough for today's children. I'm against all this new folderol.

2. What this younger generation needs is good, hard discipline. In my day, when you stepped out of line, you got it—right where it did the most good.

3. A simple but sure solution to the school dropout problem: require a high-school diploma of all automobile drivers.

4. The founders of this country did a pretty good job of writing a Constitution. I'm against this constant tinkering and changing.

5. Look at that man wobbling down the street. He must be drunk.

6. Ever since we started testing these atom bombs we've had unusual weather. It's obvious they are the cause of it.

7. Senator Hart's bill would enforce clear labeling of the contents and quantity offered in boxes and cans. The use of oversized or half-filled containers would be eliminated. Such a bill would also (1) be an infringement on free enterprise; (2) increase production costs and consumer costs, say the spokesmen for industry.

8. Opponents of freedom of debate in the senate would give full and easy sway to the majority because, they say, a minority can paralyze legislative action. . . . The American people are not to be governed by unbridled majority rule: nor were they ever meant to be.

9. Passage of the so-called "Civil rights" bill by the Senate should be absolutely prevented. . . . This bill would do no good to anyone, but would destroy all our rights by turning our Government into a dictatorship. No doubt the dictator would place our country under one-world government under the U.N. This organization, being communist conceived and controlled, we would really be under communist slavery.

10. With the President's announcement of the A-11 reconnaisance plane, reaction immediately set in . . . one magazine indicated that the

new high-speed craft has already served as a valuable tool for gathering intelligence information over communist territory. . . . The question raised by all this is, why are the American people not informed of its achievements until after we've shown off to Nikita? Is it asking too much of our government to clarify exactly what is top secret from whom?

11. The entire history of this nation shows us to be a peace-loving people. Since the very beginning days we have fought wars only to protect ourselves, our homes, and our families. We never began a war for profit, for territorial gain.

12. Madame, may I have just a moment of your time? I know how busy you are, but I want to offer you a wonderful opportunity. I am working my way through college by selling subscriptions to ————. Mrs. Brown, your next-door neighbor, and Mrs. Smith up on the corner were just kind enough to take a subscription. As Mrs. Smith said, "I just couldn't pass up such a bargain."

13. All worthy politicians put the country's best interests ahead of their own. Richard Bundy puts the country's interest and your interests first. Richard Bundy is worthy of your vote in the coming election.

14. EL PRADO, TEXAS—I feel I must write you a letter of gratitude for bringing Sloan's Little Bile Salts to my attention. For years, I doctored for all sorts of ills—headaches, nagging backache, constant fatigue, pains in my joints, and flutters of the heart. Two bottles of Sloan's Little Bile Salts cured me completely. I won't ever waste my money on a doctor again. SINCERELY YOURS, MRS. S————.

15. Ladies and Gentlemen of the Jury: Just look at Mrs. J————, my client. How could she possibly have committed this terrible crime? You can see she is a good, Christian mother with two lovely, healthy children. She has given these children and her poor dead husband the best years of her life. Happily married for twenty years, now she must face life without her helpmate.

16. I have absolute proof that an auto inspection law could save many lives in our state. In 1947, the year prior to the passage of such a law in a neighboring state, the accident fatalities in that state were 836. The next year when an inspection law was in effect, fatalities were 734. The law was repealed and in 1949 fatalities rose to 843. I firmly believe saving 109 lives in 1965 would be most worth while.

17. The Moscow representatives at the Geneva disarmament conference reacted negatively to the American offer to join in destroying medium bombers from each of their fleets. They insisted such bombers were obsolete and worthless. As a counter-proposal, they suggested two-power destruction of all strategic bombers (without, of course, any arrangements for inspections that would guarantee against the building of replacements).

In each of the selections we have offered thus far in these two chapters we have labeled the propaganda device present. In other materials that you will read critically in the future, you can't expect to find this type of guide to the thinking involved. Here are several selections in which no suggestions are offered. Read them to discover what the writer is trying to say to you and why he is saying it; note also how he uses words to accomplish his purpose. The questions on each piece may help you to determine whether you have read critically.

The following paragraph is taken from a government publication offered to help its personnel to make their communications more readable.

> The present movement toward simplification of language and direct-ness of statement in government writing and the elimination of jargon and unnecessary wordiness as well as the use of short, direct statements instead of long sentences which are difficult to understand because the reader is apt to get lost before he arrives, if he ever does, at the meaning intended by the writer, is a valuable attempt to achieve economy and intelligibility, for many pamphlets, instruction sheets, ordinary mem-oranda and assorted missives circulated through the War Department fail of their primary purpose through befogging their contents by use of pseudo-official phraseology which only the initiated can hope to under-stand and of which even they cannot be certain without reference either to the key works needed for translating them or to their own garbled and confused memories of dealing, usually without much success and always after a long period of time and travail, with similar kinds of wording in similar situations, so, though don't be too hopeful, for some-one with unusual gifts and energy in applying them will manage triumphantly to misunderstand you no matter what you say or how you say it, try saying what you have to say as simply and as briefly as you can, and then after you've said it, stop saying it and don't say it any more.*

Which of these ideas has the author tried to convey to his readers?

a. The need for simple language in government writings. b. The fact that most readers can't understand government publications. c. The difficulty that many writers have in expressing themselves in a simple style. d. The need for short, simple sentences in government writing.

The author is, of course, stressing both *a* and, even more so, *d* in this selection. How does he achieve the emphasis upon *d*? By deliberately vio-lating the principle he is offering? Do you think that this was an effective way of making his point? Or, should he have said simply, "Don't ————, Don't ————, Do ————."

If you recognize the irony in this satire on government writing, you will probably remember the author's points better than if he had simply preached about the value of simple writing. If you didn't recognize this as satire, you may be one of those readers he mentions with the unusual gift of misunderstanding almost any style of writing. Did you allow the run-on sentences and the complexity of this one long sentence to interfere with your getting the facts? Were you reacting emotionally to the style and difficulty and thus losing sight of the author's intentions? Remember that reacting to the material or the author's implications before you have clearly identified the facts will prevent you from learning to read critically.

---

* Adapted from *War Times*, pamphlet published by the War Department, U.S.A.

The short story that follows was distributed widely by a large corporation. Since it was often enclosed with a bill, many receivers tended to read it carefully. As you read it, ask yourself what public image this corporation was trying to project in the minds of its subscribers.

> Here's a question with which most of us are familiar: "Who pays the bill?" Well, the answer to this was a life-saver in one case at least. A little girl in suburban Chicago couldn't seem to find anything to swallow but silver polish. This wasn't too healthful. Father rushed her to Resurrection Hospital and was informed an hour later that she wasn't staging much of a comeback. Father had lived with telephones all his life. It came natural for him to reach. He reached twice, once for the silver polish with the label on it and once for the telephone. He got a voice and read the label to it. Then there were other voices. A telephone in the offices of the manufacturer in New York began to ring but no one answered—closed for the weekend. No emergency numbers were listed, but the telephone girls were thinking all along the line and someone asked, "Who pays the bill?" "Who pays the bill?" routed out of bed an accountant for the telephone company in New York. He raced to the office where records showed a name. Eleven calls in the five boroughs finally located an executive. Seconds later the polish formula and antidote were being dictated to the doctors. The child recovered, probably to grow up to be the mother of someone who sometime will do something that will send Mother flying to the telephone.

Do you believe this melodrama, or do you think it was just the imagination of some clever staff writer? Do you think the humane concern shown by the telephone employees was a matter of corporation policy or was it really an indication of their personal feelings of sympathy for a human in distress? If the employees had actually been instructed by their superiors in handling this sort of emergency would they have employed such a roundabout solution? Would they not have called first on the Poison Control Center which is now a part of many hospitals? If you had received this piece with your telephone bill, would it have increased your respect for the company?

Many of the materials that you will need to read critically in the future may be longer, more difficult, and less interesting than the selections we have used in this book. Hence, for the final bit of practice in critical reading we have selected two speeches that may prove more challenging to your reading ability.

▶   *CRITICAL-READING EXERCISE*

The following is a pro and con discussion of the tidelands oil question between Senators Spessard L. Holland of Florida and Herbert H. Lehman of New York.* The question is whether Congress should return title to the

---

* Adapted from *Faster Reading for Business* by George D. Spache and Paul C. Berg. Copyright © 1958 by George D. Spache and Paul C. Berg, pp 160–7. Reprinted by permission of Thomas Y. Crowell Company, New York, publishers.

submerged lands adjoining coastal states to the state governments. The critical point in the debate is the fact that oil deposits are present in part of this land.

First, here are remarks by Senator Holland on Senate Joint Resolution 13, providing for giving the states "property rights in the submerged lands beneath navigable waters."

Tidelands Property Rights†
—SPESSARD L. HOLLAND

It will be noted that this joint resolution provides that nothing therein shall be deemed to affect in any wise the rights of the United States to the natural resources of the portion of the subsoil and seabed of the continental shelf lying outside the boundaries of the respective states, and it confirms the jurisdiction and control of the Federal Government over those natural resources. In other words, this measure clearly emphasizes that nine tenths of the submerged lands off the coast of the United States is under the control and jurisdiction of the Federal Government and that the other one tenth, which lies inside the boundaries of the states, and immediately adjoining the coasts of the states, should be owned and controlled by the respective states. . . .

In closing, it is interesting to note that many of those who oppose this proposed legislation are the very ones who have been active proponents of an ever larger Federal Government and who seem to think that an all-powerful Federal Government is a panacea for all the ills of the people of this country. Those of us who support the proposed legislation are strongly opposed to the nationalization of resources—and that is what they are attempting to do to us—in the five-thousand-mile shoestring of coastal waters which throttles the shores of our coastal states. The resources in this narrow belt are vital to the states and to local growth and prosperity, and we feel that the ownership and control of these resources should remain in the states and be subjected to state and local control where it will be very close to the people who are so greatly affected.

We are now talking about fundamental philosophy. We are talking about local self-government. We are talking about the opportunity of a citizen to see the very officials who serve him in the regulation of lands which may represent the total investment of his lifetime savings. We think it is sound government to keep such regulation, control, and ownership just as close to home as is possible.

We strongly feel that our position is sound and just, that it will receive as it has already received, the approval of the vast majority of our people who, we believe, as indicated by the result of the recent Gallup poll, agree with us that the important rights enjoyed by these states for a hundred and fifty years should be restored and safeguarded, and that such action would be in the interest of soundly economic and democratic government. These rights and the immense values already developed and to be developed in the coastal belt, plus the similar values

† Adapted from *Congressional Record* 99 (April 6, 1953), pp. 2848 and 2877.

in the inland waters and in the Great Lakes, involve problems which are so clearly local in nature that we shall continue with all of our strength to fight to prevent their transfer to a Federal Government which is already too big, too wasteful, and too far from the people.

Mr. President, there is not a senator within the sound of my voice who does not know that much of the body of ills which afflict us on the domestic front flows directly from the fact that the Federal Government is too big, and that there is no finite mind which can grasp all its implications or all its details, even though it is the responsibility of senators and representatives to make laws for the government of our huge, swollen Federal system, as well as of our people, and it is our duty to provide appropriations whereby those immense pieces of uncoordinated machinery can attempt to function.

It is our hope that the joint resolution will speedily pass the Senate and be enacted into law.

Answer these questions to show how critically you read Senator Holland's arguments.

1. Senator Holland suggests that his resolution refers to what portion of the submerged lands off the coast of the United States?
   a. Nine tenths.   b. One tenth.   c. One-half.   d. All.
2. Why does he stress this point?
   a. To confuse his listeners.   b. To play down the magnitude of the transfer of the title.   c. Because the transfer of title affects only an insignificant portion of the submerged lands.   d. Because the lands being transferred are of little value.
3. Where does Senator Holland claim that these lands really lie, and how does he use this claim as an argument for returning them to the states?
   a. Adjacent to the coast and hence part of the United States.
   b. Within the navigable waters of the states, and should belong to the states.   c. Within the boundaries of the states and hence are part of the states.   d. Close by the states, and having once been their property should be returned to the states.
4. What other arguments are offered by the Senator without sufficient proof of their validity?
   a. These are local lands and should be supervised locally.   b. Local governments do a better job than state governments.   c. Every man should be free to supervise his own business.   d. What happens to these lands is the concern of only those living near them.
   e. All of these arguments.
5. How does the Senator try to gain the approval of his listeners for local rather than federal government of the submerged lands?
   a. By proving the inefficiency of a large government.   b. By referring to the Federal government as "swollen," "wasteful."   c. By

claiming that the lands are only a small part of the total area in question.   d. By failing to mention the presence of oil on these lands.

6. How does the Senator attempt to help his listeners identify their interests with the small, local government?
a. By claiming that everyone understands local government better than the federal system.   b. By drawing an analogy—the state and the submerged lands are like every man and his possessions.
c. By pointing out the advantages of local or state supervision.
d. By claiming that each person is first a citizen of a state.

7. Which of Senator Holland's arguments would influence you most to agree with him?
a. The area in question is only a small part of the submerged lands.
b. The lands are within the boundaries of the states.   c. Local lands and projects should be supervised locally.   d. The federal government is too inefficient to administer these lands properly.
e. These lands rightfully belong to the people near them.

Before we point out the kind of fallacy by which you may have been influenced in answering question 7, read the following excerpts from a speech in opposition to this bill; then answer the subjoined questions.

Tidelands Oil°

—HERBERT H. LEHMAN

We must not lose sight of the main question before us, much as the proponents of this legislation would like to have us lose sight of that question.

That question is: Why should we give these rights away? Why should we give these billions away?

Under the rulings of the Supreme Court these rights and this great wealth belong to all the states—to New York, and Connecticut, and Virginia, and Ohio, and Wisconsin, and Minnesota, and North Dakota, and Iowa—to all the forty-eight states and all the people of this country and to their descendants.

Why should Congress vote to take these rights away from all the people, from the nation as a whole, and give them to three states?

The proponents of this legislation have not given the answer. In my remarks today, Mr. President, I shall try to state why the Congress should not give these rights away. I propose to argue what I deeply believe, that the national interest and the national need require the retention of these rights, and that the alienation of these rights—this proposed giveaway—is a denial of the national interest, and a handicap to our national security.

° Adapted from the *Congressional Record*, **99** (April 13, 1953), p. 3077.

What we should be doing, Mr. President, in the proper exercise of our obligations as members of the national Congress, is to be debating how best to use these rights to promote the national interest and to advance the national security—not what manner we can legally follow in giving away these rights which lawfully belong to the nation.

The Anderson bill offers a method of using the rights lawfully vested in the national government—to develop our oil resources, to expand our oil production, to promote the national defense, and incidentally to award to the states adjacent to these resources a very generous share of the benefits from the development of these resources, within the three-mile area.

The Hill amendment offers a way of using the benefits accruing to the national government to promote the general welfare of the nation by advancing the cause of education throughout our land, by investing part of the Federal Government's share of the proceeds from this development in the future of America, in the education of our young. In my opinion, nothing could possibly be more important.

The Holland joint resolution neglects these needs entirely. It concentrates on a confused and questionable formula for giving away what can be given away, and for paralyzing the national government's access to those rights which cannot, even under the most extreme stretch of the legal imagination, be given away.

The national rights of the three-mile belt are proposed to be given away. The bill proposes to give away title, but comprehends the strong possibility that title cannot be given away, and so provides for the contingency that this part of the giveaway will be declared illegal. So the Holland joint resolution proposes to give away the rights to the resources in the three-mile belt, even if the courts find that Congress could not legally hand over the legal title to this area.

Then the Holland measure goes further, and edges out beyond the three-mile zone, into the international zone, and seeks to give to certain states title to areas in the open sea beyond any limits which our country has ever claimed to be the exclusive territory of any country, even our own.

We have protested and resisted the claims of Russia, Ecuador, and Mexico, among other nations, to exclusive territorial rights beyond the three-mile zone off their shores; but today it is proposed to give to certain states proprietary rights to ocean areas far beyond our coasts—rights which we as a nation have never claimed to possess.

What a travesty on national responsibility. How irresponsible we will seem in the eyes of the world if we approve this legislation.

Try these questions based on Senator Lehman's remarks.

1. How does the Senator attempt to prejudice his listeners against the Holland resolution?
   a. By disproving all of Senator Holland's arguments.   b. By the use of satire and ridicule.   c. By describing it in such terms as *con-*

fused, questionable, irresponsible, travesty.　　d. By offering the argument that the lands never did belong to the states.

2. What emotional appeal does Senator Lehman use to sway his audience to approval of the Hill amendment?
a. By showing the greater value of the Hill amendment.　　b. By the emphasis upon the "future of America," "education of our young." c. By trying to anger the audience against his opponent.　　d. By implying that the states are selfish in trying to secure these lands for their own ends.

3. How does the Senator attempt to show that the lands do not belong to the states?
a. By claiming that they should be supervised by the federal government.　　b. By proving that the lands are not within the states. c. By showing that supervision of the lands is not properly a local problem.　　d. By citing the Supreme Court decision that they belong to the nation.

4. What is Senator Lehman's main argument against giving the lands to the state?
a. That administration of these lands is the concern of the entire nation.　　b. That these lands do not belong to the states.　　c. That the lands are too valuable to turn over to the states.　　d. That the federal government would be more efficient in supervising these lands.　　e. That passing this resolution would expose Congress to criticism from foreign countries.

5. How does the Senator emphasize the importance of the exact area to be transferred?
a. By disproving the assertion that only one tenth of the submerged lands would be transferred.　　b. By showing that such action would be contrary to the law.　　c. By claiming that the land would include areas never claimed for the United States.　　d. By demonstrating the tremendous value of these lands.

6. Which of these facts would you like to know before agreeing with one of the Senators?
a. To whom the lands originally belonged.　　b. How much money is likely to be realized from the oil on these lands.　　c. What would be done with the income derived from the oil rights.　　d. I have already decided against the Holland resolution.　　e. I am in favor of the Holland resolution.　　f. The detailed provisions of the Holland, Hill, and other resolutions.　　g. Why it was necessary to have a Supreme Court ruling on the ownership of the lands.

Now return to your answer to question 7, following Senator Holland's remarks. If you choose *a, b, c,* or *e,* you permitted an argument with insufficient evidence to sway your thinking. The size of the lands, as in *a,* proves nothing about their real value or importance, or how they should be supervised. The fact that the lands immediately adjoin the states or, in a sense, are within the states' boundaries as in *b* does not necessarily prove that they belong to or should be administered by the state. The control and supervision of the coastal waters of a nation have long been considered the rightful province of the central government because of the international nature of the problem. States, counties, or other local political units have seldom been permitted to enter into agreements or treaties about such waters with other such units or with foreign nations.

Federal supervision of local lands and projects (opposed in *c* and *e*) is a principle certainly now completely accepted in our country. Dams, national parks, canals, hydroelectric projects, flood control, the TVA, Indian reservations, and many other federal projects exist within various states but remain under federal control.

The efficiency of our central government can certainly be questioned in many details, as in *d,* but, in our opinion, the raising of this issue does more to cloud the question under discussion than to clarify it. If the members of Congress were afraid of inefficient federal administration of the revenues to be derived from the lands in question, it was well within their power to direct the exact way the revenues should be administered. Senator Holland has created a false dilemma as though the only choice for Congress was between ineffective federal administration or local supervision, which presumably would be better. Several alternative courses are open, such as more detailed legislation concerning the administration of the lands, delaying action until a committee has explored all the problems in the situation, or leaving the lands under federal control with strict instructions from Congress regarding their administration.

Summary

The process of critical reading to which we have tried to introduce you might be described in these steps:

1. Identifying the facts—recognizing clearly what the author or speaker is saying.

2. Examining the source—looking critically at the author, his competence, reliability, his probable viewpoints or biases.

3. Analyzing the material—examining the author's assumptions and the logic and accuracy of these assumptions and conclusions; recognizing the inferences the reader is supposed to make; detecting the implications present in the author's diction, style or tone; recognizing his use of propaganda tricks and emotional appeals.

In addition to the three steps we have tried to illustrate here, you may find a fourth step necessary in college assignments: the comparison of a selection with other sources that may present conflicting viewpoints. You will find this fourth step profitable in such areas as political science, history, psychology, sociology, law, and journalism, as well as biography, essays, and much expository material.

We might sum up critical reading by saying that it implies an attitude in the reader that helps him to change his beliefs as he reads, but not by accepting totally an author's viewpoint. It enables him to react to each strong viewpoint with a contrasting or opposing view based on his own logic and beliefs. The critical reader reads widely, but constantly resists the efforts that are being made to manipulate his thinking, his purchases, his beliefs, his life.

Help Yourself

If you need additional practice materials to improve your skills in critical reading, these are good sources. Ask your instructor for help in selecting those best suited to your needs.

Altick, Richard D. *Preface to Critical Reading*. New York: Holt, Rinehart and Winston, 1961. *A very thorough study of critical and analytic reading. With many examples.*

Casty, Alan. *The Act of Reading*. Englewood Cliffs, N. J.: Prentice-Hall, 1962. *Each short article is followed by questions asking the reader to evaluate the thinking underlying the presentation.*

Diederich, Paul B., and Osmond E. Palmer. *Critical Thinking in Reading and Writing*. New York: Holt, Rinehart and Winston, 1955. *The questions accompanying each reading selection demand very careful, thorough reading.*

Graves, Harold F., and Bernard S. Oldsey. *From Fact to Judgment*. New York: Macmillan, 1963. *Offers a wide variety of selections for critical reading.*

Hummel, William, and Keith Huntress. *The Analysis of Propaganda*. New York: Holt, Rinehart and Winston, *A readable study of propaganda techniques, with examples.*

Kay, Sylvia C. *Reading Critically in the Fields of Literature and History*. New York: Twayne, 1952. *Brief selections from literature and history to be read critically, in a class or group.*

Sherbourne, Julia Florence. *Toward Reading Comprehension*. Boston: Heath, 1966. Chapter V. *Gives a number of short selections demanding critical reading, and some exercises in this skill.*

Stroud, James B., Robert B. Ammons, and Henry A. Bamman. *Improving Reading Ability*. New York: Appleton-Century-Crofts, 1956. Chapter VIII. *Offers a number of brief exercises in detecting author's purpose, viewpoint, and appeal to emotions of the reader.*

PART II

Promoting Vocabulary Growth

CHAPTER 8

ANALYZING DIFFICULT WORDS

The average adult reader has one favorite technique for determining the meanings of unknown words—the guess. This technique is formally known as finding meanings from context. It may be sheer guesswork in which the reader tries to sense the meaning implied by the rest of the sentence or paragraph. Or, the meaning may actually be given in a phrase or clause following the word so that no real analysis is necessary. The reader may use any of several other aids, such as working out the meaning from his own experience, or using the footnotes or glossary of the text.

However, no matter what technique the average reader uses to get the meaning of an unknown word, he is not likely to be very effective or systematic. His use of the context is apt to be a fumbling, hit-or-miss process that fails more than half the time. Because he has had no instruction in varied means of using the context, he is unable to derive meanings from context even when they are clearly given. The average student is forced to use more time-consuming methods of deriving meanings, such as using affixes and roots, the dictionary, or the textbook glossary.

Because of this lack of facility in deriving meanings from context, we think it essential to offer some suggestions and practice in this and related vocabulary skills.

Contextual Clues in General Reading

What is the process of deriving a meaning for an unknown word from the context or general reading? Basically it is a series of trial-and-error efforts at recognizing and understanding the unknown word. It may include such steps as the following:

Read this sentence.

The lecturer droned on and on: his *divagations* led him away from one point after another until the audience was thoroughly confused.

What is your first guess for the meaning of *divagations*?

Read on to see whether you need to refine this guess.

Some of the audience dozed, others openly chatted with their neighbors. Only a few tried desperately to follow the *divagations* of the speaker and to organize these into a coherent set of notes.

Now what do you think divagations means?
a. Remarks.   b. Illustrations and examples.   c. Disorganization.   d. Wanderings.

The process of deriving meanings of unknown words from context sometimes involves a series of guesses or trials with possible synonyms. For example, in answer to the first question above, your first guess may have been "remarks" or "examples" or "statements." But the sentence implied that the speaker was led away from his own points of emphasis by his *divagations,* and that the audience was unable to follow him. Therefore, the word must mean something more than these first guesses. If you recognized this clue, your first guess may have been "digressions." "deviations," "detours," or "ramblings," all of which are superior guesses.

The rest of the paragraph again implies that those who were really listening found it difficult to follow the speaker—in other words, he *wandered.* Almost any of the more intelligent guesses you may have made is a reasonable synonym for *divagations.*

This crude process of refining guesses as you read is perhaps the commonest way of using the context to derive meanings of difficult words. If the reader has a wide vocabulary and knows many words of similar meanings, this way of using the context is fairly effective. He tries several meanings until he finds one that seems to make sense. If the reader's vocabulary is limited, he must resort to other approaches. Among the steps such a reader may take are the following:

Skipping the Word.   Some readers simply skip a difficult word and read on, hoping that either of two things will happen: (1) they will be able to understand the selection without recognizing the unknown word, or (2) the reading material will eventually clarify its meaning.

For example, in the following sentence the reader might skip trying to find the meaning of the word in italics and still understand the sentence:

On his right hand, the gentleman wore a *gauntlet* of heavy leather with an embroidered cuff.

It isn't essential to know that a gauntlet is "a medieval glove, as of mail, plate, or leather, with a cuff-like extension for the wrist" in order to understand the meaning of this sentence. A simple guess that a gauntlet is some kind of covering for the hand may be sufficient to enable the reader to continue reading with comprehension. In reading situations like this, some idea of the meaning of an unknown word is gained by intuition or by inference. Actually the reader hasn't entirely skipped the word or ignored it, for he does react with a crude idea of the meaning. This may be enough to enable him to understand this particular sentence.

Whether this approximate meaning is really enough for good comprehension of the paragraph depends upon a number of elements of the reading task. The reader may suddenly discover that because of the vague meaning given to the word, he is missing the train of thought of the selection. In such a case, he can't continue to ignore the exact meaning but must return to the word to refine his guess. Or, he will have to reread to find more clues to the meaning of the bothersome term.

The reader can avoid this sort of confusion and rereading if he follows through with the second type of reaction we have mentioned. Having reacted once with an approximate meaning, the reader goes on, expecting the material to clarify or refine his original guess. He is particularly alert to discover a further definition in the rest of the sentence or the paragraph in which the unknown word appears.

Skipping a word thus doesn't actually mean ignoring it. Rather, the reader reacts immediately with a reasonable guess and then reads on to refine that guess, if he can.

One significant point to remember in using the context to derive word meanings is the advisability of reading enough of the context to get a variety of clues. Many readers tend to stop reading as soon as they meet a difficult term and to attempt to define its meaning immediately. In many sentences, stopping at the unknown word defeats any effort to obtain its meaning.

For example, read this sentence for the meaning of *patronage*.

> Andrew Jackson is accused by many historians of promoting, more than any other previous President, an undesirable type of political *patronage*.

If you didn't know the meaning of *patronage*, and if you stopped reading at this point, would you be able to figure it out?

Patronage means—
   a. double-talk.   b. chicanery, trickery.   c. false promises.
   d. undercover gifts.   e. nepotism.   f. control of offices.

At this point, *patronage* has not really been defined, and logically it could mean any of these six answers. Let's read on for other clues.

> Jackson's system of *patronage* was called the spoils system, after the expression "To the victors belong the spoils."

At this point, you may decide to find *patronage* in the dictionary. Which of these four dictionary definitions will fit the context? Do you know enough about the word to make a choice?

> *Patronage* means—
>   a. a condescending air or favor.   b. the patrons or clientele of a business.   c. support given by, or asked from a patron.   d. control of nomination to political offices.

You might guess that the last answer is probably right, because it has some relationship to politics. But do you really understand the term? If so, can you explain why Jackson was criticized for promoting patronage? Have you read enough to know why patronage is undesirable? Finish reading the paragraph to see whether you can refine your understanding.

> Such a system, with its awarding of government jobs to loyal minor politicians regardless of their qualifications, is the enemy of an efficient civil service and a source of inefficiency and corruption in public offices.

Now, perhaps, you have a clearer comprehension of the meaning and the implications of *patronage*.

If you are trying to derive the meaning of a word from context, read beyond the word before attempting a complete definition. Watch for additional clues, explanations, or repeated use of the term. Use the context for all it will give, before turning to the dictionary or deciding upon a meaning.

Digging for Contextual Clues.   In many selections, particularly those in literary materials, the clues given to an unknown word are not very obvious. Often the meaning is implied by figures of speech, or by the tone or mood of the selection, or is dependent upon the reader's previous experiences. Often the author gives no further clues in the paragraph. In such cases, the reader may have to get whatever meaning he can from careful reading of the single sentence in which the word appears.

Read this sentence for the meaning of *specious*.

> His argument was as *specious* as the words of the snake who beguiled Adam and Eve in the Garden of Paradise.

In this sentence, specious means—
>   a. money or currency.   b. unusual or different.   c. deceptively plausible.   d. wide open or widely spaced.

Obviously, as used in this sentence, *specious* does not relate to *specie* ("coin" or "currency") or *spacious* ("wide open" or "roomy"). The reference to the beguiling snake implies that the argument was more than just unusual or different. It must have been deluding or deceptive, or only apparently truthful. Both the allusion to the snake and the use of the word *beguiling* lead us to recognize that *specious* must mean "deceptively plausible."

Read this sentence for the meaning of *inculcate*.

> Music, drama, novels, pictures, sculpture, and architecture *inculcate* into the rising generation the values, ideals, and hopes of the people who produced them.

What is the meaning of *inculcate?*
  a. Enter.   b. Initiate.   c. Implant.   d. Force.

Trying each of the answers in the context as a substitute for *inculcate* would speed up the selection of the best synonym. "Enter" and "force" would be eliminated, for when we insert these into the context they seem inappropriate. The arts mentioned just can't "enter" the rising generation nor can they "force" the values, ideals and hopes upon them. This leaves the choice between answers *b* and *c*. By definition, *initiate* means to begin, to instruct, to admit to a club. However, the presence of the word *into* interferes with the substitution of *initiate* for *inculcate*. We can't "begin into" or "instruct into," although we can "admit into"; but this last possible meaning is obviously too weak for the true meaning of the sentence. The final possible answer, "implant," can be fitted into the context as a logical substitute for *inculcate*.

In this type of context, there is no direct explanation, and all clues may be concentrated in one sentence. The reader must recognize the clues—the allusions, figures of speech, and choice of words selected to create imagery or impressions—to the extent that these are meaningful from his previous knowledge. The novelist, the dramatist, and most frequently, the poet assumes that his clues are within the experience of his reader and will be integrated to convey the meaning he intends. Some readers may feel that this is a very great assumption or even an unfair one. But, after all, if writers could make no assumptions about the vocabularies of their readers, their efforts would certainly be terribly infantile and dull.

Recalling the Word.   In addition to trying to use contextual clues to meaning, many readers attempt to aid their recognition of a word by pronouncing it. This can be helpful if the reader has heard the word frequently enough to have formed some mental associations with it. Saying it aloud may help to recall auditory memories for the sound and meaning of the word. It is essential in this effort that the reader's analysis of the word be correct and that he pronounce it properly. If he does not duplicate the usual pronunciation of the word as he has heard it, he may not recognize it.[1]

Pronunciation as a help to word recognition is usually more effective with general terms than with technical words. The reader is more likely to have heard such general words in lectures or ordinary conversation. But there is always the possibility that he may have heard a technical term in the classroom or lecture hall, and pronouncing it may help to recall this experience.

There is another advantage in trying to pronounce an unknown word besides the possibility of recalling it. By pronouncing it or reading aloud the

---

[1] See the Appendix for specific help with principles of pronunciation.

sentence in which it appears, the reader creates another association with the word, in addition to its visual form. He forms an auditory memory for the word that may help him to retain the meaning and recall it on other occasions. It is true that this auditory impression is a temporary one. But if the word is important and recurs fairly often, the effort to pronounce it can start the process of learning this word.

Using the Dictionary.   Some readers turn immediately to the dictionary each time they meet a new word. It is true that the dictionary is the most authoritative source for the exact meaning, spelling, pronunciation, and other facts about a word. But many readers turn to the dictionary too hastily and too often. Looking up a word becomes a substitute for any real attempt to analyze the context for possible clues. Some readers become dependent upon the dictionary and thus lose many opportunities for reasoning out meanings by their own efforts. By avoiding the thinking involved in using contextual clues, these readers also fail to form the mental associations that would help them to retain and recall unknown words. Each time they meet a difficult word, they must again turn to the dictionary for lack of any useful memories attached to the word. For these reasons, although the dictionary is a very useful tool, as we shall point out in a later chapter, its excessive use can be a handicap to vocabulary growth. In our opinion, using the dictionary is the last step in finding a word meaning, coming after we have exhausted the other possibilities in the context, pronouncing the word, or studying its parts. After deriving some meaning from the context, the dictionary may serve to confirm a guess or to reveal other meanings for the unknown word.

Contextual Clues in Technical Reading

The use of contextual clues for word meaning is somewhat different in technical reading from what it is in general materials. Here the word may not have a common meaning, because it may be the name for a process, an object, a form of life, an element, and so on. Or the word may be a common one that is used in a special technical sense, such as *cape, charge, force,* or *minute.* These differences may be illustrated by the word *Vorticella* in the following selection.

> One of the most interesting forms of microscopic life is the *Vorticella.* If you look at one of these under a microscope, you will note that it has a head and stem. The head looks somewhat like a bell attached to a stalk. The stem of the *Vorticella* coils and uncoils like a spring to raise and lower the bell-shaped head. The *Vorticella,* unlike some other microscopic animals, lives in a colony with many of its genus.
>
> The food-getting activities of the *Vorticella* are more complicated than those of the Amoeba. The stem straightens to raise the head and bring it into contact with food in the water. The food is washed or pushed by cilia into the mouth or gullet of the *Vorticella* and then on to a food vacuole, where it is digested.

This kind of reading doesn't show an inherent meaning for the term *Vorticella.* Yet, if you read carefully you could define, or rather describe, a *Vorticella,* couldn't you? Your description might include mention of the head and stem, the cilia, and its microscopic size. If you wished to differentiate it from other microscopic animals, you would mention the colony and the rudimentary gullet. Such a definition would be as complete as you are likely to find in most dictionaries. Perhaps the only other significant fact for which you might need a dictionary would be the pronunciation of the term. Most important of all, by combining the clues given in the context, you have formed a number of associations that will help you recall the term.

Many textbook authors are aware of it when they are using a word that the reader may not know. They may then deliberately explain or illustrate the meaning to aid the reader.

Try to read this selection for the meaning of *contiguous:*

> During the time of Pericles, plans were made to rebuild the marble Parthenon on the Acropolis. The first set of plans occasioned much debate, for they differed from the original design of the temple in many details. For example, the new plans proposed that the pillars were to be almost immediately *contiguous,* with scarcely space enough between for a hand to enter, much less a human. Fortunately, this plan was dropped in favor of a rebuilding according to the original design.

What does *contiguous* probably mean, according to this selection?
a. Close.　　b. Touching; in contact.　　c. Parallel.　　d. Alongside each other.

Answers *a, c,* and *d* correctly describe the pillars, of course. But they could be used to describe any set of pillars, without conveying the exact meaning intended here. The objection to the new set of plans was that the pillars would be too close or almost "touching" or "in contact." Careful reading of the later part of the sentence in which *contiguous* appears clarifies the exact meaning intended. Another way of checking your choice of a definition would be to insert it into the context, to try it for fit, as it were. Here again, "touching" and "in contact" are the closest substitutes that would preserve the full meaning of the sentence.

If you are not concerned about learning the new words you meet and thus enlarging your vocabulary, you may be satisfied with only an approximately correct meaning. In this instance, "close," "near," or "alongside" as definitions of *contiguous* might have met your need to get the meaning of the sentence. For any person who wants to improve his ability to read or to communicate with others, however, approximate meanings are a short-range and inadequate solution. Words are among the most valuable tools we have to use in the process of thinking, and they are essential for learning ideas. Vague, fuzzy understandings of words result in fuzzy thinking and learning.

Retaining New Words

Someone has estimated that the number of new technical words a student must learn in each high school and college area, such as biology, chemistry, or American history, is about 300 to 500. This word count includes only words that recur frequently, are significant for learning the subject, and also have some social usefulness. The sciences impose the greatest vocabulary load, with biology demanding over 500, physics about 375, and chemistry about 350. Mathematical courses are easiest in this respect, with geometry requiring about a hundred and algebra only about fifty, largely because most of the mathematical terms used are learned in the earlier study of arithmetic.

What is the significance of this technical word count? Simply that each year of college study is likely to demand the learning of 600 to 800 technical terms, plus an undetermined but greater number of general words. The weekly load is perhaps 50 to 60 new words. How is the student to learn and retain these?

A few students can learn most of the new vocabulary by paying careful attention to their uses and meanings as the words are encountered in reading or in listening in classrooms and lecture rooms. Most other students, however, would benefit from a more systematic effort to retain the new vocabulary. Research in this area has indicated that underlining terms, checking them in the margin, or looking them up in the dictionary is *not* very effective. Memories for words learned in these ways are very fleeting. A more active and systematic method is decidedly superior to these casual steps.

One system that rates high among serious students is a collection of vocabulary cards. On one side of a card, you write the word and a sentence or phrase that illustrates its use and meaning. On the back of the card, write a brief dictionary definition and, if you need them, some indications of the pronunciation and the meanings of the parts of the word. Words can be collected from textbooks, the classroom or lecture hall, and from your supplementary reading. If you keep the cards sorted according to their subject matter, you can review them before studying, before examinations or written assignments. As you learn one group of cards, put them away and replace them with the new ones you have prepared. If a particular examination covers all the work in the course up to the time it is given, you may find it profitable to review all the cards you have collected in that subject.

Another variation of this method of learning new terms involves making a word list in each of your notebooks. As in the case of the card file, new terms are added, illustrated, and defined, and then reviewed until they are learned. (The frequency with which some students lose their notebooks during the year makes this variation seem a little less practical than the card file.)

If you can devise some system of learning the five to ten words per day that are essential, and if that system suits you better than those we have suggested, by all means use it. Your success in college and afterwards will depend heavily on your vocabulary skills.

Summary

We have outlined the steps that the interested reader will employ in attempting to discover the meaning of an unknown word. These steps are taken so quickly that you may be unaware that you have already been using some of them. In fact, most readers can complete all of them, except the use of the dictionary and the entry in the card file, in about one second. Compare the steps again with your system.

When you meet a difficult new word:

1. *Skip it:* Take a guess, then read on, because you can probably comprehend well enough the word. Expect the context to clarify the meaning later.

2. *Use the context:* Look for explanation or clarification in the immediate context. Try a synonym or two for the approximate meaning. Refine these guesses as you read on. Watch for allusions, figures of speech, and other clues.

3. *Pronounce it:* Say the word aloud, if you can. (See the Appendix if you need help with this step.)

4. *Analyze it:* Look for clues to the meaning in the root and affixes. (See Chapter 9 for help in this step.)

5. *Define it:* In technical materials, use the given facts to form your own definition.

6. *Use the dictionary:* If none of the preceding steps suffice, look up the word in the dictionary. (See Chapter 10 for help in this step.)

7. *Retain it:* Add the word to your card file or word list for future review.

Help Yourself

If you need practice materials to help you improve your ability to use the context, the following are excellent aids. Ask your instructor to suggest ways in which you might use one of these sources.

Brown, Marion Marsh. *Learning Words in Context.* San Francisco: Chandler Publishing Co., 1961. 222 pages. *Most of this book is devoted to the study of word meanings in a variety of contexts.*

DeVitis, A. A., and J. R. Warner. *Words in Context.* New York: Appleton-Century-Crofts, 1962. 332 pages. *Promotes vocabulary growth by emphasizing use of context, word derivation.*

Nathan, Norman. *The Right Word.* Boston: Houghton Mifflin, 1962. 191 pages. *Offers a wide variety of interesting exercises in judging, using, and reacting to words in context.*

Taylor, Stanford E., Helen Frankenpohl, and Arthur S. McDonald. *Word Clues.* Huntington, N.Y.: Educational Developmental Laboratories, 1963. 168 pages. *Each of these programed, self-correcting workbooks permits the student to derive and evaluate his meanings for 300 words. Book L or M in this series would be suitable for the college student or adult.*

CHAPTER 9

WORD CLUES FROM AFFIXES
AND ROOTS

One of the steps in recognizing word meanings recommended in Chapter 8 was an analysis of a word in terms of its parts. Undoubtedly you were introduced to this type of word attack some time ago. But, in all probability, you have not recognized the importance of this skill, for it is not often demanded in elementary and secondary reading. Now that you are attempting to deal with more difficult and more technical terms, we strongly urge you to make a vigorous attempt to acquire skill in this technique.

Knowing a number of affixes and roots and using this knowledge when reading result in quicker and better understanding. Use of such word elements also strongly promotes vocabulary growth, an indispensable part of learning. Comprehension and speed are both improved by increased skill in handling difficult words and by development of a wider reading vocabulary.

Problems in Using Affixes and Roots

There are certain problems in using affixes and roots to unlock word meanings. These difficulties may have interfered with or discouraged your development of this vocabulary-building skill. First, there is the problem of the number of possible roots and affixes. Some vocabulary books offer hundreds of such elements, enough to make their learning appear impossible to the average person. Trying to learn all roots and affixes is impractical, in our opinion; for although there are perhaps a thousand or more Latin and Greek bases for English words, no one knows how many of these the literate reader needs to know. Probably it is more realistic to learn a brief, selected list useful in general reading, and to give some attention to learning those word parts that occur often in certain technical areas.

A second problem is that some word elements have variations in spelling and meaning, which confuse some readers who attempt to use affixes and roots. For example, the prefix *ad-* meaning "to" or "toward" has the following variations:

a-	ascribe	al-	allude
ab-	abbreviate	an-	annex
ac-	acquire	ap-	append
ad-	adhere	ar-	arrive
af-	afferent	as-	associate
ag-	agglutinate	at-	attract

A given affix or root also may have a number of distinctly different meanings. Leading dictionaries give at least four or five meanings for the prefix *a-*, such as "in," "on," "up," "away from," "without," "not," and "apart from." These variations in spelling and meaning, which have occurred as an element has moved from one language to another, sometimes result in a loss of the literal meaning of the word part. The meanings and usage of many present-day words no longer bear much relationship to the meanings of their original bases. Illustrations of this are the words *precise* and *abuse*. *Precise* is derived from *prae*, meaning "before," and *caedere*, "to cut." *Abuse* comes from the prefix *ab*, "away," and *uti*, "to use." The literal meanings of "cutting before" or "using away" that can be derived from the parts of *precise* and *abuse* are irrelevant to current meanings.

Finally, in some English words, elements that appear to be actual suffixes or prefixes are not such at all. The element *dis* is not a true prefix in *disciple* or *discipline*, nor does *un* mean "not" in *unanimous*, to give only a few examples. These difficulties in interpreting affixes and roots have led many to discontinue their use in studying words. However, the problems are not insurmountable, as we hope to show.

In practice, the analysis of words in terms of their roots and affixes is really a process of (1) separating and identifying syllables and (2) looking for possible meanings. Both prefixes and suffixes form separate syllables and are often readily distinguished from the stem or other central part of the word. Sometimes a prefix or suffix doesn't explain very much or have a great deal of meaning. For example, *-tion* and *-ment* merely make a noun out of a verb and indicate that the action implied in the verb is present or continuing. However, separating these word elements from the main part of the word and recognizing the meaning or effect they may have is a step toward better understanding of the word. Often the remaining central portion of the word—the root or stem—is thus pointed out and can be easily recognized. You may remember the fun you had as an intermediate grade pupil in dealing with that monster nonsense word,

anti-dis-establish-ment-ar-ian-ism

This puzzler was probably coined by some teacher to demonstrate that regardless of size or number of elements, many words can be separated and analyzed in meaningful units.

We have no intention of offering a complete list or even a list of the most important word elements you as an individual should know. No such list is available, because the needs of each reader are determined by the demands of the materials he must comprehend. Our list offers those of significance to most persons reading in general materials. Suggestions for individualizing the learning of important roots and affixes as they occur in technical areas will be offered later.

A Working List of Word Parts

Combining Forms. Combining forms, as their name implies, are word elements that can be combined with roots and affixes and other combining forms to build meaningful words. The accompanying list gives some of the more important ones.

Element	Meaning	Example
anti	against, opposed to.	antisocial
audio	pertaining to hearing.	auditorium
auto	arising from within, self-activating.	automaton
biblio	books.	bibliography
bio	life, living.	biology
centro, -i	center.	concentric
form	like.	cruciform
geo	ground, earth.	geography
gram, graph	writing or record.	photograph
hetero	other, different.	heterogeneous
homo	same, alike.	homonym
hydro	water or hydrogen.	hydroplane
iso	equal, alike.	isotopes
log, logue	speech or science of.	monologue
macro	large.	macrocosm
meter, metry	device for measuring.	thermometer
micro	small.	microfilm
mono	single, alone.	monogamy
neuro	nerve.	neurotic
omni	all.	omnipotent
pan	all, every.	panorama
psycho	mind, soul.	psychology
philo	like, fond of.	philosophy
phobia	exaggerated fear.	claustrophobia
phono	sound, voice.	telephone
poly	many, several.	polygon
soph	knowledge, wisdom.	sophisticated
tele	far off.	telegraph

Combining forms occur in many familiar words, as you can see. They also can be combined with other roots and affixes or with each other to form new words, as our needs arise. For example, combining forms appear in such recent words as *telemetry, antibiotic,* and *isotope.*

Word Prefixes and Suffixes.   There is a group of very simple and obvious prefixes and suffixes derived from common words. Among those used frequently are these:

out	outward, throughout	*self*	self-blame, herself
over	overflow, moreover	*way*	roadway, wayfarer
under	underwater	*wise*	clockwise, otherwise
up	upcurve, tune-up		

The last of these word affixes, *wise,* is currently being used excessively and without precision in business jargon—for example, in *businesswise.*

Prefix	Meaning	Example
ante-	preceding in time, in front of.	antedate
circum-	around, revolve around.	circumference
contra-, -o-,	against, opposite.	contradict
equi-	equal.	equidistant
extra-	beyond, outside of.	extracurricular
inter-	together, between.	interclass
intra-, -o-,	within.	intramural
mal-, male-	bad, wrong.	malformation
mis-	badly, not.	misprint
non-	not	nonathletic
post-	after, following in time.	postcollege
pre-	before, prior to.	precollege
re-	back, again.	readmit
super-, sur-	above, more than normal.	superhuman, surpass

In addition to these common prefixes, several others merit mention. The prefix *un-* is often affixed to verbs to convey the sense of reversal of the action of the verb, as in *unchained.* When attached to nouns, *un-* has a negative force or meaning, as in *un-American* or *unacademic.* The prefix *in-* may also mean "not," as in *inadmissible,* or it may mean "into," as in *incise,* "to cut into." The prefix *sub-,* meaning "under," is a third useful element that may be added to the list above.

The prefixes *in-* and *sub-* both have a number of spellings that have arisen in an attempt to make the pronunciation of words smoother and easier. In most cases, the variation in spelling consists of making the last letter agree with the consonant at the beginning of the root. *In-* may be spelled *im, il, ir,* as in *immaterial* or *impossible, illegal, irregular.* In words coming from Greek or French, *in-* may be spelled *em-* or *en-;* it commonly means "into" in these words, as in *encamp, embank, embrace.*

Sub- changes in similar fashion to agree with the base of the word, as in *suppress, suffix, succumb, suggest, suspect.* Fortunately for its ready recognition, however, *sub-* maintains its original form in a great many words, such as *subarea, subbranch, subpolar, subsection.*

Noun Suffixes. Noun suffixes contribute very little to the meanings of the roots they are attached to, other than an indication that the complete words are nouns. Their common meaning is "action or result of an action" or "quality, state or condition"—for example, *contentment* means the state or condition of being content; *rejection* means the action of rejecting.

Noun suffix	Examples
-acity	pugnacity
-ance, -ence	assistance, occurrence
-ation, -tion, -ion, -sion	affirmation, admission
-bility	probability
-dom	freedom
-hood	manhood
-mony	matrimony
-ment	excitement
-ness	happiness
-ship	friendship
-tude	altitude
-ty	paternity

In dealing with these and other noun suffixes, the reader simply separates the suffix from the core of the word and looks for the main meaning in that central portion. The meaning of the word is present mainly in the word or root to which the suffix has been added.

Another group of noun endings refers to the person or thing that performs the action of the root or base of the word. As in the case of the endings in the preceding list, the reader looks for the major part of the meaning of the word in the base or root.

Noun suffix	Examples
-ard, -art	braggart
-ee, -eer, -ier	grantee, engineer, financier
-er, -or, -ar	maker, actor, scholar
-ist	accompanist
-ster	trickster
-ess, -stress, -tress	songstress, actress
-trix	aviatrix

You will note that *-ster* is the masculine form corresponding to *-stress* and *-tress,* and *-trix* is the feminine counterpart of *-or* or *-tor.*

Adjective Suffixes. Adjective suffixes are commonly added to words to form adjectives, those words that limit or qualify nouns.

Adjective suffix	Meaning	Examples
-able, -ible, -ble	likely to, fit to.	changeable, readable
-acious	full of.	pugnacious
-est	superlative degree.	biggest
-less	without, not able to.	harmless, countless
-like	similar to.	childlike
-most	most.	innermost
-ose, -ous, -ious, -eous	full of.	verbose, glorious
-ward, -wards	toward.	upward

Roots or Bases.   The following list gives a number of roots or bases of words, most of which are derived from Latin or Greek words. They appear in literally thousands of English words, both of general and technical nature. As we have pointed out, many such roots have lost their original meanings and acquired a great variety of new meanings and, sometimes, new spellings as they have moved from one language to another and from one usage to another. Of the hundreds of available roots we have tried to select those of consistent meaning and spelling so that the reader may use them with confidence. Other roots of use in special areas will be pointed out later in this chapter.

Root	Meaning	Examples
aer, air	air.	aerial, airlift
aqua, aque	water.	aquatic, aqueous
commun, common	common.	community, common
corp	body.	corporal, corporation
cred	belief in.	credible, credit
dei	god.	deity, deist
domin	rule over.	dominate, predominant
ego	the self.	egotist
mit, miss	to send.	mission, emit
mort	death.	immortal, postmortem
ped, pede	foot.	pedestal, centipede
scrib, script	to write.	inscribe, prescription
vid, vis	to see.	visible, provide

Special Word Elements.   The roots and affixes we have listed thus far are effective in deriving meanings mainly in general or nontechnical reading. Each subject-matter area in secondary school or college and almost every specialized field of work uses a wide variety of roots and affixes as bases for its own terms. Some of these word parts are commonly used in several fields; on the other hand, the student or worker in each field will meet many that have applications peculiar to that field. We are limited by space to listing only a representative few in several subject areas. The reader must discover for himself those word elements that are significant for each area in which he reads or studies. He must learn to use these word parts effectively if he is to function intelligently in each subject.

One group of special prefixes and combining forms referring to number or quantity occurs widely in mathematics, the sciences, and other fields. This group includes the following:

Prefix	Examples	Subject
un-, uni-	unicelled	(biology)
	uniform	(physics)
bi-, di, dis-	biofoliate	(botany)
	binomial	(mathematics)
	diabasic	(chemistry)
	dicotyledons	(biology)
tri-	triangular	(mathematics)
	triassic	(geology)
	triatomic	(chemistry)
	triclinic	(geology)
quad-, quadri-	quadrant	(mathematics)
	quadriceps	(anatomy)
	quadrivalent	(chemistry)
tetra-, tetr-	tetrachloride	(chemistry)
	tetrabranchiate	(zoology)
quint-, quinque-	quindecagon	(mathematics)
	quinquefoliate	(botany)
penta-	pentagon	(mathematics)
	pentose	(chemistry)
ses-, sex-	sestina	(English)
	sexpartile	(mathematics)
	sextile	(mathematics)
hexa-	hexane	(chemistry)
	hexameter	(English)
sept-	septilateral	(mathematics)
	septuple	(mathematics)
hepta-	heptane	(chemistry)
	heptamerous	(botany)
oct-	octahedron	(mathematics)
	octamerous	(botany)
	octane	(chemistry)
	octopod	(biology)
non-	nonagon	(mathematics)
	nones	(religion)
	nonuple	(mathematics)
dec-, deca-, (deka-)	decagram	(physics)
	decandrous	(botany)
	decane	(chemistry)
	decapod	(biology)
centi-	centipede	(biology)
	centigram	(physics)
	centile	(mathematics)

Each profession tends to emphasize its own group of word elements drawn largely from Latin, Greek, and other sources. In some instances, these represent a very real learning problem for the beginner.

For example, word elements are particularly numerous in the medical and related sciences. A representative group* for nurses, physicians, technicians, and others is the following:

Combining Forms:
> *crani, pneum, gastr, cervic, trache.*

Prefixes:
> *antero-, endo-, meso-, peri-, hypo-.*

Suffixes:
> *-algia, -itis, -osis, -plasty, -tome.*

How to Learn Affixes and Roots

The several lists of affixes and roots given in this chapter can be combined to form the basis of the more complete list you will eventually need for your own use. The number of items in our combined list immediately raises the question of the most efficient way of learning them. One method that will occur to some readers is that of simply memorizing the list. Other readers will eliminate items that are already familiar and attempt to memorize the remainder. Unfortunately, neither of these approaches is particularly intelligent or effective. Items learned in a list are often forgotten very rapidly, particularly if they are not frequently reviewed or encountered over and over again in learning situations. Instead of futile memorizing, we suggest the following uses of the list.

1. *As a basic reference list.* When you meet a root or affix frequently in your reading, consult the list for its meaning. Because ours is not a complete list, you may not find the word element there. If this is the case, and you are meeting the element again and again, you should add the item to your own personal list.

2. *As a tool for learning new words.* Try to learn one or two of the word parts in the list each day or two. Use the list to learn the meaning and the various forms or spellings of each word part. Then, as you read, look for examples of this affix or root. Try to acquire a curiosity about word parts and an alertness in seeing them. Once you become more aware of these elements of words you will be surprised at the number of times you meet and recognize them. Each word part you learn will soon become an old friend, a familiar portion of a new word that helps you deduce the whole meaning. As your familiarity with the items in the list grows, so will your vocabulary and your skill in deriving meanings for new words.

3. *As material for practice in analyzing words.* Most of your skill in analyzing words in terms of the meanings of their parts will develop be-

---

* See C. J. Birtcher, *The Birtcher Word Book* (Los Angeles: The Birtcher Corporation, for a more complete list.

cause of your attitude toward this skill. Practicing with the list of word parts will help. But more important is the attempt to cultivate an active interest in the exact meanings of words. The more attention you pay to word elements and the more often you try to use them for meanings, the easier and more effective this skill will become.

You can practice mentally with almost any given word part to increase your familiarity with its usage or its effect upon word meanings. For example, using the various forms of *in-*, meaning "not" or "into" (*im-, il-, ir-, em-, en-*) add these to common words, such as *pass, force, power, regular,* and so on. What does the prefix do to the total meaning? Try the same exercise with such suffixes as *-ance, -ence, -ment, -dom* added to common verbs.

Other types of mental practice with word parts in order to improve your vocabulary are possible. To become more familiar with the roots or bases, you may practice thinking of as many words as you can that contain a given root, such as *cred* or *scrib* or *vid*. What do they mean? Or if you feel more creative, try adding one or more affixes to each item in the list of roots. What words can you make in this fashion? Are they words in ordinary use? What would they mean? Try the same sort of mental gymnastics in putting any two of the combining forms together. When a common suffix is added to these two, does the combination form a logical word? Is it a familiar word?

Learning to use any great number of affixes and roots as an effective vocabulary aid is not an easy or short-term process. Most individuals who are interested enough to pay attention to them keep on learning new word parts in the particular materials they read in connection with their work or for recreation. The keynote of such continued growth is the interested attitude of the reader who enjoys discovering the bases of new words, and the added skill in communicating ideas that comes as a result. Space does not permit us to provide as much practice with these word parts as you may need. Fortunately, a number of books and other materials that are especially valuable for this purpose are available. Decide how much further practice is advisable with your instructor's help.

HELP YOURSELF

If you need additional practice in learning roots and affixes, these aids are particularly helpful. Ask your instructor which would be best for you.

Brown, Marion Marsh. *Learning Words in Context.* San Francisco: Chandler Publishing Co., 1961. pp. 193–220. *Offers a number of exercises with stems, prefixes and suffixes.*

Brown, James I. *Programmed Vocabulary.* New York: Appleton-Century-Crofts, 1964. p. 240. *Provides self-instructional materials mainly on affixes and roots.*

DeVitis, A. A., and J. R. Warner. *Words in Context.* New York: Appleton-Century-Crofts, 1962. pp. 243–302. *Gives practice in using words containing Latin, Greek, and French parts, in sentences.*

Jennings, Charles B., Nancy King, and Marjorie Stevenson. *Consider Your Words.* New York: Harper and Row, 1959. pp. 21–77. *Gives practice in interpreting the effect of various affixes upon word meanings in context.*

Holt, Alfred H. *Phrase and Word Origins.* New York: Dover Publications, 1961. *Traces the origins of over 1,200 common words and phrases.*

Learning, Inc. *Vocabulary Growth—Divide and Conquer Words.* Chicago: Coronet Instructional Films. *A programmed step-by-step approach to word analysis. For self-instruction.*

Monson, Samuel. *Word Building.* New York: Macmillan, 1958. *Offers practice materials in vocabulary through the use of the dictionary, Latin and Greek roots, and other word elements.*

Norwood, J. E. *Concerning Words and Phrasing.* New York: Prentice-Hall, 1956. pp. 2–90. *Offers a wide variety of exercises in word building and word analysis.*

Ward, Earl F. *Spelling and Vocabulary: Reinforce Your Learnings.* San Francisco: Chandler, 1961. pp. 77–172. *Part 2 of this workbook is devoted to a large number of exercises on endings, accent and prefixes.*

CHAPTER 10

HOW TO USE A DICTIONARY

This chapter is intended to sharpen your understanding of the true functions of a dictionary and its proper uses. The results we have obtained on the Dictionary Test, given in the Appendix, in junior and senior high schools indicate that skill in use of the dictionary does not increase greatly as students advance through school. The norms for the test show that college students answer about 76 per cent of the test correctly, which is only 24 per cent more than ninth graders. It appears that despite early introduction to the dictionary, many college students and adults do not have a high degree of skill in using it. You may wish to take the Dictionary Test before reading this chapter to learn which functions you need to review.

What Is a Dictionary Supposed to Do?

There are two conflicting concepts of the proper function of a dictionary: (1) that it simply describes the ways in which our language is being used, and (2) that it prescribes exactly how the language should be used. Most dictionary users seem to believe in the prescriptive function, for they depend upon the dictionary as an arbiter of correct usage. When disagreements arise regarding the correct pronunciation of a word such as *rationale* or the spelling of *idyl,* or the pronunciation of *short-lived,* most of us expect the dictionary to supply the final answer. After all, we reason, what good would a dictionary be if it didn't answer such questions?

The concept of the prescriptive function of the dictionary probably dates from the attitudes of several of the early lexicographers, or dictionary makers. It certainly was the avowed purpose of Samuel Johnson in 1755 and Noah Webster in 1828. Both set out to bring some sort of order and stability into our spelling and pronunciation. As Johnson pointed out, "every language has its improprieties and absurdities, which it is the duty of the lexicographer to correct or proscribe." We may judge how scientifically Johnson approached this goal by such definitions of his as that offered for *oats;* he defined *oats* as "a grain which in England is generally given to horses, but in Scotland supports the people." Webster's contributions were more clear and concise, but even he failed to simplify our spelling in such words as *women* and *tongue,* which might more logically be spelled *wimmen* and *tung.*

Despite these strong precedents, in 1857 the *Oxford New English Dictionary on Historical Principles* was planned to offer an inventory of the entire language, correct and incorrect, obsolete and current. Although it was not completed until 1933, the prestige of the thirteen-volume *Oxford* established the descriptive function of the dictionary. As expressed in the seventh edition of *Webster's New Collegiate Dictionary,*

> The function of a pronouncing dictionary is to record as far as possible the pronunciations prevailing in the best present usage, rather than to attempt to dictate what that usage should be. Insofar as a dictionary may be known and acknowledged as a faithful recorder and interpreter of such usage, so far and no farther may it be appealed to as an authority.

If the purpose of the dictionary is simply to describe language in terms of current best usage, how and when is the puzzled student to use it? Is there a danger of becoming too dependent upon it? In our opinion, there is such a danger. We have seen students whose only recourse for discovering meanings or pronunciation was to turn immediately to this source. Because of this dependence, such students had no powers of analysis or of retention. Every difficult word was sought in the dictionary every time it was met. Vocabulary growth was at a standstill, and most of these students found college or high-school study impossible.

Overdependence upon the dictionary is fostered not only by the belief in it as an absolute authority but also by several other common misconceptions. Many students act as though they believe that each word has *one meaning* or *a correct pronunciation,* which, of course, they expect to find in the dictionary. Furthermore, they seem to think that either they know a word (that is, that single meaning) or they don't know it.

As any intelligent user of the dictionary knows, hardly any word has a single meaning; many have variant pronunciations in various sectors of the country or in other English-speaking countries. Because of the multiplicity of meanings, we have a group of ideas about each word's meanings, rather than a precise knowledge of one meaning.

These impressions of word meanings, however vague, should be called upon when meeting a word in context. These ideas, plus the clues present in the context and the information present in the parts of the word, should be our first resources in attacking a new or difficult word. In an earlier chapter, we have emphasized a pattern of attack upon new words that includes delving into the context, pronouncing the word, looking for clues in its parts, and, in the case of technical terms, searching for a descriptive definition in the context. All these analytical steps should be employed before resorting to the final aid, the dictionary.

Let us sum up our concepts of what a dictionary is supposed to do. We have pointed out that its major function is to describe words in terms of their best and most frequent current usage. The dictionary is a very useful study aid, but overdependence upon it may stifle essential vocabulary growth or, in other words, retard the reader's ability to think.

What a Dictionary Can Do for You

Before we can hope to realize the values of a good dictionary, it is important that we understand why it is constructed as it is and what kinds of information it offers.

Vocabulary. Mark Twain is supposed to have remarked that the dictionary makes pretty dry reading. Yet it is probably the best single source for growth of vocabulary and hence for ability to deal with ideas. Where else could you obtain at a relatively inexpensive cost a list of 100,000 to 150,000 items—technical terms, dialect words, slang expressions, proper names, abbreviations, foreign phrases, literary allusions, idiomatic phrases, and other types of words? When we consider the wealth of information given for each of these terms, we can appreciate the dictionary as a wonderful source of ideas and ways of expressing them.

Spelling. Can you use the dictionary to find the spelling of a word? Some say not. How can you find a word when you don't know the letters it contains? But the task is really not this difficult, for you usually know what letters the sounds can represent. Let us say that in yesterday's class in religion, the professor used a word that sounded like *akĕlight*. You might try to find it in the dictionary, somewhat in this fashion.

1. The first syllable could be spelled *ack* or *ac* or *ak* or even *acc*. Suppose you decide to check *ac* and *acc* first.

2. The middle vowel is rather indefinite—it could be *a* or *e* or *o* or even *i*. No. It couldn't be *e* or *i* or the *c* preceding it would sound like *s*. It must be *a* or *o*, if *ac* or *acc* is correct.

3. The last syllable could be spelled *light* or *lite* or even *lyte*.

4. Let's start with *aca* and then go on to *aco*, checking *acca* and *acco* on the way.

After looking over less than half a page of words beginning with *aca*, you find the word you are seeking under *aco—acolyte*. The definitions clarify that this is a term used in religion to refer to an assistant or attendant. Now you know you have found the correct term.

What have you done to find the spelling of an unknown word? You have tried to guess how the sounds might be represented, then looked in the logical places in the dictionary, and, finally, checked your selection by the relevance of the meanings given for the term. If you have almost no ideas regarding the sounds of the beginning letters of a word you wish to spell, most college dictionaries offer a list of the common spellings of English sounds. Other spelling problems—the use of the hyphen, as in *un-American* or *unAmerican;* compound words or separates, such as *wind-up* or *windup;* capitals, as in *brussels sprouts* or *Brussels sprouts;* and numbers, such as *twenty one* or *twenty-one*—are readily solved by consulting the dictionary.

Some individual sounds of English can be represented in writing by a variety of letters or letter combinations. The long *a* sound, for example, can be spelled as in *rain, rein, break, trey, day, gauge,* as well as other ways. Even the same letter may have several different sounds, as the *s* in *sun, easy, vision,* and *sure.** But the dictionary makes one of its greatest contributions to our language despite these variations by stabilizing our spelling. Picture the confusion, as in George Washington's time, when everyone spelled according to his own ideas, as in *was, wuz, wuze, waz.* English never was a really phonetic language in that each letter stood for a single sound. The Latin alphabet, which forms the basis of our words, didn't have enough letters to represent such sounds as *v,* for example. Furthermore, the sounds in our language have changed considerably during its history, often without corresponding changes in ways of spelling. As a result we have such anachronisms as *bough, though, through, thought* and many others. Difficult though our language may be, you can learn to spell it better with the aid of your dictionary.

Meaning.   Some individuals would probably be happier if present-day dictionaries resembled some of the earlier versions in giving a single meaning for each term listed. If we only had simple, single definitions, students might feel reassured that they "knew the meaning." After all, words got their meanings a long time ago, some say. Why keep adding to them?

Unfortunately for such peace of mind, since 1750 dictionaries have recognized that words constantly change their meanings, acquiring new meanings through new uses and invention and losing old meanings as customs and habits change. Take the word *engine* as a typical example of a word that has lost its original meaning, acquired new ones, and is still changing. At one time *engine* meant anything that was used to effect a purpose, any means or method. A man or a broom might once have been the *engine* to accomplish something. Later the word came to mean a mechanical tool, such as rack used in torture or a ram used in warfare.† With the invention of the steam locomotive and gasoline engine, *engine* came to mean a piece of machinery used to produce power. Today we use the word in everyday speech to mean a locomotive or the engine of an automobile. In the near future, the word may come to mean simply an

---

* See the Appendix for detailed information on letter sounds in English.

† Note that these very examples, *rack* and *ram,* have, like *engine,* lost their original meanings.

apparatus operated by atomic power or jet propulsion. As we think back over these changes, we recognize a common idea in all of them—that an engine was something man used to do things. Who knows what *engine* may mean in the year 2000?

There are constant trends in the use of words that result in modification of their meanings. A word may become specialized and thus change from a broad, general concept to a special, narrow meaning. This type of change was present in *engine* and in such words as *gear, fission,* and *briefing.* An opposite trend in word meanings is the trend toward generalization. In this process, words lose their original specific significance and gradually broaden to cover many connotations. Words that have become highly generalized include *thing* (originally meaning an assembly), *clerk* (a clergyman), *line* (cord or rope), and *cell* (a small room).

Word meanings may shift toward more proper or elevated meanings or become degraded to lower, vulgar denotations. Among those evidencing elevation are *pastor* (originally a shepherd), *minister* (a servant), and *alderman* (an old man). The slang terms *hip* and *cool* may achieve elevated meanings, if they persist in common use. Degenerated words include *swear* (to take an oath) and *swell* (to enlarge or expand). In current slang, *square* now exemplifies this degenerative trend. Other changes in word meaning involve a successive substitution of related meanings. The word *cardinal* illustrates this trend. It began with the Latin *cardo,* meaning hinge or turning point, and in turn progressed through the successive meanings of main or chief; officer of the church (who wore a red robe); short hooded cloak of scarlet cloth; and currently, a color, cardinal red, or a bird, the male of which species has a bright-red plumage.

Still another trend in word meanings is that in which the denotation of a simple word radiates outward to express many variations on the original idea. *Care,* for example, meant mental suffering or grief but has been extended to mean: heavy anxiety, watchful attention, caution, liking, management, or supervision. Other words that have grown by the process of radiation include *power, force, rank, order* and *law,* to mention only a few.

The problem of how to handle these changes in meaning is still present, if you will scan closely several modern dictionaries. Some present the older meanings first and modern ones later in the entry. Others offer the most recent definition first. Some dictionaries label meanings that have long since passed out of common use as *archaic* or *obsolete.* Others simply drop such ancient uses to save space for the addition of more modern terms and definitions. If you use any dictionary consistently, and even more so if you jump from one to another, you must familiarize yourself with the practice observed in that source. Otherwise you may find yourself trying to use definitions now obsolete for some modern terms you meet. No matter how you feel about it, the dictionary offers a wealth of historical information in the growth of language as shown in the order and variety of meanings.

The use of a dictionary for meanings presents problems of interpretation and substitution. A given word may be used in a particular sense by the writer, and we must seek an interpretation of this use in the context. If it is not clear which sense of the word is intended, we try to substitute the meanings offered by the dictionary. This dual approach to word meanings lays the foundation for future vocabulary growth. But you will stultify this development if you constantly substitute the dictionary for the effort to use your own interpretation from context.

Synonyms and Antonyms.   At the end of the definitions of many words in college dictionaries you will find a list of words with meanings similar to that of the main entry. In some dictionaries, these are prefaced by the abbreviation *syn.* for *synonyms.* In others, they are simply listed in small capitals or some other distinctive type.

Woodrow Wilson is supposed to have said that no two words in English have precisely the same meaning. This statement is probably quite true, although we often treat words as though they were interchangeable in meanings. For example, *Webster's New Collegiate Dictionary* lists these words as synonyms for *secret: covert, stealthy, furtive, clandestine, surreptitious, underhand.* The implication is that they all have a common meaning. But do they? Only one of these synonyms would be correct in each of these sentences.

1. The spies met in ———— meetings in obscure parts of the city. (*underhand* or *clandestine* or *furtive?*)

2. The arrested man had a ———— look when he faced the court. (*secret* or *covert* or *furtive?*)

3. In a recent national election, the ———— funds of one of the candidates caused considerable comment. (*clandestine* or *secret* or *stealthy?*)

4. Some people seem incapable of frank relationships and apparently must deal in a ———— manner. (*covert* or *surreptitious* or *stealthy?*)

5. Most black-market dealings must be carried out in a ———— fashion. (*surreptitious* or *covert* or *furtive?*)

6. The sneak thief made his ———— way through the darkened house. (*secret* or *stealthy* or *clandestine?*)

7. "I think John's telling on the other children after they had gone home was a contemptible, ———— act." (*secret* or *furtive* or *underhand?*)

These examples demonstrate that synonyms are not interchangeable in meaning. Your answers should have been (1) clandestine; (2) furtive; (3) secret; (4) covert; (5) surreptitious; (6) stealthy; and (7) underhand. If synonyms are not really synonymous, then why does the dictionary list them? Simply to promote more precise use of words and to enable the reader to make fine discriminations in meanings as he reads or in his own speech or writing.

This help in making fine discriminations in meanings is also the reason for the inclusion of antonyms in many college dictionaries. Again, these words are not always the precise opposites of the meaning of the main entry, for they may be only approximately antonymous. Some authorities say there is only one exactly opposite meaning for any word. But, as with synonyms, the antonyms help to broaden and deepen the group of related ideas we have regarding a word's meaning. Thus they contribute to our understanding of words in their many uses and contexts and, in turn, to our comprehension of what we read.

Derivation. The colonists who came to America were for the most part from England and, of course, spoke their mother tongue in the form characteristic of that time. They soon found, however, that their English words were inadequate for naming things they met in the New World or for expressing some of the ideas they developed. The colonists were continually meeting new animals, new plants, different trees and fruits, unusual land formations different from those they had evolved names for in England. Therefore they began to develop many, many words to express their new ideas, their discoveries, and new ways of life.

From the Indians they borrowed names of animals, plants, places, and foods. They learned to recognize the opossum and racoon and to eat hominy, succotash, and pone. They discovered how to use the tomahawk and toboggan, to play lacrosse, and to recognize the hickory, butternut, and persimmon trees. They learned to speak of the Indian's customs with his own words, such as *squaw, papoose,* and *sachem.* They learned to use tobacco and to plant corn and squash and to use the Indian's words for these activities.

Other nations that sent settlers to our shores also contributed to the growth of the American language in Colonial times. From the Dutch we acquired such words as *patroon, snoop, waffle,* and *cruller;* from the Spanish settlers, *canoe, potato, tomato, chocolate,* and *barbecue.* In addition, the colonists invented new terms for a variety of new things such as *clearing, bottom land, bluff, hoecake, crazy quilt, spelling bee, mush.* The swarms of immigrants who came to America during the eighteenth and nineteenth centuries also brought with them many new words and terms. The total number of words contributed by these groups is not large, but it forms an integral, picturesque part of the American language.

In 1828 Noah Webster published the first real tabulation of the words used in America, in his *American Dictionary of the English Language,* which included some 70,000 words. Successive editions of this dictionary brought out by the Merriam-Webster Company have grown until they now reach a figure of over half a million entries.

Most of this growth in new words and terms has been due to the development of the arts and sciences, of industry, and of commerce, particularly in the nineteenth century. Thousands of these new words are due to the activities of scientists, finding new names for new processes, new products, new inventions and discoveries. Such sciences as entomology, chemistry, and botany are continually contributing new names, drawn largely from the classical languages.

Other significant sources of new words are blends or combinations of old words used to describe new ventures, such as *beanery, lubritorium, dogdom, preschool;* or new behaviors, such as *jaywalker, rubberneck;* or new inventions, such as *radar, sonar, jeep, bazooka, half-track, flak, mimeograph, Audiograph, Redi-whip.* American writers and newspapermen have given us *quake, Jap, Nazi, spellbinder,* and such clipped words as *gas, cab, bus* and *taxi.* Famous persons and places are a prolific source of words, as in *Listerine, pasteurize, cardigan* (after the Earl of Cardigan), *sandwich* (after the Earl of Sandwich, who wouldn't stop gambling for a regular meal), *Mae West* (a lifesaving jacket), and *madras* (after Madras, India).

Because the words of our language have come from so many sources, it has been necessary to evolve some way of labeling the sources. Most dictionaries use symbols or abbreviations to indicate the various sources from which a word has been derived. Here are examples of the manner in which etymology is treated in *Webster's New Collegiate Dictionary:*

> **channel** [OF *chanel* fr. L. *canalis.*]
> **check** [OF *eschec, eschac,* through Ar. fr. Per. *shāh,* king.]

These indicate that *channel* is derived from the Old French word *chanel,* which in turn came from the Latin term, *canalis.* In the second example, our word *check* began as a Persian word meaning king, was used in Arabic, then in Old French as *eschec* or *eschac.* In like manner, a simple derivation of each English or American word is given. Of course, the entire history of changes in each word or even all the languages in which a word has been used differently are not given in the ordinary dictionary. Such a study would take much more space than the average dictionary can give to etymology. Moreover, the full history of a word or the story of its various usages is not exactly what one expects to find in the usual dictionary. The average person using a dictionary has little use for such information. Complete etymologies, therefore, are found only in special dictionaries such as the *Oxford English Dictionary, A Dictionary of American English on Historical Principles,* and the *Dictionary of Americanisms.* Some of the more interesting stories of changes in words can be found in such books as G. and C. Merriam Company's *Picturesque Word Origins,* Barfield's *History in English Words,* and Weekley's *The Romance of Words.*

Some find the etymological information in their dictionaries both interesting and useful. Others are bored by it or ignore it completely, for they see no practical values. For the latter, we offer this reminder. Correct use of words and hence clear thinking cannot be achieved without some depth of understanding of word meanings and their evolution. For example, why are *eminent–imminent, amiable–amicable,* and *mobile–movable* not equivalent or interchangeable? What is the difference between *equity* and *equitation,* or between *chateau* and *castle,* or among *prophesy, presage, predict,* and *foretell?* Only by knowledge of their respective derivations can we make these essential discriminations.

Pronunciation. Several reading researchers have explored the feelings of college students regarding their earlier training in various reading skills. When asked to identify abilities in which they were inadequately trained, many college students mention skill in pronouncing long or difficult words. If we may read between the lines, these students are telling us that they are concerned because they cannot work out pronunciations on their own— that is, without using a dictionary.

Assuming that students are reflecting a real difficulty, there are several possible explanations for this problem. One is that they have not been taught to spell the common sounds of English, or how to use syllabication, or the basic principles for these two skills. This possible reason has been seized upon by a number of self-appointed critics of American schools and emphasized excessively in many popularized articles and books. Unfortunately, it is not true except in isolated cases. Every system of teaching reading in wide use in America has taught the sounds of English, and every American school child has been taught something about syllabication in his readers, his English texts, and his spellers. The self-reports of college students collected in the research mentioned earlier show that over 50 per cent of the students thought their training in syllabication had been adequate (or even excessive).

Another explanation for students' difficulties with pronunciation—one with twofold implications—is possible. First, although reasonably trained in phonics (letter sounds) and syllabication, many students have failed to make use of these skills in word analysis; these ideas just have not functioned in the students' attempts to pronounce words. Second, for unknown reasons, some students do not or cannot employ the dictionary as an aid to pronunciation. Both of these problems may reflect the way in which syllabication and phonics have been taught, indicating that their direct application to word analysis and pronunciation have never been made obvious. For example, many of the rules for syllabication and even some phonic rules have literally nothing to do with pronunciation. Some serve no other useful purpose than to tell us how to divide a word at the end of a line. You may know enough to divide into syllables between double consonants, or to join a consonant between two vowels to the second vowel, or to split adjoining consonants that don't form a blend; but does that knowledge help you pronounce an unknown word? You may know from the principles of phonics that when *y* is the final letter it has a vowel sound, and that the vowel in an accented syllable is usually short; but how much help is this information when it comes to pronunciation? *What* vowel sound will a final *y* have— long *i* as in *sky*, short *i* as in *pity*, or the vanishing vowel as in *they?* How do you know which is the accented syllable in which the vowel will be short, in an unknown word? Which of the many syllabic or phonic principles you once memorized now help you to pronounce an unfamiliar word?

If you are one of those students who have difficulty in attacking and pronouncing the new words you meet, we suggest the following steps:

1. Review the rules for letter sounds and for syllabication listed in the Appendix. Don't just try to memorize them; try them out on familiar words, or, if you like, on difficult words chosen from the glossary of one of your textbooks.

2. Work with each rule or convention until you have a feeling for it and can apply it almost unconsciously (without having to recite it to yourself).

3. If you own a good college dictionary, familiarize yourself with the pronunciation key it offers on the inside of the front cover and also at the bottom of each page. Again, *don't* try to memorize this material but rather to learn its arrangement and how to interpret it when you need it.

4. After you have tried your best to work out the probable pronunciation of a word, use your dictionary as a final guide, if you wish to avoid the embarrassment of public mispronunciation.

5. If you don't own a dictionary, but do consult one upon occasion, you may expect some problems in interpretation. Dictionaries vary in their marking of words to indicate pronunciation. *The Funk and Wagnalls* doesn't bother to mark short vowel sounds as in *end* or *pet*, whereas the *Merriam-Webster* and the *American College Dictionary* do. *The Funk and Wagnalls* and the *American College* use one symbol for all unstressed vowels, as in so*ci*al or so*f*a, whereas *Merriam-Webster* has a special symbol for each vowel when it is unstressed or indefinite. These variations are just another reason for having the dictionary you prefer on your bookshelf.

Usage.   The usage labels and information offered in the dictionary are not highly related to reading success. Discovering whether the word we have sought in the dictionary is usually a noun or a verb or some other part of speech does not often contribute to its interpretation in context. Because of our auditory experiences with sentence patterns, we can usually sense the function of the word, without having to check with the dictionary. We realize from its place in the sentence (or the intonation, pitch, or stress if we hear the sentence) that the word is representing the name of something, or an action, or has a descriptive or other function.

Similarly, we are not dependent in reading on recognizing whether a word is standard, slang, dialect, or obsolete in order to comprehend its meaning in context. These dictionary facts regarding word usage are not highly significant for the reading act. At best, their significance bears upon our word usage in writing or in speech and, to a very small degree, to deepening the group of associations we accumulate regarding a word; associations that may in the future aid in the interpretation of recurrences of a word in our reading.

We have included a section on usage in the Dictionary Test offered in the Appendix, not because such information is significant in reading, but because it is essential to completely adequate use of the dictionary as a resource tool.

Selecting a Dictionary

The selection of your own dictionary is largely a matter of your personal reactions to the leading college dictionaries. You will want to compare the five leading college dictionaries for yourself, perhaps at your nearest bookstore. To help in this direct comparison, here are a few statistics and descriptive facts regarding each.

American College Dictionary. New York: Random House, 1962.

More than 132,000 entries; 1,500 illustrations and spot maps; 1,472 pages; weight, 4 pounds.

Each entry has pronunciation; part of speech; inflected forms; area of usage; definitions, arranged from most common through special, general to obsolete and archaic; variant spellings; etymology; synonyms and antonyms.

Outstanding in variety of definitions, in medical terms, biographical and geographical entries.

Appendices: Signs and Symbols, A Guide to Usage, Colleges and Universities (in the United States).

Funk and Wagnalls' Standard College Dictionary. New York: Harcourt, Brace, and World, 1963.

More than 150,000 entries; 1,000 illustrations; 1,606 pages; weight, 4 pounds.

Each entry has pronunciation; etymology; inflected forms; restrictive labels; part of speech; definitions; variant spellings; synonyms and antonyms.

Outstanding in phrases, tables, abbreviations, and coverage of people and places.

Appendices: Vocabulary Building; Mechanics of English; Colleges and Universities of the United States and Canada; Signs and Symbols; Preparing a Manuscript for Publication.

Webster's New World Dictionary of the American Language, College Edition. Cleveland, Ohio: World Publishing Company, 1962.

142,000 entries; 3,100 illustrations and maps; 1,760 pages; weight, 4 pounds.

Each entry has pronunciation; part of speech; area of usage; inflected forms; etymology; definitions; usage labels; variant spellings; synonyms and antonyms.

Outstanding in foreign words and phrases; large type; large number of illustrations and maps; names of persons and places.

Appendices: Colleges and Universities in the United States; Junior Colleges of the United States; Canadian Colleges and Universities; Forms of Address; Tables of Weights and Measures; Special Signs and Symbols.

Webster's Seventh New Collegiate Dictionary. Springfield, Mass.: G. & C. Merriam Co., 1963.

130,000 entries; 1,000 illustrations; 1,220 pages; weight, 3 pounds.

Each entry has pronunciation; variant spellings; inflected forms; etymology; part of speech; usage label; synonyms and antonyms; principal parts; usage examples. Biographical and geographical material under separate alphabet.

Outstanding in coverage of physical and natural sciences, including scientific names; frequency and scientific thoroughness of revisions; forematter and appendices.

Appendices: Abbreviations; Symbols and Proofreader's Marks; Proof of Lincoln's Gettysburg Address; Biographical Names; Pronouncing Gazetteer; Forms of Address; Pronouncing Vocabulary of Common English Given Names; Vocabulary of Rhymes; Mechanics of English (spelling, plurals, punctuation, compounds, capitalization, italicization); Colleges and Universities in the United States and Canada.

Winston Simplified Dictionary, College Edition. New York: Holt, Rinehart and Winston, 1957.

More than 100,000 entries; 3,000 illustrations and maps; 1,280 pages; weight, 3½ pounds.

Each entry has pronunciation; part of speech; inflected forms; variant spellings; definitions; area of usage; etymology; synonyms and antonyms (some).

Outstanding in foreign phrases, Biblical words; characters in fiction and myth; maps.

Appendices: Signs and Symbols; Tables of Weights, Measures, and Standards; Foreign Words and Phrases; Names of Persons and Places; Concise Atlas of the World.

Summary

In this chapter, we have tried to present a simple interpretation of the true purpose of a dictionary and to review all the common uses and functions of a college dictionary. Finally, we have provided a brief overview of the five leading hard-cover college dictionaries to aid you in making a selection. Despite the tendencies of some students to be unduly impressed by the authoritative air of most dictionaries, or to be overdependent upon this tool as a vocabulary aid, we urge you to purchase the dictionary of your choice. If you use it sparingly but intelligently, your dictionary will be a very profitable investment during and after college years.

HELP YOURSELF

Some readers may have already developed a real interest in words and their history and in sources of information about this topic. Others will discover from the Dictionary Test in the Appendix that they are not very knowledgeable in the common uses of a dictionary. The sources listed here may serve both these types of students. Your instructor will be glad to help you select the references most suited to your needs.

Practice in Using a Dictionary

Braddock, Richard. *The University Self-Teaching Dictionary Guide.* New York: Holt, Rinehart and Winston, 1963. 24 pages. *A good brief review of dictionary use.*

Brown, Marion Marsh. *Learning Words in Context.* San Francisco: Chandler Publishing Co., 1961. *Devotes the first chapter to exercises on using the dictionary.*

Jennings, Charles B., Nancy King and Marjorie Stevenson. *Consider Your Words.* New York: Harper and Row, 1959. *Pages 84–139 provide a variety of exercises.*

Norwood, J. E. *Concerning Words and Phrasing.* New York: Prentice-Hall, 1956. *Several short chapters are devoted to the dictionary and certain of its functions.*

Sherbourne, Julia Florence. *Toward Reading Comprehension.* Boston: Heath, 1966. *Pages 44–74 and 219–25 offer a number of exercises on letter sounds and the dictionary.*

Triggs, Frances Oralind, and Edwin W. Robbins. *Improve Your Spelling.* Mountain Home, N.C.: The authors, 1944. *An excellent review for college students of English spelling. A self-teaching tool.*

Books on Word Origins

Bombaugh, C. C. *Oddities and Curiosities of Words and Literature.* New York: Dover, 1961. *A fascinating study of play with words in prose and poetry.*

Greenough, J. B., and G. L. Kittredge. *Words and Their Ways in English Speech.* New York: Macmillan, 1900, 1901, 1928, 1929, paperback 1961. *A classic.*

Holt, Alfred H. *Phrase and Word Origins.* New York: Dover, 1961. *Traces the origins of over 1,200 common words and phrases, in a very readable fashion.*

Shipley, Joseph T. *Dictionary of Word Origins.* Patterson, N.J.: Littlefield, 1961.

Weekley, Ernest. *The Romance of Words.* New York: Dover, 1961. *Style is unattractive, but the book contains much information on word origins.*

Books on Dictionaries

Gray, Jack C. *Words, Words and Words about Dictionaries.* San Francisco: Chandler Publishing Co., 1963. 207 pages. *A collection of excellent articles on dictionaries, their makers and their troubles.*

Mathews, M. M. *Words: How to Know Them.* New York: Holt, Rinehart and Winston, 1956. 121 pages. *Discusses dictionaries, their functions, and their values in vocabulary building.*

PART III

Applying Reading Skills

CHAPTER 11

READING IN COLLEGE SUBJECTS

In earlier chapters of this text, you have been introduced to a number of reading techniques that you will probably employ in your college work. In this part of the book, we would like to help you to gain skill in using these techniques in the different ways they will be needed in different college subjects. We intend that this part will help you realize, even more clearly than you now do, that the successful adult reader achieves his goals primarily because he is flexible in his reading habits.

Planning Purpose

The flexible reader does not approach each piece of material with the purpose of simply reading the best he can. Rather, he first tries to visualize the real purpose he is trying to accomplish, recognizing that purposes vary from one type of material or one type of content to the next. He attempts to establish this purpose by trying to answer the question, "What am I supposed to remember (or talk about or recite on) after having read this?" or "What sort of questions am I likely to have to answer?"

This planning of purpose is an essential first step in attempting to read almost any type of college material. Without this planning, the student may not control his rate of reading and hence may not achieve the degree or type of comprehension he intends. Without this prereading thinking, the student is literally reading blindly or, if you prefer, stupidly. How can one intelligently discuss or recite on a piece of material, or answer questions on it, if he doesn't know while he is reading what he is supposed to be able to recall? Comprehension isn't an automatic result of reading, as many experiments show. The reader retains only what he thinks is expected of him, and when he is not very clear in this expectation, he retains almost nothing of real value. For example, one experiment at Harvard University showed that most students, although able to answer a few superficial, multiple-choice questions on a selection, could not actually summarize it in their own words. In all probability, the reason for the inadequacy of depth of comprehension among these competent students was the lack of explicit directions prior to the reading. The students did not know what they were expected to retain and thus remembered only a few significant facts. They hadn't anticipated being asked to write an organized summation that would include their own reactions. Like most students, they just read as best they could for some general ideas.

Among the classes of one of the authors at the University of Florida, it has been found that when students are permitted (or urged) to read the questions before beginning a practice selection, comprehension is much improved. The group average in comprehension of a selection usually rises 20 to 25 per cent above that in trials in which prereading of questions is not stressed. The questions are often too numerous and detailed to remember precisely, but even a general idea of what the reader is expected to recall makes for markedly improved comprehension.

The purposes for reading any assignment, as evidenced by the instructor's expectations regarding students' learning, may be identified in any of a number of ways:

1. By reading any related questions in the syllabus, or course outline.

2. By paying careful attention to the remarks or questions offered by the instructor when he makes the assignment.

3. By reading any questions found in the textbook or in the accompanying workbook or laboratory manual.

4. By previewing related questions in a college review book or guide.

If none of these sources are available or very helpful, then preview the material to construct your own questions that will guide your reading. If necessary, write these into your outline as the major headings for each section of the assignment. Try consciously to imitate the kinds of questions usually demanded in this type of material by your instructor in class or in exams. Be sure to distinguish among questions that—

1. Stimulate discussion, such as "On what grounds could the British government defend its sales of rubber to the Chinese Communists during the Korean War?" or "Be prepared to discuss . . ." or "What is your viewpoint of . . ."

2. Demand inferences or implications, such as "What recent events may lead you to believe that many Northern urban dwellers do not favor complete civil rights for Negroes?" or "What happened as a result of . . . ?" or "What were the probable causes of . . . ?"

3. Ask for relationships or sequences, such as "What series of events led to . . . ?" or "What trends contribute to . . . ?" or "What economic changes resulted from . . . ?"

4. Emphasize the central thought or main idea, such as "What is the author's major thesis in this essay?"

5. Stress significant details, such as "Name the three . . ." or "Give the formula for . . ." or "State the principle of . . ." or "Among his major compositions, Beethoven's best known works are . . ." or "Sketch the life of a prominent American writer of the last half of the nineteenth century."

6. Involve your personal reactions, such as "Discuss . . ." or "What were your impressions of . . . ?" or "Contrast Pepys' concept of his role as a government worker with the concept you think is characteristic of modern civil-service employees."

Using Different Ways of Reading

Having planned the purposes for reading, the next logical step is to employ a method or way of reading that will result in accomplishing these goals. Five ways of reading were introduced in the opening chapters of this book. You practiced these methods in various types of reading situations. Presumably, you are now sufficiently familiar with each to use it when you think it appropriate. But how do you decide when to skim or to scan or to simply read rapidly? When do you combine all of these together into the complete act of study, as in the *PQRST* method?

Some of these distinctions are fairly obvious, no matter what college subject you are reading. You will preview almost everything you read, in order to clarify your purposes for reading and to decide on a method you will then use to complete the reading. Even such literary forms as poetry and drama and such esoteric materials as mathematical problems should be previewed for the best results in comprehension and accuracy. Some of these forms of reading do not lend themselves to previewing by reading topic and summary sentences, and so on, because their style does not follow a paragraph-by-paragraph arrangement. Even in some forms that do follow a paragraph arrangement, such as the short story, novel, letter or biography, there may not be a strict use of topic and summary sentences. In both of these types of material, you will probably preview by a kind of skimming—reading selectively at high speed to gain an over-all impression, as in a poem, a play, or a problem, or perhaps in a novel, a biography, or a short story.

The next step following the previewing to plan purposes is to choose a reading rate and method that will achieve the degree of comprehension necessary in this type of material. The rate at which you read and the manner in which you do it (skimming, scanning, studying, or reading rapidly) are dependent upon a number of factors. Your approach is determined by your answers to such questions as these:

How difficult is this material for me?
Very difficult—requires careful, slow reading or studying.
Somewhat familiar or easy—requires selective reading or skimming.
Very familiar or very easy—requires rapid reading.

What sort of questions will I have to answer?

Questions on details—require studying.

Questions on central thoughts, general impressions, personal reactions, leading to discussion—require some selective skimming or rapid reading, some careful reading.

Questions on relationships, inferences, outcomes, sequences—require some skimming or rapid reading, some careful reading.

Questions on specific details, names, dates, statistics—require scanning after complete reading.

Questions on author's organization, diction, use of figures of speech or symbolism, viewpoint, or bias—require some scanning or skimming after complete reading.

Questions on diagrams, figures, tables, charts, illustrations—require scanning after careful reading of related textual sections.

In purely recreational reading and in some types of supplementary reading where no specific report will be expected, your reading approach may well be selective, rapid reading for the most part. Occasionally you will want to read some portions more slowly and analytically.

You will notice that we are *not* saying that there is one best way to read each type of material, such as to study a textbook assignment, to skim a historical novel, to scan a reference book. The individual differences among readers and the variations in difficulty, style, and format of reading materials make it impractical to lay down hard and fast rules on reading techniques. Each time you read or study, it becomes your responsibility to choose a speed of reading and one or several methods of reading that will accomplish what you believe are the goals for the assignment.

Achieving Reading Flexibility

All the practice and suggestions in this book have only one significant goal—to help you to achieve reading flexibility. Our definition of the flexible reader is quite obvious. He is one who adjusts his rate, concentration, and method of reading to the specific purposes of each reading and to the difficulty of the material, as these appear to him. Are really good readers flexible in using varying approaches and rates of reading? Does this flexibility have any effect upon their academic success? Does it contribute anything to them personally in terms of enjoyment of reading, freedom from feelings of anxiety about grades, and so on? The answer to all these questions is a most emphatic "Yes!"

The flexible reader does his daily academic work more easily, without "blood, sweat, and tears." His grade average is significantly better during college years; his likelihood of dropping out much lower. College life takes on new dimensions of depth and meaning, because of the leisure time for active participation in campus activities and the freedom from tension, worry, and drudgery.

Can a college student be inflexible, a one-reading-method person, and still succeed in and enjoy college? Such an individual can struggle through college; our research indicates that not all poor readers necessarily drop out. Whether he really enjoys this struggle and does more than barely exist during this period is a very debatable point. In our work with college students, we have seen some who retained only one main idea in a three-minute skimming test, whereas the average retention was over seven ideas. Some students take nearly thirty minutes to scan for ten significant details (and then find only a few), whereas the average adult takes less than eight minutes to find eight of the ten details. Some read at a rate of less than one hundred words per minute, whereas the average for college students in materials of moderate difficulty is usually in the neighborhood of three hundred words per minute. In other words, some inflexible readers can't really skim for main ideas; they take three and one half times as long to scan for details (and then can't find them); and they read generally about one-third as fast as the average. Using these comparisons, it appears that the inflexible reader needs about three times as much time to complete his daily academic work, and yet often understands or retains less than the average. Some of these readers do get through college, particularly if they have one area of strong interest and aptitude, such as science or mathematics, which is not highly dependent upon flexibility. But their college years are hardly halcyon or as pleasantly memorable as those of more fortunate students.

Summary

We have tried again to emphasize the importance of achieving flexibility in reading, for greater ease and enjoyment of your work in college. We have also stressed the primary importance of planning your purposes in each reading and, consequently, of using different methods of reading or studying to accomplish these purposes. We have outlined various ways of planning purposes and related them to instructors' expectations for students' reading. We have suggested different ways of reading, in keeping with the difficulty of the material and the types of questions to be answered. Finally, we have mentioned some of the advantages that accrue to the flexible college or adult reader.

Selections for Reading Practice

Each reading selection in this chapter has been chosen as a sample of materials commonly used in each college or adult reading area. Each selection is planned as a complete exercise in planning your purpose, applying an appropriate reading method, demonstrating comprehension, and learning new vocabulary. The comprehension check on each reading will include a variety of questions phrased in the form of a short classroom quiz. The questions will resemble those often used by college instructors in each area in order to make the exercise as realistic as possible. Purposes for reading will be varied according to the subject and the common practices of instructors. Thus, the several exercises will give you a sample of the kinds of reading tasks you will face in different college subjects. Each will be an opportunity for you to test your ability to adopt your rate and comprehension and way of reading to college reading situations. At the close of each quiz, a Self-Appraisal section will aid you in evaluating your performances and your progress.

These college reading exercises need not be done in any set sequence in order for you to realize their values. If your instructor agrees, you might begin with the selections in areas of immediate concern to you, and progress later to other related subjects. If you need more exercises in reading in a certain area, you may make a selection from the sources in the list that follows.

HELP YOURSELF

These sources contain a number of sample reading selections from different college subjects. Most of them include a comprehension check, but you will have to make your own appraisal of your successes.

Bloomer, Richard H., *Reading Comprehension for Scientists.* Springfield, Ill.: C. C. Thomas, 1963. 213 pages. *Offers twenty scientific selections, arranged in order of difficulty. Comprehension is measured by the reader's skill in supplying omitted words.*

Cherington, Marie R. *Improving Reading Skills in College Subjects.* New York: Bureau of Publications, Teachers College, Columbia University, 1961. 141 pages. *Offers samples from nine major college subjects.*

Cosper, Russell, and E. Glenn Griffin. *Toward Better Reading Skill.* New York: Appleton-Century-Crofts, 1959. 268 pages. *Contains 26 selections from a half dozen fields. Comprehension and vocabulary checks plus discussion questions are appended to each.*

Glock, Marvin D. *The Improvement of College Reading.* Boston: Houghton-Mifflin Co. 1954. 307 pages. *In addition to samples from college fields, contains a number of selections for practice in skimming, rapid reading, detailed reading, and critical reading.*

Howland, Hazel Pope, Lawrence L. Jarvie, and Leo F. Smith. *How to Read in Science and Technology.* New York: Norman W. Henley, 1950. 264 pages. *Contains a great many short scientific selections offering practice in following directions, details, main ideas, problem-solving, graphic materials and so on.*

McDonald, Arthur S., and George H. Zimny. *The Art of Good Reading.* Indianapolis: Bobbs-Merrill, 1963. 426 pages. *Besides the 32 college reading selections, the authors offer a number of short chapters on how to read more efficiently and flexibly in college.*

Shaw, Phillip B., and Agatha Townsend. *College Reading Manual for Class and Individual Training.* New York: Thomas Y. Crowell, 1959. 237 pages.

Offers about 100 brief exercises from the fields of English, social science, and science. Each is followed by a comprehension check.

Wedeen, Shirley Ullman. *College Reader* and *Advanced College Reader.* New York: G. P. Putnam's Sons, 1958 and 1963. 250 and 252 pages. *Each book contains 50 short readings from a wide variety of college subjects. The advanced book is offered for upperclassmen.*

Instructions for Reading the Selections

1. Read the introductory material for suggestions on how to read each selection.

2. Follow the method of reading outlined in these directions.

3. Record the time required to read the entire selection.

4. Compute your actual reading rate by means of the Chart for Determining Rate of Reading at the back of this book.

5. Then answer the various types of questions after each selection.

6. Check your answers with the Answer Key and determine your score on each part of the quiz.

7. Read the Self-Appraisal section after each selection and evaluate your own reading performances.

Anthropology

This 1,000-word selection points up some needed refinements in the methods used by present-day anthropologists. Preview the selection and its questions, then read it for detailed, critical comprehension. After previewing, estimate your probable reading rate in words per minute. Write down the time when you begin reading and when you finish, in order to compute your actual rate later.

STARTED _____   FINISHED _____

TOTAL TIME _____

Needed Refinements in the Biographical Approach*

—CLYDE KLUCKHOHN

In some quarters during the past decade there has flourished uncritical enthusiasm over life histories. There has been a great overestimation of the place of the hastily gathered document set in only a general cultural context.

The personal document requires many safeguards of objectivity in the collecting and analysis of data, techniques of presentation, and rigorous, explicit interpretation. At best the life-long retrospective biography is an imperfect alternative to the contemporaneous, on-going life history, controlled by current observations and the current testimony of others. If, from a single culture, retrospective autobiographies, contemporaneous life histories, and episodic documents were collected by a number of observers of both sexes from a representative sample of the society, the gains to the study of culture and personality could be enormous. Commensurate energy and skill would, of course, also have to be expanded upon annotation, analysis and interpretation. Multiple techniques, carried out by multiple observers and analysts, are the key to the problem of "subjectivity."

Until recently, biographical materials collected by anthropologists have represented in most cases somewhat incidental by-products of field work oriented to an over-all description of a culture. Where life history documents have been taken at all they have been seen as a means to this end of ethnography. The majority of the published results are sketchy and too limited to objective events and description of customs. They do not give even the shadow of a life—merely the partially outlined skeleton, for the subject's reactions to these happenings has seldom been sought. Annotation has been limited and almost entirely restricted to cultural points. Hence we have, for the most part, merely interesting curiosities, enlivening material for teaching anthropological courses. A few ethnographic footnotes have been gleaned from them; a pitifully few theoretical questions have been asked. Internal contradictions have been dismissed as due to "inconsistency" in the informant rather than analyzed in personality terms. But if one end of a piece of paper reacts to sulphuric acid in one way and the other end to hydrochloric acid in another, this does not prove that the paper is inconsistent.

With the growth of interest in culture and personality and the development of field approaches, a few individuals have pioneered in establishing biographical research as a major objective of anthropological field work in its own right. During the past ten years four substantial biographies have appeared. Du Bois has published brief autobiographies of four men and four women from a single culture with the individual's dreams and associations, with Rorschachs, and with interpretations by a Rorschach expert and by a psychiatrist. Opler has almost ready for publication an extremely rich and long autobiography which will be intensively analyzed in both cultural and psychological dimensions. Much carefully designed field work is completed or under way. For example, John Adair and Evon Vogt have collected autobiographies from a large number of Zuni and Navaho veterans respectively and from an equal number of men in the same age group who did not leave their communities for the armed services. A clinical psychologist, Burt Kaplan, obtained Rorschachs and Thematic Apperception Tests from the same individuals.

In other words, a few anthropologists are no longer content to treat biographical work as a somewhat romantic diversion. The utility for cultural studies is generally accepted. It has been shown that life histories are not only helpful in establishing the range of conformity to patterns but also in indicating broad resemblances between groups of cultures. Still, most anthropologists do not show too much imagination in getting biographical materials. They continue to follow a flat and colorlessly standardized pattern. This is, in some measure, because the prestige

rewards within the anthropological profession are based upon the production of ethnographies or of scrupulous monographs on accepted topics
such as kinship, basketry, and the like. Unless the biographical approach
receives a comparable recognition, only an occasional field worker will
treat this area seriously. Actually, somewhat different professional training
is required for first-class work in the ethnographic and culture and personality fields. The gentle techniques that promote a free flow of spon-
taneous reminiscence are often incompatible with getting the specific
details and the cross-checking of data required in good ethnographic
work.

Refinements are required in two main areas of biographical research.
The first is that of library research, the second that of the design and
carrying out of field studies. With some honorable exceptions, American
anthropologists are notorious among social scientists for their neglect of
library research. Future field work could be much more specifically
pointed if intensive analyses of present materials were made and published. For the Navaho, for instance, personal narratives of at least a
hundred individuals are now available. They were collected by seven
different field workers and the age of the subjects ranges from grade
school children into old age. The variation in length and quality is great,
but at least eight of the documents are extremely substantial. One of the
most pressing needs of contemporary anthropology is extensive, sustained,
and high-quality library research upon collections of this sort. Unless a
greater proportion of available source materials is collated and synthe-
sized, field research will suffer materially, for the right questions will
not be asked.

Library research must get abreast of field research if investigations
in the personal document field are not to be dismissed by future historians of science as "much-advertised in some decades of the twentieth
century, often pretentious, but essentially unscientific in content, form,
and utility." Among other things, the studies of reliability which psychologists have carried out on personal documents are wanting in anthropology. A special phrasing of the problem might be to discover the
varying reliabilities of groups of judges who: (a) knew the culture of
the subject first-hand; (b) had done no field work but had studied the
relevant literature intensively; and (c) had no specialized preparation in
anthropology but training in social or clinical psychology. Other analyses
should consider systematically different subjects' accounts of the same
events, the varying selectivity or consistent emphasis in documents obtained from different subjects by the same field worker, the effects of a
given culture on the systematic distortion of verbal material, etc. Standardized techniques for content analysis also need to be developed.

Questions—Needed Refinements in the Biographical Approach

Main Ideas

1. The author suggests that life histories or biographies of persons drawn
   from a certain culture—
   a. may give a completely distorted view of that culture.   b. do not

permit adequate comparisons with other cultures.   c. must be supplemented by other types of records, for the sake of objectivity.
d. are the primary investigative tool of anthropologists.

2. One of the author's major objections to the biographical or life-history records is that—
a. they are entertaining but not informative.   b. they have served merely as subjective, general descriptions of a culture and its customs.   c. they fail to present a contemporary view of the culture.   d. their analysis is always limited to the enumeration of events in the life of the individual described.

3. Two necessary major changes in biographical research emphasized here are— (choose two)
a. better and more careful library research.   b. less romantic and more factual material.   c. more careful planning of the design of field studies.   d. more scientific, less pretentious records.

4. What do you conceive to be the author's main purposes in writing this selection?_____

_____

_____

_____

_____

_____

Details

5. Other objections to the biographical materials mentioned are— (choose as many as you wish)
a. their sparseness of details.   b. the tendency to ignore important theoretical questions.   c. their failure to recognize the interaction between the individual and the events of his life.   d. the lack of parallel, corroborative materials that permit more objective study.
e. the marked variations in clarity, style, and coherence among the recorders.   f. their emphasis upon the chronology of an individual's life.

6. The author praises several anthropologists who have used biographical research for—
a. including a complete life history of the individual.   b. including psychological and interpretative material in their reports.   c. attempting to reconcile the frequent inconsistencies among informants.   d. using a more logical organization of the life-history materials.

7. In the author's opinion, better library research by anthropologists would include—
a. more detailed analyses of all available parallel materials.
b. more attention to the specific details of ethnographic work.

c. concurrent studies of culture and personality.   d. more detailed studies on specific customs, such as basketry, agriculture, kinship.

8. The author is critical of the fact that professional prestige in anthropology is often based on—
a. the quality of the field studies reported.   b. the quantity of materials produced on unimportant details such as basketry.   c. the depth of the library research in related materials.   d. the complexity of the design or plan of the current field studies.

Vocabulary

Some of the following terms may have been new to you in this selection:

retrospective   collated
subjectivity   kinship
anthropologist   objectivity
culture   episodic
ethnography   annotation
Rorschach
Thematic Apperception
   Test

Check those you knew before reading the selection. Choose the correct definition or synonym for each word as used here to show how accurately you now understand these terms.

1. retrospective
   a. in inverse order.   b. applying to an earlier time.   c. looking back in time.

2. subjectivity
   a. dependence upon personal opinion.   b. lack of reliability.
   c. substantiality.

3. anthropologist
   a. a scientist.   b. student of natural man.   c. one who studies races and traits of man.

4. culture
   a. refinement.   b. behavior typical of a group.   c. excellence of taste and judgment.

5. ethnography
   a. study of guiding beliefs.   b. a branch of anthropology.
   c. study of moral principles of man.

6. Rorschach
   a. a cultural record.   b. an abbreviated life history.   c. a personality test.

7. Thematic Apperception Test
   a. a psychological test.   b. a detailed life history.   c. physical measurements.
8. collated
   a. recognized.   b. collected and compared.   c. piled in order.
9. kinship
   a. relationships among persons of common ancestry.   b. relationships among friends and relatives.   c. relationships among kissing cousins.
10. objectivity
   a. dependence upon factual grounds.   b. realism.   c. existence independent of mind.
11. episodic
   a. consisting of a series of loosely connected events.   b. a disease of animals.   c. consisting of a series of writings or letters.
12. annotation
   a. glossary or appendix.   b. critical or explanatory comments.   c. bibliography.

Check your answers with the Answer Key. Write down in the Self-Appraisal the total credits you receive for each portion of the test.

Self-Appraisal

Record your predicted and actual reading rates.
Predicted rate: ———— wpm.
Actual rate: ———— wpm.
What were your approaches to this material? Check those steps you used.

1. Previewed selection.
2. Previewed questions.
3. Wrote preview questions.
4. Skimmed some.
5. Took notes.
6. Underlined.
7. Reread some.
8. Skipped over some.

Was this an effective pattern of reading for you? What was your final sum of points in—

Main Ideas	————	(16 points or better?)
Details	————	(24 points or better?)
Vocabulary	————	(21 points or better?)
TOTAL	————	(61 points or better?)

Did you use steps 1, 2, 7, and possibly 3 or 5 in your pattern? Or did the material seem easy enough to let you omit some of these? Does your score on the test support your choice of steps?

Was your comprehension adequate in each type of question? If not, what steps should you be taking to improve it?

Was your rate controlled to result in adequate comprehension? Was your predicted rate within 25 to 50 words per minute of your actual rate?

Did you know the terms you thought you knew? Did you learn others by reading the selection? The context was not very helpful here in clarifying the meaning of many of the new terms, was it? But you might have obtained some clues to their meanings by structural analysis, or attention to their roots and affixes. For example, did you recognize the combining forms *anthrop-*, meaning "manlike," and *-logy*, "science of"; *ethno-*, "race," and *-graphy*, "record"; or the stem *episode* in *episodic;* or the addition of *an-* to *notation* to give *annotation*, "notes or marks"; or *retro-*, meaning "back" plus *spect*, meaning "look" in *retrospective?*

Did you make any mistakes in handling this material effectively, such as the following?

Reading too rapidly for detailed comprehension. (See your score in Details.)

Reading too cautiously or in too great detail. (Failing to get minimum score on Main Ideas?).

Failing to get the main ideas by previewing. (Compare your questions with the instructor's.)

Overestimating your actual reading rate. (Because of failure to recognize the real difficulty of the material while previewing?)

Paying too little attention to new or technical words. (See your score in Vocabulary.)

Failing to try to organize the material in order to retain it. (Omitting all such organizational steps as 3, 5, 6, or 7 from your pattern?)

Art

This 1,000-word selection reviews some of the trends in early Japanese art and architecture. Preview the selection and its questions, then read it for detailed comprehension. After previewing, estimate your probable reading rate in words per minute. Write down the time you begin reading and when you finish, in order to compute your actual rate later.

STARTED ——————————   FINISHED ——————————

TOTAL TIME ——————————

Japanese Art[*]

The arts of Japan have neither the stylistic continuity of the Indian nor the wide variety of the Chinese. A series of foreign influences sporadically affected the course of Japan's artistic evolution. Yet, no matter how overwhelming the impact of new forms and styles, the indigenous

[*] From Helen Gardner's *Art Through the Ages*, Fourth Edition, Revised by Sumner McK. Crosby, copyright, 1926, 1936, 1948, © 1959, by Harcourt, Brace & World, Inc.; copyright 1954, by Louise Gardner, and reprinted by permission of the publishers.

tradition invariably reasserted itself. Hence the artistic pattern evolved in a rhythmic sequence of marked periods of borrowing, of absorption, and of return to native patterns.

Japan and its nearby islands are of volcanic origin so that there is little stone suitable for carving or building. In architecture this lack led to the development of wooden construction, carefully devised to withstand the frequent earthquakes and tempests. In sculpture, figures were either modeled in clay, which was often left unfired, or cast in bronze by the *cire perdue* process, familiar to many other cultures, or constructed of lacquer. Although the technique of lacquer probably originated in China, Japanese artists excelled in creating large, hollow lacquer figures by placing hemp cloth soaked in the juice of the lacquer tree over wooden armatures. The surfaces were gradually added to and finished, but the technique remained one of modeling rather than of carving. Such figures were not only light but very durable, being hard and resistant to destructive forces. Hollow lacquer was gradually superseded by carved sculpture done in wood, with unusual sensitivity for grain and texture.

The earliest arts of Japan were produced by a people of an ethnic group different from that of the later Japanese. The first artifacts known in Japan are pottery vessels and figurines from a culture designated as Jomon, which apparently flourished in the first millennium B.C. These objects are associated with Neolithic tools, although they persisted in northern Japan as late as the fourth or fifth century A.D. while a metal culture was being fully developed in the south. The Jomon arts may have been produced by the Ainus, a people who still survive on Hokkaido, Japan's northern-most island. The Ainus did not paint their pottery, as most Neolithic peoples did. Instead, they carved the clay with geometric and curvilinear patterns, some of which were apparently taken from designs on Chinese bronzes of the Late Chou period. Grotesque figurines with stubby arms, accentuated hips, and goggle-shape eyes are another strikingly original aspect of Jomon pottery which contrasts strangely with later Japanese art.

The development of more typically Japanese forms began about the same time as the advent of the Christian era. Objects from this period fall into three categories: (1) those imported from the Asian mainland, (2) those copying imported articles, and (3) those of Japanese invention. There are, for instance, bronze mirrors from Han China as well as replicas made in Japan. Some of the replicas are adorned with a Japanese innovation—spherical rattles attached to the perimeter of the disk. From Korea, on another wave of continental influence, came a gray pottery known as *yayoi*, which was soon copied, and small comma-shaped stones (*magatama*) used as necklaces. A third area—Indo-China—was the source of motifs used on bell-shaped bronzes known as *dotaku*. Houses and boats depicted on these bronzes are the same as those on contemporaneous drums of Annam in Indo-China. Within this heterogeneous culture the Japanese spirit began to assert itself in the production of *haniwa*. These are sculptured tubes made of pottery and placed fencelike around burial mounds, possibly to control erosion and also to act as protectors of the dead. The upper parts of these curious objects are usually modeled in human form, but sometimes they are in the shape of a horse, a bird, or even a house. Simple pottery cylinders were used similarly in Indo-China, but the sculptural modeling of *haniwa* is uniquely Japanese. The form of the tube so conditioned the representation that arms and legs as well as the mass of the torso in most instances recapitulated the cylindrical base of the *haniwa*. The tubelike character of some later monumental sculpture and even of the common wooden dolls may have been derived from these remote ancestors.

Architecture was first limited to pit dwellings and simple constructions of thatched roofs on bamboo stilts, but we learn from *haniwa* models that wooden architecture was fully developed by the fifth century, some buildings containing such features as two stories, saddle roofs, and decorative gables. There may have been monumental constructions of wood, but nothing remains from this early period except for colossal mounds which were the tombs of rulers. The *tumulus* of Nintoku, who, according to legends, reigned from ca. 395–427, has an over-all length of 1,600 feet and rises 130 feet from the ground. Three concentric moats protect the mound, which once must have been surrounded by *haniwa* guardians.

The native traditions which were being established at this time were interrupted in 552 by an event of paramount importance to Japan. In that year the ruler of Kudara (Paikche), a kingdom in Korea, sent a gilt bronze figure of the Buddha to Kimmei, emperor of Japan. With the image came the gospels. For half a century the new religion met with opposition, but at the end of that time Buddhism and its attendant arts were firmly established in Japan. Among the earliest examples of Japanese art serving the cause of Buddhism are a bronze sculpture of Yakushi, the Buddha of medicine, and a triad of Shaka (Sakyamuni); the first was cast in 607, the second in 623. Both were made by Tori Busshi, a third-generation Korean living in Japan. Tori's style is that of the mid-sixth century in China. His work proves how tenaciously the formula for a "correct" representation of the icon had been maintained since the introduction of Buddhism almost a century earlier. Yet at the same time a new influence was coming from Sui China. This may be seen in the cylindrical form and flowing draperies of the wood sculpture known as the Kudara Kwannon (Chinese: Kuan-yin). The two types were blended, and in the middle of the seventh century they coalesced in one of Japan's finest sculptures, the *Miroku* (Sanskrit: Maitreya) of the Chuguji nunnery at Horyuji. In this figure the Japanese artist combined a gentle sweetness with formal restraint in a manner unknown in Chinese sculpture.

Questions—Japanese Art

Main Ideas

1. The author's general purpose in this selection was to—
   a. emphasize the lack of originality in much of Japanese art.
   b. show that Japanese artists were largely imitators of other artists.   c. indicate that the Japanese artists and architects had

a unique, distinctive style.   d. illustrate that Japanese art had its own traditional style, despite its periods of borrowing from other cultures.

2. Because most of the islands of Japan are of volcanic origin—
   a. architects and sculptors had to depend upon wood or clay rather than stone for their medium.   b. houses must be built of the most durable materials to withstand frequent earthquakes.   c. the hardships in deriving a living from the poor soil delayed development of the native arts.   d. few examples of early Japanese architecture are available for study today.

3. It would appear to be characteristic of Japanese art that—
   a. most of its form and style were simply imitations of other cultures.   b. the forms and styles sometimes borrowed were rapidly modified and improved by Japanese creativity.   c. there were no outstanding forms and styles peculiar to these people.   d. each new trend in art was stimulated by an idea or artifact imported from a neighboring country.

Details

4. Name three other cultures from which Japanese artists borrowed ideas at various times and give at least one concrete example of a form or style or object that was imitated in each case._____

   _____

   _____

   _____

   _____

   _____

   _____

   _____

   _____

   _____

   _____

   _____

5. The earliest arts of Japan were—
   a. very similar to the contemporary work.   b. borrowed from the Chinese.   c. produced by a group called the Ainus.   d. of unknown origin.

6. Japanese lacquer figures were made by—
   a. building a hollow figure of successive layers of cloth soaked in lacquer.   b. modeling many layers of lacquer-soaked cloth on a wooden core.   c. shaping the stiffened cloth (soaked in lacquer) into various figures.   d. applying layers of lacquer to carved wooden figures.

7. The Jomon pottery and figurines produced by the Ainus—
   a. were decorated by many cabalistic figures and designs.   b. were finished in a variety of bright paints.   c. were carved with geometric patterns and left unpainted.   d. were similar to the work of other peoples of the Neolithic period.

8. Jomon figurines were—
   a. quite similar to those of contemporary peoples in other parts of the world.   b. carved with geometric and curvilinear patterns.   c. much like those produced in later periods of Japanese art.   d. goggle-eyed and grotesquely shaped in body.

9. The haniwa represent an example of—
   a. typical Japanese borrowing.   b. early Japanese art.   c. decorations of Japanese burial mounds.   d. typical Japanese artistic improvement of a simple artifact borrowed from another culture.

10. The introduction of the Buddhist religion to Japan—
    a. delayed markedly the spread of Christianity.   b. resulted in many Japanese art objects devoted to this faith.   c. brought with it a strong Chinese influence upon Japanese art.   d. had little or no impact upon the traditional style.

Vocabulary

Several of the following terms may have been new to you:

indigenous   armatures
artifact   ethnic
haniwa   curvilinear
coalesced   recapitulated
sporadically   icon

Check those you knew before you read the selection. Choose the correct synonym or definition for each term as used in this selection to show how well you now understand these terms.

1. indigenous
   a. natural.   b. native to the group.   c. foreign.

2. artifact
   a. pottery.   b. primitive art object.   c. figurine.

3. haniwa
   a. carved tubes.   b. grave markers.   c. hollow lacquer figures.

4. coalesced
   a. dissolved.   b. resulted in.   c. blended or merged.

5. sporadically
   a. significantly.   b. slightly.   c. at irregular intervals.

6. armature
   a. wire wound on a core.   b. a crude form used as the base of a built-up sculpture.   c. a carved wooden figure finished in lacquer.

7. ethnic
   a. pertaining to a racial group.   b. pertaining to foreigners.
   c. proper or ethical.

8. curvilinear
   a. composed of geometric shapes.   b. composed of curved lines.
   c. based on Chinese design.

9. recapitulated
   a. repeated.   b. recounted.   c. surrendered.

10. icon
    a. model.   b. statue.   c. representation of a deity.

Check your answers with the Answer Key. Write down in the Self-Appraisal the total credits you receive for each portion of the test.

Self-Appraisal

Record your predicted and actual reading rates.
Predicted rate: ———— wpm.
Actual rate: ———— wpm.
What were your approaches to this material? Check those steps you used.
1. Previewed selection.
2. Previewed questions.
3. Wrote preview questions.
4. Skimmed some.
5. Took notes.
6. Underlined.
7. Reread some.
8. Skipped over some.
Was this an effective pattern of reading for you? What was your final sum of points in—

Main Ideas   ———— (16 points or better?)
Details   ———— (28 points or better?)
Vocabulary   ———— (18 points or better?)
  TOTAL   ———— (62 points or better?)

Did you use steps 1 and 2 as instructed? Did the difficulty of the material or the detailed nature of the questions alert you to the need for step 7 and possibly 3 or 5?

Was your comprehension adequate in each type of question? If not, why not? Was your predicted rate within 25 to 50 words per minute of your actual rate? Was your rate appropriate to detailed comprehension?

Did you know the terms you thought you knew? Did you learn some of the new ones in reading the selection? Most of them should have been clarified by the context, if you read carefully.

Did you make any mistakes in handling this material effectively such as the following?

Reading too rapidly for detailed comprehension. (See your score in Details.)

Reading too cautiously or in too great detail. (Failing to get minimum score on Main Ideas?)

Failing to get the main ideas by previewing. (Compare your questions with the instructor's.)

Overestimating your actual reading rate. (Because of failure to recognize the real difficulty of the material while previewing?)

Paying too little attention to new or technical words. (See your score in Vocabulary.)

Failing to try to organize the material in order to retain it. (Omitting all such organizational steps as 3, 5, 6, or 7 from your pattern?)

Astronomy

This 1,000-word selection offers a brief review of recent changes in our concepts of space. Preview the selection and its questions, then read it for detailed comprehension. After previewing, estimate your probable reading rate in words per minute. Write down the time you begin reading and when you finish, in order to compute your actual rate later.

STARTED _____   FINISHED _____

TOTAL TIME _____

The Nature of the Universe*

Man's view of the universe has been enormously expanded during the decades since the close of the second world war, primarily because of the new techniques of radio astronomy and the space probe. It was, however, the introduction of the great optical telescopes which led to the major revolution in our ideas about the size and organization of the cosmos. Until twenty-five or thirty years ago we still believed that the system of stars visible in the sky on any clear night, and known as the Milky Way, was confined in space and itself represented the totality of the universe. Even so short a time ago we believed that the sun, the earth, and the attendant planets were situated at the centre of this system of stars, and that the sun was a typical star and seemed bright because it was close to us. The stars appeared faint, not because they were small and insignificant, but because they were at great distances. Nevertheless we believed that we were privileged to be situated in the centre of this assembly. It was estimated that there were many thousands of millions of stars in this Milky Way system and they were believed to be distributed in an approximately spherical enclosure of a size such that it

* Pp. 1–4, "The Nature of the Universe" from *The Exploration of Outer Space* by Sir Bernard Lovell. Copyright © 1962 by A. C. B. Lovell. Reprinted with permission of Harper & Row, Publishers, Incorporated, and Oxford University Press.

would take a ray of light travelling 186,000 miles a second a few thousand years to traverse it. These ideas have been changed completely.

The investigations which were carried out by the American astronomers in the few years after 1920 following the opening of the 100-inch telescope on Mount Wilson showed that this egocentric view was wrong; that, in fact, the stars of the Milky Way were arranged in a disc of extent such that a ray of light would take a hundred thousand years to traverse the distance separating the extremities of the stars, and that the system was asymmetrical. If one could remove oneself from the Milky Way system and look back on it through a large telescope then the stars would appear to be arranged in a flattened disc with the stars concentrated in spirals radiating from the central hub like a giant octopus. It was realized too that the sun, far from being at the centre of this disc of stars, was situated in an unfavourable position somewhere near the edge of the disc.

We know that this Milky Way system or local galaxy contains about one hundred thousand million stars. The earth is a planet of the sun's family, 93 million miles away. The most distant planet in our solar system, Pluto, is a few thousand million miles distant, so far away that the light from the sun takes about 6½ hours on its journey towards the planet Pluto. These distances, which are still just conceivable in terrestrial terms, are minute compared with the distance which separates our solar family from the nearest star in space. In order to describe these distances it is convenient to use the expression known as the "light years," which is the distance which a ray of light travels during the course of a year. The speed of light is 186,000 miles per second; the light from the sun takes 8 minutes on its journey, therefore the sun is at a distance of 8 light minutes. The light from Pluto takes 6½ hours on its journey to earth so Pluto is 6½ light hours away. On the other hand the nearest star is enormously more distant, so far away that the light from it takes 4½ years on its journey.

It is important to realize that our knowledge in astronomy is almost entirely of time past. We have no knowledge whatsoever of time present. Our knowledge of the sun is 8 minutes old, our knowledge of the nearest star is 4½ years out of date, and our knowledge of some of the stars which we see in the Milky Way may be a hundred thousand years out of date because the light from these stars has taken a hundred thousand years on its journey through space towards us. The presence in the sky of faint nebulous patches had been known for a very long time and in fact Herschel speculated in the nineteenth century that these nebulae might indeed be other systems of stars outside our Milky Way system; but it was not until the 100-inch telescope on Mount Wilson came into use that Hubble was able to show that this was indeed the case. There is such a nebulous object, visible to the naked eye under good conditions, in the constellation of Andromeda. We know that this object is not a nebulous region of gas amongst the stars of the Milky Way but another great system of stars so far away that the light from it has taken 2 million years on its journey towards us. This M_{31} nebula in Andromeda is outside our own galaxy or Milky Way system, 2 million light years distant. In many respects it seems that our own Milky Way system is very similar to this spiral galaxy in Andromeda, not only in the spiral arrangement of the stars but also in size and stellar content. As seen through the great optical telescopes, space appears to be populated everywhere with these galaxies of stars. Extragalactic nebulae are scattered to such great distances that at the limit of our penetration the light from the galaxies has been thousands of millions of years on its journey through space towards us. Within this observable region of the cosmos there must be trillions of galaxies of stars which are bright enough to be recorded on the photographic plate of the 200-inch Palomar telescope.

These tremendous changes in our view of space have been brought about largely because of the introduction of the big optical telescope. It is over 300 years since Galileo first used a small telescope to look into space and since that time man has appreciated that his penetration into space increases with the size of the telescope. The development of the optical telescope, although pioneered in the eighteenth and nineteenth centuries by Lord Rosse and Herschel in the United Kingdom, became the prerogative of the American continent in the twentieth century. The 100-inch telescope on Mount Wilson came into use in 1918, and the 200-inch on Mount Palomar twenty years later.

Questions—The Nature of the Universe

Main Ideas

1. One of the more dramatic results of the use of large telescopes was the realization that—
   a. the sun is not the center of our local galaxy.   b. we learn astronomical facts long after they have occurred.   c. the universe is infinitely larger and more complex than we had imagined.   d. the earth is simply a planet of the sun's family.

2. A second important discovery arising from use of large telescopes was the fact that—
   a. we had miscalculated the distances among the members of the sun's family.   b. the distances between us and other stars was greater than we had thought.   c. light travels much faster than we had estimated.   d. our system of stars, the Milky Way, is only one of many such galaxies.

3. Much of our knowledge in astronomy is composed of facts about events long past, because—
   a. astronomy is an ancient science.   b. light from the stars we see has taken a long time to reach us.   c. our early telescopes were too small for accuracy.   d. the nearest star is 4½ light years away.

Details

4. By the use of great telescopes, the size of the Milky Way was finally established as—
   a. several thousand light years.   b. at least 100,000 light years.
   c. 4½ light years.   d. 8 light minutes.

5. The constellation of Andromeda includes—
   a. a nebulous region of gas.   b. another group of stars in the Milky Way.   c. another solar family.   d. a spiral galaxy as great as the entire Milky Way.

6. It is quite possible that we shall discover that—
   a. some other planets are populated.   b. most stars are farther away than we thought.   c. space is populated with many galaxies like our Milky Way.   d. some stars are 2 million light years from us.

7. What other recent developments are contributing to our knowledge of space, besides large telescopes?_____

   _____

   _____

   _____

   _____

Vocabulary

Some of the following terms may have been new to you in this selection:

cosmos   nebula
galaxy   Milky Way
terrestrial   light year

Check those you knew before reading this article. Choose the correct definition or synonym for each term as used here, to show how accurately you understand these terms.

1. cosmos
   a. the world.   b. the entire universe.   c. the solar family.

2. galaxy
   a. a system of stars.   b. the Milky Way.   c. Andromeda.

3. terrestrial
   a. of the earth.   b. human.   c. astronomical.

4. nebula
   a. vague.   b. area of apparent gas or dust in space.   c. a complex constellation or galaxy.

5. Milky Way
   a. the universe.   b. a local galaxy.   c. system of stars visible from earth.

6. light year
   a. distance traveled by light from the sun to the earth.   b. distance traveled by light in one year.   c. time elapsed for passage of light from a star to earth.

Scanning

To answer these questions, go back over the selection quickly, if you need to. Time yourself for the answering of these questions.

1. The speed of light is—
   a. 93 million miles per minute.   b. 186,000 miles per second.
   c. 100,000 miles per year.   d. 186,000 miles per minute.
2. The size of the Milky Way is estimated to be—
   a. 100,000 light years.   b. a few thousand years.   c. 2 million light years.   d. 4½ light years.
3. The distance from earth to the sun is—
   a. 100,000 light years.   b. 93 million miles.   c. 4½ light years.
   d. 8 light years.
4. The distance from earth to the nearest star is—
   a. 8 light minutes.   b. 2 million miles.   c. 4½ light years.
   d. 93 light years.
5. The Milky Way probably includes about—
   a. 93 million stars.   b. 100,000 stars.   c. 2 million stars.
   d. 100,000 million stars.

Check your answers to these questions with the Answer Key. Write down in the Self-Appraisal the total credits you receive for each part of the test.

Self-Appraisal

Record your reading rates and scanning time.
Predicted rate ———— wpm.
Actual rate ———— wpm.
Time for scanning ————.
What were your approaches to this material? Check those steps you used.
1. Previewed selection.
2. Previewed questions.
3. Wrote some preview questions.
4. Skimmed some.
5. Took some notes.
6. Underlined.
7. Reread some.
8. Skipped over some.
Was this an effective pattern of reading for you? What was your final sum of points in—

Main Ideas   ————   (26 points or better?)
Details   ————   (16 points or better?)
Vocabulary   ————   (12 points or better?)
Scanning   ————   (9 points or better?)
TOTAL   ————   (63 points or better?)

Did you use steps 1 and 2 as directed, and possibly 3, 5, or 7 also? Was your comprehension adequate in every area? If not, why not? What might you do to improve in any of the types of questions?

Was your rate appropriate for detailed comprehension? Did you estimate your rate within 25 to 50 words per minute?

Did you really know the vocabulary terms you thought you knew? Did you learn any others in reading the selection?

How long did it take you to find the answers in the Scanning section— two or three minutes? Did you find all the correct answers in this section? Do you need to improve this skill?

Did you make any mistakes in handling this material effectively, such as the following?

Reading too rapidly for detailed comprehension. (See your score in Details.)

Reading too cautiously or in too great detail. (Failing to get minimum score on Main Ideas?)

Failing to get the main ideas by previewing. (Compare your questions with the instructor's.)

Overestimating your actual reading rate. (Because of failure to recognize the real difficulty of the material while previewing?)

Paying too little attention to new or technical words. (See your score in Vocabulary.)

Failing to try to organize the material in order to retain it. (Omitting all such organizational steps as 3, 5, 6, or 7 from your pattern?)

Biology

This 1,250 word selection is drawn from the lectures of a famous zoologist. It contrasts several interpretations of the causes of mutations. Preview the selection and its questions, then read it for detailed comprehension. After previewing, estimate your probable reading rate in words per minute. Write down the time you begin reading and when you finish, in order to compute your actual rate later.

STARTED   _____   TOTAL TIME _____
FINISHED   _____

Definition of Mutation*

The mutation concept has had a tortuous history. Not only has the term changed repeatedly in meaning, but even now it is being used in at least two different senses. Alternatives to the term "mutation" have been proposed, but all of them have failed of adoption. Many years ago Waagen (1869) designated as mutations the smallest perceptible changes

* Theodosius Dobzhansky, *Genetics and the Origin of Species,* Second Edition (New York: Columbia University Press, 1941). Reprinted by permission.

in the temporal series of forms in a species of ammonites; these changes have a definite direction, and their gradual accumulation with the passage of time leads to the appearance of types progressively more distinct from the progenitor. To what extent Waagen's mutations correspond to the mutational steps observed by geneticists is an open question.

The creators of the mutation theory were Korjinsky and De Vries. The latter (De Vries, 1901) defines it as follows: "As the theory of mutation I designate the statement that the properties of organisms are built from sharply distinct units . . . Intergrades, which are so numerous between the external forms of plants and animals, exist between these units no more than between the molecules of chemistry." A mutation is, then, a change in one of the units which at present are known as genes. The comparison of genes with chemical molecules may prove to be a truly prophetic one. Thus far De Vries's statements have a decidedly modern ring. De Vries proceeds, however, to define the distinctions between his mutation theory and Darwin's selectionism: "The latter [selectionism] assumes that the usual or the so-called individual variability is the starting point of the origin of new species. According to the mutation theory the two [individual and mutational variabilities] are completely independent. As I hope to show, the usual variability cannot lead to a real overstepping of the species limits even with a most intense steady selection . . ." On the other hand, each mutation "sharply and completely separates the new form, as an independent species, from the species from which it arose." Since De Vries's "species" are evidently not identical with the usual, or Linnaean, ones, an attempt was made to introduce the term "elementary species" for the former. This attempt has met with little sympathy, not only because the word species was here used in an entirely new sense, but especially because in sexually reproducing organisms one would have to consider almost every individual an elementary species. Furthermore, it is clear at present that the individual variability, in so far as it is hereditary at all, is due to the fact that the populations of most species are mixtures of types differing from each other in one or in several genes. Finally, the mutants obtained by De Vries in his classical investigations with Oenothera proved to be an assemblage of diverse changes, including gene alterations, segregation products due to a hybridity of the initial material, and chromosomal aberrations.

The studies begun by Morgan in 1910 on mutability in the fly *Drosophila melanogaster* constitute a turning point in the history of the mutation theory. Although mutations occur as sudden changes, in the sense that no gradual passage through genetic conditions intermediate between the original and the mutant types is observed, the distinction which De Vries has attempted to draw between individual and mutational variability does not exist. The amount of change produced by a mutation, as measured by the visible departure from the ancestral condition in the structural and physiological characters, varies greatly. Since mutants which are recognizable even to an untrained eye are most useful in experiments, such mutants are preserved while the slight ones are generally discarded; this has created a false impression among some biologists that all Drosophila mutants show striking visible alterations. Slight mutants, falling well within the normal range of individual variability, have been observed by Johannsen (1909) in beans, and Morgan (1918) has repeatedly emphasized that they occur in Drosophila as well. Baur (1924) found small mutations to be very common on the snapdragon (*Antirrhinum majus*). Small and large mutations are not distinct classes as some writers have implied.

From the very beginning of the work on *Drosophila* it has become clear that most mutations behave as changes in single Mendelian crosses between the ancestral and the mutant type. Since Mendelian segregation and recombination constitute the twin bases on which the existence of genes is inferred, the conclusion is drawn that most mutations represent gene changes. The nature of these changes is, however, a different problem. If a gene is a self-reproducing unit in a chromosome endowed with a definite chemical structure, alterations of this structure which permit the changed particle to retain its autosynthetic functions might be a source of the mutational variability. It would seem reasonable to restrict the term "mutation" to apply to this, and only to this, kind of change. Such a restriction leads, however, to grave difficulties in practice, since no methods are available for a direct comparison of the chemical structures of the ancestral and the mutated genes. The sole evidence of the occurrence of a change in the gene is the appearance of a phenotypic variant, a mutant, which follows Mendel's law in inheritance. Yet a loss (deficiency) or a reduplication of a part of a chromosome likewise results in phenotypic alterations that show Mendelian inheritance. Similar effects may be produced by rearrangements of the genic materials within the chromosomes (inversion, translocation). Finally, reduplications and losses of whole chromosomes may simulate Mendelian units.

Mutational changes fall, consequently, into two large classes: those presumably caused by chemical alterations in the individual genes (mutation proper, otherwise known as point mutation, transgenation, or genovariation), and those of a grosser structural kind, involving physical destruction, multiplication, or spatial rearrangement of the genes (chromosomal aberrations). An attempt to discriminate between these classes by examination of the chromosomes of the mutant types under the microscope breaks down because of the limitations of the existing cytological techniques. For example, a loss of a chromosome section may be detectable in a species with large and well-differentiated chromosomes, but not in one with small and compact ones. The giant chromosomes in the larval salivary glands of *Drosophila* and certain other flies unquestionably offer the most favorable material for such studies, but even there one cannot be certain that very small structural changes (for example, losses or additions of single discs) are not overlooked. Stadler (1932) has correctly emphasized that what is described as gene mutations is merely the residuum left after the elimination of all classes of hereditary changes for which a mechanical basis is detected.

Goldschmidt (1938, 1940) takes the extreme view that all the supposed mutations are rearrangements in the chromosomal materials. All that one can say regarding this view, which has been espoused by some earlier writers without finding many adherents, is that the postulated mechanical changes have not been shown to exist in most mutants. Admittedly, the inability to detect such changes in any one mutant is not a proof that this particular mutant is caused by a chemical, rather than a mechanical, change, but it remains nevertheless probable that many mutants do belong to this class. It would be strange indeed if the hereditary materials possessed an eternally immutable chemical constitution. Discovery of a method that would permit a separation of the intragenic from the intergenic changes is a goal for the future. For the time being the term mutation subsumes a variety of phenomena. In a wide sense, any change in the genotype which is not due to recombination of Mendelian factors is called mutation. In the narrower sense, it is a presumed change in a single gene, a Mendelian variant which is not known to represent a chromosomal aberration. Unless otherwise specified, the term will be used below in the latter sense.

Questions—Definition of Mutation

Main Ideas

1. Of the various possible theories of mutation, the author accepts only the belief that it is—
   a. a change in one of the units known as genes.   b. any variation from the characteristics of the basic species.   c. a series of minor changes over a period of time that eventually result in a new form or species.   d. individual variations and mutational variations in a species.

2. The author rejects De Vries' definition of mutation on the grounds that it—
   a. is too vague and inaccurate.   b. is contrary to the observed facts in such species as *Drosophila melanogaster*.   c. considers individual variations and mutational variations as different phenomena.   d. does not consider the principle of natural selection.

3. Mutations fall into two large classes—
   a. natural selection and individual variations.   b. individual variations and gene changes.   c. alterations in individual genes and structural changes among the genes.   d. individual variations and mutational changes.

4. These classes of mutations might be described as—
   a. the sum of changes and drastic variations.   b. mechanical and chemical changes in genes.   c. small variations and marked mutations.   d. ancestral and inherited changes.

Details

5. Individual variations or slight changes are held to be due to—
   a. structural changes in the genes.   b. chemical changes in the

genes.   c. sexual reproduction.   d. mixtures of types of the species varying in one or several genes.

6. Three possible causes of changes within a species are— (choose three)
   a. mixtures of types varying in genes.   b. dramatic mutations.
   c. asexual reproduction.   d. slight individual variations.   e. inheritance of characteristics imposed by the environment.   f. natural selection of the fittest types.

7. A mutant is a variant from the species that—
   a. differs slightly in certain traits.   b. differs markedly in many traits.   c. follows Mendel's law in perpetuating its variation.
   d. appears only once.

8. The view that mutations are simply rearrangements of the chromosomal materials—
   a. is widely held at this time.   b. cannot be verified with our present techniques.   c. is accepted by the author.   d. is indefensible in light of our present knowledge.

Vocabulary

Some of the following terms may have been new to you in this selection:

mutation	gene
selectionism	progenitor
phenotype	chromosome
genotype	species

Check those you knew before reading the selection. Choose the correct definition or synonym for each word as used here, to show how accurately you understand these terms.

1. mutation
   a. a phenotypic variant.   b. a genotypic variant.   c. any change.

2. selectionism
   a. small individual variations.   b. Darwin's theory to explain mutations.   c. a series of changes that leads to an independent species.

3. phenotype
   a. hereditary constitution.   b. gene arrangement.   c. observable characteristics of a species.

4. genotype
   a. hereditary factors that characterize an organism.   b. acquired characteristics.   c. the observable traits of a species.

5. gene
   a. basic unit of heredity.   b. a chemical molecule.   c. a cell.

6. progenitor
   a. phenotypic variant.   b. male of the species.   c. ancestor.

7. chromosome
   a. genetic-containing material.   b. staining material.   c. material forming a cell.

8. species
   a. a type.   b. a genotype.   c. a class of organisms.

Check your answers to these questions with the Answer Key. Write down in the Self-Appraisal the total credits you receive for each portion of the test.

Self-Appraisal

Record your predicted and actual reading rates.
Predicted rate ———— wpm.
Actual rate ———— wpm.
What were your approaches to this material? Check those steps you used.
1. Previewed selection.
2. Previewed questions.
3. Wrote preview questions.
4. Skimmed some.
5. Took notes.
6. Underlined.
7. Reread some.
8. Skipped over some.
Was this an effective pattern for you? What was your final sum of points in—

Main Ideas   ————   (20 points or better?)
Details   ————   (18 points or better?)
Vocabulary   ————   (20 points or better?)
TOTAL   ————   (58 points or better?)

Did you use steps 1, 2, and 7 at least, and possibly 5 in your reading? If not, why not?

Was your comprehension adequate in all types of questions?

Was your rate controlled to result in detailed comprehension? Was your predicted rate within 25 to 50 words per minute of your actual rate?

Did you really know the terms you thought you knew? Did you learn some of the others? How did you learn them—by noting, for example, the common root in *gene, progenitor, genotype,* or by memorizing the author's definitions?

Did you make any mistakes in handling this material effectively, such as the following?

Reading too rapidly for detailed comprehension. (See your score in Details.)

Reading too cautiously or in too great detail. (Failing to get minimum score on Main Ideas?)

Failure to get the main ideas by previewing. (Compare your questions with the instructor's.)

Overestimating your actual reading rate. (Because of failure to recognize the real difficulty of the material while previewing?)

Paying too little attention to new or technical words. (See your score in Vocabulary.)

Failing to try to organize the material in order to retain it. (Omitting all such organizational steps as 3, 5, 6, or 7 from your pattern?)

Business Administration

This 1,500-word excerpt from a government bulletin provides a detailed review of certain types of business insurance. Preview the selection and its questions, then read it to be prepared to discuss the content in detail. After previewing, estimate your probable reading rate in words per minute. Write down the time when you begin reading and when you finish, in order to compute your actual speed later.

STARTED _____   TOTAL TIME _____

FINISHED _____

Business Insurance*

FIDELITY, FORGERY, AND SURETY BONDS

Fidelity and surety bonds are important to the businessman because they deal with guaranteeing the reliability of human beings in business relationships. Forgery bonds are important because they protect the businessman against loss resulting from forgery or alteration of checks and other securities.

Fidelity and surety bonds differ from other insurance contracts in that they involve three parties: (1) the *principal*, or bonded party, who promises to fulfill certain obligations; (2) the *beneficiary*, or insured, who requires the bond, and (3) the *surety*, or insuring company, which reimburses the beneficiary if the principal defaults on his promise. In the case of forgery bonds, only two parties are involved: The person to whom the bond is issued and the insuring company.

Fidelity Bonds. A fidelity bond protects the businessman against loss caused by employee dishonesty. Although the average employer finds it hard to believe that any of his employees could be dishonest, losses from employee dishonesty cost American business more than $400,000,000 each year, according to the estimate of some authorities.

Only about one eighteenth of the loss is covered by insurance. Losses by individual firms sometimes have been large enough to force the firm into bankruptcy. Good business management requires that every officer and employee of an enterprise be covered under a fidelity bond, regardless of whether he handles money, securities, or merchandise as a part of

* From *Management Aids for Small Business: Annual No. 1* (Washington, D.C.: Small Business Administration, January 1955). Reprinted by permission.

his duties. Fidelity bonds serve to deter employees who are tempted to dishonesty and, if the employees are dishonest, enable the businessman to recover his loss.

The following types of fidelity bonds are available to the businessman:

1, *Primary commercial blanket bonds.* This form is used to bond all a businessman's employees, making it unnecessary to select certain ones to be covered. This is particularly useful if a business has considerable employee turnover. Coverage of all employees is important, also, because "trusted" (and therefore often uninsured) employees usually cause the losses. When two or more dishonest employees work together in stealing from a business, this bond reimburses only up to the limit of the bond. Since losses under these circumstances may be very substantial, it is important to carry a bond that gives adequate coverage.

2. *Blanket position bonds.* This form is broader than the primary commercial blanket bond in that it automatically covers each employee up to the limit of the bond. In a case of collusion (where two or more employees work together to steal from the business) each employee who can be shown to have contributed to the loss is covered up to the full amount of the bond. Thus, if an employer carries a $5,000 bond, and 2 employees are found responsible for a $10,000 loss, the insurance company will pay the full $10,000.

3. *Individual or name schedule bonds.* This type of bond is used to cover one or more designated employees. The employees can be insured for different amounts.

4. *Position schedule bonds.* This form covers specific positions, rather than specific individuals. Each position is covered for a stipulated amount, and the person holding the position is automatically covered. This bond is especially designed for businesses which have high employee turnover.

5. *Discovery bonds.* This type of bond is similar to the name schedule and position schedule form of bonds but applied retroactively to the original date of employment of the bonded employee. It is a particularly desirable type for employers who, in the past, have carried inadequate fidelity insurance or none at all.

Forgery Bonds. A forgery bond covers loss caused by forged or altered checks and other securities. Businessmen are constantly exposed to losses of this kind because of the tremendous volume of checks, drafts, notes, securities, and other written instruments used in modern business. No one knows the total dollar loss suffered each year by commercial and industrial organizations and individuals through forgery, but crime authorities estimate it at some $300,000,000. The following types of forgery bonds are available:

1. *Depositors' forgery bonds.* This form of bond is available to both individuals and businesses, with the exception of savings banks and loan associations. It is the principal form of forgery bond used by business concerns. Under the terms of the bond, the insured and his bank are

reimbursed for forgery losses which occur and are discovered while the bond is in force. Coverage for the businessman's bank is important, because in many instances a bank is not legally liable for forged checks which it honors. The bond protects against loss from forged or altered checks, drafts, and similar instruments issued by the insured or his agent. The depositor's forgery bond concerns itself with outgoing checks, drafts, and other instruments.

2. *Incoming check rider.* This rider is attachable to the depositor's forgery bond and protects the insured against loss from forged or altered instruments he receives as payment for personal property sold and delivered, or for services rendered.

3. *Securities bonds.* This type of bond is particularly valuable for banks, investment houses, and other financial institutions which are their own transfer agents. Two forms are available. One form applies to persons engaged in buying securities for themselves or who buy or sell securities for others. The second form covers persons who act as issuing agents, transfer agents, or registrars for corporations.

Surety Bonds. A surety bond guarantees performance of an obligation or contract. The premise underlying surety bonds is that no losses are expected, and the premium amounts to a service charge to compensate the insurance company for pledging its credit. Many surety bonds are in the nature of financial guarantees. When applying for a bond of this type, the businessman must be prepared to furnish the insurance company with financial information and possibly collateral security to support his application.

In most cases, the purpose of a surety bond is not to protect the businessman; rather, it is legally required of him, as a means of protecting others. In turn, surety bonds make it possible for the businessman to operate his business, pursue an action or defense in litigation, or obtain benefits for himself which would not otherwise be possible.

The following are among the many types of surety bonds which are of interest to the businessman:

1. *License and permit bonds.* These are required by Federal, State, and local governments in the case of certain types of businesses. They guarantee that the bonded person will comply with the law or ordinance governing the types of operation for which the license or permit is issued. They enable the bonded person to engage in a certain line of activity and enjoy certain privileges and, at the same time, protect the public from any loss resulting from noncompliance with the law.

2. *Supply contract bonds.* These usually are required by Federal and State purchasing offices, and guarantee that the bonded person will fulfill the conditions of a contract for furnishing supplies. If the supplier defaults, the insurance company reimburses the buyer.

3. *Customs bonds.* These bonds are required by the Federal Government to insure compliance with regulations governing importation of certain merchandise. They guarantee that the owner of the merchandise will pay any required taxes or duties and will comply with the applicable

Federal statutes, thereby enabling him to obtain immediate possession of the merchandise.

4. *Internal revenue bonds.* The Federal Government requires these bonds in order to insure compliance with specific regulations or payment of certain Federal taxes.

5. *Court bonds.* Various courts require individuals engaged in lawsuits to post these bonds.

6. *Performance bonds.* This form of bond guarantees that the principal or bonded person will faithfully perform the terms of a contract, such as for constructing or remodeling a building. The insurance company assumes responsibility if the bonded person defaults on his obligation.

7. *Payment bonds.* A payment bond is a supplementary agreement to a performance bond, usually in connection with a building contract, and guarantees to the insured that the finished structure or product will be turned over to him free of labor and material costs incurred by the mechanics and subcontractors. This bond, like the performance bond, is particularly important to a business firm which is planning to expand its facilities by constructing new buildings or remodeling existing plants.

Questions—Business Insurance

Main Ideas

1. Briefly discuss the two basic purposes of bonds such as those mentioned in this selection._____

_____

_____

_____

_____

_____

_____

_____

_____

_____

_____

2. Name the primary purpose of a fidelity bond, a surety bond, and a forgery bond. Be certain to point out the intrinsic differences among these three types._____

_____

_____

_____

_____

_____

_____

_____

_____

_____

_____

Details

3. If an employee is found to have misappropriated property or funds from his employer, which general type of coverage will recover this loss for the employer?
   a. Fidelity bond.   b. Forgery bond.   c. Surety bond.
   d. Burglary insurance.

4. A contractor, hired to build an office building, goes bankrupt during the period of the contract, and the work is left incomplete. What general type of protection must the employing agency have if it is to recover for this loss?
   a. Fidelity bond.   b. Forgery bond.   c. Surety bond.
   d. Burglary insurance.

5. The chief difference between the primary commercial blanket and blanket position fidelity bond is—
   a. in the extent of retroactive coverage.   b. in the number of employees covered.   c. the extent of the coverage in thefts involving more than one employee.   d. the first covers all employees; the second, those in certain positions.

6. Which type of employee most often causes the greatest losses through dishonesty?
   a. The "trusted" employee.   b. The short-term or part-time employee.   c. The underpaid "white collar" worker.   d. The known suspects.

7. Which type of surety bond guarantees that the bonded person will furnish the merchandise purchased by another?
   a. Supply contract bond.   b. Customs bond.   c. Performance bond.   d. Payment bond.

Vocabulary

Some of the following terms may have been new to you in this selection:

fidelity	stipulated
surety	instruments
principal	rider
beneficiary	retroactively
collusion	securities

Check those that you knew before reading this article. Choose the correct definition or synonym for each term as used in this selection, to show how accurately you understand these terms.

1. fidelity
   a. loyalty of two parties to a contract.   b. a type of protection against dishonesty.   c. the trustworthiness of employees.

2. surety
   a. positive payment.   b. a guarantee of an obligation or contract.   c. a protection against deceit or fraud.

3. principal
   a. the insuring company.   b. the bonded party.   c. the businessman or his company.

4. beneficiary
   a. the businessman or his company.   b. the insuring company.   c. the insured party.

5. collusion
   a. deceit or fraud.   b. action by two or more employees resulting in loss to the employer.   c. secret agreement among employees.

6. stipulated
   a. promised.   b. agreed upon in a contract.   c. agreed upon by the opposing lawyers in a trial.

7. instruments
   a. tools or utensils.   b. mechanical or musical devices.
   c. legal documents.

8. rider
   a. an additional guarantee.   b. a type of forgery bond.   c. a statement added to a contract.

9. retroactively
   a. applying to a prior time.   b. in reverse.   c. to make up for the past.

10. securities
    a. documents showing debt or property.   b. protection.
    c. measures taken to guard against sabotage.

Scanning

To answer these questions, go back over the selection quickly, if you need to. Time yourself for the answering of these questions.

1. Approximately how much money is lost each year to the American public through forgery?
   a. $300,000,000.   b. $400,000,000.   c. $500,000,000.
   d. $600,000,000.

2. What is the approximate amount of money lost to business each year by employee dishonesty?
   $200,000,000.   b. $300,000,000.   c. $400,000,000.   d. $500,-000,000.

3. What is the name of the bond that insures the federal government's receipt of taxes and duties levied on certain imported merchandise? a. Performance bond.   b. Internal revenue bond.   c. Payment bond.   d. Customs bond.

4. What is the purpose of fidelity and surety bonds? a. To protect against loss resulting from unauthorized alteration of securities.   b. To guarantee the reliability of another in business relationships.   c. To protect against loss from the larceny of unprotected property.   d. To protect against loss of valuable papers and records.

5. What type of bond insures against the dishonesty of a person holding a specific position: teller, cashier, and so on? a. Blanket position bonds.   b. Individual or name schedule bonds.   c. Securities bonds.   d. Position schedule bonds.

After you have finished answering all these questions, turn to the Answer Key and check them. Write down in the Self-Appraisal the total credits you receive for each part of the test.

Self-Appraisal

Record your reading rates and scanning time.

Predicted rate ———— wpm.

Actual rate ———— wpm.

Time for scanning ————.

What were your approaches to this material? Check those steps you used.

1. Previewed selection.
2. Previewed questions.
3. Wrote preview questions.
4. Skimmed some.
5. Took notes.
6. Underlined.
7. Reread some.
8. Skipped over some.

Was this an effective pattern of reading for you in this material? What was your final sum of points in—

Main Ideas	————	(20 points or better?)
Details	————	(15 points or better?)
Vocabulary	————	(12 points or better?)
Scanning	————	(12 points or better?)
Total	————	(60 points or better?)

Did you use steps 1, 2, and 7, at least, and possibly 3 or 5 in your pattern of reading? If not, why not? Was your comprehension poor in any area? If so, why? What could you do to improve in any of the types of questions in which you scored poorly? Was your rate too rapid for detailed retention?

Did you estimate your rate within 25 to 50 words per minute? If not, why not?

In the vocabulary review, did you really know the terms you thought you knew? Did you learn any more in reading the selection? How did you discover their meanings—by context or structure? If this subject area were your major field, how would you go about learning those terms you missed in the test?

In the Scanning section, how long did it take you to find the answers— three to four minutes? How many correct answers did you find by scanning —four or five? Do you need to improve this skill?

Did you make any mistakes in handling this material effectively, such as the following?

Reading too rapidly for detailed comprehension. (See your score in Details.)

Reading too cautiously or in too great detail. (Failing to get minimum score on Main Ideas?)

Failing to get the main ideas by previewing. (Compare your questions with the instructor's.)

Overestimating your actual reading rate. (Because of failure to recognize the real difficulty of the material while previewing?)

Paying too little attention to new or technical words. (See your score in Vocabulary.)

Failing to try to organize the material in order to retain it. (Omitting all such organizational steps as 3, 5, 6, or 7 from your pattern?)

Chemistry

This 1,250-word selection from a commercial bulletin explores some of the implications for agriculture of sulphur in our soil. Preview the selection and its questions, then read it for detailed comprehension. After previewing, estimate your probable reading rate in words per minute. Write down the time when you begin reading and when you finish, in order to compute your actual rate later.

STARTED ———————————

FINISHED ——————————— TOTAL TIME ———————————

Sulphur-Deficient Soils*

Sulphur occurs naturally in most soils in varying amounts, principally in complex organic compounds and in the form of sulphates of calcium, potassium, magnesium, and sodium. Sulphur is added to soil in rainfall as absorbed sulphur from industrial gases, in irrigation water as sulphates, in animal manures, and in sulphur-containing fertilizers such as

* From *Sulphur and Soils* (Houston: Texas Gulf Sulphur Company, July 1950). Reprinted by permission.

normal superphosphate, sulphate of ammonia, and sulphate of potash. Soil amendments such as elemental sulphur and gypsum also add to the soil's supply of sulphur.

Sulphur-deficient soils, though uncommon, do occur in some areas. Such soils have been found in parts of Minnesota, Idaho, California, Washington, Oregon, and Canada. Where a deficiency of sulphur exists in soils, crops fail to grow normally but respond to sulphur fertilization. A sulphur-deficient plant is characterized by loss of green color in the leaves. In mild cases, only the younger leaves may be affected. In more severe cases all of the leaves may be yellow in color. The symptoms resemble nitrogen deficiency except that the lower leaves do not dry up. If sulphur deficiency is acute, the plant will die prematurely regardless of the abundance of other plant food elements. Sulphates, which constitute the source of supply of plant-available sulphur in soils, are soluble. Due to their solubility tremendous losses of sulphates from the soil occur through leaching and erosion. Crop removal also accounts for the loss of large amounts of sulphur from the soil.

Notwithstanding the fact that sulphur is added to soils through absorbed sulphur in rainfall, through sulphate-bearing irrigation waters, and in sulphur-containing fertilizers, it has been estimated that there is a net annual loss of sulphur from the soils of the United States of approximately 3,000,000 tons. Were it not for the fact that American fertilizer usage has included nitrogen, phosphate, and potash carriers which also contain sulphur then sulphur-deficient soils would be more commonplace. One hundred lbs. of 20% superphosphate contain 20 lbs. of phosphoric acid and approximately 12 lbs. of sulphur. One hundred lbs. of 20% sulphate of ammonia contain 20 lbs. of nitrogen and approximately 24 lbs. of sulphur. In the case of each of these fertilizers the purchaser pays for the material on the basis of its phosphate or nitrogen content and receives the sulphur at no additional cost.

In recent years there has been a trend toward the production and use of highly concentrated fertilizers which contain little, if any, sulphur. For instance, anhydrous ammonia, ammonium nitrate, and urea are nitrogen fertilizers used for the same purpose as sulphate of ammonia. Also, treble superphosphate and calcium metaphosphate are phosphorus fertilizers used for the same purpose as normal superphosphate. If, in the future, the non-sulphur-containing fertilizers should predominate, sulphur deficiencies in soil will become prevalent and sulphur in some form will of necessity have to be included in our fertilizer program for normal crop production.

SULPHUR AND SOIL REACTION

Sulphur, in addition to being an essential plant food element, is also a soil-acidifying agent. Soils are classified according to their chemical reaction as acid, neutral, or alkaline. Differences in acidity and alkalinity are represented on what is known as the pH scale. This scale is divided into units from 1 to 14. A pH of 7 is neutral and, in ascending order, from 7 to 14 is increasingly alkaline. Conversely, a pH below 7, in descending order to 1, is increasingly acid. Most economic crop plants thrive in soils with a pH between 6.5 and 7.5. Such soils may be designated as slightly acid, neutral, or slightly alkaline.

Soils which are too acid for normal crop production may be corrected by the application of agricultural lime. This is a standard practice in certain sections of the country. Soils which are too alkaline or are not sufficiently acid may be corrected by the application of some acidifying agent such as sulphur, sulphur dioxide, sulphuric acid, aluminum sulphate, or iron sulphate. The choice of an acidifying agent depends somewhat upon the economics involved and the ease of handling. Because of its low cost, sulphur is the only one of these materials used for large-scale soil acidification purposes. Recently, sulphuric acid and sulphur dioxide introduced into irrigation water have been tried. The results are promising, although costs have been excessive compared to elemental sulphur.

Broadcast applications of sulphur are more effective on soils having a relatively low calcium content. It is neither practical nor necessary to attempt to change the pH of the entire soil mass in high-calcium soils. In moderately and highly alkaline soils with a high calcium content, sulphur, for purposes of acidification, should be applied in narrow bands or, in the case of orchards, in holes placed around the trees.

Sulphur when applied to soils is oxidized to sulphur dioxide by sulfofying bacteria. The sulphur dioxide combines with water to form sulphuric acid in the soil, resulting in acidification. One lb. of sulphur will produce approximately 3 lbs. of sulphuric acid. Optimum conditions for the oxidation of sulphur in soils are an abundance of sulfofying bacteria, a warm soil with sufficient organic matter, a well aerated soil, and a sufficient moisture supply. If any one of these factors is limited, then the oxidation process will be slowed down. Most soils contain a sufficient supply of the proper type of bacteria. When the bacteria are limited in number, the addition of barnyard manure will usually insure their presence in sufficient quantity.

Acidification of alkaline and neutral soils tends to increase the availability of other plant nutrients, particularly phosphorus and the minor elements. Lack of iron in plants may cause chlorosis, a yellowing of the foliage. Many investigators have considered that this was responsible for all cases of iron chlorosis. Recent tests have shown that soil applications of sulphur will correct so-called iron chlorosis in calcareous soils by increasing the activity of iron in the plant although the total iron uptake might not be affected.

Questions—Sulphur-Deficient Soils

Main Ideas

1. Sulphur-deficient soils are found in—
   a. most parts of the United States.   b. only a few areas of the United States.   c. only the eastern section of the United States. d. hot, humid areas of the United States.   e. sections associated with little rainfall.

2. The continued use of fertilizers lacking in sulphur may—
   a. result in the loss of much useful farm land.   b. cause increase in the areas characterized by sulphur-deficient soils.   c. necessitate a reevaluation of the importance of sulphur for soil acidification.   d. require the search for new and different fertilizing agents.

3. It is difficult to identify sulphur-deficient plants because—
   a. the plants' leaves dry up.   b. the leaves become yellow.
   c. the yellowing of the leaves resembles nitrogen insufficiency.
   d. the plant tends to die quickly, before an analysis can be made.

4. Sulphur may be used not only as a plant food but also—
   a. to acidify only noncalcareous soils.   b. in conjunction with lime to correct soil conditions.   c. to correct alkaline or nonacid soils.   d. to stimulate the sulfofying bacteria.

5. Name at least three ways in which sulphur is added naturally to soils. Where these conditions are usually present, may we assume that sufficient sulphur for plant growth will be present?_____
   _____
   _____
   _____
   _____
   _____
   _____

Details

6. Sulphur is lost from the soil by— (choose two)
   a. plant removal.   b. oxidation.   c. evaporation.   d. continuous planting of low-sulphur-content crops.   e. leaching.

7. The addition of sulphur to soils tends to make them more—
   a. calcareous.   b. alkaline.   c. acid.   d. neutral.

8. A sulphur-deficient plant is characterized by—
   a. loss of green leaf color.   b. drying of the leaves.   c. lack of seed production.   d. late budding in the spring.   e. early loss of leaves in the fall.

9. Loss of sulphur from American soil would be even greater and perhaps a real problem, were it not for the fact that—
   a. most farmers add sulphur to their soils.   b. sulphur is present in most common fertilizers.   c. many crops do not depend highly upon the presence of sulphur in the soil.   d. applications of sulphur enable plants to make better use of their iron intake.

10. Sulphur may be applied to soils in these ways: (choose at least two)
    a. leaching or erosion.   b. by adding some form of it to irrigation water.   c. by mixing it with agricultural lime.   d. by spreading

it over the soil.   e. by using a phosphorus or concentrated fertilizer.

Vocabulary

Some of the following terms may have been new to you in this selection:

leaching   sulphate
anhydrous   acidifying
alkaline   pH
chlorosis   sulfofying
calcareous   amendments

Check those that you knew before reading this selection. Choose the correct definition or synonym for each word as used in this selection to show how accurately you understand these terms.

1. leaching
   a. washing away by rain, ground water, and so on.   b. causing loss of color.   c. the action of wind and rain.

2. anhydrous
   a. an oxide that forms an acid.   b. without water.   c. extra strong.

3. alkaline
   a. dry, bitter.   b. a salt.   c. the opposite of acid.

4. chlorosis
   a. a plant disease.   b. yellowing of plant leaves.   c. sulphur deficiency.

5. calcareous
   a. containing calcium.   b. hard, brittle.   c. dry, rocky.

6. sulphate
   a. some form of sulphur.   b. raw sulphur.   c. a salt of sulphuric acid.

7. acidifying
   a. making sour or acid.   b. any use of sulphur.   c. changing the pH.

8. pH
   a. the symbol for hydrogen.   b. the scale of acidity or alkalinity.   c. the abbreviation for philosophy.

9. sulfofying
   a. sulphur-producing.   b. replacing oxygen with sulphur.
   c. nitrogen-producing.

10. amendments
    a. a revision in a bill or law.   b. changes or additions.   c. substances added to the soil.

Check your answers to these questions with the Answer Key. Write down in the Self-Appraisal the total credits you receive for each portion of the test.

Self-Appraisal

Record your reading rates here.

Predicted rate ———— wpm.

Actual rate ———— wpm.

What were your approaches to this material? Check those steps you used.

1. Previewed selection.
2. Previewed questions.
3. Wrote preview questions.
4. Skimmed some.
5. Took notes.
6. Underlined.
7. Reread some.
8. Skipped over some.

Was this an effective pattern of reading for you? What was your final sum of points in—

Main Ideas	————	(20 points or better?)
Details	————	(20 points or better?)
Vocabulary	————	(21 points or better?)
TOTAL	————	(61 points or better?)

Did you use steps 1, 2, and 7 at least, and possibly 5 in your pattern of reading? If not, why not?

Was your comprehension adequate in each type of question? If not, what should you be doing to improve?

Was your rate controlled to result in detailed comprehension? Was your predicted rate within 25 to 50 words per minute of your actual rate?

Did you really know the vocabulary terms you thought you knew? How about the others—did you learn some by reading the passage? Did you react to the structure of *anhydrous*—*an*, "without"; *hydro*, "water"? Did you recognize the base *calci*, "calcium," in *calcareous*, or the obvious parts of *acidifying*?

Did you make any mistakes in handling this material effectively, such as the following?

Reading too rapidly for detailed comprehension. (See your score in Details.)

Reading too cautiously or in too great detail. (Failing to get minimum score on Main Ideas?)

Failing to get the main ideas by previewing. (Compare your questions with the instructor's.)

Overestimating your actual reading rate. (Because of failure to recognize the real difficulty of the material while previewing?)

Paying too little attention to new or technical words. (See your score in Vocabulary.)

Failing to try to organize the material in order to retain it. (Omitting all such organizational steps as 3, 5, 6, or 7 from your pattern?)

Education

Suppose you were asked to read this 1,500-word article in an introductory course in education. The instructor did not give any specific directions; hence you will have to plan your own goals in reading the article. Preview it, outlining on paper the written questions you intend to be able to answer, or that you think he will ask. *Don't* read the questions at the end of the article. After previewing, estimate your rate of reading in words per minute. Write down the time when you begin reading and when you finish, in order to compute your actual rate later. Then read to answer the questions you have outlined. When you have finished, compare your questions with those given.

STARTED _____   FINISHED _____

TOTAL TIME _____

SEVEN PRINCIPLES OF LEARNING*

Have you ever refinished a piece of furniture? If so, you know that one swipe of the sander across the grain may mean hours of work removing the resulting scratches. The refinishing expert knows how necessary it is to work with the grain of the wood. Yet many teachers fail to realize the importance of working with, not against, the grain of the pupils. Too often the scratches drastically interfere with the learning process. Teachers need to know the characteristics of young people—their needs, interests, motivations, drives—what makes them act and feel as they do. Every effort should be made to capitalize upon such knowledge in planning and creating a classroom atmosphere conducive to learning.

How may we provide the learning situation that will bring about desirable change? How may we efficiently choose the textbook? The supplementary reading material and visual symbols? The films and other audio-visual aids? How may our lectures, class discussions, demonstrations, and group reports be more effective? How may the key to the learning process—the assignment—be made most vital? How may we evaluate any procedure or material that has been used? The seven principles of learning emphasized in this article may serve as criteria that will help us answer these questions. For each principle the *why* justifies its

* Stanley L. Clement, "Seven Principles of Learning," *The Clearing House,* September 1961, pp. 23–26. Reprinted by permission.

importance and the *how* illustrates how it may be carried out. (Only a few samples are cited of the many activities possible.)

I. LEARNING SHOULD BE AN ACTIVE PROCESS

Why: Students must participate in order to react. We cannot simply pour in knowledge, but we must draw it out. It would be interesting to know what goes on in the minds of students sitting passively in class with their books closed. Young people like action; they want to be doing something. It is better to make outlines, to simulate meetings, and to demonstrate processes than merely to describe them. We learn through actual living rather than just reading about it in books. Teachers are not needed mainly to give answers but to help students find the answers.

How:

(1) Greater care in making assignments—indicating a problem to be solved, definite questions to answer, people to find out about, something definite to do besides just read so many pages.

(2) Discussion, role playing, demonstration (by students), laboratory work in all subjects.

(3) Film evaluation, tape-recorder use (language laboratory), teaching machines, field trips.

(4) Notebooks, scrapbooks, diagrams, charts, graphs, projects.

(5) Group work, debates, pupil-teacher planning.

II. LEARNING SHOULD BE MEANINGFUL

Why: Understanding precedes mastery. Learning and understanding are reciprocal. Students learn only what they understand. While essential facts need to be memorized for automatic recall, the students' concern for remembering will be minimized by the tendency to retain what they understand. Memorizing the steps of a geometry proof or a chemistry process will have little value unless the student understands what he is doing.

How:

(1) Teaching the new in terms of the old—connecting it to previous learning and past experience both within and outside the course.

(2) Application to life situations.

(3) Emphasis on assignment making.

(4) Pictures, graphs, charts, maps, models, specimens.

(5) Demonstration, laboratory work, films, field trips.

III. LEARNING SHOULD BE USEFUL

Why: A goal provides a motivating force. If class work seems important to the student—if it will make a difference and bring success—he will have a greater desire for achievement. And he should gain satisfaction here and now, not just entertain a promise for the future. Will it help him to get the most out of school? Will it aid in getting into and succeeding in college? Will it help in earning a living? Will it aid him in the ability to express himself? To get along with people? Will it help avoid embarrassment because of ignorance? Whatever we do should have as its basis the meeting of the needs of the individual and the welfare of society.

How:

(1) Establishing aims for subjects, units, and daily lessons which relate to needs, drives, motives, and desires of young people—aims which seem worth while and are accepted by them—which relate to problems arising in life with which they can identify themselves.

(2) Planning and evaluation work in terms of these aims.

(3) Making students conscious of these aims—starting and ending each course, each unit, and each daily lesson with emphasis on the aims.

(4) Pupil-teacher planning.

(5) Determining from school alumni what learning they found most useful in school and what they thought was neglected.

IV. Learning Should Be Interesting

Why: Interest precedes effort. Students learn more rapidly when they are highly motivated. Curiosity can be a driving force. Learning does not have to be painful. It does not lose prestige because it is interesting. This does not mean a lowering of standards. Work may only appear to be less difficult because it is pleasant and purposeful.

How:

(1) Planning stimulating assignments.

(2) Using a variety of methods and materials, such as films and demonstrations.

(3) Increasing pupil participation in class through discussion and debates.

(4) Capitalizing on desire for social approval—having group activity.

(5) Appealing to rivalry and pride through competition.

V. Learning Should Be Individualized

Why: An opportunity should be provided for each pupil to realize his potential. The school used to put all students in the same mold—fitting the child to the school. Emphasis was on teaching subjects, not children; the same curriculum and methods were used for all. Teaching was beamed at the average student while the bright student became bored and the slow became frustrated. With almost everyone going to secondary school now, the ability of the average student is considerably below what it used to be.

In any grade, a large number of students are below the average of the grade below and approximately the same number are above the average of the grade below. There is often a spread of six years in any grade above the fourth and this spread becomes greater as teaching becomes better.

Adolescence is a period of rapid growth. Not only do students mature at different rates, but different aspects of the same individual vary as well. Even with ability grouping there is no such thing as a homogeneous class, only one that is relatively more so.

How:

(1) Knowing strengths and weaknesses of pupils—using grouping within a class and adapting content to the various levels.

(2) Using a variety of methods and materials.

(3) Having differentiated assignments—minimum and maximum, standard and optional.

(4) Basing group work on student interests.

(5) Capitalizing on supervised study and help sessions to aid slow students and challenge bright ones.

VI. LEARNING SHOULD BE SATISFYING

Why: Students will repeat satisfying experiences and shun unpleasant ones. Satisfaction may be both extrinsic and intrinsic. Because of their lack of adult maturity, young people often do not have a true sense of values. Outside motivations can be justified as long as they do not become ends in themselves and there is a chance for all to be rewarded.

How:

(1) Having the amount of praise handed out to students at least balance the amount of criticism which is leveled at them.

(2) Offering incentives—honors, awards, privileges.

(3) Providing opportunity for all to succeed, to hold status in the group.

(4) Keeping pupils aware of their progress in relation to their ability.

(5) Using negative approaches as a last resort for some cases—detention, scolding, failures.

VII. LEARNING SHOULD BE UNIFIED

Why: The total learning situation is important. The student does not learn merely with his mind but physically, socially, and emotionally. All of the senses must be used. The environment or setting for learning is vital. Improper physical conditions, uninspiring teachers, and unplanned lessons are still too much in evidence.

Whole learning is more effective than part learning. We tend to divide school up into too many isolated subjects and each subject into individual doses, with resulting lack of emphasis on perspective or relationships.

How:

(1) Good room atmosphere—light, heat, ventilation, bulletin boards, etc.

(2) Being aware of the importance of teacher appearance, enthusiasm, voice, posture, and attitude.

(3) Consideration of pupil health and home situations.

(4) Long-range planning and long-range assignments—the unit method.

(5) Setting stage, reviewing, and summarizing each day and for each unit.

As we select and as we judge each of our procedures and materials, let us ask ourselves: Is it useful? Does it promote a desirable goal? Is it meaningful? Will the student understand it? Is it interesting? Will it arouse curiosity? Does it involve action? Will student participation be high? Is it individualized? Is it adapted to interests and abilities? Is it satisfying? Will it be a pleasant experience? Is it unified? Is there a clear relationship to the whole unit? If we can answer these questions in the affirmative, not only will we be teaching but the students will really learn.

Questions—Seven Principles of Learning

The most obvious questions a teacher might ask on this selection are these:

1. What are the seven principles of learning? (*Answers:* a, active process; b, meaningful; c, useful; d, interesting; e, individualized; f, satisfying; g, unified.)
2. Give an example of the application of each principle as it might be seen in the classroom. (See the article for a variety of possible answers.)
3. Which of these principles do you consider to be the most important? Why? (Your answers would, of course, reflect your own preferences.)
4. Give an example of a common classroom practice you have witnessed that violates each of these principles. How might such practices be improved?

Did you anticipate that the instructor might also ask questions such as the following?

5. Give an example of each principle as it might be applied in your field of interest, the field in which you intend to teach.
6. Which of these principles is most significant in dealing with elementary pupils? With secondary pupils? With college students? Or are they equally applicable?
7. Can the mature student of secondary-school or college age do anything to promote the operation of these principles in his own learning? Can he, for example, do anything to make learning an active process? A meaningful process? And so on.
8. Do you believe there is any duplication among these seven principles? Which principles overlap, in your opinion? How would you rewrite them?
9. Are there any major principles or concepts of learning from other learning theories that you think might be added to this list? Name and illustrate them, and justify their inclusion.
10. For which of his principles does the writer offer the weakest illustrations and defense? Can you improve on his ideas?

11. In most of these principles, the author discusses only extrinsic motivation, or what the teacher might do to motivate pupil learning. From what other angle might these principles have been approached? Illustrate this viewpoint.

Vocabulary

Here are some of the terms that may have been new to you. Check those you knew before you read the article.

audio-visual
role playing
homogeneous
individualized
classroom atmosphere

Choose the synonym or definition for each term as it is used in this selection.

1. audio-visual
   a. pertains to speed-reading devices.   b. pertains to games that appeal to the ear or eye.   c. pertains to teaching devices, such as filmstrips.
2. role playing
   a. a classroom game.   b. an activity like charades.   c. reenacting life situations in the classroom.
3. homogeneous
   a. including only one type.   b. a group of similar ability, age, or other major trait.   c. blended into a smooth mixture.
4. individualized
   a. attempting to meet individual differences.   b. separated, one by one.   c. teaching each child.
5. classroom atmosphere
   a. room temperature.   b. basic pupil-teacher relationship.
   c. control of classroom lighting, climate, and so on.

Self-Appraisal

Even without any prereading instructions, it is apparent that the basic aim in reading this article would be comprehension and applications of the seven learning principles. Did the questions you framed while previewing resemble those we think the instructor would ask? If not, why not? Did you anticipate only factual questions?

Patterns of Reading

Record your reading rates here.
Predicted rate: ———— wpm.
Actual rate: ———— wpm.

What were your approaches to this material? Check those steps you used.
1. Previewed selection.
2. Previewed questions.
3. Wrote preview questions.
4. Skimmed some.
5. Took notes.
6. Underlined.
7. Reread some.
8. Skipped over some.

Did you use steps 1 and 3 as instructed? The simplicity of this article probably permitted you to use step 4 or 8 also. If you took any notes, you might well have written simply a key word to identify each principle. Or you may have underlined each key word, although this approach is not as effective for remembering as actually writing the words.

Did you estimate your actual reading rate within 25 to 50 words per minute? Was your rate appropriate to the purposes you outlined for yourself—that is, were you able to answer your own questions?

In the vocabulary review, did you really know the terms (as they are used by educators) that you thought you knew? Did you learn any of the others in reading the article?

If you are an education major, it would be profitable to examine closely the questions we have proposed, and perhaps to try to answer them at least to your own satisfaction. You will face such questions frequently in this area of study, and you should learn to anticipate them by your reading approach.

English

This 1,350-word selection is drawn from a handbook widely used in college freshman English courses. It deals with a bit of the history of the development of the English language. Preview the excerpt and its questions, then read it for detailed comprehension. After previewing, estimate your probable reading rate in words per minute. Write down the time when you begin reading and when you finish, in order to compute your actual rate later.

STARTED _____   FINISHED _____

TOTAL TIME _____

The Development of English*

THE MIDDLE ENGLISH PERIOD

About a century and a half before the end of the Old English Period, another Scandinavian people, the Normans (Norsemen), landed on the

* Extracts reprinted by permission of the publisher from *The Macmillan Handbook of English,* by John M. Kierzek and Walker Gibson. Fifth edition © The Macmillan Company, 1965.

Normandy beaches of France, took over the country, settled down, and adopted the language and culture of the French. It was done gradually, of course, with many intrigues and the usual political deals and battles. In 1066, William, Duke of Normandy, after a tempestuous and unsavory career in his own country, laid claim to the English throne. The Norman Conquest followed his decisive victory in the Battle of Hastings. What eventually happened to the language of England can be better understood if we remember that the Norman Conquest was not a mass migration of one people intent upon displacing another, but rather the personal adventure of a dictator grasping for more power and distinction. William the Conqueror, like other ambitious lords of his day, was interested primarily in defeating possible rivals to his throne and eliminating them by imprisonment, torture, and death. Their positions of power he filled with his own henchmen. To pay for his campaigns it was necessary for him to take what property was worth taking. Meanwhile, life went on; the work was done, crops were grown, trade revived, and the common people continued to speak the native Anglo-Saxon speech. The language of the court and the upper classes was Norman French. The language of the church was Latin, the universal language of that day.

For a time England continued to be trilingual. In the course of years a number of things happened that tended to separate the English people from their neighbors across the Channel. For the rulers it became increasingly important to be kings of England rather than to remain dukes of a small French province. Wars with France and Scotland, the Crusades, a break with the Church of Rome, a rise in the middle classes, all encouraged a sense of national unity and importance. By the middle of the fourteenth century, English, not French and Latin, became the accepted language of the ruling classes, the law courts, and the church. More than that, one dialect of the three that had persisted since the earliest Anglo-Saxon times, the East Midland dialect of London and its governmental agencies, emerged as the leading language of England, a position it has held to this day. The fact that Chaucer, a Londoner, wrote his popular stories in this dialect may have helped to establish it.

Naturally, the English that emerged was greatly enriched by additions of Norman French words. As one might expect, most of these words came out of the social, political, and economic life in which the Normans dominated. From the language of government we get such words as *parliament, crown, duke, sovereign;* from the law courts, *judge, jury, justice, jail, plaintiff;* from feudal life and the life of the higher social classes, *castle, count, baron, vassal, liege, war, prison, barber, grocer, tailor, mantle, labor, chamber.* A Norman word did not necessarily displace an Anglo-Saxon word. Quite often two sets of words survived; thus for the native Saxon words *work, stool, swine, sheep, cow, calf,* and *deer* we have parallel Norman French words *labor, chair, pork, mutton, beef, veal,* and *venison.*

MODERN ENGLISH

The year 1500 has been arbitrarily set as the beginning of the Modern English Period because near that time two events of superlative importance took place: William Caxton set up his printing press in England in 1476, and England began to feel the first impulses from the continental European Renaissance. The history of the English language since 1500 is one of gradual growth and enrichment, not of violent change, mainly because no foreign invader has again succeeded in setting foot on the tight little island. There have been, it is true, literary fashions or movements, like the swinging of a pendulum, which hurried or retarded the changes. The Elizabethan Age enriched the language in both flexibility of structure and added vocabulary. The Classical Period, which followed, stressed correctness, conciseness, and simplicity. In the Romantic Period the pendulum swung to the other extreme. In addition to this rhythmic swing from the liberal attitude to the conservative and back to the liberal, there were other influences at work. The simple dignity of the King James Bible of 1611 acted as a brake upon the exuberancy of both Romanticists and Latinists. From time to time some writer or group of writers rediscovered the virtues of the speech of the common people. England became first a world empire and then the mother country of a world commonwealth of nations, and the speech of a people who inhabited one half of a little island became a world language.

Several other profound influences upon the course that the English language has taken must be mentioned here. One is the standardizing influence of the dictionaries, the grammars, and the printing houses, which beginning in the Eighteenth century set up standards of correctness first in spelling, then in pronunciation and meaning, and more recently in good usage. Another is the influence of almost universal education. A third, and now probably the most powerful influence, is that of television, radio, the theater, and motion pictures. The speech of the radio and television announcer and newscaster has emerged as the standard speech of our nation today—and tomorrow, it seems probable, of the whole English-speaking world. This standardizing influence is extremely powerful; regional differences in America, although they may always remain, tend to grow less prominent and less important. Two world wars have done their bit to scramble dialects in this country, and, on the international scene, to mix Australians, Americans, and British; hence it need not be a rash prophecy to assume that national differences in pronunciation and usage will in time become less noticeable.

OUR CHANGING LANGUAGE

When one looks back upon the fifteen hundred years that are the life span of the English language, he should be able to discern a number of significant truths. The history of our language has always been a history of constant change—at times a slow, almost an imperceptible change, at other times a violent collision between two languages. Our language has always been a living growing organism; it has never been static. Another significant truth that emerges from such a study is that language at all times has been the possession not of one class or group but of many. At one extreme it has been the property of the common, ignorant folk, who have used it in the daily business of their living, much as they have used their animals or their kitchen pots and pans. At the other extreme it has been the ward of those who have respected it as an instrument and a sign of civilization, and who have striven by writing it down to give it some permanence, order, dignity, and, if possible, a little beauty.

As we consider our changing language, we should note here two developments that are of special and immediate importance to us. One is that since the time of the Anglo-Saxons there has been an almost complete reversal of the different devices for showing the relationship of words in a sentence. Anglo-Saxon was a language of many inflections. Modern English has few inflections. We must now depend largely on word order and on function words to convey the meanings that the older language did by means of changes in the forms of words. Function words, you should understand, are words such as prepositions, conjunctions, and a few others that are used primarily to show relationships among other words. A few inflections, however, have survived. And when some word inflections come into conflict with word order, there may be trouble for the users of the language, as we shall see later when we turn our attention to such matters as *who* or *whom* and *me* or *I*. The second fact we must consider is that as language itself changes, our attitudes toward language forms change also. The eighteenth century, for example, produced from various sources a tendency to fix the language into patterns not always in accord with the way people actually used it. Gradually a reaction against this authoritarian attitude set in and grew, until at the present time there is a strong tendency to restudy and re-evaluate language practices in terms of the ways in which people speak and write.

Questions—The Development of English

Main Ideas

1. The major influence for change in the English language during the Middle English period was—
   a. the cruelty of William the Conqueror.   b. the use of Latin by the clergy.   c. the introduction of Norman French.   d. the extinction of the landed Anglo-Saxon noblemen.

2. The amalgamation of Norman French, Anglo-Saxon, and Latin into the single language we know as English was fostered by—
   a. the development of England and its colonies as a commonwealth of nations.   b. the gradual development of a new ruling class in England, the Norman French.   c. the developing sense of national identity that distinguished the English people from their French relations.   d. the leveling influence of the appearance of a middle class of Englishmen.

3. In the Modern English period, the history of the English language indicates that—

a. national differences among English-speaking nations gradually disappeared.   b. the East midland dialect became the common form of English.   c. the language gradually matured into the present form.   d. English was most markedly influenced by the Elizabethan Age.

4. One of the most significant facts about the development of our language is—
a. the speed with which it has evolved.   b. the steady pace at which it has gradually evolved.   c. the substitution of word order for inflections in conveying the meanings and functions of words. d. the large proportion of common words drawn from Norman French.

5. In contrast to the early lexicographers and grammarians, modern linguists—
a. are attempting to continue the standardization of our language.
b. evaluate language practices in terms of current speech rather than standard or proper patterns.   c. are more concerned with the improvement of our language than its analysis or history.   d. are quite familiar with the impact of other languages and cultures upon our speech patterns.

Details

Mark the following statements True or False according to the facts given in the selection.

_____ 1. When the Normans migrated to England, they introduced a number of French customs.

_____ 2. By replacing the Anglo-Saxon noblemen with his Norman followers, William the Conqueror made French the language of the upper classes.

_____ 3. At one period of their history, the English people lacked a common language.

_____ 4. The writings of Chaucer were offered in the East Midland dialect of London.

_____ 5. The East Midland dialect, which became the leading form of English, originated during the Chaucerian period.

_____ 6. The gradual separation of England from its ties with the continent fostered the development of a separate language.

_____ 7. The Norman French words added to the Anglo-Saxon language dealt only with the customs and activities of the upper classes.

_____ 8. The Middle English period can be dated roughly from 1000 to 1500 A.D.

—— 9. The Modern English period began in about 1500 A.D.

—— 10. Influences upon the language during the Modern English period included the standardizing effect of dictionaries and grammars.

—— 11. Universal education in English-speaking countries has tended to stabilize and standardize the language.

—— 12. Regional and dialectal differences within America are being minimized by the influence of the standard speech pattern offered by television, radio, and motion pictures.

—— 13. Soon all Americans will sound like radio and television announcers and newscasters.

—— 14. Our language has been and still is in a state of relatively constant change.

—— 15. In the not-too-distant future, the many standardizing influences upon our language will probably result in a stabilized condition with little subsequent change.

Vocabulary

The following terms may have been new to you in this selection. Check those you already knew. Then choose the correct definition or synonym for each, in terms of the manner in which it was used here.

promulgating   function words
trilingual   structure
dialect   Latinists
inflections   static

1. promulgating
   a. furthering or advancing.   b. declaring or stating.   c. suggesting.

2. trilingual
   a. using a polyglot language.   b. having many languages.
   c. using three languages

3. dialect
   a. employing poor usage.   b. colloquial speech.   c. regional or local speech.

4. inflections
   a. changes in the forms of words.   b. changes in speech patterns.
   c. changes in pitch or tone.

5. function words
   a. words that have different purposes.   b. words used to clarify meaning.   c. all words other than nouns and verbs.

6. structure
   a. the arrangements and functions of words.   b. the making of complete sentences.   c. the scientific study of language.

7. Latinists
   a. the clergy of the Middle English period who spoke and wrote Latin.   b. students of Latin.   c. those who promoted the introduction of Latin terms into English.

8. static
   a. interfering noise in radio reception.   b. in a state of change.
   c. at rest, without change or movement.

Check your answers to these questions with the Answer Key. Write down in the Self-Appraisal the credits you receive for each portion of the test.

Self-Appraisal

Record your reading rates here.
Predicted rate: ——— wpm.
Actual rate: ——— wpm.

What were your approaches to this material? Check those steps you used.
1. Previewed selection.
2. Previewed questions.
3. Wrote preview questions.
4. Skimmed some.
5. Took notes.
6. Underlined.
7. Reread some.
8. Skipped over some.

Was this an effective pattern of reading for you? How did you score in—

Main Ideas	———	(18 points or better?)
Details	———	(27 points or better?)
Vocabulary	———	(15 points or better?)
TOTAL	———	(60 points or better?)

Did you use steps 1 and 2 in your pattern of reading, as instructed? To secure detailed comprehension, you may have also employed steps 3 or 5 or 7.

Was your score acceptable in all three types of questions? If not, why not? What can you do about it?

Was your rate appropriate to good comprehension as measured by your total score? Was your actual rate within 25 to 50 words per minute of your predicted rate? If not, why not?

Did you really know the terms you checked as familiar? Did you learn some of the others or some new meanings for others as a result of reading the selection? How did you discover the meanings of *trilingual, inflections,* and *function words?* Did you recognize that these were defined by the context?

Did you make any mistakes in handling this material effectively, such as the following?

Reading too rapidly for detailed comprehension. (See your score in Details.)

Reading too cautiously or in too great detail. (Failing to get minimum score on Main Ideas?)

Failing to get the main ideas by previewing. (Compare your questions with the instructor's.)

Overestimating your actual reading rate. (Because of failure to recognize the real difficulty of the material while previewing?)

Paying too little attention to new or technical words. (See your score in Vocabulary.)

Failing to try to organize the material in order to retain it. (Omitting all such organizational steps as 3, 5, 6, or 7 from your pattern?)

Geology

This 1,500-word selection discusses the problem of one of our disappearing mineral products—coal. Preview the selection and its questions, then read it for detailed comprehension. After previewing, estimate your probable reading rate in words per minute. Write down the time you begin reading and when you finish in order to compute your actual rate later.

STARTED   ——————————   FINISHED   ——————————

TOTAL TIME   ——————————

Mineral Resources*

Modern civilization is strikingly dependent on mineral resources. Many mineral products are essential in peace and in war, and those essential minerals in which a nation is not self-sufficient are coming to be termed strategic minerals. The United States, more fortunate than other nations, is deficient only in about seven essential mineral supplies: manganese—the "vitamin" of the steel industry—tin, platinum, nickel, and a few others.

The world's mineral supplies are being consumed at an unprecedented rate. The amount mined during the first quarter of the present century was greater than that in all previous history. This enormous draft on our mineral resources means that the known supplies are being rapidly depleted and that as fast as they are depleted new supplies must be discovered in order to maintain the present rate of production. The easily found mineral deposits have already been found, so that more ingenuity and more work are necessary to find new deposits. Therefore the cost of

* Chester R. Longwell, Adolph Knopf, and Richard F. Flint, *Outlines of Physical Geology* (New York: John Wiley & Sons, 1941). Reprinted by permission.

finding new deposits is steadily rising. It is the counsel of prudence, then, to enlist all possible aids to minimize the financial risks of the search and discovery of new deposits. Applying the principles of geology to the search for valuable mineral deposits is one of the main functions of economic geology. To aid in this search there have recently been developed powerful auxiliaries, such as the seismograph for "seismic prospecting," the torsion balance, and other geophysical instruments. We call these instruments auxiliaries advisedly, because the results obtained by their use must be interpreted in the light of the geology of the area that is being explored before the results can be practically applied.

Even more important than the aid given by applied geology to the finding of new deposits is its power to guide intelligently the development and exploitation of the deposits already found.

COAL

Occurrence and Nature of Coals. Coals are compact masses of carbonized plant debris. Peat is the embryonic form of coal. Between peat and anthracite there is a complete series of gradational varieties of coals, and this gradation leads to the conclusion that all coals, no matter how structureless and amorphous they may seem, consist of carbonized plant remains. This conclusion is confirmed by the results of microscopic study, which show that coals are not amorphous but consist of plant debris in various stages of alteration. Fragments of wood, bark, leaves, roots, spores, seedcoats, and lumps of resin have been recognized in coals. Even in such highly carbonized material as anthracite the plant ingredients can be made visible, and, unexpectedly enough, are found to be so well preserved that the species of many of the plants can be identified.

Coals occur in beds which are generally inclosed between strata of sandstone and shale. Their occurrence between strata of this kind harmonizes with the other evidence that most coal beds accumulated in freshwater swamps. Limestones are rare, either immediately above or below a coal bed, and where they do occur they indicate that the coal-forming swamp was near the sea and at sea level and therefore was likely to be inundated at intervals by the sea.

Most beds of coal are underlain by a layer of clay, the underclay, which, because it contains the roots of plants, is interpreted as a fossil soil. Stumps of large trees, with their root systems penetrating the underclay, are abundant in some coal fields. These features support the prevailing idea that most coal beds were formed from plant matter that accumulated where it grew.

Chemical Composition of Coals. It is customary to ascertain the chemical composition of coals to determine their value as fuels, and ordinarily the following constituents are reported: (1) fixed carbon, which is the carbon left after the gas has been driven off; (2) volatile matter, mainly combustible hydrocarbons (gas) but including some inert gases, such as carbon dioxide; (3) water; (4) ash; and (5) sulphur. The value of a coal as a fuel depends on its content of fixed carbon and volatile combustible matter, whereas the water, ash, and sulphur are undesirable ingredients. Coals containing much ash are termed low grade.

Classification of Coals by Ranks. Coals are classified according to ranks by a combination of their fixed-carbon content and their physical properties. As there is a continuous gradation from low-rank to high-rank coals, the divisions adopted are necessarily arbitrary.

The lowest-rank coals are the lignites, so called because of their obviously woody appearance, or brown coals, in reference to their color. They are highly immature coals. When taken from the mine they may appear to be perfectly dry, but may contain as much as 30 to 40 per cent of water. On exposure they lose most of this water; they slack and crumble to pieces and are likely to take fire spontaneously.

The medium-rank coals are the bituminous. They do not slack on exposure and generally have a prismatic jointing perpendicular to their banding. As there is no hard and fast line between lignite and bituminous coal, the intermediate varieties are termed sub-bituminous. Their black color and nonwoody structure distinguish them from the lowest-rank lignites, and their tendency to slack distinguishes them from the high-rank bituminous coals.

The highest-rank coal is anthracite. It differs physically from the bituminous varieties by its conchoidal fracture and absence of cross-jointing. Water and volatile matter are extremely low, and nearly all the carbon is fixed carbon.

The increase in the rank of a coal, then, is marked by the progressive increase in the fixed-carbon content and by the diminution of the content of water.

Relation of Rank of Coal to the Geologic History of the Coal. Coals have formed in all the geologic periods since flora began growing on the lands. Most of them have formed in forested coastal swamps. The requisite conditions for the accumulation of a coal bed are at least two: (1) the swamp must be stagnant, hence the water cover under which the plant remains are accumulating is poorly aerated, thus preventing the plant debris from being oxidized to carbon dioxide; and (2) the swamp must be slowly sinking, thus permitting progressive accumulation of the plant remains.

The nature of the environment in which the coals were formed is inferred from the botanical character of the coal-forming flora and from the character of the inclosing sedimentary strata. Modern analogues of coal-forming swamps are the Dismal Swamp of Virginia, the Everglades of Florida, and, above all, the dense mangrove swamps of coastal Sumatra.

There are two stages in the transformation of plant matter into coal. The first stage consists of a bacterial fermentation, which after a longer or shorter interval becomes arrested by the toxic products formed during the bacterial activity. During this stage the plant debris is carbonized and compacted; it is transformed to peat.

In the second stage the further changes in the immature coals are determined by geologic activities. If the coal beds remain geologically unacted upon—if they remain horizontal, undisturbed—the coal does not advance in rank. The most influential factor in raising the rank of a coal is folding of the inclosing strata, which raises the rank of the coal by eliminating the water and volatile combustible matter. Nowhere is this better shown than in the Appalachian belt. In Ohio and western Pennsylvania the coal-bearing strata are horizontal, but eastward across the coal belt they become more and more closely folded. Concurrently the fixed-carbon content of the coal rises more than 40 per cent. The anthracite fields of Pennsylvania, which furnish 99.9 per cent of this country's supply of anthracite, are in the highly folded portion of the Appalachian coal field, and the coal of these fields consists almost wholly of fixed carbon, the moisture and gas having been nearly completely eliminated.

Questions—Mineral Resources

Main Ideas

1. The application of the science of applied geology to mineral resources is most important in—
   a. finding new resources.   b. developing and exploiting resources as they are found.   c. discovering new uses for common minerals.   d. finding substitutes for our vanishing resources.
2. What is the basic composition of all coal?
   a. Carbonized plant remains.   b. Resinous deposits.   c. Hydrocarbon.   d. Fixed carbon.

Details

3. The use of the seismograph and torsion balance for finding mineral resources gives the geologist data—
   a. that may be objectively interpreted irrespective of the particular area.   b. that must be interpreted in relation to the peculiarities of the particular area.   c. more quickly but no more accurately than older methods.   d. that is more accurate but less rapid than the older methods.
4. What type of rock formation usually incloses coal beds?
   a. Clay and limestone.   b. Shale and limestone.   c. Sandstone and limestone.   d. Sandstone and shale.
5. Which type of geologic activity within a coal field produces the highest grade of coal?
   a. A folding of the coal strata.   b. A lowering of the coal strata.   c. A relatively undisturbed environment during the time of coal formation.   d. An over-all rising of the coal strata.
6. The most completely carbonized form of coal is—
   a. peat.   b. lignite.   c. bituminous.   d. anthracite.
7. Which chemical produces the highest fuel value in coal?
   a. Fixed carbon.   b. Carbon dioxide.   c. Sulphur.   d. Hydrocarbon.
8. What is the first step in coal formation?
   a. Bacterial fermentation of plant matter.   b. Toxic activity upon

plant matter.   c. Carbonization of plant matter.   d. Ossification of plant matter.

Vocabulary

Some of the following may have been new to you in this selection:

embryonic   bituminous
amorphous   aerated
volatile   oxidized
lignite   sedimentary

Check those you knew before reading this selection. Choose the correct definition or synonym for each word as used in this selection to show how accurately you understand these terms.

1. embryonic
   a. underdeveloped.   b. beginning or earliest form.   c. unborn.
2. amorphous
   a. without form or shape.   b. broken into pieces.   c. combustible.
3. volatile
   a. gaseous.   b. carboniferous.   c. easily vaporized.
4. lignite
   a. plant debris.   b. brown coal.   c. wet coal.
5. bituminous
   a. medium-rank coal.   b. highly volatile coal.   c. wood-like coal.
6. aerated
   a. stagnant.   b. covered with water.   c. mixed with air.
7. oxidized
   a. carbonized.   b. mixed with oxygen.   c. combustible.
8. sedimentary
   a. very ancient.   b. plant debris.   c. formed by deposits.

Check your answers to these questions with the Answer Key. Write down in the Self-Appraisal the total credits you receive for each portion of the test.

Self-Appraisal

Record your reading rates here.
Predicted rate: ——— wpm.
Actual rate: ——— wpm.
What were your approaches to this material? Check those steps you used.

1. Previewed selection.
2. Previewed questions.

3. Wrote preview questions.
4. Skimmed some.
5. Took notes.
6. Underlined.
7. Reread some.
8. Skipped over some.

Was this an effective pattern for you? What was your final sum of points in—

Main Ideas	_____	(10 points or better?)
Details	_____	(30 points or better?)
Vocabulary	_____	(20 points or better?)
TOTAL	_____	(60 points or better?)

Did you use steps 1, 2, and possibly 5 or 7 in your pattern of reading?

Was your comprehension adequate in each type of question? If not, what can you do about it?

Was your rate controlled to yield detailed comprehension? Was your predicted rate within 25 to 50 words per minute of your actual rate?

Did you know the terms you thought you did? Did you learn any of the others while reading the selection?

Did you make any mistakes in handling this material effectively, such as the following?

Reading too rapidly for detailed comprehension. (See your score in Details.)

Reading too cautiously or in too great detail. (Failing to get minimum score on Main Ideas?)

Failing to get the main ideas by previewing. (Compare your questions with the instructor's.)

Overestimating your actual reading rate. (Because of failure to recognize the real difficulty of the material while previewing?)

Paying too little attention to new or technical words. (See your score in Vocabulary.)

Failing to try to organize the material in order to retain it. (Omitting all such organizational steps as 3, 5, 6, or 7 from your pattern?)

History

This 1,200-word selection reviews some of the basic contributions of the Greeks to man's understanding of the universe and some of its sciences. Preview the selection and its questions, then read it for detailed comprehension. After previewing, estimate your probable reading rate in words per minute. Write down the time when you begin reading and when you finish, in order to compute your actual rate later.

STARTED _____   FINISHED _____

TOTAL TIME _____

Science and Exploration in Hellenistic Culture*

Many Hellenistic Greeks found science more rewarding than philosophy or religion. Building on Aristotle's works and the vast data from Alexander's explorations, they expanded known sciences or created new ones. For instance, they enlarged and perfected geometry. Euclid (fl. c. 300 B.C.) produced a systematic textbook which was standard until about 1900. Later scientists, chiefly Eratosthenes of Cyrene, Archimedes of Syracuse, and Apollonius of Apamea made geometry the key to algebra, quadratic equations, and trigonometry. Archimedes was a genius both in pure and applied mathematics. He invented the windlass, the double or compound pulley, and the endless screw to serve as water pump. He improved catapults and used concave glass to burn Roman ships besieging his native Syracuse and grapnels to dash them against the rocks. He applied the principle of the lever to launch by himself the largest ship built in ancient times. "Give me where to stand, and I will move the Earth." Since slaves were cheap, machinery seemed pointless. Even so, Hellenistic scientists invented the water mill, water clock, and water organ, discovered the principles of compressed air, and used steam for motive power.

Greek astronomy learned even more from Babylonia when it became part of the *oecumene*. Babylonian astronomers had computed the length of the year to within 7 minutes 16 seconds. Building on Babylonian science, Aristarchus of Samos (310–230 B.C.) put forward the heliocentric theory, though he posited a circular, not an elliptical, movement and thought the sun was stationary. Most important, following Aristotle he emphasized observation as essential to science. Hipparchus of Nicaea (fl. 161–126 B.C.) calculated the mean lunar month within one second. Eratosthenes (275–194 B.C.), using astronomy, mathematics, and geography, measured the earth's circumference at the equator. Assuming the earth was round, he took the distance between two north-south points, that is, Alexandria and Syene (modern Aswan). Using two poles of the same length, and observing the length of their shadow on given days and hours in both Alexandria and Syene, he was able to calculate the earth's curvature between these points, and from that the circumference of the globe. His answer was 24,662 miles at the equator (the modern figure is 24,857). His error arose from supposing Syene to lie due south of Alexandria, whereas it is 2½ degrees east.

Explorations, east and west, by traders and at the bidding of land-hungry kings enlarged the knowledge of geography. While Alexander was pushing his armies to India, Pytheas, a Massiliot Greek, ventured into the North Sea and possibly the Baltic, coasting along Scotland, Scandinavia, or both, and discovering the Arctic Ocean. He may have established the moon's influence on tides, as against Aristotle's view that tides were due to winds raised by the sun. The Ptolemies, eager for war-elephants, encouraged trade with India, both by sea and overland across

* From *The Ancient World* by Vincent M. Scramuzza and Paul L. MacKendrick. Copyright © 1958 by Holt, Rinehart and Winston, Inc. Reprinted by permission of the publishers.

northern Arabia from Mediterranean ports, in particular Tyre. Later they used African elephants, and limited Indian imports to spices, muslins, perhaps silks, and other precious articles for which Hellenistic and growing Roman wealth was creating an increasing demand. When they lost southern Syria, they diverted Indian trade to a new route, free from Seleucid interference, via the Indian Ocean, east Arabian ports, and the Red Sea. They established trading posts on the African coast as far south as Somaliland and possibly even farther. Carthaginian sailors explored the Atlantic as far west as the Azores and south to the Cape Verde Islands. A Greek or Carthaginian ship from Cadiz in Spain may have rounded the Cape of Good Hope, finally landing in Somaliland.

Eratosthenes, abreast of these developments, mapped Europe, Asia, and Africa as a single land mass surrounded by the sea. He may have suspected the existence of a north-to-south continent dividing the Atlantic. Eighteen hundred and fifty years later men were to call it America. Finally he thought of reaching India by sailing westward from Spain. Picked up by medieval scholars, especially Roger Bacon, and by them transmitted to the intrepid fifteenth-century navigators, this idea was partly tested by Columbus and fully by Magellan. Eratosthenes' world map, complete with lines of latitude and longitude, looked more like a modern one than any until the fifteenth century. Unfortunately, later generations returned to the geocentric concept of the universe, following Ptolemy, a compiler of the second century A.D.

Cicero's teacher, the Syrian Posidonius of Apamea (c. 135–51 B.C.) rivaled Eratosthenes as the greatest Hellenistic polymath. He undertook a *Summa Hellenistica* integrating all knowledge: science, philosophy, popular worship and a higher religion based on Stoic-Platonic ideas, Hellenic reason and Oriental mysticism, astronomy and astrology, gods and demons, men and beasts. For him, the earth was a copy or counterpart of heaven; and the entire mineral, vegetable, and animal kingdoms were directed from heaven. Man was both an earthly and a heavenly creature; a compound of clay and spirit while on earth, a spiritual or daemonic being after death. A Stoic Nature-Providence guided even psychological phenomena, including man's thinking: both that based on fact and deduction and that which reflected his fears and hopes. The latter category included heavenly guidance by dreams, divination in all its forms (stargazing, hepatoscopy, bird flights, thunder and lightning), or magic and love potions. While Posidonius' serious influence rivaled Aristotle's he also perpetuated superstition under the guise of encyclopedic science. His influence, both good and bad on the Romans, was enormous. In fact it was Hellenistic culture on which the Romans modeled their ideas, their arts, and their lives, and which they transmitted to posterity, though in time they also imitated the writers, philosophers, and the plastic arts of earlier Greek centuries.

There was progress in medical theory and practice. Hippocratic search for symptoms plus Aristotelian regard for observed facts produced the "Scientific School" of medicine, which flourished especially in Alexandria, under a royal endowment for research. Vivisection of animals and dissection of cadavers led Herophilus to important discoveries in the anatomy of the liver, the lungs, and the generative organs. He established that blood is propelled by the heart, and he contrived an instrument to measure pulse-beats. He almost anticipated William Harvey's seventeenth-century discovery of the circulation of the blood. He discovered the nerves and understood that they received their stimulation from the brain. He understood also the function of the spinal cord. Another school, the "Empiric," or practical, cured or relieved sickness by new drugs, including opium, and by dieting, cold baths, massage, and exercise. In short, Hellenistic physicians startlingly anticipated modern medicine. Surgery too progressed: new instruments were invented and more serious operations performed.

Aristotle's disciple Theophrastus (c. 369–285 B.C.) like his master, observed facts carefully and presented them in scientific treatises. His *Inquiry on Plants* deals with the problems and principles of methodology and classifies scientifically all the varieties he knew. His *Aetiology of Plants* describes their physiology with a precision and acuteness remarkable without the microscope. Botany as an analytic science was his special province as zoology had been Aristotle's. Royal subsidies helped to establish zoological and botanical gardens in response to growing public interest, especially in exotic specimens.

Questions—Science and Exploration in Hellenistic Culture

Main Ideas

1. It is probably the author's main purpose in this selection to show that the Greeks made significant contributions to civilization in— a. philosophy and religion.   b. the arts of war.   c. applied mathematics and the sciences.   d. geometry and algebra.

2. The author implies that one of the reasons for the dramatic progress of Hellenistic culture and science was— a. the ability of the Greeks to think independently.   b. the freedom from the distractions of war.   c. the capacity to build upon the work of earlier Greeks and other cultures.   d. the system of widespread higher education.

3. Some of the scientific facts and principles discovered by the Greeks remained relatively unchanged until modern times. Among these more enduring contributions were— (choose as many as you need) a. the Euclidean system of geometry.   b. various simple machines, such as the compound pulley.   c. the geocentric concept of the universe.   d. the discovery of the circulation of blood in the human body.   e. the calculation of the shape and size of the earth. f. various surgical techniques.

4. Match the men named in the left-hand column with their areas of interest or contributions. Write the number of the related item in the right-hand column after the appropriate name.

Euclid   ———   1. An encyclopedia.
Archimedes   ———   2. Systematic geometry.
Eratosthenes   ———   3. Human anatomy.
Posidonius   ———   4. Botany.
Herophilus   ———   5. Size of the earth.
Theophrastus   ———   6. Applied mathematics.
                               7. Astronomy.

5. The period of Hellenistic culture referred to in this selection extended
from—
a. 300 B.C. to 100 A.D.   b. 375 B.C. to 50 B.C.   c. 310 B.C. to
400 A.D.   d. 200 B.C. to 100 A.D.

Vocabulary

Some of the following terms may have been new to you in this selection:

heliocentric   motive
geocentric   oecumene
divination   polymath
treatises   vivisection

Check those you knew before reading this selection. Choose the correct
definition or synonym for each word as used here to show how accurately
you now understand these terms.

1. heliocentric
   a. centered around the sun.   b. in ever-widening circles.
   c. concentrically oriented.

2. geocentric
   a. concentric.   b. centered around the earth.   c. a geometric
   theorem.

3. divination
   a. of divine nature.   b. foretelling.   c. science of astrology.

4. treatises
   a. articles or writings.   b. books.   c. speeches.

5. motive
   a. involving force.   b. involving power.   c. involving motion.

6. polymath
   a. mathematician.   b. scientist.   c. master of all knowledge.

7. oecumene
   a. Greek colonies.   b. civilized world.   c. known world.

8. vivisection
   a. dissection of live animals.   b. study of live animals.   c. anatomy of live animals.

Check your answers with the Answer Key. Write down in the Self-Appraisal the total credits you receive for each portion of the test.

Self-Appraisal

Record your reading rates here.

Predicted rate: ———— wpm.

Actual rate: ———— wpm.

What were your approaches to this material? Check those steps you used.

1. Previewed selection.
2. Previewed questions.
3. Wrote preview questions.
4. Skimmed some.
5. Took notes.
6. Underlined.
7. Reread some.
8. Skipped over some.

Was this an effective pattern of reading for you? What was your final sum of points in—

Main Ideas	————	(9 points or better?)
Details	————	(30 points or better?)
Vocabulary	————	(20 points or better?)
TOTAL	————	(59 points or better?)

Did you use steps 1 and 2 as instructed, and after previewing the questions, also use steps 5 or 6 to aid your retention of the details? Or, didn't the material seem that difficult? Do your scores on the test support your choice of steps? Was your comprehension adequate in each type of question? If not, why not?

Was your rate controlled to result in sufficient comprehension? Was your predicted rate within 25 to 50 words per minute of your actual rate?

Did you know the terms you thought you knew? Did you learn some others by reading the selection? Did you notice the similarities in *heliocentric* and *geocentric?* in *vivisection* and *dissection?* Were you able to derive the meanings of *oecumene, polymath,* and *divination* from the context?

Did you make any mistakes in handling this material effectively, such as the following?

Reading too rapidly for detailed comprehension. (See your score in Details.)

Reading too cautiously or in too great detail. (Failing to get minimum score on Main Ideas.)

Overestimating your actual reading rate. (Because of failure to recognize the real difficulty of the material while previewing?)

Paying too little attention to new or technical words. (See your score in Vocabulary.)

Failing to try to organize the material in order to retain it. (Omitting all such steps as 3, 5, 6 or 7 from your pattern?)

Literature

This 3,600-word selection is the author's effort to portray the traditions of the Old South and the decay of those traditions following the Civil War. Preview the questions to the selection. Then read, keeping in mind that there are several levels of meaning. There is the concrete, or objective level, which may be found in the clear details of the story. There are the more abstract inferences set by the tone and mood, which give the reader a feeling about the customs and traditions of a community. There is also an allegorical quality—the description of transition in a social system depicted in the lives of the characters in the story.

After previewing, estimate your probable reading rate in words per minute. Write down the time when you begin reading and when you finish, in order to compute your actual rate later.

STARTED ————————————   FINISHED ————————————

TOTAL TIME ————————————

A Rose for Emily*

—WILLIAM FAULKNER

I

When Miss Emily Grierson died, our whole town went to her funeral: the men through a sort of respectful affection for a fallen monument, the women mostly out of curiosity to see the inside of her house, which no one save an old man-servant—a combined gardener and cook—had seen in at least ten years.

It was a big, squarish frame house that had once been white, decorated with cupolas and spires and scrolled balconies in the heavily lightsome style of the Seventies, set on what had once been our most select street. But garages and cotton gins had encroached and obliterated even the august names of that neighborhood; only Miss Emily's house was left, lifting its stubborn and coquettish decay above the cotton wagons and the gasoline pumps—an eyesore among eyesores. And now Miss Emily had gone to join the representatives of those august names where they lay in the cedar-bemused cemetery among the ranked and anonymous graves of Union and Confederate soldiers who fell at the battle of Jefferson.

Alive, Miss Emily had been a tradition, a duty, and a care; a sort of hereditary obligation upon the town, dating from that day in 1894 when Colonel Sartoris, the mayor—he who fathered the edict that no Negro woman should appear on the streets without an apron—remitted her taxes, the dispensation dating from the death of her father on into perpetuity. Not that Miss Emily would have accepted charity. Colonel Sartoris invented an involved tale to the effect that Miss Emily's father had loaned money to the town, which the town, as a matter of business, preferred this way of repaying. Only a man of Colonel Sartoris' generation and thought could have invented it, and only a woman could have believed it.

When the next generation, with its more modern ideas, became mayors and aldermen, this arrangement created some little dissatisfaction. On the first of the year they mailed her a tax notice. February came, and there was no reply. They wrote her a formal letter, asking her to call at the sheriff's office at her convenience. A week later the mayor wrote her himself, offering to call or to send his car for her, and received in reply a note on paper of an archaic shape, in a thin, flowing calligraphy in faded ink, to the effect that she no longer went out at all. The tax notice was also enclosed, without comment.

They called a special meeting of the Board of Aldermen. A deputation waited upon her, knocked at the door through which no visitor had passed since she ceased giving china-painting lessons eight or ten years earlier. They were admitted by the old Negro into a dim hall from which a stairway mounted into still more shadow. It smelled of dust and disuse —a close, dank smell. The Negro led them into the parlor. It was furnished in heavy, leather-covered furniture. When the Negro opened the blinds of one window, they could see that the leather was cracked; and when they sat down, a faint dust rose sluggishly about their thighs, spinning with slow motes in the single sun-ray. On a tarnished gilt easel before the fireplace stood a crayon portrait of Miss Emily's father.

They rose when she entered—a small, fat woman in black, with a thin gold chain descending to her waist and vanishing into her belt, leaning on an ebony cane with a tarnished gold head. Her skeleton was small and spare; perhaps that was why what would have been merely plumpness in another was obesity in her. She looked bloated, like a body long submerged in motionless water, and of that pallid hue. Her eyes, lost in the fatty ridges of her face, looked like two small pieces of coal pressed into a lump of dough as they moved from one face to another while the visitors stated their errand.

She did not ask them to sit. She just stood in the door and listened quietly until the spokesman came to a stumbling halt. Then they could hear the invisible watch ticking at the end of the gold chain.

Her voice was dry and cold. "I have no taxes in Jefferson. Colonel Sartoris explained it to me. Perhaps one of you can gain access to the city records and satisfy yourselves."

"But we have. We are the city authorities, Miss Emily. Didn't you get a notice from the sheriff, signed by him?"

"I received a paper, yes," Miss Emily said. "Perhaps he considers himself the sheriff . . . I have no taxes in Jefferson."

"But there is nothing on the books to show that, you see. We must go by the—"

"See Colonel Sartoris. I have no taxes in Jefferson."

"But, Miss Emily—"

"See Colonel Sartoris." (Colonel Sartoris had been dead almost ten years.) "I have no taxes in Jefferson. Tobe!" The Negro appeared. "Show these gentlemen out."

II

So she vanquished them, horse and foot, just as she had vanquished their fathers thirty years before about the smell. That was two years after her father's death and a short time after her sweetheart—the one we believed would marry her—had deserted her. After her father's death she went out very little; after her sweetheart went away, people hardly saw her at all. A few of the ladies had the temerity to call, but were not received, and the only sign of life about the place was the Negro man—a young man then—going in and out with a market basket.

"Just as if a man—any man—could keep a kitchen properly," the ladies said; so they were not surprised when the smell developed. It was another link between the gross, teeming world and the high and mighty Griersons.

A neighbor, a woman, complained to the mayor, Judge Stevens, eighty years old.

"But what will you have me do about it, madam?" he said.

"Why, send her word to stop it," the woman said. "Isn't there a law?"

"I'm sure that won't be necessary," Judge Stevens said. "It's probably just a snake or a rat that nigger of hers killed in the yard. I'll speak to him about it."

The next day he received two more complaints, one from a man who came in diffident deprecation. "We really must do something about it, Judge. I'd be the last one in the world to bother Miss Emily, but we've got to do something." That night the Board of Aldermen met—three graybeards and one younger man, a member of the rising generation.

"It's simple enough," he said. "Send her word to have her place cleaned up. Give her a certain time to do it in, and if she don't . . ."

"Dammit, sir," Judge Stevens said, "will you accuse a lady to her face of smelling bad?"

So the next night, after midnight, four men crossed Miss Emily's lawn and slunk about the house like burglars, sniffing along the base of the brickwork and at the cellar openings while one of them performed a regular sowing motion with his hand out of a sack slung from his shoulder. They broke open the cellar door and sprinkled lime there, and in all the outbuildings. As they recrossed the lawn, a window that had been dark was lighted and Miss Emily sat in it, the light behind her, and her upright torso motionless as that of an idol. They crept quietly across the lawn and into the shadow of the locusts that lined the street. After a week or two the smell went away.

That was when people had begun to feel really sorry for her. People in our town, remembering how Old Lady Wyatt, her great-aunt, had gone completely crazy at last, believed that the Griersons held themselves a little too high for what they really were. None of the young men was quite good enough for Miss Emily and such. We had long thought of them as a tableau: Miss Emily a slender figure in white in the background, her father a spraddled silhouette in the foreground, his back to her and clutching a horsewhip, the two of them framed by the back-flung front door. So when she got to be thirty and was still single, we were not pleased exactly, but vindicated; even with insanity in the family she wouldn't have turned down all of her chances if they had really materialized.

When her father died, it got about that the house was all that was left to her; and in a way, people were glad. At last they could pity Miss Emily. Being left alone, and a pauper, she had become humanized. Now she too would know the old thrill and the old despair of a penny more or less.

The day after his death all the ladies prepared to call at the house and offer condolence and aid, as is our custom. Miss Emily met them at the door, dressed as usual and with no trace of grief on her face. She told them that her father was not dead. She did that for three days, with the ministers calling on her, and the doctors, trying to persuade her to let them dispose of the body. Just as they were about to resort to law and force, she broke down, and they buried her father quickly.

We did not say she was crazy then. We believed she had to do that. We remembered all the young men her father had driven away, and we knew that with nothing left, she would have to cling to that which had robbed her, as people will.

III

She was sick for a long time. When we saw her again, her hair was cut short, making her look like a girl, with a vague resemblance to those angels in colored church windows—sort of tragic and serene.

The town had just let the contracts for paving the sidewalks, and in the summer after her father's death they began the work. The construction company came with niggers and mules and machinery, and a fore-man named Homer Barron, a Yankee—a big, dark, ready man, with a big voice and eyes lighter than his face. The little boys would follow in groups to hear him cuss the niggers, and the niggers singing in time to the rise and fall of picks. Pretty soon he knew everybody in town. When-ever you heard a lot of laughing about the square, Homer Barron would be in the center of the group. Presently we began to see him and Miss Emily on Sunday afternoons driving in the yellow-wheeled buggy and the matched team of bays from the livery stable.

At first we were glad that Miss Emily would have an interest, because the ladies all said, "Of course a Grierson would not think seriously of a Northerner, a day laborer." But there were still others, older people, who said that even grief could not cause a real lady to forget *noblesse oblige* —without calling it *noblesse oblige*. They just said, "Poor Emily. Her kinsfolk should come to her." She had some kin in Alabama; but years ago her father had fallen out with them over the estate of Old Lady Wyatt, the crazy woman, and there was no communication between the two families. They had not even been represented at the funeral.

And as soon as the old people said, "Poor Emily," the whispering began. "Do you suppose it's really so?" they said to one another. "Of course it is. What else could . . ." This behind their hands; rustling of craned silk and satin behind jalousies closed upon the sun of Sunday afternoon as the thin, swift clop-clop-clop of the matched team passed: "Poor Emily."

She carried her head high enough—even when we believed that she was fallen. It was as if she demanded more than ever the recognition of her dignity as the last Grierson; as if it had wanted that touch of earthiness to reaffirm her imperviousness. Like when she bought the rat poison, the arsenic. That was over a year after they had begun to say "Poor Emily," and while the two female cousins were visiting her.

"I want some poison," she said to the druggist. She was over thirty then, still a slight woman, though thinner than usual, with cold, haughty black eyes in a face the flesh of which was strained across the temples and about the eye-sockets as you imagine a lighthouse-keeper's face ought to look. "I want some poison," she said.

"Yes, Miss Emily. What kind? For rats and such? I'd recom—"

"I want the best you have. I don't care what kind."

The druggist named several. "They'll kill anything up to an elephant. But what you want is—"

"Arsenic," Miss Emily said. "Is that a good one?"

"Is . . . arsenic? Yes, ma'am. But what you want—"

"I want arsenic."

The druggist looked down at her. She looked back at him, erect, her face like a strained flag. "Why, of course," the druggist said. "If that's what you want. But the law requires you to tell what you are going to use it for."

Miss Emily just stared at him, her head tilted back in order to look him eye for eye, until he looked away and went and got the arsenic and wrapped it up. The Negro delivery boy brought her the package; the druggist didn't come back. When she opened the package at home there was written on the box, under the skull and bones: "For rats."

IV

So the next day we all said, "She will kill herself"; and we said it would be the best thing. When she had first begun to be seen with Homer Barron, we had said, "She will marry him." Then we said, "She will persuade him yet," because Homer himself had remarked—he liked men, and it was known that he drank with the younger men in the Elks' Club—that he was not a marrying man. Later we said, "Poor Emily" behind the jalousies as they passed on Sunday afternoon in the glittering buggy. Miss Emily with her head high and Homer Barron with his hat cocked and a cigar in his teeth, reins and whip in a yellow glove.

Then some of the ladies began to say that it was a disgrace to the town and a bad example to the young people. The men did not want to interfere, but at last the ladies forced the Baptist minister—Miss Emily's people were Episcopal—to call upon her. He would never divulge what happened during that interview, but he refused to go back again. The next Sunday they again drove about the streets, and the following day the minister's wife wrote to Miss Emily's relations in Alabama.

So she had blood-kin under her roof again and we sat back to watch developments. At first nothing happened. Then we were sure that they were to be married. We learned that Miss Emily had been to the jeweler's and ordered a man's toilet set in silver, with the letters H.B. on each piece. Two days later we learned that she had bought a complete outfit of men's clothing, including a nightshirt, and we said, "They are married." We were really glad. We were glad because the two female cousins were even more Grierson than Miss Emily had ever been.

So we were not surprised when Homer Barron—the streets had been finished some time since—was gone. We were a little disappointed that there was not a public blowing-off, but we believed that he had gone on to prepare for Miss Emily's coming, or to give her a chance to get rid of the cousins. (By that time it was a cabal, and we were all Miss Emily's allies to help circumvent the cousins.) Sure enough, after another week they departed. And, as we had expected all along, within three days Homer Barron was back in town. A neighbor saw the Negro man admit him at the kitchen door at dusk one evening.

And that was the last we saw of Homer Barron. And of Miss Emily for some time. The Negro man went in and out with the market basket, but the front door remained closed. Now and then we would see her at a window for a moment, as the men did that night when they sprinkled the lime, but for almost six months she did not appear on the streets. Then we knew that this was to be expected too; as if that quality of her father which had thwarted her woman's life so many times had been too virulent and too furious to die.

When we next saw Miss Emily, she had grown fat and her hair was turning gray. During the next few years it grew grayer and grayer until it attained an even pepper-and-salt iron-gray, when it ceased turning. Up to the day of her death at seventy-four it was still that vigorous iron-gray, like the hair of an active man.

From that time on her front door remained closed, save for a period of six or seven years, when she was about forty, during which she gave lessons in china-painting. She fitted up a studio in one of the downstairs rooms, where the daughters and granddaughters of Colonel Sartoris' contemporaries were sent to her with the same regularity and in the same spirit that they were sent to church on Sundays with a twenty-five-cent piece for the collection plate. Meanwhile her taxes had been remitted.

Then the newer generation became the backbone and the spirit of the town, and the painting pupils grew up and fell away and did not send their children to her with boxes of color and tedious brushes and pictures cut from the ladies' magazines. The front door closed upon the last one and remained closed for good. When the town got free postal delivery, Miss Emily alone refused to let them fasten the metal numbers above her door and attach a mailbox to it. She would not listen to them.

Daily, monthly, yearly we watched the Negro grow grayer and more stooped, going in and out with the market basket. Each December we sent her a tax notice, which would be returned by the post office a week later, unclaimed. Now and then we would see her in one of the downstairs windows—she had evidently shut up the top floor of the house— like the carven torso of an idol in a niche, looking or not looking at us, we could never tell which. Thus she passed from generation to generation —dear, inescapable, impervious, tranquil, and perverse.

And so she died. Fell ill in the house filled with dust and shadows, with only a doddering Negro man to wait on her. We did not even know she was sick; we had long since given up trying to get any information from the Negro. He talked to no one, probably not even to her, for his voice had grown harsh and rusty, as if from disuse.

She died in one of the downstairs rooms, in a heavy walnut bed with a curtain, her gray head propped on a pillow yellow and moldy with age and lack of sunlight.

V

The Negro met the first of the ladies at the front door and let them in, with their hushed, sibilant voices and their quick, curious glances, and then he disappeared. He walked right through the house and out the back and was not seen again.

The two female cousins came at once. They held the funeral on the second day, with the town coming to look at Miss Emily beneath a mass of bought flowers, with the crayon face of her father musing profoundly above the bier and the ladies sibilant and macabre; and the very old men—some in their brushed Confederate uniforms—on the porch and the lawn, talking of Miss Emily as if she had been a contemporary of theirs, believing that they had danced with her and courted her perhaps, confusing time with its mathematical progression, as the old do, to whom all the past is not a diminishing road but, instead, a huge meadow which no winter ever quite touches, divided from them now by the narrow bottleneck of the most recent decade of years.

Already we knew that there was one room in that region above stairs which no one had seen in forty years, and which would have to be forced. They waited until Miss Emily was decently in the ground before they opened it.

The violence of breaking down the door seemed to fill this room with pervading dust. A thin, acrid pall as of the tomb seemed to lie everywhere upon this room decked and furnished as for a bridal: upon the valance curtains of faded rose color, upon the rose-shaded lights, upon the dressing table, upon the delicate array of crystal and the man's toilet things backed with tarnished silver, silver so tarnished that the monogram was obscured. Among them lay a collar and tie, as if they had just been removed, which, lifted, left upon the surface a pale crescent in the dust. Upon a chair hung the suit, carefully folded; beneath it the two mute shoes and the discarded socks.

The man himself lay in the bed.

For a long while we just stood there, looking down at the profound and fleshless grin. The body had apparently once lain in the attitude of an embrace, but now the long sleep that outlasts love, that conquers even the grimace of love, had cuckolded him. What was left of him, rotted beneath what was left of the nightshirt, had become inextricable from the bed in which he lay; and upon him and upon the pillow beside him lay that even coating of the patient and biding dust.

Then we noticed that in the second pillow was the indentation of a head. One of us lifted something from it, and leaning forward, that faint and invisible dust dry and acrid in the nostrils, we saw a long strand of iron-gray hair.

Questions—A Rose for Emily

Main Ideas

1. How does Faulkner present this story?
   a. As a character study.   b. As a study of a culture.   c. As a mystery story.   d. As a series of chronological events.

2. What was the principal portrayal Faulkner attempted to make in this story?
   a. A picture of life in a small Southern town.   b. The curiosity of neighbors.   c. The resistance of people to change in their social system.   d. The influence of one person on a community.

3. What or whom did Emily represent symbolically?
   a. The culture and traditions of a society.   b. The people within the Southern culture.   c. The new generation bent on change.   d. All the families of the South immediately following the Civil War.

4. Why was Emily in death referred to by Faulkner as "a fallen monument"?
   a. Symbolically, in and through her life, the townspeople had worshipped the dead but unburied past.   b. She was the last of an aristocratic family.   c. She had been a strong political force in the community.   d. Her generation was being replaced in the town by the younger people with more modern ideas.

5. Why did Faulkner use the first person plural as the narrator?
   a. The *we* represented the outside world viewing the South.
   b. The *we* represented the involvement of an entire society in Emily's intrigue.   c. Faulkner meant it simply as an editorial *we*.
   d. The *we* represented those persons not in sympathy with the social system Emily represented.

Inferences and Interpretations

6. What was most important to the people of Jefferson?
   a. Climbing the "social ladder."   b. Holding to their traditions.
   c. Earning a living.   d. Keeping "up to date" in appearances.

7. What gave Emily her influence over the townspeople?
   a. Her beauty.   b. Her money.   c. Her social position.
   d. Her knowledge of their weaknesses.

8. What did the townspeople expect Emily to do with the arsenic?
   a. Kill herself.   b. Kill Homer Barron.   c. Rid the house of
   rats.   d. They didn't have any idea of her intentions.

9. Why was the Board of Aldermen unable to collect taxes from Miss
   Emily?
   a. She simply refused to pay any taxes.   b. They were incapable
   of convincing her that she owed taxes.   c. They were afraid to
   press her for payment.   d. The townspeople didn't believe she
   should pay taxes.

10. Some of the neighbors viewed Emily's female cousins as—
    a. intruders.   b. simply there to help prepare for Miss Emily's
    wedding.   c. having come to try to stop the gossip about Miss
    Emily.   d. coming to claim their share of the Grierson estate.

11. Why may we suppose that the townspeople suspected that Homer
    Barron may have been killed by Emily?
    a. They knew that there was a history of insanity in Emily's family.
    b. They knew that Homer Barron had disappeared suddenly.
    c. At first Emily had not admitted to her neighbors that her father
    had died.   d. They knew that she had purchased arsenic and
    that afterward there was an odor about her house.

12. Why did the townspeople fail to do anything about their suspicions
    that Emily had killed Homer Barron?
    a. The Grierson family was wealthy and powerful politically.
    b. Homer Barron was a Yankee.   c. Tradition could not allow
    an "old" family to fall into disrepute.   d. They were afraid of
    Emily.

13. What may be assumed by the failure of the neighbors to discover
    earlier the body of Homer Barron?
    a. Emily had kept him well hidden.   b. The neighbors assumed
    the murder would have been committed elsewhere.   c. The
    neighbors secretly sympathized with Emily's act.   d. Emily did
    not allow the neighbors to visit her.

14. Read again the last sentence in Part II: "We remembered all the
    young men her father had driven away, and we knew that with
    nothing left, she would have to cling to that which had robbed her,
    as people will." Whom does Faulkner imply had robbed Emily?
    a. Homer Barron.   b. Her father.   c. Her neighbors.
    d. An unknown assailant.

15. How does Faulkner portray Emily's Negro manservant?
    a. As a trusted friend.   b. As a partner to her crime.   c. As a

bearer of tales to the community.   d. As only a part of her way of life.

Vocabulary

Several of the following words may have been new to you:

cupolas	temerity
edict	tableau
remitted	condolence
calligraphy	cabal
motes	cuckolded

Check those you knew before you read the selection. Choose the correct synonym or definition for each term as used here to show how well you now understand these words.

1. cupolas
   a. domes.   b. columns.   c. towers.
2. edict
   a. axiom.   b. ruling.   c. idea.
3. remitted
   a. refusal.   b. abolished.   c. pardoned.
4. calligraphy
   a. handwriting.   b. scribbling.   c. sentences.
5. motes
   a. clouds.   b. specks.   c. tiny insects.
6. temerity
   a. foolhardiness.   b. courtesy.   c. rashness.
7. tableau
   a. imaginary scene.   b. French play.   c. figures arranged to portray an incident.
8. condolence
   a. expression of sympathy.   b. gifts of friendship.   c. domestic assistance.
9. cabal
   a. plan.   b. secret sympathetic group.   c. plot.
10. cuckolded
   a. killed.   b. deprived of manhood.   c. betrayed.

Check your answers with the Answer Key. Write down in the Self-Appraisal the total credits you receive for each portion of the test.

Self-Appraisal

Record your reading rates here.
Predicted rate ———— wpm.
Actual rate ———— wpm.
What were your approaches to this material? Check those steps you used.

1. Previewed selection.
2. Previewed questions.
3. Wrote preview questions.
4. Skimmed some.
5. Took notes.
6. Underlined.
7. Reread some.
8. Skipped over some.

Was this an effective pattern of reading for you? What was your final sum of points in—

Main Ideas ———— (18 points or better?)
Inferences ———— (24 points or better?)
Vocabulary ———— (18 points or better?)
TOTAL ———— (60 points or better?)

Did you use step 2 as suggested? The involved style so often characteristic of Faulkner may have necessitated your rereading occasionally for clarity, as in step 7. In other places, you may well have skimmed or read rapidly, as in step 4.

Was your comprehension adequate in both main ideas and the inferences or implications? Was your predicted rate within 25 to 50 words per minute of your actual rate?

Did you know the terms you thought you knew? Did you learn some of the new ones in reading the selection? Most of them should have been clarified by the context, if you read carefully.

Did you make mistakes in handling this material effectively, such as the following?

Reading too rapidly for detailed comprehension. (See your score in Inferences.)

Reading too cautiously or in too great detail. (Failing to get minimum score on Main Ideas?)

Overestimating your actual reading rate.

Paying too little attention to new words. (See your score in Vocabulary.)

Mathematics

This 1,300-word selection offers a simple explanation of directed numbers, a concept that puzzled great mathematicians for centuries. You might be asked by your mathematics instructor to read such a passage as an introduction to the topic. Preview the selection and its questions, then read it, particularly for comprehension of its main idea. After previewing, estimate your probable rate in words per minute. Write down the time when you begin reading and when you finish, in order to compute your actual rate later.

STARTED ————————   FINISHED ————————

TOTAL TIME ————————

The Invention of Algebra*

The origin of the minus sign − is not known. It was used by merchants to indicate a *deficiency* long before it was used by mathematicians. Thus, "8 − 3" written on a bale would indicate a deficiency of 3 (yards, or whatever it might be). Clearly, no merchant would be likely to come across the puzzling statement "3 − 8"! This would indicate that the bale contained material that was 8 yards short of the correct length of 3 yards, which just doesn't make sense. But mathematicians from very early times ran up against statements like this in their process of solving "equation" problems. For centuries they ignored such statements as being absurd. Like the merchant, being accustomed only to the primitive number-scale 1, 2, 3, 4, 5 . . . they were at a loss to explain such a statement. In the *Arithmetica* of Diophantus the equation (in modern symbols) $4x + 20 = 4$ is curtly dismissed as "absurd," since no number on the only number-scale known to Diophantus would serve for the value of the unknown x. Before a statement like "3 − 8" could have any meaning, another mathematical concept had to be invented: the idea of *direction* on the number-scale. We shall deal with this aspect of *minus* (and of *plus*) later in this chapter. All through mathematics we find one generation labeling some idea as "absurd" just because it doesn't make sense to them. A few generations later, the same idea is accepted as obvious. All that has happened is that some bright individual has thought out some new line of approach to the problem, and perhaps invented some mathematical device that makes it all crystal clear. Maybe our grandchildren will smile in kindly incredulity when they read that only a few extremely skilled individuals really understood Einstein's theory of relativity in 1948. As we shall see, even the great Descartes labeled some numbers as "imaginary." Today, those numbers are no more imaginary than the bread and butter they earn for electricians.

Let us now see how mathematicians overcame the difficulty that caused Diophantus to declare that the equation $4x + 20 = 4$ was "absurd." We shall see the difficulty lay, not with the equation, but with the inability of the primitive number-scale to handle any but numbers starting with zero and continuing through 1, 2, 3, 4 . . . in an endless series. After being dubbed "absurd" for thousands of years, equations like the one just quoted at last came into their own, as mathematicians slowly came to realize that in many problems the essential idea is not merely magnitude, but the *order* in which things lie. If the non-mathematically-minded reader will bear with an example that looks particularly trivial and childish, he may quickly grasp the idea of the new concept that was introduced into the primitive number-scale. By this new concept, the ideas of *direction* and *relative position* were linked to the number-scale, which was now extended into one having *no beginning* as well as no end.

Imagine we are among a crowd of onlookers watching a large hotel on fire. We hear a cry of distress. We see a would-be rescuer emerge

---

*From *Makers of Mathematics* by Alfred Hooper. Copyright 1948 by Random House. Reprinted by permission.

from a sixth floor window on to the fire escape. He rushes up 18 steps, peers through a window, evidently sees nothing, and then climbs down 5 steps to look in at another window. Here we shall leave him, since, as mathematicians, we are, of course, supposed to be interested only in calculations.

Even a small child would know that the would-be rescuer is now 13 steps above his starting point. How would he know this? By working the calculation $18 - 5 = 13$. Like Diophantus, he would say that the minus sign shows that 5 is to be subtracted from 18.

But there is another, and quite different interpretation possible. The facts we have considered make it clear that in the statement $18 - 5 = 13$, the number 18 indicates an upward movement in this particular problem, and the number 5 a downward movement. *So the minus sign may be regarded as indicating that the number following it is to be measured in a direction exactly opposite to that indicated by the number 18.*

How would this idea have worked if our would-be rescuer had run 5 steps up and then 18 steps down the fire escape? We should have indicated these movements by writing $5 - 18$. This gives us the kind of problem that baffled ancient mathematicians. Obviously, if *minus* can only indicate subtraction, we, too, must remain baffled. But since we have agreed that a minus sign also indicates a change of direction, the statement makes sense, since it tells us that the climber, having gone up 5 steps, then took 18 steps *in the opposite direction*. But can there be any answer to "$5 - 18$"?

Well, let the would-be rescuer make his 18 downward steps in two movements, the first a downward movement of 5 steps, the second, another downward movement of the remaining 13 steps. We can now say that the number of steps from his starting point at which he finishes his three movements can be indicated by $5 - 5 - 13$. Clearly, the first two of these movements bring him back to his starting point, so the "$5 - 5$" part of the statement can be ignored, leaving the answer -13. So $5 - 18 = -13$. But what meaning can be attached to this -13? Obviously it indicates *the number of steps below his starting point at which the climber finishes*. If then we agree that when calculating distances up and down a ladder, or any graduated scale, a *minus* sign may indicate either a downward movement or a position below some starting point, the expression $5 - 18 = -13$ has a meaning which it could not have with the elementary number-scale of arithmetic.

Now let us consider another case. Suppose the climber had run up 4 steps, paused, then run up another 7 steps. We should then calculate his final position, relative to his starting point, as $4 + 7 = 11$. What does this + sign indicate? Diophantus would have answered "addition." We should now say "Yes, but it may also indicate an *upward* movement." So if we agree that a *minus* sign indicates a downward movement or a position below some fixed starting point, a *plus* sign will indicate either an upward movement or a position above that same starting point. We can now label the starting point as 0, the steps above the starting point as $+1, +2, +3, +4, \ldots$ and the steps below that starting point as -1,

−2, −3, −4, . . . Numbers marked like this, with a + or − sign, are called *directed numbers,* or *signed numbers.* A directed number having a + sign is called a *positive* number; one having a − sign, a *negative* number. As we have seen, Cardan was the first mathematician to deal clearly with the meaning of negative numbers.

Let us now return to the equation $4x + 20 = 4$, which Diophantus considered "absurd." Using our new concept, it is clear that x must stand for a negative number, the number −4. A possible problem that would lead to this equation would be "What movement must be made by a man standing on a ladder, if four times that movement combined with twenty steps upward would bring him to a position that was four steps above his starting point?" Since the answer is "4 downward steps," we see that the equation makes perfectly good sense after all.

These directed or signed numbers may be used whenever two movements occur in exactly opposite directions. Thus, on a horizontal scale, movements to the right, or positions to the right of a fixed starting point can be indicated by positive numbers; movements to the left, or positions to the left of that starting point, by negative numbers.

Questions—The Invention of Algebra

Main Ideas

1. Early mathematicians were unable to deal with negative numbers because they—
   a. had not discovered the minus sign.   b. did not understand algebra.   c. used a number system beginning with zero.   d. had no system for recording such quantities.

2. The basic concept that early mathematicians lacked was that—
   a. some numbers could be less than zero.   b. numbers have a beginning and an end.   c. zero is simply a place-holding figure.
   d. numbers indicate direction or relative position.

3. A man standing on the side of a steep hill attempts to climb. Because of the steepness, each time he climbs upward five steps he slides back the distance equal to about six steps. After three trials at climbing, how far would he have progressed?_____

   _____

Details

4. The minus sign attached to a number indicates that the number—
   a. is to be measured in a direction opposite to the next number.
   b. is to be subtracted from the next number.   c. is below zero in the number scale.   d. is part of an equation.

5. If you understand directed numbers, you can do these simple problems.

   a. Add −8 and +5. ——   b. Add +13 and −5. ——

  c. Multiply −6 by +4. ———   d. Subtract −2 from +17. ———
  e. Subtract −6 from −12. ———

6. Early mathematicians understood the use of the minus sign—
   a. long before merchants or others using numbers.   b. only to indicate subtraction.   c. as indicating a quantity below zero.   d. as
   a means of solving certain equations.

Vocabulary

Several of the following terms may have been new to you:

deficiency   signed numbers
equation   positive number
direction

Check those you knew before you read the selection. Choose the correct
synonym or definition for each term as used in this selection to show how
well you now understand these terms.

1. deficiency
   a. the act of subtracting.   b. something lacking or missing.
   c. a negative amount.

2. equation
   a. a chemical formula.   b. matching two things.   c. a statement of a mathematical problem.

3. direction
   a. order of objects or numbers.   b. guidance or supervision.
   c. an instruction.

4. signed numbers
   a. numbers greater than zero.   b. numbers with superscription,
   such as 4^2.   c. positive or negative numbers.

5. positive number
   a. any number.   b. +4 or −4.   c. number preceded by plus
   sign.

Self-Appraisal

Record your reading rates here:
Predicted rate: ——— wpm.
Actual rate: ——— wpm.
What were your approaches to this material? Check those steps you used.

1. Previewed selection.
2. Previewed questions.
3. Wrote preview questions.
4. Skimmed some.
5. Took notes.
6. Underlined.

7. Reread some.

8. Skipped over some.

Was this an effective pattern of reading for you? What was your final sum of points in—

Main Ideas   ———   (19 points or better?)
Details   ———   (25 points or better?)
Vocabulary   ———   (15 points or better?)
     TOTAL   ———   (59 points or better?)

Did you use step 1 and 2 as directed? The simplicity of this selection might have permitted you to use step 4 or 8 also. You probably found little need for steps 3, 5, 6, or 7.

Was your comprehension adequate in each type of question? Was your predicted rate within 25 to 50 words per minute of your actual rate?

Did you know the terms you thought you knew? Did you learn any terms in reading the selection?

Did you make any mistakes in handling this material effectively, such as the following?

Reading too rapidly for detailed comprehension. (See your score in Details.)

Reading too cautiously or in too great detail. (Failing to get minimum score on Main Ideas?)

Failing to get the main ideas by previewing. (Compare your questions with the instructor's.)

Overestimating your actual reading rate. (Because of failure to recognize the real difficulty of the material while previewing?)

Paying too little attention to new or technical words. (See your score in Vocabulary)

Psychology

This 1,000-word selection compares common-sense knowledge with that derived from scientific psychology. This topic is often treated in the opening chapters of textbooks in the introductory course in psychology. Let us assume that you were asked to read this in such a course. Your instructor did not give any specific directions; hence you will have to plan your own purposes in reading the excerpt.

Preview it, outlining on paper the written questions you intend to be able to answer, or that you think will be asked in class. *Don't* read the questions at the end of the article. After previewing, estimate your probable rate of reading in words per minute. Write down the time when you begin reading and when you finish, in order to compute your actual rate later. Then read to answer the questions you have outlined. When you have finished, compare your questions and answers with those given.

STARTED   ————————   FINISHED   ————————
TOTAL TIME   ———————

Folk Psychology*

This approach may also be called *popular psychology* because it consists of the notions of the average person as to why men and women behave as they do. These notions are said to be self-evident truths because anyone can see for himself that they are correct. It is self-evident to many people that "sparing the rod spoils the child," that "slums breed crime," and that "haste makes waste." It is just plain common sense that "one has to work hard in order to succeed," that "honesty is the best policy," and that "accidents are caused by carelessness." A common-sense explanation is one that appeals to reasonable men and women as distinguished from fools, lunatics, and experts. Freud, for example, aroused the ire of people when he proclaimed in 1905 that young children possessed sexual desires, for such an idea ran counter to the popular notion regarding the innocence of the child. Likewise, Darwin shocked the sensibilities of Victorian England when he proposed the outrageous doctrine that man had not been specially created by a divine power but had evolved from lower forms of life.

It is sometimes said, or at least implied, that popular opinion is almost invariably wrong and that common sense is likely to be unmitigated nonsense. This is as absurd as to insist that the so-called truths of folk psychology are invariably right and that common sense is an infallible source of knowledge. After all, popular beliefs are based upon repeated observations by countless generations of people, and it is unlikely that all of these observations are inaccurate or distorted. Folk psychology undoubtedly contains a great deal of wisdom. The trouble is that it is difficult to separate the wisdom from the nonsense. This is where scientific psychology enters the picture and offers something that popular psychology does not possess. Scientific psychology provides the means for testing the beliefs of folk psychology to find out whether they are *probably* true or *probably* false. We say probably because man's knowledge of the truth falls within certain limits of probability; rarely, if ever, does one arrive at complete certainty even when using the most advanced methods of science.

One might ask—why test something that any sensible person can see for himself is true? Is not the best test of truth the consensus of reasonable people? Not always, as history reminds us again and again. At one time, sensible people believed that the earth was flat and that the sun moved around the earth. You could see with your own eyes that these were "true" facts. Why fly in the face of the solid, indisputable evidence of one's senses? Consensus did not prevent these ideas from being proved false by Columbus and Copernicus although it took a long time for people to accept their "new-fangled" notions. One is reminded that when Galileo was tried by the Inquisition in the seventeenth century for subscribing to the Copernican theory of the solar system, he was forced to repudiate the findings of his own scientific experiments. Consensus is an index of

* From *Psychology: An Introductory Textbook* by Calvin S. Hall. Published by Howard Allen, Inc. Copyright 1960 by Calvin S. Hall. Reprinted by permission.

the popularity of an idea; it is not necessarily a guarantee of its truth. Even agreement among experts is not a satisfactory criterion of validity, for unpopular ideas have sometimes had hard sledding against the traditional views of scientific men.

For instance, the great English scientist, Isaac Newton, demonstrated in 1672 that white light is not a simple wave length but a mixture of all the colors of the spectrum. He did this by passing sunlight through a prism, which broke down the light into the colors of the rainbow. It was many years before the scientific fraternity accepted Newton's findings; even as late as 1810, Goethe, the immensely influential German thinker, wrote a book to prove Newton was wrong. Another example of a discovery that ran counter to the beliefs of traditional science was Freud's demonstration of the existence of unconscious processes in behavior; although this theory was not widely accepted by psychologists for years, it is now a cornerstone of modern psychological theory.

Today, an overwhelming number of psychologists simply do not believe in the reality of mental telepathy and clairvoyance. Is this still another example of the way in which scientific orthodoxy erects and maintains a road-block against the recognition of reality? Perhaps the future will show that the unorthodox minority who now believe in the truth of so-called psychic phenomena are right and that the conservative traditionalists are wrong. In any event, the lesson that history teaches of the fate of unpopular ideas in science should discourage us from being too dogmatic and should make us less susceptible to the bandwagon effect of the fashionable idea. Progress in science, as in any other sphere of human endeavor, is often the result of healthy skepticism for the most cherished assumptions and convictions of the crowd, whether the crowd is the people in general or a group of scientists.

A shortcoming of the ideas of folk psychology is their overgeneralization and oversimplification, which make very poor prescriptions for action. For example, take the familiar rhyming maxim, "Haste makes waste." Sometimes it does, sometimes it does not. When a person is learning a new skill, such as running a machine, speed is likely to have a detrimental effect on his performance. But if he is highly skilled in the operation of the machine, haste is an asset rather than a liability. Only careful observations of a large number of people working under a variety of conditions and with different amounts of experience can reveal when haste does and when it does not make waste. A rule of thumb often contains an element of truth, but even this element has to be qualified before it can be applied. Folk psychology contains some very shrewd insights, but it also includes a number of superstitions. Sorting out the insights from the superstitions is a task for scientific psychology.

STOP TIMING HERE

Here is a group of widely-accepted popular beliefs. Most of them are based on repeated observations of most of us. Some are found to be true on the basis of scientific evidence, as well as "common sense." Others are false. Place a T or an F before each to show your belief regarding their validity.*

    ——— 1. The color red is especially exciting to a bull.

    ——— 2. American Indians have keener vision than white peoples.

    ——— 3. The majority of adult criminals are feeble-minded.

    ——— 4. People tend to grow more conservative as they pass the age of forty.

    ——— 5. Cats can see in complete darkness.

    ——— 6. Men and boys are more often color-blind than women and girls.

    ——— 7. Most great men are born of poor but honest parents.

    ——— 8. Long, slender fingers indicate artistic ability.

    ——— 9. Staring at a person's back will cause that person to turn his head.

    ——— 10. Women are inferior in intelligence to men.

    ——— 11. Blondes are more aggressive than brunettes.

    ——— 12. Suspicious people and people who like to keep their personal affairs from the world reveal this trait in their handwriting by the use of *a*'s and *o*'s which are completely closed.

    ——— 13. The shape of the head is a good index of moral character.

    ——— 14. Coffee in small amounts increases efficiency in learning.

    ——— 15. Babies instinctively fear the dark.

    ——— 16. A mother's thoughts during pregnancy can birthmark her child.

    ——— 17. Even moderate tobacco smoking can produce feebleminded-ness.

    ——— 18. Most psychologists believe that man's instinct to fight causes wars.

    ——— 19. Phrenologists can tell what line of work a man is best suited for by feeling the bumps on his head.

    ——— 20. All cats, rats, and rabbits are color-blind.

    ——— 21. To get the most work from men it is better to criticize a poor performance than to praise a good one.

    ——— 22. If a person is hard of hearing, his vision will be unusually good.

    ——— 23. An expectant mother can cause her child to be a boy if she engages in typical masculine activity during pregnancy.

    ——— 24. The brightest Negro is inferior in intelligence to the dullest white.

    ——— 25. The first-born child is usually the brightest child in the family.

    ——— 26. All men are created equal in inborn capacity for achievement.

    ——— 27. People with green eyes are less trustworthy than blue-eyed people.

* Adapted from *Working with Psychology* by Floyd L. Ruch and Neil Warren. Published by Scott, Foresman and Company, 1938. Used by permission of the copyright owners.

—— 28. If a man had enough faith, he could cure a broken leg instantly.

—— 29. The study of mathematics gives one a logical mind.

—— 30. Men judge by reason; women, by feeling and intuition.

—— 31. A person with sufficient will-power can overcome any physical defect.

—— 32. Too much study can cause a college student to become feeble-minded.

—— 33. The average person past the age of forty can learn nothing new.

—— 34. On the average, the children of a white mother and an American Indian father are lower in intelligence than either parent.

—— 35. As men pass their fortieth year, they become increasingly interested in attending musical comedies.

—— 36. A person's character is influenced by the position of the stars and planets at the time of his birth.

—— 37. The children of marriages of first cousins are usually feeble-minded.

—— 38. Cold hands are the sign of an affectionate disposition.

—— 39. There is clear evidence that the increased complexity of modern life has caused an increase in the rate of insanity.

—— 40. Children who are unusually advanced in their school work generally become feeble-minded when they grow up.

—— 41. Underprivileged children who have to fight their way through life are usually more aggressive than the children of rich parents.

Questions—Folk Psychology

Some of the obvious questions an instructor might ask are the following. See the Answer Key for possible answers.

1. What name is given to the beliefs of the general public regarding the behavior of man?

2. Since many popular beliefs about the behavior of men are correct, what more has scientific psychology to offer in this area?

3. Why is it necessary or desirable to test the accuracy of beliefs based upon the observations of generations of sensible people?

4. Give two examples of early scientific findings that were not generally accepted because they were contrary to common-sense beliefs.

5. What current psychological theories are still considered as popular but unscientific theories by most behavioral scientists?

Other questions you may not have anticipated, but should try to answer, are these:

6. Give an example of a common popular belief regarding the meaning of human size, weight, hair color, or some other physical characteristic. Do you subscribe to this belief? If so, be prepared to offer some personal evidence in support of it.
7. Was it the author's intention here to convince you that most popular beliefs were unsound or untrue? Or did he have some other motive?
8. Do you believe that some kinds of people are inclined to cling to popular beliefs, even when there is scientific evidence against them? If so, why?
9. What are the two basic flaws in logic present in most common-sense beliefs?
10. How do you compare with the average college student in the number of false popular beliefs that you subscribe to? Check your answers to the 41 beliefs with the Answer Key.

Vocabulary

Some of the following terms may have been new to you. Check those you knew before reading the selection.

probability   orthodoxy
fraternity   psychic
telepathy   bandwagon effect
clairvoyance   ire

Choose the synonym or definition for each term as it was used here.

1. probability
   a. possibility.   b. mathematical possibilities of the occurrence or truth of an event.   c. likelihood.
2. fraternity
   a. a Greek-letter club.   b. a social organization.   c. any group with common beliefs or training.
3. telepathy
   a. communication over great distances without using any of the common senses.   b. foretelling coming events.   c. communicating with the dead.
4. clairvoyance
   a. foreseeing the future.   b. communicating with the dead.
   c. black-magic practices.
5. orthodoxy
   a. highly conservative views.   b. body of beliefs held by the majority.   c. a group of religious beliefs.
6. psychic
   a. physical phenomena.   b. relates to the science of physics.
   c. pertaining to the supernatural rather than the physical world.

7. bandwagon effect
a. preperformance circus parade.　　b. tendency to conform to popular opinion.　　c. use of prestige to appeal to the reader.
8. ire
a. amusement.　　b. hatred.　　c. anger.

Self-Appraisal

Did the questions you framed during the preview resemble those most likely to be asked by the instructor? Did you anticipate any of the other questions? How did yours differ: in being too factual or in failing to realize that some questions might draw upon your previous learning?

Patterns of Reading

Record your reading rates here.

Predicted rate: ——— wpm.

Actual rate: ——— wpm.

What were your approaches to the material? Check those steps you used.
1. Previewed selection.
2. Previewed questions.
3. Wrote preview questions.
4. Skimmed some.
5. Took notes.
6. Underlined.
7. Reread some.
8. Skipped over some.

How did you score on the tests?

Comprehension　　———　　(49 points or better?)
Vocabulary　　———　　(10 points or better?)
　Total　　———　　(59 points or better?)

Did you use steps 1 and 3 as instructed? This selection is not very difficult reading, and thus you may have been able to use steps 4 or 8 also. It would hardly seem necessary for you to take any notes, to underline, or to reread in this relatively simple material.

Did you estimate your actual reading rate within about 25 to 50 words per minute? Was your rate apparently appropriate as measured by your comprehension?

In the vocabulary review, did you really know those terms you thought you knew? Did you learn any of the others in reading the article?

Speech

This 1,700-word selection is drawn from a textbook on speech communication, similar to those used in the introductory course on speech. Assume that your instructor has asked you to read it to answer these basic questions: (1) By what means other than speech does a speaker convey his messages to the listener? (2) How may these means of communication function both positively and negatively?

Preview the selection, with these two questions in mind. Write down any other questions you believe may be answered in the reading, or those that may arise in the classroom discussion of it. Preview also the questions at the end of the selection. After previewing, estimate your probable reading rate in words per minute. Write down the time when you begin reading and when you finish, in order to compute your actual reading rate. Then read to answer the questions you anticipate as well as those offered at the end of the selection.

STARTED ——————————— FINISHED ———————————

TOTAL TIME ———————————

Being Seen, Heard, and Understood*

A speaker is like a fish in a glass bowl. He is before everybody's eyes, and everything he does is magnified. The things we ordinary mortals do consciously or unconsciously may be pretty bad, yet we get by fairly well off the platform. On the platform it is another story; we've got to do now what we ought to do otherwise. The seeing-of-the-speaker by the audience is an inherent part of the speech itself. We cannot hide behind the miserable excuse that "how a speaker says it is not important; it is what he says that counts," because the audience cannot know what the speaker says except by how he translates it into light waves and sound waves.

THE BASIS OF BODILY COMMUNICATION

What do we think with? Only the brain? Hardly. The brain is like a telephone exchange. Without the lines running to it from the outside, it is useless. It is the switchboard, but not the whole system. Its function is to receive incoming signals, make proper connections, and send the messages through to their destination. For efficient service, the body must function *as a whole*.

We have spoken in the preceding chapter of the speaker's "mental attitude." A good phrase, but where is the "mind?" Is it in the brain? Or perhaps in the nervous system? After all, can we say that the mind is in any particular *place*? It is not a thing, like a leg, or even the brain. It is a function, an activity. Aristotle, twenty-three hundred years ago, observed that *the mind was to the body what cutting was to the ax.* When the ax is not in use, there is no cutting. So with the mind, "Mind," said Charles H. Woolbert, "is what the body is doing." We think, not with the cortex, with the brain, or even with the nervous system, but with the brain, the nerves, the glands, and the muscles, working together as a whole.

* From *Speech Communication* by William Norwood Brigance. Copyright, 1947, F. S. Crofts & Co., Inc. Reprinted by permission of Appleton-Century-Crofts.

If this total activity is necessary for thinking, *it is also necessary for carrying thought from one person to another.* Observe how people go about the business of ordinary conversation. If you have never done this painstakingly, you have a surprise in store, for good conversationalists are almost constantly in motion. Their heads are continually nodding and shaking sometimes so vigorously that you wonder how their necks can stand the strain. The shoulders shrug; the torso stretches, bends, turns, swings, and droops—constantly changing position and attitude. Even the legs and feet are active. As for the hands and arms, they are seldom still for more than a few seconds at a time.

These people, remember, are not making speeches. They are merely common folk trying to make others understand what they have in mind. They are not conscious of movement. Their speech is not studied. They are just human creatures in a human environment, trying to adapt themselves to a social situation. Yet they converse, not only with oral language, but with visible actions that involve practically every muscle in the body.

In short, because people really think all over, a speaker must talk all over if he succeeds in making people think.

Language Demands a Visible As Well As an Audible Code

Visible, or sign, language is older than the spoken code. It is written more deeply into our organisms. It carries the basic or stronger impressions. Today, with all our refinement of spoken communication, *the eye is still quicker than the ear.*

For example, before the speaker utters a word, he begins to carry meanings to all who see him. Does he stand in a timid, withdrawing attitude, or thrust out his jaw belligerently, or smile with winning grace? The audience senses at once the meaning conveyed by the approach. Throughout the speech he carries fine shades of meaning to the audience merely by movements of the body, shoulders, hands, and head; by the laugh, the smile, the play of features. Even friendliness of manner and charm of personality are carried as much by what is seen as by what is heard. These communications directed to the eye are caught instantly by the audience, whereas those addressed to the ear unfold themselves more slowly. The eye *is* quicker than the ear.

But the real use of visible signs is to supplement and to interpret words rather than to take their place. Many times words fail completely in conveying meaning unless accompanied by signs. "When you call me that, smile!" said Owen Wister's character in *The Virginian* to a man who addressed him with an epithet. Some words are fighting words unless interpreted by a smile. Yet with a smile a friend may call me "an old crook" and make the words a term of affection. Then again, words take on added or stronger meaning if accompanied by certain movements, such as a nod of the head or a stroke of the hand. One reason why conversationalists use gestures so freely is to intensify and amplify their processes of social adaptation. They do not have to be told to gesture; they do it instinctively. At least, *good* conversationalists do.

THE EFFECT OF ACTION ON THE AUDIENCE'S ATTENTION

Think back over your experience. Did you ever lean forward, muscles tense, while watching an athletic contest? Did you ever feel your muscles pulling and pushing as if to throw a ball, make a catch, shoot a basket, or do any of the things the players are doing? Whether you know it or not, you assuredly have engaged in this sort of mimicry. It is the spectator's basis of understanding and enjoyment.

This phenomenon is known as *empathy*. It may be defined as *feeling ourselves into* whatever we perceive. All perception, in fact, involves this participation. We not only wind up with the pitcher, swing with the batter, and breast the tape with the sprinter, but also feel ourselves into static situations. When we see a painting or stand before a cathedral, our like or dislike hinges largely on whether the object evokes pleasant or unpleasant stresses and tension in our bodies. To be sure, we are unconscious of this participation, as we are of our breathing or our heartbeat. But it nevertheless influences our behavior profoundly.

Now apply this to the audience hearing a speech. *Unconsciously they are imitating the speaker.* The speaker has no option whatever on whether or not his gestures will affect the audience, for his gestures *must* affect them in one of three ways:

1. If he uses too little action, empathy in the audience will be weak. Because of its weakness, the audience will not remain physically alert, but will relax more and more into physical (and therefore mental) inaction. But the more one relaxes, the less active the mind becomes, until in complete inactivity one goes to sleep—complete relaxation. So the speaker who does not gesture puts his audience into a state too near to sleep for them to follow alertly what he is saying. They will sit and half listen, but, when he is through, they will recall little of what he has said.

2. If the speaker uses uncontrolled gestures, gestures that he never intended to use and often does not know he is using, the audience will be drawn into fitful and distracting responses. We have all seen the speaker who buttons his coat and then unbuttons it, or twists a handkerchief in his hands, or rocks up and down on his toes, or moves an object on the table before him from one place to another, then to another . . . and to another. "If he moves that watch again, I'll scream," whispered a woman after a speaker had put his watch in twelve or fifteen places over the table. She did not scream, but neither did she listen to what he was saying. She was waiting for his watch to be moved again. So with all people. They are distracted by their empathic reactions to a speaker's uncontrolled movements.

3. If the speaker uses controlled and communicative action, the audience is aroused to an enjoyable participation. They are lifted to alert attention and find it easier to follow what the speaker is saying.

SHALL THE SPEAKER USE GESTURE?

We are now in a position to answer the question "Must I use gesture?" If people think all over, and if action is a part of the thinking process, the speaker who uses no action is inhibiting his own thinking. If gesture comes so naturally to the good conversationalist that he cannot converse effectively without it, it will also be of value in the more important and larger conversations that the public speaker carries on with his audience. If gesture is the means of arousing the listeners' attention, then surely it is a foolish speaker who would talk without action.

The question should be restated: "Can I afford to try speaking without gesture—since it is so vital a part of the means of social adaptation?" The answer is "No!" The public speaker, in his capacity of leader, needs every possible means of effectiveness. He cannot afford to deny himself anything that will assist in getting the responses that he wants. If he would hold his place among his fellows, if he would justify his leadership, he must use every possible means of effectiveness, and this inevitably includes bodily action.

Questions—Being Seen, Heard, and Understood

Main Ideas

1. According to the author, thinking is—
   a. solely a brain function.   b. a psychic phenomenon.   c. a function of the nervous system.   d. the sum total of bodily activity.

2. To transmit thought or ideas from one person to another, it is essential not only to employ speech, but also—
   a. to employ eye control.   b. to speak directly to the other person.
   c. to employ a variety of bodily movements.   d. to be certain that he is listening.

3. It is the author's contention that—
   a. what a speaker says is more important than how he says it.
   b. the speaker's bodily actions are reacted to more quickly than his words.   c. it is easy for an audience to sense a speaker's meaning.
   d. the speaker's meaning is conveyed better by his movements than his words.

4. The basic function of gestures in speech is to—
   a. convey the speaker's meaning.   b. amplify or intensify his spoken words.   c. attract and hold the attention of the listener.
   d. induce the listener to experience the emotions of the speaker.

Details

1. Describe three positive or negative types of gestures and the effects they may have upon an audience._____

_____

_____

_____

_____

_____

_____

_____

2. Why does the author believe that gestures are an essential part of communication by speech? Give at least two of his arguments.

3. Do you agree with the author's definition of thinking as the total of bodily activity? Do we really "think" with our muscles? Give your reasons for or against this concept and support them with at least one example or illustration.

Vocabulary

Some of the following terms may have been new to you. Check those you knew before reading the selection.

inherent	mimicry
painstakingly	phenomenon
torso	empathy
belligerently	option
epithet	inhibiting

Choose the synonym or definition for each term as it was used here.

1. inherent
   a. an integral part of.   b. important.   c. unavoidable.
2. painstakingly
   a. accompanied by pain.   b. very carefully.   c. staking out pain areas.
3. torso
   a. shoulders.   b. waist.   c. trunk of the body.

4. belligerently
   a. aggressively, in a warlike manner.   b. automatically.   c. unconsciously.
5. epithet
   a. greeting.   b. an uncomplimentary or disagreeable word.
   c. salutation.
6. mimicry
   a. excitement.   b. emotion or feeling.   c. imitation.
7. phenomenon
   a. an unusual happening.   b. any incident or behavior.   c. a gesture.
8. empathy
   a. imitating emotions or feelings.   b. muscle tension.   c. identifying with or experiencing the feelings or actions of others.
9. option
   a. choice.   b. a right or privilege.   c. control.
10. inhibiting
    a. promoting.   b. directing.   c. interfering with.

Self-Appraisal

Were you able to answer the preview questions suggested by the instructor? How about the other questions on main ideas and details?

Patterns of Reading

Record your reading rates here.
Predicted rate: ———— wpm.
Actual rate: ———— wpm.
What were your approaches to this material? Check the steps you used.
1. Previewed selection.
2. Previewed questions.
3. Wrote preview questions.
4. Skimmed some.
5. Took notes.
6. Underlined.
7. Reread some.
8. Skipped over some.
How did you score on the tests?

Main Ideas	————	(30 points or better?)
Details	————	(24 points or better?)
Vocabulary	————	(12 points or better?)
TOTAL	————	(66 points or better?)

Did you use steps 1, 2, and 3 as instructed? Did the questions you wrote while previewing resemble those of the instructor? This selection is a relatively simple one, and you may have also used step 4 or even 8. Was your pattern effective in all three types of questions? If not, why not?

Did you estimate your actual rate within 25 to 50 words per minute? If not, why not? Did your actual rate promote effective comprehension?

In the vocabulary section, did you actually know those terms you thought were familiar? Did you learn some of the others in reading the selection?

Statistics

Most of us are quite uncritical or even gullible in reading the statistical matter we encounter. This 1,400-word selection may help sharpen your critical thinking abilities in dealing with such topics. Preview it to discover its main ideas, and read the questions at the end. Estimate your probable rate of reading in words per minute. Write down the time when you begin reading and again when you finish. Then read the selection to understand the author's purpose and his examples of deceptive statistics.

STARTED ——————————   FINISHED ——————————

TOTAL TIME ——————————

The Misleading Average*

What is an average? Is it the most common characteristic of a relatively large number of people, or a point that divides the population into two equal halves of "haves" and "have-nots"? Or, is it the total amount of a certain trait divided equally among the entire population? Well, it is and it isn't. It may be any or all of these.

The word *average* is used loosely to describe any of three measures known technically as the mode, the median, and the mean. When we discuss such human traits as height and weight, it doesn't matter much which we use, for these characteristics are distributed normally throughout the population. But if we talk about incomes or income taxes, wattage consumption or divorce rates, it matters a great deal which average is selected.

Let's take a case in point. The ABC Electronics Company tells us that their average employee earned $4,000 last year. Sounds fairly good, doesn't it? But what does this average mean? Was $4,000 the most common salary among the employees? No, because the greatest number of employees earning any one salary, or the mode, is found at $2,500. Did half of the help earn more and half less than $4,000? Is this a median? No. All but about a half dozen employees are hourly workers at a basic wage of $2,500. Then what does the $4,000 mean? It must be an average of the salaries paid to the two partners who own the company ($23,000 each); the two engineers ($12,000 each); a technician and a production manager ($8,000 each); two foremen ($3,000 each); and the forty hourly workers who earn about $2,500 per year. All these salaries add up to $192,000 which divided by forty-eight employees averages $4,000. Neat, isn't it? Would you have thought of adding in the owners' shares to raise the average yearly salary? But the labor union isn't likely to use this mean in asking for a better salary scale. They are more apt to use the mode, the point at which most of the employees fall on the scale of $2,500. In this case, the union could also use the median of $2,500 since more than half of the workers earn this amount or less.

Graphically, these data could have been presented something like Figure 1 (but of course no statistician attempting to please the owners of the ABC Electronics Company would have used such a method of presenting the facts):

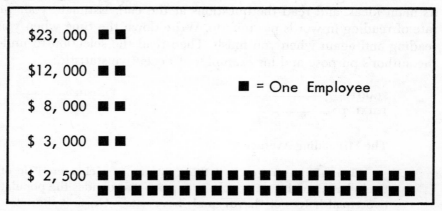

FIGURE 1.   Average Yearly Salary—ABC Electronics Company.

The next time you read something about an average, ask yourself, "What average—mean, mode, or median?" or "Average of what? Who and what is included here?" Here are typical "average" figures found in a recent publication. Just what do they mean?

Changing Times for June, 1956, reports an average of 6.02 hours of televiewing per day in the American home. Last year's figure is given as 5.81 hours per day. It concludes, "The glass screen is really taking over."

These figures have an artificial note of authenticity because of the use of the decimal figures. It sounds much more accurate to say 6.02 hours rather than simply 6 hours. But how many homes were involved in this survey? The fine distinctions implied in the decimals are absurd unless the sample was quite large.

How was the survey done? By whom? By calling on the phone and asking how many hours a day the TV set was used? Were reliable time-sampling measures used to determine actual amount of televiewing? Are these figures offered by TV manufacturers or broadcasting chains who, perhaps, have an ulterior motive? As for monopolizing the televiewer's day, how much of a real difference is the .21 of an hour (thirteen minutes)? Is the conclusion based on a significant difference? Do these facts add up to anything at all? Do they even indicate a reliable trend?

THE DECEPTIVE SAMPLE

Many statistics are based upon a sample of the population. But no statistic is any better than the sample on which it is based. This sample may be too small, or biased by obvious or hidden factors, or deliberately chosen to prove the writer's point. Take the case of the *Literary Digest* pool of 1936 that predicted the presidential election of Alfred Landon. The sample was composed of ten million telephone and *Digest* subscribers who had been used in a correct presidential prediction in 1932. Such a sample seemed large enough and apparently free from bias. But the people who could afford telephones and magazine subscriptions just weren't representative of the American public in 1936. Most Americans were still struggling with the effects of the depression at the later date. Telephones and magazines were luxuries for many trying to make both ends meet. The sample was economically biased and reflected the voting preferences of a select group, not the general public.

To yield an accurate statistic, a sample must be representative of the total group. It should be selected by pure chance under circumstances in which every person or thing in the total group has an equal chance of being selected. This is called a random sampling. However, because it involves so great a cross section of the total population, true random sampling is almost prohibitive in time and cost. In its place, a stratified sample composed of a small group possessing those traits characteristic of the general population is commonly used. Public-opinion polls, surveys of users of a certain product, sales predictions for a proposed new product, views of magazine-readers, preferences of radio listeners and televiewers are commonly based on this stratified sampling technique.

But how does the researcher know that his stratified sample is really a random sample of the total population? The truth is, he doesn't. His conclusions may be distorted by any of a dozen factors such as the very questions asked, the emotional reactions of those interviewed to the questions or the interviewer, the extent to which social prestige or the ego of the respondent is challenged, and the like. How accurate, for example, can a survey of such personal matters as income, church attendance, racial discrimination, or wife-beating really be?

By this time, you have recognized that our purpose is to make you look more critically at any statistic based on sampling. Most poll results are apt to be biased, even when they are not deliberately distorted. This bias is likely to be toward reflecting the thinking and actions of the person with better-than-average economic and social status. As Darrel Huff expresses it, if you were the interviewer waiting outside a factory, which man would you stop—the surly-looking fellow plowing along with his head down, or the cleancut, smiling chap walking leisurely homeward?

To help you read and interpret statistics based on sampling, we suggest you "ask" the writer such questions as: How many people are involved in these data? What kind of people were they? How were they selected? What are some of the factors that may have influenced the results? What do the results prove, if anything? What kind of sense do they make? For example, the manufacturer of a popular brand of cigarettes claims that more doctors smoke this brand than any other. Are doctors better judges of taste, mildness, and other cigarette qualities than other people? Aside from the fact that we don't know how many doctors were sampled, just what does this statistic prove? The implication is, of course, that medical training makes one a better judge of cigarettes and more aware of the possible harmful effects. Therefore, if more doctors smoke X brand, it must be better and less harmful than other brands. Only a moment's thought will demonstrate that if X is a widely sold brand, it is likely to sell well among most groups, plumbers as well as doctors. This is a common type of two-pronged propaganda device, this use of the prestige of the medical profession in impressing the public, and questionable statistics.

Or take the claim of a toothpaste manufacturer that six out of eight people prefer the taste of his product to that of others. Does he tell you how many people were sampled before these results were secured? Usually not, because his researchers probably waited until they found such a result in one small group rather than reporting on the preferences of the entire population sampled. If two toothpastes were being compared, we would expect five out of ten people to prefer Z paste, purely on a basis of chance. Flipping a coin several hundred times is likely to result in half heads and half tails. But in a small sample, the law of probability does not operate in the same fashion. The first ten tosses of your coin may all be heads. Thus, if the surveyors for Z toothpaste took a number of small samples, it is quite possible that they would find one in which the results were the kind they wanted. This may not be dishonest reporting of research but it certainly is rigged to produce the desired results.

Questions—The Misleading Average

Main Ideas

1. The author's purpose is to—
   a. urge the reader to read statistical material more carefully.
   b. alert the reader to common, deceptive statistical presentations.
   c. teach the reader how to read any statistics.   d. help readers who have problems in mathematics.

2. This selection implies that readers may be fooled by— (choose as many as you need)
   a. false reporting of research.   b. the loose use of mathematical terms.   c. unwarranted conclusions from statistical data.
   d. statistics that are outright lies.   e. reports based on samples of unknown size or validity.

Details

Mark these statements True or False in terms of the facts given in the selection.

——— 3. An average is the same as a median or mode.

———— 4. Most reports involving statistics are misleading.

———— 5. Advertisements or reports based on large samples are usually dependable.

———— 6. A stratified sample is selected to be representative of the entire population.

———— 7. Many current reports based on sampling use stratified samples.

———— 8. Polls and opinion samples are often biased by the nature of the sample.

———— 9. Some advertisements may use a deliberately biased sample in order to impress the reader.

———— 10. Only a statistician can judge the validity of a sampling report or opinion poll.

———— 11. In the ABC Electronics Co. report the "average" employee's salary was inflated by averaging in the management salaries.

———— 12. By reading analytically, the average person can avoid being misled by questionable statistical reports.

Vocabulary

Several of the following terms may have been new to you:

average	random sample
mode	statistic
median	probability
stratified sample	

Check those you knew before you read the selection. Choose the correct synonym or definition for each term as used in this selection.

1. average
   a. the mode. b. the median. c. the mean.

2. mode
   a. the most frequent value or score in a large group of such.
   b. the archetype or model. c. the average.

3. median
   a. the mean. b. the exact midpoint in a large group of values.
   c. the most frequent value in a large group of such.

4. stratified sample
   a. a small but representative population sample. b. a random sample. c. a sample chosen by the social classes included.

5. random sample
   a. a small but representative population sample. b. an accidental sample. c. a sample selected without plan or purpose.

6. statistic
   a. a chart or diagram. b. any single figure or arithmetical fact.
   c. the study of mathematics.

7. probability
   a. likelihood.   b. the mathematical chances for a given event to
   occur.   c. tossing coins.

Check your answers with the Answer Key. Write down in the Self-
Appraisal the total credits you receive for each portion of the test.

Self-Appraisal

What were your approaches to this material? Check those steps you
used.

Record your reading rates here.

Predicted rate: —————— wpm.

Actual rate: —————— wpm.

1. Previewed selection.
2. Previewed questions.
3. Wrote preview questions.
4. Skimmed some.
5. Took notes.
6. Underlined.
7. Reread some.
8. Skipped over some.

Was this an effective pattern of reading for you? What was your final
sum of points in—

Main Ideas	_____	(20 points or better?)
Details	_____	(24 points or better?)
Vocabulary	_____	(16 points or better?)
TOTAL	_____	(60 points or better?)

Did you use steps 1 and 2 in your pattern of reading? Was your comprehension adequate in each type of question? If not, what should you be doing to improve?

Was your predicted rate within 25 to 50 words per minute of your
actual rate? If not, why not?

Did you know the vocabulary words you thought you knew? How about
the others—did you learn some by reading the passage?

CHAPTER **12**

USING YOUR READING
SKILLS FOR REVIEWING

One thing of which you can be certain is that you will soon forget much of anything you read. In just eight hours, although you may remember roughly 85 per cent of the main ideas, you will probably recall only 20 per cent of the details. Without an intervening review, two weeks after a reading you will retain only about 20 per cent of what you originally comprehended. After memorizing facts, such as lists of foreign vocabulary, formulas, dates and other figures, you are apt to lose as much as 50 per cent in twenty-four hours. Without some methods of review to stop it, the curve of forgetting drops faster than the upward curve of accumulated learning.

Reviewing not only will help to overcome the effects of forgetting, but it will aid in certain other situations that commonly occur in college life. Many times, even though you have carefully studied an assignment by the *PQRST* method, you may not be quizzed or tested on it for some time. Because of the speed of forgetting, the only solution to this situation is an adequate review. Sometimes your examinations are cumulative in that they cover several successive assignments that may be several weeks apart. Again, a review of the entire body of materials is the only possible way of preparing for this type of examination. Some assignments are too difficult or too detailed for you to retain all the facts you may need, even by the *PQRST* approach. These assignments must be restudied or reviewed, perhaps several times, for adequate retention. Finally, reviewing is perhaps the only practical way of integrating what you have learned from the textbook, your lecture or laboratory notes, your outside reading, and all the other sources you may have used for study purposes.

Fortunately, the very reading and study techniques you have learned earlier in this book—previewing, skimming, scanning, summarizing, and so on—can be used just as effectively for review purposes. Here are some specific suggestions for utilizing them in reviewing.

How to Review

Psychologists and others who have experimented with and studied the art of reviewing have discovered a number of basic facts and principles. You will notice, as we discuss these principles, that the reading skills presented in this book were carefully selected to prepare you to follow the fundamental rules for studying and reviewing.

Get Yourself Ready for Study.   Pick a sensible, uncluttered space for study. It need not be absolutely soundproof, for most of us are so used to some natural noise that we can't stand complete silence. Rather, find an area of relative quiet, without frequent distractions of noises or persons, an area well lighted and well ventilated, and with moderately comfortable chair and table.

Get together all the materials you may need before you begin—pencils, paper, notes, texts, and reference books. Don't distract yourself during study by having to hunt for things you need.

Study at first alone; then, if you find it profitable, talk over the material with another student; quiz each other or just have a bull session to reinforce and crystallize your ideas.

Review After Reading.   To prevent forgetting, you have three built-in aids in the *PQRST* approach: (1) *summarizing* in your own words, writing down the answers to the questions framed in the *P-Q* step, (2) writing down the main ideas as you read, and (3) *testing* yourself by answering your own questions or those supplied by your instructor or textbook. All are significant aids to retention. Self-recitation after reading has demonstrated its value for memory in almost every experiment in which it has been involved. These steps tend to increase comprehension by almost 25 per cent over that obtained just by reading.

Anticipate Questions.   In many of the earlier exercises, we emphasized practice in trying to frame questions such as your instructor might ask. Although some students find this difficult, most can learn it by being attentive to the types and variety of questions used in class recitations, quizzes, and examinations. Don't forget that in many colleges copies of previous examinations can be obtained from the bookstore, the library, or your instructor.

Use also the questions you frame during the *P-Q* step as a means of review. If you have forgotten some of the answers, find them by *skimming* over the chapter, then *scanning* a section or page to locate the precise fact or concept.

Space Your Review.   Distributed review is far superior to last-minute cramming before an examination. Make frequent reviews a definite part of your study schedule. For example, it is desirable to *skim* through the preceding material each time before reading the new assignment. At the end of a large unit, or at least two or three times before a mid-term or final examination, tie all the earlier assignments of a course together by quickly skimming them. If you have made notes on each chapter, or an outline of main ideas in the *P-Q* and *R-S* steps, study all these briefly again. Such cumulative reviewing will keep your retention high and make all-night cramming sessions unnecessary.

Review Critically. In two earlier chapters, you were introduced to some basic ideas about critical reading. If you try to read "with a questioning attitude" you will certainly help your retention. We tend to remember only those facts we agree with and to forget quickly those that run contrary to our usual beliefs. Guard against retaining only what meets your approval or fits your prejudices. Question the author, argue with him, judge his accuracy and his motives constantly, and thus strengthen your comprehension of both sides of his arguments.

We grant that somewhere in your college work you may have to study subjects in which you are not greatly interested. But don't let your inability to recognize the ultimate place of such content in your education lead you to failure. If you can, accept it as just another obstacle or challenge on the way to your goal of a degree. Approach it critically, inquire about its place in the scheme of things, and try to see it in a perspective of its contribution or relevance to other areas. You may well find some satisfaction in solving this problem, even though you may never do more than pretend or force an interest.

Memorize. Almost every subject has some content that must be memorized "cold." Fortunately, this aspect of learning has had a great deal of study. We know that it is more efficient to study some things as a whole, rather than part by part; this approach is useful in learning poetry, the periodic chart of the elements, and other such items. Building understanding and meaningful associations also help, as in recalling formulas or involved processes. A card file for drilling oneself is useful with foreign vocabulary, formulas, technical terms, important dates, and time or chronology lines.

Mnemonic devices such as "30 days hath September . . ." are not generally approved by many authorities. But they may be helpful in some instances of memorizing a series of almost unrelated facts, such as the bones of the spine or cranium. If you use a device such as "In 1492 Columbus sailed the ocean blue," however, be careful it doesn't turn into "In 1493 Columbus sailed the deep blue sea." Try to weave it into a definite order or sequence with some logical interrelationships. Try to visualize or to build images of the process or series you are memorizing.

Organize Your Resources. After skimming the text, read your lecture or laboratory notes on the same subject. Consult your notes from supplementary reading and other sources. Review all of these at the same sitting. Test yourself by answering questions based on all the resource material you have available.

Keep It Short. Don't waste time in rereading whole chapters or similar portions. Rereading that is not in direct answer to a series of questions is almost wasted effort. Simple rereading as a review technique will yield only about 5 per cent more than you gained from the first reading.

If a long period has elapsed since the first reading, refresh yourself by skimming for main ideas and by answering the questions framed in the *P-Q* step. If you have forgotten the facts, then reread selectively only the pertinent portions.

Don't study too long at one sitting. Concentration can't be maintained at a high, efficient level for long periods. Use two or three sittings of two to three hours each rather than one long cramming session when covering a large body of content.

Help Yourself

There are many fine books to help you improve the efficiency of your studying and reviewing habits. Your instructor will aid you in selecting one of the following, if you need more details in this area.

Cole, Luella. *Students' Guide to Efficient Study.* Fourth edition. New York: Holt, Rinehart and Winston, 1960. 67 pages. *Good chapters on methods of study, notetaking, and other topics.*

Farquhar, William W., John D. Krumboltz, and C. Gilbert Wrenn. *Learning to Study.* New York: Ronald, 1960. 243 pages. *Simple, clear discussion of many aspects of study.*

McDonald, Arthur S., and George H. Zimny. *The Art of Good Reading.* Indianapolis: Bobbs-Merrill, 1963. 426 pages. *Chapter 7 and 8 are excellent.*

Pauk, Walter. *How to Study in College.* Boston: Houghton Mifflin, 1962. 132 pages. *Many original, practical illustrations of study techniques.*

Robinson, Francis P. *Effective Study.* Revised edition. New York: Harper & Row, 1961. 278 pages. *Extended treatment of higher-level work skills and educational deficiencies.*

APPENDIX

Using Letter Sounds and Syllables to Pronounce Words

For most students, the use of letter sounds and syllables is very familiar. But if you have difficulty in analyzing or pronouncing words new to you, it will be profitable to review this section. No attempt has been made to include the spelling or pronunciation of every English sound or every rule for phonics or syllabication. Rather, we have selected only those items that will help in word analysis and pronunciation, and those that recent research indicates are true and reliable.

Vowel Sounds.   In most dictionaries the following conventions are used:
1. A long line over a vowel means the long sound (usually just like the name of the letter) as in *fāme, ēven, īce, ōld, cūbe.*
2. A short, curved line over a vowel means the short sound, as in *ăt, ĕnd, ĭt, ŏdd, ŭp.*
3. Other marks over a vowel indicate variations of the short sound, as in *ärt, âir, ȧsk.*
4. Unstressed or indefinite vowels may be represented by the schwa symbol, as in *əbove, sickər, charəty, melən, focəs.*

Consonant Sounds.   Some consonants have several sounds. Here are the more frequent variants. Those consonants not listed usually have only one common sound.

Consonant	*Sound*	*Example*
c	s	cede, civil, force (before *e, i,* or *y*)
	k	collect, cargo, cry (before any letter except *e, i,* or *y*)

289

Consonant	*Sound*	*Example*
	sh	ocean, vicious
ch	ch	church
	j	Greenwich (grĭnĭj)
	sh	machine
	k	echo
d	d	drop
	t	dropped
	j	soldier
f	f	fame
	v	of
g	g	go, ghost, guard
	j	engine
	zh	mirage
gh	g	ghastly
	f	cough, laugh
j	dzh	jar
	y	hallelujah
ph	f	phantom
	v	Stephen
q	kw	quake
	k	liquor
s	s	sun, pass
	z	easy, trees
	sh	sure, mansion
	zh	vision, Asia
t	t	note
	ch	question
th	voiceless (soft)	tooth
	voiced (hard)	either
	t	Thomas
x	ks	box
	gz	exact
	ksh	anxious
	gzh	luxurious
	z	anxiety

Consonant	Sound	Example
y	y	yes
	i	sky
	e	ready, martyr
	u	Myrtle
z	z	zeal, buzz
	zh	seizure

Silent Letters. Many letters are silent in the normal pronunciation of words. Here are a few examples of these silent letters and the rules governing them.

Silent letter	Examples
b	dumb, climb (after *m*), *also* subtle, debt
c	czar, indict
ch	yacht
d	handsome, Wednesday
g	sign, gnat (before *m* or *n*)
gh	high, taught
h	forehead, shepherd
k	knot, know (before *n*)
l	would, salmon
n	hymn (after *m*)
p	raspberry, psalm, pneumonia
t	mortgage, listen, whistle
w	write, wren, two (before *r* or *oo*), *also* answer, toward

Phonic and Syllabication Principles. The rules for letter sounds and syllabication are closely interrelated. The sounds of the vowels, for example, depend on the manner in which the word is divided into syllables and where the accent falls in the word. The same vowel may have different sounds when at the beginning or end of a syllable, when it alone forms a syllable, or when in the middle of a syllable. In other words, in order to work out the pronunciation of a word, it is essential to divide it first into its proper syllables.

There are a large number of rules or conventions governing phonics and syllabication. One recent study listed forty-five rules for these combined areas and still did not include all those commonly taught. Obviously a number of these have nothing to do with pronunciation, and others are of very questionable validity. Therefore, we have attempted to condense the number to a few basic principles.

The first problem to be solved in attempting to pronounce a word is to determine the sounds of the vowels. These letters vary most in their values and are the greatest source of difficulty. Consonants, on the other hand, are more often regular than variable in their sounds. The decision regarding each vowel involves choosing either a long sound or one of several short sounds. There may be as many as five or six short sounds for the vowel, but the differences are very slight. Most of us who are not linguists or speech majors can't hear much difference among these short vowel sounds. Thus the decision for each vowel sound boils down to selecting the long sound or a rather indefinite short sound. Some of the following principles will help in making this choice:

Rule 1. A vowel usually has its long sound (like its name) when—
a. it is the only vowel and occurs at the end of the word: *hi, sky, so, he.*   b. it is the first vowel in the digraphs *oa, ee, ay, ea,* and *ai: boat, speed, clay, eat, paint* (not true in many other vowel combinations).   c. it is an accented syllable: cr*e*ator, re*a*gent.   d. it is at the end of an accented syllable (called an open syllable): bi*r*acial, *p*athos.   e. When the word or syllable ends in a silent *e: bone,* chromo*some.* (This rule works only about two out of three times.)

Rule 2. A vowel usually has its short sound in most other situations, as—
a. in the middle of a syllable or a one-syllable word: *hat, cut, consonant.* (This is called a closed syllable.)   b. at the end of an unaccented syllable: con*s*titute, *d*igestion.   c. at the beginning of a syllable: *at*tack, *or*bit. (This is also called a closed syllable.)

But how does the poor reader know which syllables are accented or unaccented, or where they begin or end, when he can't pronounce the word? He must first know some basic facts about syllable formation, before he can decide on a long or short sound for each vowel.

Accent.

Rule 3. In most two-syllable words, the first syllable is accented: *cho'sen, du'al.*

Rule 4. If the first syllable is a prefix, it is usually unaccented: *accli'mate, detract', exhume', inflate', retain'.*

The accent in English is so variable that in other situations than those covered by these two rules you must depend upon your ear or the dictionary.

Syllables.

Rule 5. There are as many syllables in a word as there are sounded vowels (and most vowels are sounded except perhaps final *e*'s and the second vowel in such digraphs as *oa, ea, ai, ay,* and sometimes *ei* and *ie,* and in dipthongs such as *ou, oi,* and *oy* as in *out, oil,* and *boy.*)

In other words, the first step in syllabication is to estimate roughly the number of syllables by the number of vowels or vowel combinations present. For example, how many syllables are there likely to be in *Maori,* in *calceolaria?* There are three and six syllables respectively.

How many in these? Say each word slowly and count the vowel sounds.

luminous—three vowel sounds (*ou* is a single sound) equal three syllables.

lubricate—three vowel sounds (final *e* is silent) equal three syllables.

boiler—two vowel sounds (*oi* is one sound) equal two syllables.

terrible—three vowel sounds equal three syllables. (Note that *ble* is a syllable because there is a vowel *sound* in it ("bul"), not because of the silent *e.*

Rule 6. Syllabic divisions are usually made—
a. between double consonants: *suf-fix, cut-ter.*   b. between *any* two consonants not forming a blend or a single sound: *hob-gob-lin,* but *rath-er; pic-ture,* but *pick-et; shep-herd,* but *tel-e-phone.*   c. after a prefix or before a suffix: *pre-view, mort-al.*   d. before a consonant that comes between two vowels, when the first syllable is not accented: *pe-can,* but *ped-al; re-lieve,* but *rem-e-dy.*

Rule 6d is a variation on Rules 1d and 2a—those dealing with open and closed syllables. It simply says that a consonant between two vowels tends to go with the second vowel. This makes the first syllable an open one, with a long vowel sound in keeping with Rule 1d. Some words may be exceptions to this principle because of their history or the influence of common pronunciation. In the exceptions, the consonant between two vowels is attracted to the first syllable, making it a closed syllable and rendering the vowel sound short, as in Rule 2a.

Rule 6d tends to operate when the first vowel, before a consonant, is accented, as in the examples of *pedal* and *remedy.*

Let us review the steps you might use in attempting to pronounce *radiometeorograph.*

1. Because of the similarity to known words—*radio, meteor,* and *graph* —you will probably identify eight vowel sounds.

2. Your first estimate is eight syllables.

3. Now, try to mark the syllables so as to find which are open (long vowel sound) and which are closed (short vowel sound). Draw lines to show the syllabic divisions. Mark the syllables now.

4. You should have marked in this fashion: *ra|di|o|me|te|or|o|graph.*

5. Now decide which vowels are long. Mark them with a long line above the letter.

6. Did you mark the vowels long in syllables 1, 2, 4, and 5 (Rule 1d for open syllables) and in syllables 3 and 7 (Rule 1c for vowel as a syllable)?

7. This leaves short vowel sounds only in syllables 6 and 8 (Rule 2a for closed syllables).

8. Now, pronounce the word.

Now try the word *communalism.*

1. How many vowel sounds? Four.
2. How many syllables? Probably four.
3. Mark them with verticle lines.
4. Did you mark *com|mu|nal|ism* or *com|mun|al|ism?*
5. What familiar words should help you decide that the second syllable was open—that is, *mu?* Perhaps you thought of *communism,* or *commune.*
6. Using the same familiar words as guides, where does the accent go—on the first or second syllable? The first, of course.
7. Now, pronounce the word.

► **WORD ANALYSIS EXERCISE I**

Analyzing Words for Sounds and Syllables

Try the following exercise to sharpen your feeling for syllabication and pronunciation. In the first column, write the number of vowel sounds, as a rough estimate of the number of syllables. Then mark the syllables and the long vowel sounds. If this changes your estimate of the number of syllables, write your revised estimate in the second column.

Finally, try to pronounce the word according to your analysis. Then check yourself with the Answer Key.

	Vowel sounds *(Estimated syllables)*	*Revised estimate*
1. Maori	———	———
2. betroth	———	———
3. calceolaria	———	———
4. convolution	———	———
5. gladiolus	———	———
6. gimlet	———	———
7. mitosis	———	———
8. mitral	———	———
9. mayonnaise	———	———
10. meatus	———	———
11. behemoth	———	———
12. gumbo	———	———
13. Hanseatic	———	———
14. misdemeanor	———	———
15. orchestral	———	———
16. pellucid	———	———

	Vowel sounds (Estimated syllables)	Revised estimate
17. homeopath	———	———
18. pleonasm	———	———
19. residual	———	———
20. sisal	———	———
21. nimbus	———	———
22. cryptograph	———	———
23. contravene	———	———
24. cubicle	———	———
25. diatonic	———	———
26. sanctity	———	———
27. polychrome	———	———
28. physiology	———	———
29. cymbal	———	———
30. pannikin	———	———

You will sometimes need to turn to the dictionary to confirm your pronunciation, despite your use of these practical steps to analysis. Our language is such a mixture of nonphonetic and foreign words that it is one of the most difficult to learn. When you do turn to the dictionary, you will find that pronunciation is indicated by a phonetic respelling. Each word is respelled with the letters that will give the exact pronunciation of the word. Here is some practice in reading phonetic respelling that will help you to use your dictionary for pronunciation more easily.

► **WORD ANALYSIS EXERCISE II**

Pronouncing from Phonetic Spellings

The word at the left represents the phonetic spelling of words as found in the dictionary. Find the word at the right for which it is the proper pronunciation.

1. kwik	a. kick	b. quit	c. quick	d. wick
2. surtin	a. certain	b. contain	c. curtain	d. citron
3. garazh	a. carriage	b. garret	c. gasket	d. garage
4. thot	a. that	b. thou	c. though	d. thought
5. hed	a. herd	b. had	c. bid	d. head
6. unek	a. uncle	b. unite	c. unique	d. unicorn
7. lunj	a. lounge	b. lunge	c. lunch	d. lung
8. koral	a. choral	b. carrel	c. coral	d. curl
9. eksept	a. accept	b. except	c. echo	d. excerpt
10. faz	a. face	b. phase	c. vase	d. fash
11. trak	a. trick	b. trunk	c. track	d. truck
12. not	a. knot	b. note	c. newt	d. gnat
13. gost	a. guest	b. guessed	c. gist	d. ghost
14. ski	a. skip	b. sky	c. ski	d. skid
15. mach	a. mash	b. madge	c. match	d. Magi

►   *WORD ANALYSIS EXERCISE III*

Pronouncing with the Aid of Symbols

Try to read the pronunciation given in the first column. For what common word does each phonetic spelling stand? Write the word on the line at the right.

1. yăngkē   _____
2. bēm   _____
3. rȯng   _____
4. käntrăt   _____
5. ərgənt   _____
6. sīprəs   _____
7. turnĭkĕt   _____
8. dĭspōz   _____
9. tōerd, tōrd   _____
10. ĕkstrə   _____
11. midnīt   _____
12. səksĕs   _____
13. hĭch   _____
14. rĭzəlt   _____
15. gān   _____
16. prĕst   _____
17. pärkā   _____
18. orəjən   _____
19. īs   _____
20. mōshən   _____

A Test on Use of the Dictionary

This test is an attempt to measure your skill in using a dictionary. If you are like most students, you use a dictionary only to find meanings of words you don't know. You are apt to make little use of a dictionary for finding pronunciations or spelling or derivation, or for correct usage of a word. This test will help you to see whether you know how to use a dictionary for all these purposes.

Use the sample page from *Webster's Third New International Dictionary*[*] to help you answer the questions. This is a test to determine your skill in using such a book, not a memory or information test.

Choose one answer for each question. Check yourself with the Answer Key, and compare your scores with the Table of Percentiles.

Pronunciation

1. *picaro* is pronounced to rhyme with—
     a. *do.*   b. *too.*   c. *domino.*   d. *ado.*   e. *sue.*

[*] By permission. From *Webster's Third New International Dictionary*, copyright 1961 by G. & C. Merriam Co., Publishers of the Merriam-Webster Dictionaries.

2. The most common pronunciation of *picayune* is—
   a. *pik-i-un'*.   b. *pik'e-yoon*.   c. *pik-a-yoon*.

3. Which letter or letters in *picaresque* are silent?
   a. *ue*.   b. *u*.   c. final *e*.   d. *que*.   e. *q*.

4. The mark ' indicates—
   a. a division between two syllables.   b. a foreign pronunciation.
   c. the syllable that is spoken loudest in the word.   d. the softest syllable in the word.

5. How many pronunciations of *picine* are given?
   a. One.   b. Two.   c. Three.   d. Four.   e. Five.

6. In the pronunciation of *picador,* the accented syllable rhymes with the first syllable of—
   a. *doorway*.   b. *pica*.   c. *picture*.   d. *above*.   e. *pikestaff*.

7. The first syllable of *piccolo* has the same vowel sound as the first syllable of—
   a. *sinus*.   b. *sine*.   c. *pibroch*.   d. *sister*.   e. *pica*.

8. Name the syllables accented in *pichurim?*
   a. The first.   b. The second.   c. The third.   d. The first and third.   e. The second and fourth.

9. *picaroon* is pronounced to rhymn with—
   a. *megaton*.   b. *macaroon*.   c. *octagon*.   d. *axone*.
   e. *squadron*.

10. What letter or letters in *piazza* are silent in the American pronunciation?
    a. The final *a*.   b. One of the *z*'s.   c. Both *z*'s.   d. The *i*.
    e. The first *a*.

Meaning

11. How many meanings are given for *piciform?*
    a. Five.   b. Three.   c. Four.   d. One.   5. Two.

12. In this sentence, which of the dictionary meanings is used for the word *Piapoco?* "As we entered the clearing, we heard the strange sounds of *Piapoco,* as the natives whispered to each other."
    a. The first.   b. The second.   c. The third.   d. None of them.

13. What word means almost the same or is a synonym for the adjective *picayune,* according to this dictionary?
    a. *pike*.   b. *peck*.   c. *petty*.   d. *select*.   e. *paltry*.

14. How many combinations or phrases using the verb *pick* are noted?
    a. Seventeen.   b. Five.   c. Sixteen.   d. Four.   e. Thirteen.

15. Under what word will you find further information regarding *picine?*
    a. *woodpeckers*.   b. *birds*.   c. *piciformes*.   d. *piciform*.
    e. *pici*.

pi-an-net *or* pi-a-net \'pīə,net\ *n -s* [prob. fr. ¹*ple* + *Annet*, fr. *Ann*, feminine name + -*et*] : MAGPIE 1a

¹pi-a-no \pē'ä(,)nō, -,ä(-\ *adv (or adj)* [It, fr. LL *planus* smooth, graceful] : SOFTLY, QUIETLY — used as a direction in music; opposed to *forte*; abbr. *p*

²piano \"\ *n -s* : a softly performed passage or tone (as in a voice or instrument)

³pi-ano \pē'a(,)nō, -,na *sometimes* -'a(-\ *n -s* [It, short for *pianoforte*, fr. *piano e forte* soft and strong, fr. *piano* soft (fr. LL *planus* smooth, graceful, fr. L, even, level, flat) + *e* and (fr. L *et*) + *forte* strong (fr. L *fortis*); fr. its being chiefly distinguished from the spinet in that its tones could be made softer or stronger — more at FLOOR, FORT] 1 : a stringed percussion instrument structurally derived from the dulcimer but historically from the clavichord and harpsichord and having steel wire strings stretched over a sounding board that sound when struck by felt-covered hammers operated from a keyboard and pedals that alter or modify the quantity and quality of sound produced — called also *pianoforte*; see GRAND PIANO, UPRIGHT PIANO 2 : a machine operated by a keyboard for perforating the cards for a jacquard apparatus

piano accordion *n* : an accordion with a keyboard for the right hand resembling and cor-

piano accordion

responding to the middle register of a piano keyboard

piano as-sai \-ä'sī\ *adv (or adj)* [It] : very softly — used as a direction in music

pi-a-no-forte \pē'anə,fōr(d-ē̄), |-t(ē)-, -fȯr|, -fō(ə)|, -ˌ₊ᵃ·ᵈᵉ, *in the 4-syllable pronunc,* |d- *does not occur before consonants other than* ᵈ\ *n -s* [It] : PIANO 1

pi-an-o-fort-ist \"fȯrd-ᵊst\ *n -s* : PIANIST

pi-an-o-graph \'pēʷan·ə,graf, -ˈrä̇f\ *n* [*piano* + -*graph*] : a melo-graph applied to a piano

piano hinge *n* : a hinge having a thin pin joint and extending along the full length of the turning part — called also *continuous hinge*

pi-a-no-la \pēə'nōlə\ *n -s* [*Pianola*] 1 : a deal or hand (as in contract) that offers no difficulty in the play 2 : something easy to perform or accomplish : CINCH

Pianola \"\ *trademark* — used for an automatic piano player

piano legs *n pl* : fat or disproportionately thick legs (some were bowlegged and some were knock-kneed, some had pipestems and some *piano legs* —Esther Forbes)

pi-an-o-logue \'pē'an·ᵊ,lȯg *also* -,äg\ *n -s* [*piano* + -*logue*] : a comic monologue accompanied by piano playing

pia-no no-bi-le \pyä'(,)nōˈnōbḁ,lā\ *n* [It] : the principal story of a house

piano organ *n* : a mechanical piano built like a barrel organ and operated like a hand organ : STREET PIANO

piano player *n* 1 : PIANIST 2 : a mechanism for reproducing the playing of piano music usu. housed in a portable cabinet and consisting of an electropneumatic apparatus for turning a perforated roll representing the composition to be played and for actuating a series of levers which operate the piano keys

piano quartet *n* : a musical composition written for piano, violin, viola, and cello; *also* : the performers for such a composition

piano score *n* : a musical score having the separate instrumental parts condensed upon two staffs

pia-no-vi-o-lin \pē'anˌᵊ,ᵥₑ·ᵊ,lᵊn\ *n* : a sostinente pianoforte producing tones resembling those of the violin

piano wire *n* [so called fr. its being used for the strings of pianos] : steel wire of high tensile strength and evenness of thickness containing 0.75 to 0.85 percent carbon

pi-a-po-co *n, pl* piapocos *or* piapocos *usu cap* 1 a : an

---

associated with the Miami 2 : a member of the Piankashaw people

¹pic *var of* PIX

⁴pic \'pik\ *n, pl* pics *or* pix \-ks\ [short for *picture*] 1 : PHOTOGRAPH (these ~s tell the story —*Springfield (Mass.) Republican*) 2 : MOTION PICTURE

⁵pic \"\ *n -s* [Sp *pica*, fr. *picar* to prick] 1 : the picador's lance 2 [by shortening] : PICADOR

⁶pic \"\ *vr* pic-ed \-kt\ pic-ed; pic-ing \-kiŋ\ pics \-ks\ : to prod or thrust at (a bull) with a pic

¹pi-ca \'pīkə\ *n -s* [prob. fr. ML, collection of church rules, prob. fr. L, magpie, perh. fr. its use in printing the service book and its resemblance to the colors of the bird] 1 : an old size of type between small pica and english 2 a : at a size of type equivalent to 12 point b : a unit equal to ⅙ inch used in measuring composing materials, line and cut widths, and type-page dimensions — compare EM, LINE 9c, POINT SYSTEM 3 : a size of typewriter type providing 10 characters to the linear inch and six lines to the vertical inch

²pica \"\ *n* [NL, fr. L, magpie — more at ¹PIE] 1 *cap* : the genus containing the magpies 2 -s [prob. fr. the fact that the magpie is omnivorous; a craving for and eating of unnatural substances (as chalk, ashes, or bones) that occurs in nutritional deficiency states (as aphosphorosis) in man or animals or in hysteric or insane conditions in man : GEOPHAGY — called also *depraved appetite*; compare LICKING DISEASE, WOOL EATING

pi-ca-cho \pē'käˌ(,)chō\ *n -s* [Sp, fr. *pico* peak + -*acho* (fr. L -*aceus* -aceous)] : a large pointed isolated hill

pi-ca-dor \'pikə,dȯ(ə)r, -ˈdō(ə)r\ *n, pl* picadors \-,rz\, -(ə)z\ *or* picado-res \,pikə'dō,(ᵣ)rēz, -ˈdȯ,-, -rās\ [Sp, fr. *picado* (past part. of *picar* to prick, pierce) + -*or*] : a mounted member of the bullfighting cuadrilla who prods the bull with a lance in order to weaken the neck and shoulder muscles — compare TORERO

pi-ca-du-ra \,pikə'd(y)u̇rə\ *n -s* [Sp, fr. *picado* (past part. of *picar*) + -*ura* -ure (fr. L)]; cut tobacco for cigarettes

pi-cae \'pī,sē\ *n pl, cap* [NL, fr. L *pica* magpie] *in former classifications* : an order of birds including most of the recent order Coraciiformes together with the parrots, cuckoos, and various passerine birds

pic-ail-lon \,pikal'yōn\ *n -s* [F — more at PICAYUNE] : PICA-YUNE 1

picaninny *var of* PICKANINNY

¹pic-ard \'pikərd, -i,kärd\ *n -s cap* [F, fr. MF, fr. *Picardie*, Picardy, province of northern France] 1 : a native or inhabitant of Picardy in northern France 2 : the French dialect of Picardy

²picard \"\ *adj, usu cap* [F, fr. *Picardie*] : of, relating to, or coming from Picardy

³picard \"\ *n -s usu cap* [ML *Picardus*, fr. *picardus* inhabitant or native of Picardy, fr. MF *picard*; fr. the fact that the group was founded or driven out of France]; one of a religious group active in Bohemia around the 15th century

pic-ar-dy third \'pika(r)dē-\ *n, sometimes cap P* [trans. of F *tierce de Picardie*, fr. *tierce* third]: the major third as introduced into the final chord of a musical composition written in a minor key

pic-a-rel \,pikə'rel\ *n -s* [F] : a small European marine fish (*Spicara smaris*) of the family Maenidae

¹pic-a-resque \,pikə'resk *sometimes* ,pēk-\ *adj* [Sp *picaresco*, fr. *picaro* rogue + -*esco* -esque]; of, relating to, or being a type of prose fiction of Spanish origin in modern literature in which the principal character is a rogue or vagabond and the narrative is a series of incidents or episodes connected chronologically but with little or no motivation or complication of plot (~ *novel*) (~ *career*) (waifs of the ~ tradition —Asher Brunes)

²picaresque \"\ *n -s* : someone or something that is picaresque (forming a kind of children's ~ of loosely connected episodes —Irving Howe)

pi-car-i-ae \pī'ka·(a)rē,ē\ *n pl, cap* [NL, irreg. fr. L *picus* woodpecker — more at ¹PIE] *in former classifications* : an order of birds nearly equivalent to the Coraciiformes but often

---

²pic-e-ne \"\ *n -s cap* : a native or inhabitant of ancient Picenum

¹pi-cene \"\ *n -s* [ISV *pic*- (fr. L *pic-*, *pix* pitch) + -*ene*] : a fluorescent crystalline hydrocarbon C₂₂H₁₄ obtained from the pitchy residue of petroleum or lignite tar; benzo-chrysene

²pic-e-ni-an \(")pi'sēnēən\ *adj, usu cap* [L *picenus* Picenian + E -*an*] : of or relating to Picenum, the Picenes, or their language — compare SABELLIAN

²picenian \"\ *n -s cap* 1 : PICENE 2 : the Italic language of the Picenian people

pic-e-ous \'pisēəs, 'pīs-\ *adj* [L *piceus* fr. *pic-*, *pix* pitch + -*eus* -eous — more at PITCH] : of, relating to, or resembling pitch : PITCHY; *esp* : glossy brownish black in color

²pi-chi \'pēchē\ *n -s* [AmerSp *pichi*, *piche*, fr. Araucan *pichi*, *pichin* small thing] : a small armadillo (*Zaedyus pichiy* syn. *Z. minutus*) of southern So. America

²pichi \"\ *n -s* [AmerSp *pichi*, *piche*, fr. Araucan *pichi*, *pichin*] : a Peruvian shrub (*Fabiana imbricata*) the herbage of which yields a tonic and diuretic

pich-i-ci-a-go \,pichē'siˈ(a)gō, |ā(-\ *also* pich-i-cha-go \-ˈchē,chī-\ *n -s* [perh. fr. Allentiac] : a small burrowing So. American armadillo (*Chlamyphorus truncatus*) armored with many bands of plates that are laterally replaced by thick hair; *also* : a larger but very similar form that constitutes a separate genus (*Burmeisteria*)

pich-u-rim \'pishəˈrəm\ *or* pichurim bean *n -s* [Pg *pichurim*, fr. Tupi *pichurim*] : one of the thick strongly aromatic cotyledons of a tropical American tree (*Nectandra pichurim*) used as a substitute for nutmegs and as a flavoring agent and stimulant tonic

pi-ci \'pī,sī\ *n pl, cap* [NL, fr. L, pl. of *picus* woodpecker — more at ¹PIE] : a group of birds formerly coextensive with or more extensive than the order Piciformes comprising the woodpeckers and piculets

pic-i-dae \'pisə,dē, 'pīs-\ *n pl, cap* [NL, fr. *Picus*, type genus + -*idae*] : a family of birds (suborder Pici) comprising the woodpeckers, the piculets, and the wrynecks

pic-i-form \'pisə,fȯrm, 'pīs-\ *adj* [prob. fr. (assumed) NL *piciformis*, fr. L *picus* woodpecker + -*formis* -iform] 1 : like a woodpecker 2 [NL Piciformes] : of or relating to the Piciformes

pic-i-for-mes \,pisə'fȯr,mēz\ *n pl, cap* [NL, fr. *Picus* + -*iformes*] : an order of nonpasserine birds formerly restricted to the woodpeckers but now usu. including also the jacamars, puffbirds, barbets, honey guides, and toucans

pi-cine \'pī,sīn, -sᵊn\ *adj* [L *picus* woodpecker + E -*ine*] : of or relating to woodpeckers : PICIFORM

¹pick \'pik\ *vb* -ED/-ING/-S [ME *piken*, partly fr. MF *piquer* to prick, partly fr. MF *pic*, pick, strike & partly fr. (assumed) OE *pīcian* to prick (whence OE *pīcung* pricking); akin to MD *picken*, *pecken* to prick, hoe, pick, ON *pikka* to peck, hack — more at PIKE (weapon)] *vt* 1 : to pierce, penetrate, or break up with a pointed instrument (~*ing* the hard clay) (~ the surface of a millstone) 2 : to remove covering or adhering matter from : to remove (as the bones clean); *specif* : to remove feathers from (~ a goose) 3 a : to separate and remove with the fingers or fingertips : PLUCK (~*ing* flowers for the table) b : to take lightly, neatly, or selectively : CULL (~*ing* only the ripest berries) c : to gather one by one or bit by bit (~ apples) (~ rags) d : to take needed sorts from (standing type) (if you ~ this form chalk the chase) 4 : to select from among a group : CHOOSE, NAME (attempts to ~ an exact synonym —Johnson O'Connor) (tried to ~ the shortest route) (~*ed* his way cautiously through the swamp) (~*ed* a winner in the next race) 5 : to take the contents of (as a pocket) by stealth (suspected of ~*ing* pockets) (skilled at ~*ing* the brains of his associates) 6 : to seek and find occasion for : provoke deliberately (~ a quarrel) 7 a : to dig into or pull lightly at with fingertips or fingernails or a pointed instrument (~*ing* his teeth with a knife) (~*ed* the shoestring until it came untied) b : to pluck (the strings of a stringed musical instrument) with a plectrum or a pointed instrument (~*ing* the banjo) : to play (such an instrument) in this manner (~ a guitar) ; *broadly* : to play (a stringed instrument) (~*ing* her way through the sonata)

Arawakan people of the lower Guaviar river in Colombia, So. America **b :** a member of such people **2 :** the language of the Piapoco people
piarachnoid *var of* PIA-ARACHNOID
pi·a·rist \ˈpīərəst\ *n* -s *usu cap* [prob. fr. (assumed) NL *piarista*, fr. *piarum* (in the phrase *patres scholarum piarum* fathers of the religious schools) + *-ista* -ist] **:** a member of a religious teaching institute founded at Rome early in the 17th century by St. Joseph of Calasanza
pias *pl of* PIA
pias *abbr* piaster
pi·as·sa·va *also* **pi·as·sa·ba** *or* **pi·a·sa·va** *or* **pi·a·sa·ba** \ˌpēəˈsävə, -äbə\ *n* -s [Pg *piassaba*, fr. Tupi *piaçaba*] **1 :** a coarse brown fiber that invests the bases of the leaf sheaths of a Brazilian palm and is used in making ropes, mats, and brushes; *also* **:** the palm (*Attalea funifera*) that bears this fiber and yields the coquilla nut **2 :** a fiber from a Brazilian palm (*Leopoldinia piassaba*) common along the Amazon river; *also* **:** the tree yielding this fiber **3 :** the stiff coarse bast fiber of an African palm (*Raphia vinifera*) **4 :** coarse fiber derived from any of several palms (as tucum, gomuti, and hemp palm)
piast \ˈpyäst\ *n* -s *usu cap* [after *Piast*, legendary peasant who was believed to be the founder of the dynasty in the 9th century] **1 :** a member of the first dynasty of Polish rulers that ended with the death of Casimir III in 1370 **2 a :** a member of the native Polish nobility **b :** a man of purely Polish descent
pi·as·ter *or* **pi·as·tre** \pēˈastə(r)\ *n* -s [F *piastre*, fr. It *piastra* thin metal plate, coin, fr. OIt, fr. L *emplastra*, *emplastrum* plaster — more at PLASTER] **1 :** a Spanish dollar **:** PIECE OF EIGHT **2 a** (1) **:** any of several monetary units of some Middle Eastern countries (as Turkey, Egypt, Syria, Lebanon, Libya) equal to ¹⁄₁₀₀ pound — see MONEY table (2) **:** a Saudi Arabian unit equal to ¹⁄₂₂ rial **b :** a coin representing one of these units **3 a :** a monetary unit of Cyprus equal to ⅛ shilling or ¹⁄₁₈₀ pound sterling **b :** a coin representing this unit **4 :** the basic monetary unit of French Indochina until 1954 and of the Republic of Vietnam from 1955
pi·at \ˈpīˌat\ *n* -s [*p*rojector *i*nfantry *a*nti*t*ank] **:** a short-range antitank gun used in the British and Canadian armies weighing 33 pounds and firing a 2.75-pound projectile that explodes on impact with force sufficient to penetrate four inches of tempered armor plate
piat·ti \ˈpyädˌē\ *n pl* [It, fr. pl. of *piatto* plate, fr. *piatto* level, flat, fr. (assumed) VL *plattus* — more at PLATE] **:** CYMBALS
pi·az·za \pēˈazə, *in sense 1 usu* -atsə\ *n, pl* **piazzas** \-əz\ *or* **piaz·ze** \-t(ˌ)sā\ [It, fr. L *platea* street, courtyard — more at PLACE] **1** *pl* *piazze* **:** an open square in an Italian or other European town **:** a town square or open market **2 a :** an arcaded and roofed gallery that often surrounds an open court; *also* **:** a portico or single colonnade before a building **b** *chiefly North & Midland* **:** VERANDA, PORCH **syn** see BALCONY
pi·az·zaed \-əd\ *adj* **:** furnished with a piazza ⟨long-*piazzaed* summer hotel⟩
pib·ble \ˈpibəl\ *dial var of* PEBBLE
pib·gorn \ˈpibˌgȯrn\ *also* **pib·corn** \-ˌkȯrn\ *n* -s [W, fr. *pib* pipe + *corn* horn] **:** an obsolete Welsh single-reed woodwind instrument similar to the hornpipe

pibgorn

pi·blok·to *or* **pi·block·to** \pəˈbläk(ˌ)tō\ *n* -s [Esk *piblokto*] **:** a hysteria among Eskimos characterized by excitement and sometimes by mania, usu. followed by depression, and occurring chiefly in winter and usu. to women
pi·broch *or* **piob·aireachd** \ˈpēˌbräk\ *n* -s [ScGael *piobaireachd* pipe-music, fr. *piobair* piper, fr. *pìob* pipe] **:** elaborate variations for the Scottish Highland bagpipe on a traditional theme
¹pic \ˈpēk\ *n* -s [F, prob. fr. Sp *pico*, fr. *picar* to prick, pierce, prob. fr. (assumed) VL *piccare* — more at PIKE (weapon)] **:** PEAK 5a
²pic \"\ *n* -s [F, fr. MF *picq*, fr. *piquer* to prick — more at PIKE] **:** ³PIQUE
including the parrots and cuckoos
pi·car·i·an \-rēən\ *adj* [NL *Picariae* + E *-an*] **:** of or relating to the Picariae
pi·carii \-rēˌī\ *n pl, cap* [NL, prob. alter. of *Picariae*] *in former classifications* **:** a group of birds practically equivalent to the Picariae together with the Clamatores
pic·a·ro \ˈpikəˌrō\ *n* -s [Sp *picaro*] **:** ROGUE, TRAMP, VAGABOND, BOHEMIAN
¹pic·a·roon *or* **pick·a·roon** \ˌpikəˈrün\ *n* -s [Sp *picarón*, aug. of *picaro*] **1 :** PICARO **2 :** PIRATE, CORSAIR — used of a man or a ship
²picaroon \"\ -ED/-ING/-S *vi* **:** to act as a pirate or brigand watching or searching for a prize or victim
picas *pl of* PICA
¹pic·a·yune \ˌpikēˈyün, -kəˈ-\ *n* -s [F *picaillon* old copper coin of Piedmont, halfpenny, fr. Prov *picaioun*, fr. *picaio* money, fr. *pica* to strike, prick, sound, jingle (fr. — assumed — VL *piccare* to prick, pierce) + *-aio* -al (fr. L *-alia*) — more at PIKE (weapon)] **1 a :** a Spanish half real piece formerly current in Louisiana and other southern states **b :** HALF DIME **2 :** something of very small or of the least value ⟨not worth a ~⟩
²picayune \ˌ==ˈ=\ *adj* **1 :** of little value **:** PALTRY, MEASLY ⟨not more than two or three countries are carrying on any sort of forest research, and these programs are ~ —William Vogt⟩ ⟨compared to the total number of people employed, such cutbacks were still ~ —*Time*⟩ **2 :** concerned with trifling matters **:** petty, narrow, or small-minded in point of view ⟨within the limits of a short review it would seem ~ to be critical —W.F.Stolper⟩ **syn** see PETTY
pic·a·yun·ish \-nish, nēsh\ *adj* [¹*picayune* + *-ish*] **:** PICAYUNE ⟨a lifetime of ~ drudgery in the company of louts —H.L. Davis⟩ **syn** see PETTY
pic·ca·dil·ly \ˌpikəˈdilē\ *n* -ES [F *picadilles*, pl. of *picadille* pickadil — more at PICKADIL] **1 :** PICKADIL **2 :** a high wing collar worn by men in the late 19th century
piccage *var of* PICKAGE
pic·ca·lil·li \ˌpikəˈlilē\ *n* -s [earlier *piccalillo*, prob. alter. (perh. influenced by Sp *picadillo* hash) of ¹*pickle*] **:** a relish of chopped vegetables and pungent spices
pic·ca·nin \ˈpikəˌnin\ *n* -s [Afrik, short for *piccaninny*, fr. E — more at PICKANINNY] *southern Africa* **:** PICKANINNY
pic·ca·nin·ny \ˈpikəˌninī\ *Brit var of* PICKANINNY
¹pic·co·lo \ˈpikəˌlō\ *n* -s [It, lit., small, prob. fr. It dial. *picca*

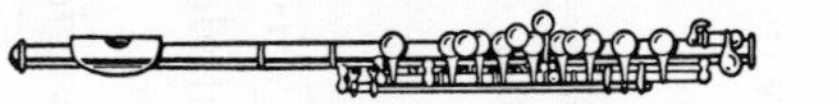
piccolo 1

little] **1 :** a small shrill flute pitched an octave higher than the ordinary flute **2 :** a two-foot labial pipe-organ stop with a high piercing tone **3 :** an apprentice waiter in a European restaurant **:** BUSBOY **4** *South* **:** JUKEBOX
²piccolo \"\ *adj* [It] *of a musical instrument* **:** smaller than ordinary size ⟨~ banjo⟩ ⟨~ cornet⟩ ⟨~ piano⟩
pic·co·lo·ist \-lōəst\ *n* -s **:** a piccolo player
pic·co·lo·pas·so red \ˌpikəlōˈpä(ˌ)sō-\ *n* [*piccolopasso* fr. It *piccolo* small + *passo* raisin wine] **:** OXBLOOD
piccotah *var of* PICOTAH
pice \ˈpīs\ *n, pl* **pice** [Hindi *paisā*] **1 a :** a unit of value of India equal before 1955 to ¼ of an anna or ¹⁄₆₄ rupee **b :** a similar unit of Pakistan — see MONEY table **2 :** a bronze or copper coin representing one pice
pic·ea \ˈpisēə, ˈpīs-\ *n, cap* [NL, fr. L, pitch pine, fr. *pic-*, *pix* pitch] **:** a genus of temperate and arctic evergreen trees (family Pinaceae) having acicular leaves that are keeled on both surfaces and borne individually on persistent peg-shaped bases and cones that become pendulous and have reflexed scales — see SPRUCE
pic·e·in \ˈpisēən, ˈpīs-\ *n* -s [NL *Picea* (genus name of the Norway spruce *Picea abies*) + ISV *-in*] **:** a bitter crystalline glucoside $C_{14}H_{18}O_7$ obtained esp. from the needles of the Norway spruce and from the barks of willows
¹pi·cene \ˈpīˌsēn\ *adj, usu cap* [L *picenus* of Picenum, fr. *Picenum*, ancient Roman province in eastern central Italy] **:** PICENIAN
also **:** to play music on (a stringed instrument) ⟨reputed to ~ a mighty mean guitar —G.S.Perry⟩ **c :** to loosen or pull apart with a sharp point ⟨~ wool⟩ ⟨~ oakum⟩ **8 :** to turn (a lock) with a wire or a pointed tool instead of the key esp. with intent to steal **9 a** *of a bird* (1) **:** to strike with the bill ⟨cruelly ~*ed* by the stronger chicks⟩ (2) **:** to take up (food) with the bill **b :** to eat sparingly or mincingly **10 :** to cause (bits of the surface of paper) to stick to type and be pulled off — used of ink **11 :** to finish (an edge of cloth) with a line of fine running stitches parallel to the edge ⟨pocket flaps ~*ed* by hand⟩ **~** *vi* **1 :** to use or work with a pick or pickax **2 :** to gather something from a plant **:** HARVEST ⟨the ~*ing* season⟩ ⟨fruit ripe for ~*ing*⟩ **3 :** PILFER, FILCH — used chiefly in the phrase *picking and stealing* **4 a** *of a bird* **:** to strike or take things up with the bill ⟨chickens ~*ing* about the yard⟩ **b :** to eat sparingly or mincingly **:** eat with little appetite ⟨~*ing* listlessly at his dinner⟩ **5 :** to lose bits of the surface by adhesion to the inked form during printing — used of paper — **pick a hole in :** to find or reveal a flaw in (as an argument) or blemish in (as a reputation) — **pick and choose :** to select with care and deliberation or with notable fastidiousness ⟨*picking and choosing*, dillying and dallying; not a man to have straightforward love for a woman —Virginia Woolf⟩ — **pick at 1 :** to try to pull or seize with the fingertips ⟨*picking at* the bedclothes⟩ **2 :** to find fault with continually **:** pick on **:** NAG, PESTER — **pick on 1 :** to pick at **:** HARASS, NAG, TEASE ⟨felt that he was *picked on* because he was better than the others —Robertson Davies⟩ **2** *or* **pick upon :** to single out for special attention **:** choose for a particular purpose or reason ⟨they had *picked on* a poor camping site⟩
²pick \"\ *n* -s **1 :** a blow or stroke with a pointed instrument **2 a :** the act of choosing or selecting **:** right or privilege of selection **:** CHOICE ⟨had the ~ of several jobs⟩ ⟨here are several brands, take your ~⟩ **b :** something that is or would be chosen first **:** the best or choicest part or member ⟨the ~ of the herd⟩ ⟨the ~ of the rebel forces⟩ **3** *dial* **a :** the taking of a bit of food **:** PECK **b :** a scanty meal **c :** a little bit **:** SCRAP **4 :** the portion or quantity of a crop gathered at one time **:** PICKING ⟨biggest berry ~ in several years⟩ ⟨the first ~ of peaches⟩ **5 :** something that is picked in with a point or pointed pencil **6 a :** a particle (as of hardened ink, dirt, or paper) embedded in the hollow of a letter and causing a spot on a printed sheet; *also* **:** the spot so caused **b :** a burr on the face of a plate or cut or of newly cast type **c :** the tendency of paper to pick **7 :** a maneuver in basketball for cutting off a player from the play **:** SCREEN
³pick \"\ *adj* [²*pick*] **:** PICKED, BEST ⟨handed out the new guns to the ~ rifle shots of his crew —F.B.Gipson⟩
⁴pick \"\ *vb* -ED/-ING/-S [ME *pykken*, alter. of *picchen* pitch, v.] *vt* **1** *obs* **:** to set up or fix in place (as a tent) **2 a** *chiefly dial* **:** to throw or thrust with effort **:** HURL ⟨high as I could ~ my lance —Shak.⟩ **b :** PITCH ⟨time to ~ the hay⟩ **3** *dial* **:** to give birth to prematurely **4 :** to throw (a shuttle) across the loom **~** *vi* **1** *dial Eng* **:** to fall or topple forward **2 :** to throw the shuttle across the loom
⁵pick \"\ *n* -s **1** *dial Eng* **a :** the act of pitching or throwing **:** CAST **b :** something that is thrown **2 a :** a throw of the shuttle — used esp. in calculating the speed of a loom ⟨so many ~*s* per minute⟩ **b :** one filling thread — used esp. in describing the fineness of a fabric ⟨so many ~*s* to an inch⟩
⁶pick \"\ *n* -s [ME *pik*, prob. alter. of ¹*pike*] **1** *obs* **a :** PIKE **b :** a sharp point **:** SPIKE **2 :** a heavy iron or steel tool pointed at one or both ends and often curved, wielded by means of a wooden handle inserted in an eye between the ends, and used by quarrymen, road makers, miners, and stone dressers **3** *dial Brit* **:** any of various pointed or pronged implements: as **a :** PITCHFORK **b :** GAFF **4 :** a sharp-pointed instrument for picking: as **a :** TOOTHPICK **b :** PICKLOCK **c :** PLECTRUM 1 **5** *dial Eng* **:** a diamond in playing cards **6 :** one of the points on the forepart of a figure skate blade
⁷pick \"\ *dial var of* PIQUE
pickaback *also* **pickback** *or* **pickapack** *var of* PIGGYBACK
pickaback plant \ˈ==ˌ=-\ *also* **piggyback plant** \ˈ==ˌ=-\ *n* **:** a glandular pubescent perennial herb (*Tolmiea menziesii*) of the family Saxifragaceae that is native to western No. America, has young plants borne at the junction of leaf blade and petiole, and is used as a foliage plant

16. A *picarel* is a—
    a. tree.   b. rogue.   c. fish.   d. female picaro.   e. horse-
    man.

17. What word could you use in place of *piaster?*
    a. *square.*   b. *coin.*   c. *castastrophe.*   d. *plastron.*
    e. *emplastrum.*

18. How many definitions are given for *piblokto?*
    a. One.   b. Three.   c. Four.   d. Two.   e. Five.

19. Which of the meanings for *pica* is used in this sentence? "The ani-
    mal was afflicted with *pica* and attempted to eat its own fur."
    a. The first.   b. The third.   c. The fourth.   d. The fifth.
    e. The second.

20. Under how many other entries can you find more explanation of
    picaro?
    a. One.   b. Two.   c. Three.   d. Four.   e. Five.

Spelling

21. The plural of *pica* is—
    a. *pica.*   b. *picaes.*   c. *picae.*   d. *picas.*   e. *piccas.*

22. When written in a sentence, the last word in the middle column is
    spelled—
    a. *pi-cene.*   b. *Pi-cene.*   c. *Picene.*   d. *picene.*

23. How would you divide *piccolo* at the end of a line of typing, if you
    had only 5 or 6 spaces left?
    a. *pi-ccolo.*   b. *pic-colo.*   c. *picc-olo.*   d. *piccol-o.*
    e. *piccolo.*

24. How many syllables are there in *picaroon?*
    a. One.   b. Two.   c. Three.   d. Four.   e. Five.

25. Which of these is spelled correctly?
    a. *piccalili.*   b. *piciform.*   c. *picarell.*   d. *piastra.*
    e. *piaza.*

26. The plural of *piazza* is—
    a. *pizzas.*   b. *piazzae.*   c. *piazza.*   d. *piassas.*   e. *piazzas.*

27. How should this word be spelled?
    a. *pianonobile.*   b. *piano nobile.*   c. *pianobile.*   d. *piano-
    nobile.*   e. *pianono-bile.*

28. How would you divide *picaresque* into syllables?
    a. *pic-a-resque.*   b. *pica-resque.*   c. *picar-esque.*   d. *pi-ca-
    resque.*   e. *pi-ca-res-que.*

29. How do you spell the plural of *picacho?*
    a. *picachos.*   b. *picachoes.*   c. *picacho.*   d. *picachones.*
    e. None of these.

30. Which of these is spelled with a capital?
    a. *piciform.*   b. *piciformes.*   c. *picine.*   d. *pick.*   e. None of these.

Derivation

31. The word *piblokto* comes from what language?
    a. Esperanto.   b. Eastern dialect.   c. Esthonia.   d. East Esquiline.   e. Eskimo.
32. The seventh word in the middle column comes originally from what language?
    a. Spanish.   b. Middle French.   c. Medieval French.   d. India.   e. Latin.
33. The technical terms *Picariae, Pici,* and *Picae* were derived from what language?
    a. French.   b. New London.   c. English.   d. North Latvia.   e. Latin.
34. The fourth word in the first column (*piano*) is identical with the same word in what language?
    a. British.   b. English.   c. Italic.   d. Italian.   e. Latin.
35. The alternate spelling of *piaster* is taken directly from what language?
    a. French.   b. Italian.   c. Latin.   d. Turkish.   e. Roumanian.
36. The spelling *picaninny* is used for *pickaninny* in what country?
    a. United States.   b. Italy.   c. France.   d. Britain.   e. Australia.
37. The word *picarel* comes directly into English from the language of what country?
    a. Britain.   b. Canada.   c. Italy.   d. Portugal.   e. France.
38. The fifth entry under *pic* is derived directly from what language?
    a. Latin.   b. Italic.   c. British.   d. Spanish.   e. English.
39. The symbol *NL* (as in the entry for *Pici*) means that the word is derived from what language?
    a. Latin.   b. North Latin.   c. New London.   d. North Latvia.   e. New Latin.
40. The symbols in brackets after *piatti* implies that the word is from what language?
    a. English.   b. Italic.   c. Latin.   d. British.   e. Italian.

Usage

41. What part of speech is *pichurim?*
    a. Neuter.   b. Noun.   c. Nominative.   d. Name.   e. None.

42. The symbol *obs.* means that the meaning so labeled is—
    a. rare.   b. uncommon.   c. obsolete.   d. obscure.   e. obscene.

43. In the second entry under *pick,* what does the abbreviation *dial* under 3a mean?
    a. Dialogue.   b. Dialectic.   c. Obsolete.   d. Dialect.
    e. Archaic.

44. What part(s) of speech can *pic* be in its various meanings?
    a. A noun.   b. An adjective.   c. A verb.   d. An adjective or a verb.   e. A noun or verb.

45. What part of speech is *picaroon?*
    a. Nominative.   b. Noun.   c. Noun or verb.   d. Neuter.
    e. None.

46. In the fifth entry under *pick,* in what country is this word used as a part of a dialect?
    a. England.   b. United States.   c. Australia.   d. Canada.
    e. France.

47. When *pibble* is used to mean *pebble,* this usage is classified as—
    a. substandard.   b. dialect.   c. obsolete.   d. standard.
    e. archaic.

48. How many parts of speech can *picayune* be?
    a. One.   b. Three.   c. Two.   d. More than four.
    e. Four.

49. The second entry under *Picard* indicates that it is—
    a. an action.   b. a place.   c. the name of something.   d. a person.   e. a descriptive word.

50. Where is the noun *picayune* commonly used to refer to a small coin?
    a. Southern U.S.   b. Piedmont.   c. France.   d. Spanish-America.   e. U.S.

Chapter 1

Previewing Exercise I:

"After the Honeymoon, What?" (pp. 8–9.)

1. a 2. a 3. b 4. a 5. a

Some possible preview questions are the following:

1. What are some of the current trends in marriage, in terms of age, parenthood, size of family, divorce, and so on?
2. What are some of the expectations of young married couples?
3. Name at least three problems that many young married women will eventually have to face.
4. During what period of the marriage do many wives find it necessary to work?
5. Which fact or facts about marriage introduced here contradict common popular belief?
6. Which of the facts offered here are, in your opinion, most significant in aiding young married couples in long-range planning?

Previewing Exercise II:

"Thunderbolts in Harness" (pp. 13–14.)

1. b 2. b 3. b 4. b 5. a 6. b

Possible preview questions are the following:

1. Who initiated the scientific study of lightning?
2. When was the first man-made lightning created?

3. What was the strength of the greatest bolt of lightning created by man? How does this compare with natural lightning?
4. In addition to the generator used in creating bolts of lightning, what other tools were useful in this investigation?
5. Did the success in creating lightning supplant any study of natural lightning? If not, why not?
6. Where is lightning research still being pursued?
7. What is the primary purpose of lightning research?

Previewing Exercise III:

"What Makes a Floor Plan Good?"   (pp. 19–20.)

1. b   2. a   3. a   4. b   5. a

Possible preview questions are the following:

1. If you make a floor plan of a house you are considering, what sort of markings might you add to the plan?
2. What tests of suitability does the selection suggest that you apply to a house?
3. Which of these tests can be decided only in terms of your own family?
4. Which of these tests are independent of family size?
5. If you lay scale cutouts of your furniture on the plan, what facts will they help to reveal?
6. What aspects of home selection does the article not touch upon?
7. Could this approach to selection of a house be applied to apartment-hunting?

Previewing Exercise IV:

"How Your Right to Vote Was Won"   (pp. 25–26.)

1. b   2. b   3. b   4. b   5. a   6. b

Some of the preview questions you may have framed are these:

1. Where and when did the idea of voting originate?
2. Under what conditions was voting permitted in the early days of American history?
3. How were voting privileges extended to all male persons?
4. When did women secure the right to vote?
5. How do present-day mechanics of voting differ from those of the early days?
6. How do the national committees of the major political parties contribute to an election?
7. Why does the organization of a national political party extend downward into the smallest political divisions?

8. If the general public does not exercise its privilege of voting, what might happen?

Previewing Exercise V:

"Understanding Our Behavior: The Psychology of Personal and Social Adjustment" (pp. 29–30.)

1. a   2. a   3. c   4. b

Possible preview questions are the following:
1. What are the major areas of personal and social adjustment, according to the author?
2. What is the author trying to accomplish by citing examples of good and poor adjustment in each of these life areas?
3. What aspects of personal and social adjustment do you believe should have been emphasized more?
4. What are some examples of good and poor adjustment in the family, education, occupation, and community areas?
5. How does adjustment in one area, such as the family, affect adjustment in other areas, such as education or the community?
6. Are there other logical interrelationships among the areas of adjustment?
7. Which area of adjustment is implied as the foundational area for all others?

Chapter 2

Skimming Exercise I:

"Our Rarest Mammal?" (pp. 37–38.)

1. b   2. c   3. c   4. d   5. a   6. d   7. d   8. a
9. b   10. a

Skimming Exercise II: (pp. 41–42.)

"Psychology for Today's Living, Part II: Love, Romance, and Marriage"

1. a   2. c   3. a   4. a   5. a   6. a   7. c   8. b
9. b   10. b

Skimming Exercise III: (pp. 46–47.)

"Letters That Get Results"

1. c   2. c   3. b   4. d   5. a   6. b   7. b   8. d
9. c   10. b

Skimming Exercise IV: (pp. 49–50.)

"Our Restless Earth"

    1. b   2. a   3. d   4. a   5. a   6. d   7. c   8. b
    9. a   10. b

Chapter 3

Scanning Exercise I: (p. 54.)

"Discoverer of the Stethoscope"

    1. c   2. a   3. a

"The Telephone"   (p. 55.)

    1. c   2. d   3. b   4. a

"1, 10, 100, 1,000 . . ."   (pp. 56–57.)

    1. d   2. a   3. c

"Focus on Norway"   (p. 58.)

    1. d   2. a   3. c

Scanning Exercise II: (pp. 60–62.)

"A Comparative Study of Problems of Married and Single Students"

    1. d   2. a   3. c   4. a   5. c   6. b

Scanning Exercise III: (p. 63.)

"Stalagmites and Stalactites"

    1. lines 16–18   2. lines 32–35   3. lines 36–37   4. lines 14–15

"Improving Cotton Fabrics"   (p. 64.)

    1. lines 2–3   2. line 16   3. lines 30–31   4. lines 33–34

"A New Concept for a Navigation Satellite System"   (p. 65.)

    1. lines 12–14   2. lines 26–27   3. line 20   4. lines 29–30

"Cooperation and the Growth of Knowledge"   (p. 67.)

    1. lines 15–17   2. lines 27–29   3. lines 32–34   4. lines 19–21

Scanning Exercise IV:

"Reasons for Dropping Out of College"   (p. 68.)

    1. b   2. b   3. a

"Attrition Among First-Semester Engineering Freshmen"   (p. 69.)

    1. a   2. b   3. b

"Statistic of the Month"   (p. 70.)

    1. b   2. a   3. b

"Needs Selections by Occupations"   (p. 71.)

    1. b   2. a   3. a

"Daily Requirements Covered by the Basic Foods"   (p. 71.)

    1. b   2. b   3. b   4. b

Chapter 4

Rapid-Reading Exercise I:

"Sound"   (p. 79.)

    1. True   2. True   3. False   4. False   5. True

Rapid-Reading Exercise II: (pp. 83–84.)

"Your Job"

1. True	6. True	11. False
2. True	7. True	12. True
3. False	8. True	13. False
4. True	9. False	14. False
5. True	10. True	15. False

Rapid-Reading Exercise III:

"The Magic Box That Tests Your Driving Skills"   (p. 86.)

1. True	6. True
2. False	7. False
3. False	8. True
4. True	9. True
5. False	10. True

Rapid-Reading Exercise IV:

"Don't Let Stereotypes Warp Your Judgment"   (p. 91.)

1. False	6. True
2. True	7. True
3. False	8. True
4. False	9. False
5. True	10. False

Chapter 5

Study Exercise I:

"Listening with the Inner Ear"   (pp. 99–103.)

Possible Preview Questions

1. How and why is bad listening a handicap to businessmen?
2. What skills are needed for effective listening?
3. Why has listening training been neglected?
4. How much time do we spend listening?
5. Why is listening so important as a business grows?
6. What are upward and horizontal flow of information?
7. How is listening important in human relations?
8. How should we listen? For facts, ideas?
9. Why is concentration in listening a big problem?
10. How and when can we practice listening?
11. Who is really responsible for good communication—the speaker or the listener?

Main Ideas of Paragraphs

1. A sampling of adult students indicates that the average person's immediate recall of what he hears is 50 per cent, with only 25 per cent recall after two months.

2. Bad listening is a handicap to businessmen.

3. Failure to listen was the cause of a workman's accident in a Long Island factory.

4. Listening, or the ability to understand and recall the spoken word, is a skill that can be and is being improved through training.

5. Listening has been the forgotten stepchild of education, whereas reading has been a favored son.

6. Although it has been assumed that reading instruction would improve listening skill, such is actually not the case.

7. Today's adults were trained in reading but not in listening.

8. A survey indicates that the average adult spends 45 per cent of his

communicating time listening, with the rest divided among reading, writing, and speaking.

9. Other studies support the previous findings regarding the time spent in listening and its importance.

10. Poor listening skills force many businessmen to rely on written directives only.

11. An overheard conversation between two businessmen illustrates the danger of entrusting verbal instructions to a poor listener.

12. Poor listening skills force people away from the faster communication of the spoken word to the slower, less economical practice of writing all communications.

13. An improvement in communication from the lower up to the higher levels in a business organization is particularly needed.

14. The upward flow in oral business communication is made useless by poor listeners along the line.

15. The smooth horizontal flow of oral business communication is more in need of good listeners than good talkers.

16. Good listening is important in human relations.

17 and 18. A Chicago plant superintendent became ineffective on his job because his plant manager would not listen to his problems.

19. With a trained counselor to listen to him, the plant superintendent was able to face his problems more realistically.

20. A businessman should be willing to listen to any level of problem a subordinate may have.

21. Just being aware of the importance of good listening will likely improve one's listening ability.

22. A farmer called a telephone operator to report an incident involving two men in a car.

23. The operator's memory of an earlier police broadcast led to the arrest of the two men.

24. Listening skills are improved by understanding what the skills are.

25 and 26. "Listening for the facts" is not the best way to learn what the speaker has to say.

27. The good listener looks for the speaker's main ideas.

28. The fact that one's listening comprehension rate is faster than a speaker's word rate poses a special communication problem.

29. The poor listener is tempted to use excess thinking time for mental excursions away from the speaker's topic.

30. The writer's improvement courses in listening suggest ways in which all the listener's thinking time may be concentrated on the speaker's ideas.

31. Try to anticipate what the speaker will say.

32. Continually summarize.

33. Weigh the speaker's evidence for his statements.

34. Listen for inferred meanings.

35. Realize that the development of good listening skills requires work and practice.

36. Practice listening to talk that requires hard work mentally.

37. Good communication requires mutual responsibility of the listener and the speaker.

Main Idea for the Selection

Businessmen poor in listening skills can learn to listen much more efficiently, thus measurably improving their over-all work effectiveness.

Study Exercise II:

"Roman Culture in the Republican Age"   (pp. 107–108.)

Preview Questions and Answers

1. How was the Greek culture introduced into the existing Roman culture?
    ANSWER: The conquest of Greece, the adoption of Greek as a language, and the use of Greeks as slaves and tutors introduced Greek culture to the Romans.

2. Why did drama dominate the early period of Latin literature?
    ANSWER: Reading was not extensively practiced.

3. What difficulties were met in adapting Greek poetry to the Roman language?
    ANSWER: The lack of flexibility in Latin hindered the imitation of Greek poetry.

4. Why is the late republican era unsurpassed for prose?
    ANSWER: Political life placed a premium on oratory.

5. Who were some of the great prose writers of the late republican era?
    ANSWER: Cicero, Sallust, Julius Caesar.

6. How was Roman religion gradually modified by Greek thought?
    ANSWER: The Roman gods were gradually identified with the Greek counterparts, and the leading schools of philosophy were borrowed directly from the Greeks.

7. By the age of Augustus, what had the old Roman religion come to be called?
    ANSWER: The poet's religion.

8. Why did the more cultured of the Roman aristocrats turn from religion to philosophy for comfort and guidance?
    ANSWER: Their interest was in practical morality, which was best answered through philosophy.

9. What were some of the philosophies followed by these early Romans?
    ANSWER: Epicureanism, Stoicism.

Study Exercise III:

"Life's Home"   (pp. 111–113.)

    1. 4 years.   2. Nothing.   3. Nuclear energy.   4. 5½ times as dense.   5. A range around 100 centigrade degrees.   6. A relationship between living things and their environment.   7. Mars. 8. None.

Chapter 6   **(pp. 120–131.)**

    1. c   2. a   3. a, b   4. c   5. a, b, c, or d   6. d   7. d
8. b   9. a   10. b   11. guaranteeing, steady

Chapter 7   **(pp. 132–145.)**

    1. The aims of any social institution such as the schools change in accordance with the progress and demands of society. What was an adequate education fifty years ago is hardly appropriate for today's needs. To cite a single example, it was sufficient 50 years ago simply to teach pupils the minimum essentials of reading skill. Today's demands require more training in this field to produce better, more rapid, and more critical reading.

    2. Society has gradually learned that good social adjustment of the individual is not produced by harsh or brutal training of children. "Spare the rod and spoil the child" thinking has been refuted by careful study of the effect of the social climate upon child behavior. This approach produces only resistance, repression, negativism, aggressiveness, and increased delinquency.

    3. The author who offers the requirement of high-school graduation before issuing drivers' licenses as a solution to school dropouts makes several faulty assumptions. Among these are the belief that this regulation would prevent the dropout of those who leave school because of insufficient intelligence, poor reading skills, lack of money, early marriages, and so on.

    4. Despite all its good intentions, the Constitution was inadequate from the very beginning. In fact, it was necessary to add such amendments as the Bill of Rights within the first five years after ratification because the Constitution failed to spell out the rights and liberties of American citizens. This process of further clarifying the rights of the individual, of the States, and of the Federal Government by amendments to the Constitution is inescapable and probably will continue as long as the United States exists.

    5. Instead of being drunk, the staggering man could be ill, faint, or suffering from heat stroke, to mention only a few possibilities.

    6. This type of reasoning is often labeled *post hoc, ergo propter hoc*—"because one event follows another it must be caused by the prior event." Even if we allow that the weather has been "unusual," whatever that means, it does not necessarily follow that its uncommonness has been caused by

atomic-bomb testing. The cause might also be sunspots, weather cycles, shift in the jet stream, and so on.

7. The speaker apparently believes that among the privileges of free enterprise are the right to deceive the consumer by false or inadequate labeling or misleading containers. His argument regarding increased consumer costs hinges on whether it costs more to fill a large box half-full, or a smaller box completely.

8. You will recognize this argument as arising from one of the honorable members of the Senate who wishes to retain the right to filibuster or unlimited debate so that he may defeat the will of the majority. Most students of American government believe that decisions by majority vote are one of the strongest evidences of democracy in our political system.

9. The confusion in the mind of this speaker is apparent. He is attempting to divert our attention away from his real reasons for opposition to civil-rights legislation by drawing a red (Red?) herring across our path, the threat of communist domination.

10. In his eagerness to criticize the government, the speaker has neglected even common sense. Does he really believe that our government could share its military and diplomatic secrets with the entire nation and still retain its security?

11. The speaker's characterization of us as a peace-loving nation is very appealing. He forgets, however, such incidents as the Mexican War, the Spanish-American War, the Panama Canal grab, and so on.

12. You will recognize this spiel of the door-to-door salesman. In addition to playing upon the sympathy of the housewife, he is using the trick of inducing his listener to get on the bandwagon, to purchase a subscription just as her neighbors are supposed to have done.

13. Even if we accept the major premise as probably correct, this does not prove anything about Mr. Bundy's motives, and the final conclusion is therefore unsound.

14. Testimonials such as this, even if sincere, prove nothing about the merits of the product. The disappearance of the writer's neurotic symptoms were probably not due to the two bottles of Salts but rather were the result of autosuggestion or unconscious relief from some personal or social pressure. The writer is headed for real trouble if she continues to substitute the patent medicine for competent medical attention.

15. This is another example of non sequitur reasoning. Her earlier qualifications as a parent, wife, or church member have nothing to do with her guilt or innocence in the death of her husband. This decision must be based solely upon the facts of the case.

16. It is true that a drop in auto fatalities in 1948 coincided with the passage of an auto-inspection law and a rise appeared after its repeal. However, is this proof that inspections reduced fatal accidents? Variations in the rate from year to year are common and may be due to a number of factors, such as changes in speed laws, new traffic regulations, exceptionally

long holiday periods at the 4th of July, Thanksgiving, and Christmas, and so on.

17. The Moscow demand to destroy all bombers may impress the naïve, as it is intended to do. But if the medium bombers the U.S. offers to destroy are worthless, would this not be a good place to begin disarmament, if the Russians are sincere?

Critical-Reading Exercise I:

"Tidelands Property Rights"   (pp. 140–141.)

    1. b   2. b   3. c   4. e   5. b   6. c   7. answer varies

"Tidelands Oil"   (pp. 142–143.)

    1. c   2. b   3. d   4. a   5. c   6. answer varies

Chapter 11

Anthropology: (pp. 193–196.)

"Needed Refinements in the Biographical Approach"

Main Ideas (4 credits each, 28 points)
    1. c   2. b   3. a, c
    4. The author's purpose was (1) to awaken his fellow anthropologists to the deficiencies in life histories and biographies, (2) to urge them to do better library research, and (3) to emphasize the need for more carefully planned and objective studies. (Score separately for each major idea.)
Details (6 credits each, 36 points)
    5. b, c, d   6. b   7. a   8. b
Vocabulary (3 credits each, 36 points)
    1. c   2. a   3. c   4. b   5. b   6. c   7. a   8. b
    9. a   10. a   11. a   12. b

Art:

"Japanese Art"   (pp. 199–202.)

Main Ideas (8 credits each, 24 points)
    1. d   2. a   3. b
Details
    4. Cultures from which the Japanese borrowed ideas at various times and examples of the borrowings are—
       China: hollow lacquer figures; geometric patterns (on Ainu pottery); bronze mirrors; wood sculpture (Kudara Kwannon).

Korea: yayoi pottery; magatama (comma-shaped stones); Buddhist
bronze sculptures.

Indo China: motifs on bronze figures; haniwa (possibly).

(5 credits for each country and at least one related art form, 16 credits
if correct in all three combinations.)

5. c   6. b   7. c   8. d   9. d   10. b (5 credits each for
numbers 5 to 10; 30 points)

Vocabulary (3 credits each, 30 points)

1. b   2. b   3. a   4. c   5. c   6. b   7. a   8. b
9. a   10. c

Astronomy:

"The Nature of the Universe"   (pp. 205–207.)

Main Ideas (13 credits each, 39 points)

1. c   2. d   3. b

Details (4 credits each, 28 points)

4. b   5. d   6. c

7. The author mentions (1) radio astronomy and (2) space probes. You
may have also named other developments currently in the news.

Vocabulary (3 credits each, 18 points)

1. b   2. a   3. a   4. b   5. c   6. b

Scanning (3 credits each, 15 points)

1. b   2. a   3. b   4. c   5. d

Biology:

"Definition of Mutation"   (pp. 211–213.)

Main Ideas (8 credits each, 32 points)

1. a   2. c   3. c   4. b

Details (6 credits each, 36 points)

5. d   6. a, b, d   7. b   8. b

Vocabulary (4 credits each, 32 points)

1. a   2. b   3. c   4. a   5. a   6. c   7. a   8. c

Business Administration:

"Business Insurance"   (pp. 217–220.)

Main Ideas (35 points)

1. The basic purposes of bonds are (1) to protect the businessman
against losses of various kinds and (2) to insure the performance of
certain obligations by employees or by the other party to a contract
(5 credits each).

2. The primary purpose of a fidelity bond is to protect against employee
dishonesty (5 credits); of a surety bond, to guarantee performance of

an obligation or contract (5 credits); of a forgery bond, to cover losses caused by forged or altered checks, drafts, and so on (5 credits).

Fidelity and surety bonds (1) guarantee the reliability of another in business dealings and (2) involve three parties: the principal (bonded), the beneficiary (insured), and the surety (insuring company) (5 credits each).

Details (5 credits each, 25 points)
3. a   4. c   5. c   6. a   7. a

Vocabulary (2 credits each, 20 points)
1. c   2. b   3. b   4. c   5. b   6. b   7. c   8. c
9. a   10. a

Scanning (4 credits each, 20 points)
1. a   2. c   3. d   4. b   5. d

Chemistry:

"Sulphur-Deficient Soils"   (pp. 223–226.)

Main Ideas (5 credits each, 35 points)
1. b   2. b   3. c   4. c   5. Rainfall; irrigation water; animal manures; sulphur-containing fertilizers (any 3).

Details (5 credits each, 35 points)
6. a, e   7. c   8. a   9. b   10. b, d

Vocabulary (3 credits each, 30 points)
1. a   2. b   3. c   4. b   5. a   6. c   7. a   8. a
9. b   10. c

Education:

"Seven Principles of Learning"   (pp. 231–232.)

Vocabulary
1. c   2. c   3. b   4. a   5. b

English:

"The Development of English"   (pp. 236–239.)

Main Ideas (6 credits each, 30 points)
1. c   2. c   3. c   4. c   5. b

Details (3 credits each, 45 points)

1. False	6. True	11. True
2. True	7. False	12. True
3. True	8. True	13. False
4. True	9. True	14. True
5. False	10. True	15. False

Vocabulary (3 credits each, 24 points)
   1. b   2. c   3. c   4. a   5. b   6. a   7. c   8. c

Geology:

"Mineral Resources"   (pp. 243–244.)

Main Ideas (10 credits each, 20 points)
   1. b   2. a
Details (8 credits each, 48 points)
   3. b   4. d   5. a   6. d   7. a   8. a
Vocabulary (4 credits each, 32 points)
   1. b   2. a   3. c   4. b   5. a   6. c   7. b   8. c

History:

"Science and Exploration in Hellenistic Culture"   (pp. 248–249.)

Main Ideas (9 credits each, 18 points)
   1. c   2. c
Details (10 items, 5 credits each, 50 points)
   3. a, b, e   4. Euclid, 2; Archimedes, 6; Eratosthenes, 5; Posidonius, 1; Herophilus, 3; Theophrastus, 4.   5. b
Vocabulary (4 credits each, 32 points)
   1. a   2. b   3. b   4. a   5. c   6. c   7. c   8. a

Literature:

"A Rose for Emily"   (pp. 258–260.)

Main Ideas (6 credits each, 30 points)
   1. b   2. c   3. b   4. a   5. b
Inferences and Interpretations (4 credits each, 40 points)
   6. b   7. c   8. a   9. b   10. a   11. d   12. c   13. c
   14. b   15. d
Vocabulary (3 credits each, 30 points)
   1. a   2. b   3. c   4. a   5. b   6. c   7. c   8. a
   9. b   10. b

Mathematics:

"The Invention of Algebra"   (pp. 264–265.)

Main Ideas (11 credits each, 33 points)
   1. c   2. d   3. —3 steps, or three steps backward.

Details (6 credits each, 42 points)
   4. c   5. a, −3; b, +8; c, −24; d, +19; e, −6.   6. b

Vocabulary (5 credits each, 25 points)
   1. b   2. c   3. a   4. c   5. c

Psychology:

"Folk Psychology"   (pp. 269–272.)

1. Folk psychology, popular psychology, common-sense beliefs (any one, 7 credits).
2. The means of testing the accuracy of these common beliefs and of distinguishing the true from the false. (either reason, 7 credits).
3. Because the consensus of opinion supporting a popular belief is evidence only of its popularity, not of its truth (7 credits).
4. (Any two, 7 credits each)
   a. Freud's discovery that children exhibit or experience sexual desires.   b. Darwin's explanation of man's evolution.   c. The pre-Columbus belief that the earth was flat.   d. Galileo's proof of the Copernican theory of the solar system.   e. Newton's analysis of the composition of white light.   f. Freud's emphasis upon the unconscious processes underlying behavior.
5. (Either one, 7 credits)
   a. The belief that certain persons have ESP—extrasensory perception, or the ability to sense or foretell certain phenomena.   b. The belief that certain persons can apparently communicate over large distances without employing any obvious sense modality.
6. You may believe and try to defend such popular beliefs as these:
   a. Redheads are more emotional than blondes or brunettes.
   b. Fat people are usually pleasant, happy, and jovial.   c. Short people usually have feelings of inferiority and consequently are more aggressive than normal.   d. Tall, lean people are less friendly than the average.

Your attempts to prove any of these or other beliefs will, of course, depend upon your own personal experiences and observations. (7 credits for the statement of the belief; 7 credits for the proof.)

7. The author's primary purpose was, undoubtedly, to raise doubts in your mind regarding the reliability of common-sense beliefs. However, he also acknowledges that some of these may prove to be true, and does not expect you to discard immediately all such beliefs. Rather, he hopes that you will realize that most such beliefs need scientific verification and, hence, hopes you will approach them more skeptically. (7 credits.)

8. Many individuals allow their thinking to be swayed by their feelings, instincts, emotions, or what they think they observe to be true. They cannot discard the beliefs they have acquired despite contrary scientific evidence, for to do so would seem to contradict the evidence of their own senses. Such individuals lack an objective or scientific attitude toward natural phenomena or the behavior of man. (7 credits.)

9. The author suggests that the commonest flaws in many popular beliefs are *overgeneralization* and *oversimplification*. Several other types of faulty logic may be observed such as "post hoc ergo propter hoc," or reasoning that an event that follows closely after a possible cause or related event is caused by the earlier event. (7 credits for each of the italicized terms.)

10. All of the items are false except numbers 4, 6, 14 and 20. College classes which have responded to these statements miss an average of ten items. How do you compare in your folk psychology beliefs?

Vocabulary (2 credits each, 16 points)
    1. b   2. c   3. a   4. a   5. b   6. c   7. b   8. c

Speech:

"Being Seen, Heard, and Understood"   (pp. 276–278.)

Main Ideas (10 credits each, 40 points)
    1. d   2. c   3. b   4. b

Details (40 points)
1. a. Too few gestures make the audience too relaxed, underreacting or inattentive.   b. Uncontrolled gestures distract the audience or even antagonize or irritate it.   c. Controlled, planned gestures keep audience thinking along with the speaker.
(5 credits each, total 15)

2. The author argues that gestures are an essential part of communication because—
a. lack of gestures inhibit the speaker's thinking.   b. gestures arouse the listener's attention.   c. gestures reinforce the speaker's words.   d. speech communication is very weak without gestures.
(Any two, 5 credits each, total 10)

3. The author's argument that we think with not only the brain but with most of the body is supported by such facts as these:
a. After watching an exciting and strenuous sports event, play, or movie, or listening to a forceful, dramatic speaker, many spectators leave with feelings of physical and emotional fatigue that have built up unconsciously during the action.   b. Many reflex or instinctive actions occur without involving thinking (the brain), such as dodging

a thrown object, jumping when startled, moving quickly when pinched or burned, readjusting one's clothing in response to excessive heat or cold.   c. The sight of an accident involving injured persons, or seeing a near accident often arouses such feelings in bystanders as pain, fear, nausea, anger, a sinking feeling in the pit of the stomach, and so on, without any obvious conscious thought about these feelings.   d. In normal conversation, the many bodily movements of the speaker show the natural tendency to communicate (or think) with the whole body. (7 credits for *d*, 8 more for any answer comparable to *a*, *b*, or *c;* total 15)

Vocabulary (2 credits each, total 20)
  1. a   2. b   3. c   4. a   5. b   6. c   7. b   8. c
  9. a   10. c

Statistics:

"The Misleading Average"   (pp. 282–284.)

Main Ideas (8 credits each, 32 points)
  1. b   2. b, c, e

Details (4 credits each, 40 points)

3. False	8. True
4. False	9. True
5. False	10. False
6. True	11. True
7. True	12. True

Vocabulary (4 credits each, 28 points)
  1. c   2. a   3. b   4. a   5. c   6. b   7. b

Appendix

Word Analysis Exercise I: (pp. 294–295.)

Analyzing Words for Sounds and Syllables

	Vowel sounds (estimated syllables)	Revised estimate
1. Mao-rē[1]	3	2
2. bē-troth or bē-trōth	2	—
3. cal-cē-o-lar-ē-a	6	—
4. con-vo-lū-tion	4	—
5. glad-ē-ō-lus or gla-dī-o-lus	4	—
6. gim-let (hard g)	2	—

[1] Short vowel sounds are not marked in these words. Where necessary, long vowel sounds have been spelled phonetically to show their actual pronunciation, as the long e sound in Maori. The answers given here are based on *Webster's New Collegiate.* If you need to check your pronunciation, use your dictionary.

	Vowel sounds (estimated syllables)	Revised estimate
7. mi-tō-sis	3	—
8. mī-tral	2	—
9. māy-on-nāise	3	—
10. mē-ātus	3	2
11. be-hē-moth or bē-he-moth	3	—
12. gum-bō (hard g)	2	—
13. Han-sē-at-ic	3	4
14. mis-dē-mēan-or	4	—
15. or-ches-tral	3	—
16. pel-lū-cid	3	—
17. hō-mē-o-path	4	—
18. plē-o-nasm	3	—
19. rē-sid-ū-al	3	4
20. sī-sal	2	—
21. nim-bus	2	—
22. cryp-to-graph	3	—
23. con-tra-vēne	3	—
24. cū-bi-cle	3	—
25. dīa-ton-ic	4	3
26. sanc-ti-tē	2	3
27. poly-chrōme	3	2
28. phys-ē-ol-o-gy	4	5
29. cym-bal	2	—
30. pan-ni-kin	3	—

Word Analysis Exercise II: (p. 295.)

Pronouncing from Phonetic Spellings

1. c	6. c	11. c
2. a	7. b	12. a
3. d	8. a *and* c	13. d
4. d	9. b	14. b
5. d	10. b	15. c

Word Analysis Exercise III: (p. 296.)

Pronouncing with the Aid of Symbols

1. Yankee	6. cypress	11. midnight	16. pressed
2. beam	7. tourniquet	12. success	17. parquet
3. wrong	8. dispose	13. hitch	18. origin
4. contract	9. toward	14. result	19. ice
5. urgent	10. extra	15. gain	20. motion

A Test on the Use of the Dictionary (pp. 296–302.)

Pronunciation	Meaning	Spelling	Derivation	Usage
1. c	11. e	21. d	31. e	41. b
2. b	12. b	22. c	32. a	42. c
3. a	13. c	23. b	33. e	43. d
4. c	14. b	24. c	34. d	44. e
5. b	15. d	25. b	35. a	45. c
6. c	16. c	26. e	36. d	46. a
7. d	17. b	27. b	37. e	47. b
8. a	18. a	28. a	38. d	48. c
9. b	19. e	29. a	39. e	49. e
10. b	20. d	30. b	40. e	50. a

Standards for the Dictionary Test. The standards or norms for the test are given in percentiles or ranks which indicate the student's standing when compared to a group of equivalent age or education. For example, a score of 9 in the Pronunciation section of the test is equal to the *60th* percentile for college students. 40 per cent of college students achieve a better score in this section, while 60 per cent are usually poorer than this score.

Since this text is often used in precollege reading-improvement courses, we have also given percentile standards for high school seniors.

TABLE 1
Percentiles for College Freshmen

	Pronunciation	Meaning	Spelling	Derivation	Usage	Total
99	10	10	10	10	10	48
90	—	—	—	9	—	44
80	—	9	—	—	9	43
70	—	—	—	8	—	41
60	9	—	—	7	8	39
50	8	8	9	—	—	38
40	—	—	—	6	7	37
30	7	—	8	—	—	34
20	—	7	—	5	6	32
10	6	6	7	3–4	5	28
5	5	5	6	2	4	25
1	0–4	0–4	0–5	0–1	0–3	0–24

TABLE 2
Percentiles for 12th Grade

	Pronunciation	Meaning	Spelling	Derivation	Usage	Total
99	10	8–10	10	9–10	10	42
90	—	—	—	8	9	37
80	9	—	9	7	8	35
70	—	—	—	6	7	33
60	8	—	—	—	6	31
50	—	7	8	5	—	29
40	7	6	—	—	5	28
30	6	—	7	4	—	26
20	5	5	6	3	4	23
10	4	4	5	2	3	20
5	3	3	4	1	2	17
1	0–2	0–2	0–3	0	0–1	0–16

TABLE 3

Chart for Determining Rate of Reading

Find length of selection in left-hand column.
Find reading time at top of chart.
Find rate in wpm where these two columns intersect.

Number of words										Reading time in minutes and seconds									
	10	9–30	9	8–30	8	7–30	7	6–30	6	5–30	5	4–30	4	3–30	3	2–30	2	1–30	1
650	65	68	72	78	81	86	93	100	109	118	130	145	163	186	217	260	325	433	650
700	70	74	78	83	88	93	100	108	117	127	140	156	175	200	233	280	350	467	700
1,000	100	106	112	117	125	133	143	154	167	181	200	222	250	286	333	400	500	667	1,000
1,050	105	110	117	123	131	140	150	162	175	191	210	233	262	300	350	420	525	700	1,050
1,100	110	115	122	129	137	147	157	169	183	200	220	244	275	314	367	440	550	733	1,100
1,150	115	121	127	135	144	153	164	177	191	209	230	255	287	328	384	460	575	767	1,150
1,200	120	126	133	141	150	160	171	185	200	218	240	267	300	343	400	480	600	800	1,200
1,250	125	131	138	147	156	167	178	192	208	227	250	277	313	357	417	500	625	833	1,250
1,300	130	136	144	153	163	173	186	200	217	236	260	289	325	371	433	520	650	867	1,300
1,350	135	141	149	159	168	180	193	208	225	246	270	300	338	386	450	540	675	900	1,350
1,400	140	147	155	165	175	186	200	215	233	254	280	311	350	400	467	560	700	933	1,400
1,450	145	152	160	171	181	193	207	224	242	263	290	322	363	414	484	580	725	967	1,450
1,500	150	158	166	177	187	200	214	231	250	273	300	333	375	428	500	600	750	1,000	1,500
1,550	155	163	171	183	194	207	221	238	258	282	310	344	388	443	517	620	775	1,033	1,550
1,600	160	168	177	189	200	213	229	246	267	291	320	356	400	457	533	640	800	1,067	1,600
1,650	165	173	182	195	206	220	236	255	275	300	330	362	413	472	550	660	825	1,100	1,650
1,700	170	178	188	200	213	227	243	262	283	309	340	378	425	486	567	680	850	1,133	1,700
1,900	190	200	211	224	238	253	271	292	317	345	380	422	476	542	634	760	952	1,268	1,900
2,500	250	262	276	294	312	334	356	384	416	454	500	554	626	714	834	1,000	1,250	1,666	2,500